Transformative Transitional Justice and the Malleability of Post-Conflict States

For Áine, forever

Transformative Transitional Justice and the Malleability of Post-Conflict States

Padraig McAuliffe

Senior Lecturer, School of Law and Social Justice, University of Liverpool, UK

Edward Elgar
PUBLISHING

Cheltenham, UK • Northampton, MA, USA

Published by
Edward Elgar Publishing Limited
The Lypiatts
15 Lansdown Road
Cheltenham
Glos GL50 2JA
UK

Edward Elgar Publishing, Inc.
William Pratt House
9 Dewey Court
Northampton
Massachusetts 01060
USA

A catalogue record for this book
is available from the British Library

Library of Congress Control Number: 2016957228

This book is available electronically in the **Elgar**online
Law subject collection
DOI 10.4337/9781783470044

MIX
Paper from
responsible sources
FSC® C013604

ISBN 978 1 78347 003 7 (cased)
ISBN 978 1 78347 004 4 (eBook)

Typeset by Columns Design XML Ltd, Reading
Printed and bound by CPI Group (UK) Ltd, Croydon, CR0 4YY

Contents

Preface

> To show that justice has its practical and ideological limitations is not to slight it. The entire aim is rather to account for the difficulties which the morality of justice faces in a morally pluralistic world and to help it recognize its real place in it – not above the political world but in its very midst.[1]

Scholars and practitioners of transitional justice have begun to articulate a sense that the field is in what might be called a 'fourth phase'[2] or fourth 'generation';[3] that is, an extension of the field's familiar three-phase paradigm of post-World War II origins, post-Cold War normalization and a millennial steady-state stage.[4] This fourth phase is primarily characterized by a willingness to reconsider the boundaries of the field, most notably by extending the scope of moral and legal inquiry to encompass a wider set of outcomes like development, poverty alleviation and redistribution. A core element of this expansion has been to rewrite the dominant scripts evident in scholarship and practice. These dominant scripts foreground familiar institutions (trials, truth commissions, reparations, lustration), familiar abuses (usually bodily integrity abuses) and familiar teleologies (liberal democracy, civil rights protection).[5] Though the alternatives to this dominant script are varied, many now cohere in a commitment to redressing economic injustice for a variety of reasons. Some wish for transitional justice to become development-sensitive,

---

1 Judith Sklar, *Legalism* (Harvard University Press 1964) 122–23.

2 Vasuki Nesiah, *Transitional Justice Practice: Looking Back, Moving Forward* (Impunity Watch 2016) 11.

3 Dustin Sharp, 'Interrogating the Peripheries: The Preoccupations of Fourth Generation Transitional Justice' (2013) 26 *Harvard Human Rights Journal* 149, 152.

4 Ruti Teitel, 'Transitional Justice Genealogy' (2003) 16 *Harvard Human Rights Journal* 69.

5 On dominant scripts, see James Cavallaro and Sebastian Albuja, 'The Lost Agenda: Economic Crimes and Truth Commissions in Latin America and Beyond' in Kieran McEvoy and Lorna McGregor (eds), *Transitional Justice from Below: Grassroots Activism and the Struggle for Change* (Hart Publishing 2008) 121 at 125.

some wish for economic, social and cultural (ESC) rights to be prioritized, some want the field to address social minima or subsistence harms. Others want it to serve as a vehicle for (re)distributive justice, while yet another group urges the field to catalyse fundamental change in the economic structures that underpin poverty, inequality and social exclusion. There is no sense of rival schools (yet), either in practice or in the developing advocacy-cum-scholarship literature. This may be because the sheer urgency felt to redirect the field towards issues of economic justice smothers disagreement over what precisely economic justice should look like. The urgency flows from a widespread acceptance that transitional justice is essentially limited, and any progress towards peace or democracy is likely to prove ephemeral, unless attention is paid to the economic root causes of conflict like poverty, horizontal inequality and underdevelopment. Field-based analysis and population surveys suggest that employment, income, public safety, clean water, housing, education and healthcare are more desired forms of justice for people than accountability and truth in relation to past atrocities. Scholars who support this re-orientation insist that transitional justice will lack credibility, appear merely symbolic or even appear 'cheap and spurious' if it does not resolve economic injustice, discrimination or deprivation.[6]

This book explores this redirection of transitional justice towards economic justice. It does not address the *what* or the *why* questions of this re-orientation. The revised normative aspirations of *what* transitional justice should emphasize (development-sensitivity, ESC rights prioritization, social minima, (re)distribution and structural change) have been outlined comprehensively in a number of articles and books in the last dozen years. These arguments are referred to throughout this book, but not recapitulated. The related question of *why* transitional justice should embrace issues of economic injustice has also been explored exhaustively in many of the same works. Again, these are referred to herein but not recapitulated in detail. This book does not address the question of *how* transitional justice as a body of practices, a base of knowledge and site of activist endeavour might go about turning these commitments into

[6] Barbara Oomen, 'Justice Mechanisms and the Question of Legitimacy: The Example of Rwanda's Multi-layered Justice Mechanisms' in Kai Ambos, Judith Large and Marieke Wierda (eds), *Building a Future on Peace and Justice: Studies on Transitional Justice, Peace and Development* (Springer 2009) 175 at 197; Yvette Selim and Tim Murithi, 'Transitional Justice and Development: Partners for Sustainable Peace in Africa?' (2011) 6 *Journal of Peacebuilding and Development* 58, 61; Alex Boraine, *A Country Unmasked: Inside South Africa's Truth and Reconciliation Commission* (Oxford University Press 2000) 357.

results. In contradistinction to the questions of the *what* and the *why*, this question of *how* has been far less comprehensively addressed in the literature.[7] As Chapter 2 argues, the fourth generation of transitional justice scholarship is characterized by a calculated opacity when it comes to demonstrating how a revised approach to justice among scholars and practitioners can translate into transformed development patterns, rights-holding or structural transformation in the site of intervention. Theory-building has far outstripped empirical exploration of the relationship between economic structures and transitional justice.[8] Even the limited theoretical work undertaken so far has generated little by way of theories of change that would articulate how and why a transitional justice intervention would effect a specific transformation of economic structures or enjoyment of socio-economic rights. As Haldemann and Kouassi put it:

> It is one thing to explain why socio-economic rights should be integrated into the transitional justice framework; it is quite another to address the question of *how* this could be done. This is a crucial issue. If the ESC rights thesis is to be more than an empty abstraction, one should be able to describe the ways and means of putting it into practice.[9]

Furthermore, there has been a conspicuous lack of non-ideal theorists who have outlined the most pervasive of the obstacles to change in those 'burdened societies' that lack the political and cultural traditions, human capital or material resources needed to be well-ordered, or proposals to overcome them.[10] The overall lack of a theory of change or programme pathway that would connect transitional justice activities to outcomes is

---

[7] As one group of scholars notes, 'Local ownership, prevention, better analysis and the "springboard thesis" are the reasons why economic and social rights matter. The "why" question has effectively been answered; the "how" question is now the biggest hurdle for our research agenda'. (Paul Gready et al. 'Transformative Justice – A Concept Note' (unpublished manuscript, October 2010) 6 <http://www.wun.ac.uk/files/transformative_justice_-_concept_note_web_version.pdf> accessed 20 July 2016.)

[8] Geoff Dancy and Eric Wiebelhaus-Brahm, 'Bridge to Human Development or Vehicle of Inequality? Transitional Justice and Economic Structures' (2015) 9 *International Journal of Transitional Justice* 51, 51 (Preamble).

[9] Frank Haldeman and Rachelle Kouassi, 'Transitional Justice without Economic, Social and Cultural Rights?' in Eibe Riedel, Gilles Giacca and Christophe Golay (eds), *Economic, Social and Cultural Rights: Contemporary Issues and Challenges* (Oxford University Press 2014), 498 at 504.

[10] Lisa Fuller, 'Burdened Societies and Transitional Justice' (2012) 15 *Ethical Theory and Moral Practice* 369, 372.

problematic because without concrete proposals for how transitional justice can achieve these aspirations, it is difficult to engage critically with, or build upon, the transformative turn as a practical endeavour.

Instead of addressing the *how* question,[11] this book might be understood as addressing a question which should logically precede it, namely *where*? It is something of a cliché that transitional justice must be context-specific and adapted to the ecology in which it is pursued. However, few generalized treatments of how the field should be re-oriented to pursue economic justice disaggregate the different contexts in which transitional justice will be secured. Post-authoritarian states obviously offer different opportunities and obstacles than post-conflict states. Both post-conflict and post-authoritarian contexts present different challenges to developed or underdeveloped states undergoing nothing recognizable as transition but which are nevertheless addressing past human rights abuses. This book addresses one particular site of transitional justice, namely post-conflict states. Post-conflict states are arguably those where transitional justice is most necessary and most common, as familiar examples from Rwanda, Guatemala, El Salvador, Bosnia, Kosovo, Nepal and Sudan make clear. Contemporary processes of transitional justice in the likes of Côte d'Ivoire, Libya and Colombia (and potential future ones like Syria or Eastern Ukraine) occur at a time when the demands made of transitional justice are ever greater but many of the generic challenges and obstacles imposed by peacemaking remain the same.

A book specifically dedicated to the challenges for fourth generation transitional justice in addressing issues of economic justice in post-conflict states is necessary as it is clear that this specific ecology raises challenges for economic justice that have barely been explored in the literature. Since at least the time of the Bosnian and Rwandan conflicts, the post-conflict ecology has been considered as one of the two paradigmatic transitions that define the field alongside post-authoritarian regime alteration. However, it is rare for any treatment of transitional justice's potential to catalyse socioeconomic change in this context to specifically engage with war, its ontological and epistemological underpinnings, and how it alters the political economy of states. Many of the assumptions made are based on rather underdeveloped concepts and causal claims that

---

[11] Readers are directed towards other work by the present author that outlines some of the more evident limitations of the field's existing institutions. See Padraig McAuliffe, 'Rhetoric and Realpolitik: Interrogating the Relationship between Transitional Justice and Socio-Economic Justice' (2012–13) 23 *Finnish Yearbook of International Law* 239.

do not capture the complexity of post-conflict ecologies and the fluid dynamics of the national political economy that shape opportunities for change. Processes that are predominantly controlled by domestic actors like the modalities of warfare and war conclusion, the means by which peace is negotiated, the terms of agreements and the use of power-sharing tend to obstruct, as opposed to facilitate, the transformation of those structures which gave rise to conflict in the first place. Scholars, activists and practitioners implore the field to address poverty, inequality or discriminatory structures, and they confidently assert that it has a (rather underspecified) potency to do so. However, one is struck by the near total failure to address obvious impediments to economic transformation like the state's weak administrative capacity, the tendency of peace agreements to consolidate the power of existing and emerging elites and the likely veto power of those powerful social forces that stand to lose from any erosion of discriminatory structures they benefit from. The fourth generation of transitional justice scholarship is premised on the assumption that transition to a post-conflict environment makes these states essentially malleable and that processes of significant change are underway that the field can inform or capitalize upon (though it should be made clear that few presume it will be straightforward or easy). What is striking about these assumptions of malleability is that none of the core domestic barriers to economic justice that development actors or peacebuilders identify as salient in the post-conflict context (spoilers, elite entrenchment, neopatrimonialism or the weak administrative capacities of under-developed states) are ever addressed in this literature.

The aspirations of fourth generation transitional justice presume that transformative outcomes can be produced, legitimized and stabilized as matters of intention and design, and that transitional justice can catalyse desired economic dynamics and outcomes. One of the main problems with this literature is that it is almost entirely concerned with transitional justice's own debates, norms, institutions and values, as opposed to the actual context to which they will apply. Though undoubtedly rooted in a moral concern for post-conflict states and the obvious needs of victims, little attention is paid to those political and economic factors that make states or the communities therein more or less malleable or amenable to change. Proposals always lay in the realm of that which we as scholars or practitioners can control – the rights that should be propagated, the bottom-up approaches we can catalyse, the reform of the mechanisms we support – but never in those state institutions, informal material relations or pre-existing social structures that obviously condition the prospects for improved insight or norm advocacy to translate into transformation on the ground.

The critical focus is seldom the limited but policy-relevant reasons endogenous to the state why aspects of justice are more or less feasible. Instead, fourth generation literature primarily addresses the theoretical, exogenous reasons why the international community does or does not propound this or that (expansive) vision of transitional justice. This is most evident in the notion that liberal peacebuilding's top-down imposition of external legal frameworks and institutional templates represent the 'foundational' limitations to a more transformative transitional justice.[12]

Transitional justice has excluded from its remit those who suffer from structural violence on account of the traditional preoccupation with violations of bodily integrity. The failure to address socio-economic rights is attributed to the prioritization of civil and political rights over ESC rights, a discourse that depoliticizes justice and marginalizes agendas of structural reform. These objections to the field's liberal bias are perfectly valid. However, they ignore the obvious point that even if transitional justice actors (and the wider peacebuilding apparatus they operate alongside or within) embrace economic injustice, this reorientation in and of itself does not make domestic structures that heretofore have underpinned poverty or structural inequality (and may endure and consolidate after conflict) any more malleable than they were before. One of the core arguments made by critics of contemporary transitional justice is that systematic, structural violence that disenfranchises distinct sectors of society must be deliberately sustained by a domestic political system that distributes power and resources unequally.[13] However, the implications of this for transitional justice in terms of endogenous barriers raised to transformation are never explored.

It is necessary, both for the coherence of fourth generation scholarship and to one day address the *how* question in detail, to better comprehend how malleable structures of poverty and inequality post-conflict societies are. Above all, it is necessary to engage in some form of power analysis of these states, given that any realization of socio-economic rights claims, redistribution or structural reform in states where there are not enough goods and services to supply all demands is likely to give rise to the

---

[12] Paul Gready and Simon Robins, 'From Transitional to Transformative Justice: A New Agenda for Practice' (2014) 8 *International Journal of Transitional Justice* 339, 340.

[13] Amanda Cahill-Ripley, 'Foregrounding Socio-Economic Rights in Transitional Justice: Realising Justice for Violations of Economic and Social Rights' (2014) 32 *Netherlands Quarterly of Human Rights* 183, 191.

perception or reality of what Boulding labels (with reference to the remark made in Wonderland to Alice) as 'the Duchess's Law': 'The more there is of yours, the less there is of mine'.[14] Any change or challenge to the structures of exploitation will inherently engage with, and run up against, opposing structures of power and interest. These structures, be they state institutions, informal elite control of the economy or social norms, have played a role in moulding extant conditions and, in conjunction with those groups and actors whose interests maintain them, may serve as obstacles to change. As Chapter 3 goes on to argue, the means by which peace is agreed often tends to reinforce such obstacles. Any model of transformative transitional justice must understand and relate to the power relations at play in the distinct post-conflict context. Without grounding theory in the realities of post-conflict states, socio-economically inclined transitional justice advocacy at times resembles what Cain describes as the 'human rights cheerleading' of international human rights organizations, a form of ideological support devoid of any realistic or pragmatic strategy to actually address the deprivations identified and with little regard for what can reasonably be accomplished.[15]

Any intervention by outside actors like transitional justice becomes itself part of the conflict system in the state and the contemporaneous attempts to build peace by international actors. This book therefore tries to answer the question of what transitional justice should look like if it was immersed in peacebuilding theory, not merely in the comfortable philosophical language of (anti) liberalism, but in the pragmatic political choices that need to be made in the real world of spoilers, institutional incapacity, elite economic control and status quo-preserving peace agreements. In so doing, I do not employ the phraseology of fourth generation transitional justice but instead label the field's ongoing reorientation as its 'transformative turn'. It may seem questionable to subsume normative goals as different as promoting ESC rights, redistributing wealth or fostering welfarism under this rubric. Nevertheless, I use this term primarily because a number of other scholars explicitly use the language of 'transformation',[16] while other conceptualizations like structural

---

[14] Kenneth Boulding, *Conflict and Defense: A General Theory* (Torch Books 1962) 190.

[15] Kenneth Cain, 'The Rape of Dinah: Human Rights, Civil War in Liberia and Evil Triumphant' (1999) 21 *Human Rights Quarterly* 265, 297.

[16] Gready and Robins (n 12); Kris Brown and Fionnuala Ní Aoláin, 'Through the Looking Glass: Transitional Justice Futures through the Lens of Nationalism, Feminism and Transformative Change' (2015) 9 *International Journal of Transitional Justice* 125; Wendy Lambourne, 'Transformative Justice, Reconciliation

justice are essentially synonyms for it.[17] I also use the language of transformation because something distinctly greater than stasis or reform, but something falling short of revolution, is being proposed in this literature. Pleas to redistribute wealth,[18] to redress subsistence harms[19] or reform social blueprints to expand life choices[20] are deeply transformative in societies where neither historical developments nor economic incentives prior to transition generated more equal economies, serious poverty alleviation or welfare. Even more circumspect pleas to make transitional justice more development-sensitive[21] or to foreground socio-economic rights may mark a significant departure from what domestic elites have historically proven willing to concede, as Chapters 3 and 4 make clear.[22]

This book, therefore, is less about a substantive notion of transformative transitional justice (after all, many have articulated visions of this, albeit with a fairly consistent vagueness) than the context in which it may or may not be realized. In order to spark a critical and constructive dialogue, I concentrate the discussion on some shortcomings evident in the supporting assumptions of the transformative turn – that the discourse adopted within transitional justice establishes the bounds of what projects can be pursued (Chapter 2), that peace agreements and post-conflict reconstruction are inherently transformative moments of constitutional reform and social reordering (Chapter 3), that liberal interventionary actors involved in transitional justice or peacebuilding exert decisive

---

and Peacebuilding' in Susanne Buckley-Zistel et al. (eds), *Transitional Justice Theories* (Routledge 2013) 19 at 19–20.

[17] Krista Thomason, 'Transitional Justice as Structural Justice' in Claudio Corradetti, Nir Eisikovits and Jack Volpe Rotondi (eds), *Theorizing Transitional Justice* (Ashgate 2015) 71. Structural justice is used throughout in Jennifer Balint, Julie Evans and Nesam McMillan, 'Rethinking Transitional Justice, Redressing Indigenous Harm: A New Conceptual Approach' (2014) 8 *International Journal of Transitional Justice* 194.

[18] Rama Mani, *Beyond Retribution – Seeking Justice in the Shadows of War* (Polity Press 2002) 10; Jane Alexander, *A Scoping Study of Transitional Justice and Poverty Reduction* (DFID 2003) 48.

[19] Diana Sankey, 'Towards Recognition of Subsistence Harms: Reassessing Approaches to Socioeconomic Forms of Violence in Transitional Justice' (2013) 8 *International Journal of Transitional Justice* 121, 121, 122, and 125.

[20] Selim and Murithi (n 6) 64.

[21] Pablo de Greiff and Roger Duthie (eds), *Transitional Justice and Development: Making Connections* (Social Science Research Council 2009).

[22] Ismael Muvingi, 'Sitting on Powder Kegs: Socio-Economic Rights in Transitional Societies' (2009) 3 *International Journal of Transitional Justice* 163.

influence on patterns of inequality and redistribution (Chapter 4), that bottom-up approaches can trickle upwards towards the larger national community (Chapter 5). The book focuses only on one particular issue, namely the impact of post-conflict and peacebuilding politics on the malleability of those structures of injustice that transitional justice supposedly addresses. Some obvious stones have therefore been left unturned, like the question of the field's loss of distinctiveness or coherence as it expands,[23] the gendered dimensions of economic violence,[24] the limitations imposed by globalization and structural adjustment that lie far beyond the control of peacebuilders or transitional justice actors, and the core question of whether the field should be abandoned for a more expansive conception of 'transformative justice'.[25] Though these are important dilemmas, an editorial decision has been made to forgo an exploration of these issues in the interests of more fully developing the book's core interests. The book is designed to contribute a more context-specific discourse on economic violence by providing a framework and language with which to analyse the experiences of structural harms in post-conflict justice. It attempts to point out some of the deficiencies in a currently fashionable discourse that has marched into new territory without securing its conceptual supply lines. Finally, it hopes to provide one way of taking a grossly simplified debate forward by make practical choices clearer and giving barriers to transformation greater exposure.

---

[23] Canvassed in Balint, Evans and McMillan (n 17) 214 and Kora Andrieu, 'Dealing with a "New" Grievance: Should Anticorruption Be Part of the Transitional Justice Agenda?' (2012) 11 *Journal of Human Rights* 537, 554.

[24] Catherine O'Rourke, 'Feminist Scholarship in Transitional Justice: A De-Politicising Impulse?' (2015) 51 *Women's Studies International Forum* 118, Fionnuala Ní Aoláin, Catherine O'Rourke and Aisling Swaine, 'Transforming Reparations for Conflict-Related Sexual Violence: Principles and Practice' (2015) 28 *Harvard Human Rights Journal* 97.

[25] Proposed in Matthew Evans, 'Structural Violence, Socioeconomic Rights and Transformative Justice' (2016) 15 *Journal of Human Rights* 1 and explored in Gready and Robins (n 12).

1. Introduction: acknowledging the complexities of post-conflict socio-economic justice

Structural inequality is deeply intertwined with the dynamics of civil war. Though political, psychological and cultural stimuli may drive the recourse to violence, it is conditioned by deeper socio-economic factors and pathologies of power that determine types of harm and who should suffer it. There is, therefore, a growing consensus in scholarship and policy implementation across numerous disciplines like peacebuilding, development and international relations that states emerging from non-international violent conflict can only enjoy a just and sustainable peace if it is consolidated on the basis of economic and social development that meets the needs of the entire population. It is assumed that a peace agreement between belligerents will not endure in the long-term without attention to the basic human needs of individuals, distinct vulnerable social groups and society as a whole. To the extent that peace endures, it will prove illusory or hollow without attention to the everyday lives of those who live within its terms. As such, interveners in post-conflict states are increasingly oriented towards what is broadly described as 'positive peace', which requires attention not only to direct violence or conflict, but to structural and cultural forms of violence in the social and economic spheres which deny access to physical and social well-being.[1] This trend is visible within peacebuilding, which manifests a definite, if imperfect and by no means uniform, migration from minimalist approaches oriented around the mere avoidance of conflict recurrence to a more maximalist approach that fosters transformation of the economic, social and political conditions that formed the background to war in the first place. Within the field of development, attention has begun to shift from narrow conceptions of economic growth to poverty alleviation, redress of horizontal inequalities and some measure of redistribution.

[1] Johann Galtung, 'Violence, Peace and Peace Research' (1969) *Journal of Peace Research* 167.

This consensus has found support within transitional justice in the last decade or so as the field expands beyond its traditional preoccupations with accountability, truth, reconciliation and non-recurrence. Over time, it has become apparent that forms of structural harm, those which occur where arrangements embedded in the political and economic organization of the social world damage people by preventing them from meeting their basic needs, have been rendered invisible in a discourse that elevated atrocities like genocide, crimes against humanity and torture over the less visceral slow violence of starvation, unemployment and poverty. The justifications for including issues of structural violence and inequality as integral components of transitional justice are pragmatic (peace can only be sustainable with attention to root causes), philosophical (an ethical preference for distributive justice and equity) and sociological (polls of survivor populations overwhelmingly demonstrate that socio-economic concerns trump the desire for criminal justice or truth in transitions).[2] This re-direction of energies both conceptually and in practice has been somewhat piecemeal. It has proceeded gradually from the empirical awareness that while transitional justice mechanisms can acknowledge, condemn or punish acts that emerge in conflict, economic and social frameworks of inequality remain in place to diminish the quality of the peace in the present and jeopardize it in the longer term. This expansion began with isolated but widely cited calls by the likes of Rama Mani for a concept of redistributive justice within transitional justice to redress the inequalities that underlie social conflict[3] and by UN High Commissioner for Human Rights Louise Arbour for a re-orientation of the field towards assisting the transformation of oppressed societies by exposing discriminatory practices and violations of economic, social and cultural rights before and during conflict.[4] Increasingly, experts have argued that structural inequalities need to be incorporated within transitional justice policy as a means of redress for structural inequalities wherein a group (or groups) of people within a state endure an unequal status in relation to other groups which is perpetuated by consistently unequal attainment of rights and opportunities in relation to land, resources, opportunities and welfare.[5] As the field transcends its legalist beginnings, justice is

---

[2] Zinaida Miller, '(Re)Distributing Transition' (2013) 7 *International Journal of Transitional Justice* 370, 377.

[3] Rama Mani, *Beyond Retribution – Seeking Justice in the Shadows of War* (Polity Press 2002).

[4] Louise Arbour, 'Economic and Social Justice for Societies in Transition' (2007) 40 *NYU Journal of International Law and Policy* 1, 3.

[5] A survey of these positions in found in the next chapter.

understood less as accountability or punishment than as a set of general principles for allocating collective benefits, opportunities and burdens. This approach complements – and builds on – existing commitments to confront issues of injustice and subsistence harms that face marginalized groups like women, children, minorities and indigenous peoples. The emerging but strikingly unchallenged assumption is that transitional justice is a 'methodology for social transformation' in the broadest sense of the term.[6]

Transitional justice scholars and practitioners (as always, the discourses between the two are fluid and intertwined) increasingly call for transitional justice to 'actively reverse the systems and attitudes that discriminate and dehumanize' across the entire society[7] and to bring economic and social needs to the foreground of its processes to address the root causes of conflict.[8] Any gains of transitional justice might not be fully realized if the structural causes of repression or conflict are left unaddressed.[9] Scholars now routinely contend that addressing mass poverty should be recognized as an object of justice.[10] The failures to analyse the structural underpinnings of violence, to critique noxious development policies or to promote redistribution mean that old grievances will inevitably transmute into new ones.[11] These aspirations are imperative not only for the societies themselves, but for the continued relevance of transitional justice – the concept risks losing credibility unless it improves overall living conditions for citizens in the transitional

---

6 Sandra Nichols, 'Reimagining Transitional Justice for an Enduring Peace: Accounting for Natural Resources in Conflict' in Dustin Sharp (ed.), *Justice and Economic Violence in Transition* (Springer 2013) 203 at 211.

7 Matthew Mullen, 'Reassessing the Focus of Transitional Justice: The Need to Move Structural and Cultural Violence to the Centre' (2015) 28 *Cambridge Review of International Affairs* 462, 477.

8 Amanda Cahill-Ripley, 'Foregrounding Socio-Economic Rights in Transitional Justice: Realising Justice for Violations of Economic and Social Rights' (2014) 32 *Netherlands Quarterly of Human Rights* 183, 183.

9 Pablo de Greiff, 'Articulating the Links Between Transitional Justice and Development: Justice and Social Integration' in Pablo de Greiff and Roger Duthie (eds), *Transitional Justice and Development: Making Connections* (Social Science Research Council 2009) 28 at 33.

10 Ruben Carranza, 'Plunder and Pain: Should Transitional Justice Engage with Corruption and Economic Crimes?' (2008) 2 *International Journal of Transitional Justice* 310, 315.

11 Lisa Laplante, 'Transitional Justice and Peace Building: Diagnosing and Addressing the Socioeconomic Roots of Violence through a Human Rights Framework' (2008) 2 *International Journal of Transitional Justice* 331, 334.

state.[12] This trend should not be exaggerated – transitional justice still remains legalistic in orientation and rooted in a civil and political rights-based framework at a policy level.[13] However, to judge from recent literature, most notably in the *International Journal of Transitional Justice* and the *Transitional Justice Review*, energy is directed towards more transformative understandings of the concept. If the history of transitional justice demonstrates anything, it is that ideas current in theory generally transfer to policy, where possible.[14] Indeed, some extant critiques of transitional justice's conservatism have been assimilated at the level of policy and practice, even if this is often superficial.[15]

This book specifically examines the prospects for transformative justice in the context of post-conflict societies. Chapter 2 examines this 'transformative turn' in detail. Though Teitel famously argued that in the present era of 'steady state' transitional justice, the field has become the normalized response to atrocity in post-conflict situations,[16] much of the theorization of transitional justice's potential to address structural sources of poverty and inequality does not specifically address post-conflict societies. Most scholarship in the area is pitched at a general level, describing aspirations for the field that apply with equal force in developed settler colonies, post-authoritarian states and states that have not undergone anything resembling transition, and so do not address the unique dilemmas of states emerging from internal armed conflict.

---

[12] Rama Mani, 'Editorial: Dilemmas of Expanding Transitional Justice, or Forging the Nexus Between Transitional Justice and Development' (2008) 2 *International Journal of Transitional Justice* 253, 253–54.

[13] See, for example, *Guidance Note of the UN Secretary-General: United Nations Approach to Transitional Justice* (2010) which maintains a traditional concern with corrective justice, albeit with some lip-service to root causes and violations of economic and social rights <http://www.unrol.org/files/TJ_Guidance_Note_March_2010FINAL.pdf> accessed 20 July 2016, or the four-limbed mandate of the Special Rapporteur on the Promotion of Truth, Justice, Reparation and Guarantees of Non-recurrence which is arguably consistent with an expanded transitional justice but underplays any desire to deal with structural issues (see the Rapporteur's Report A/HRC/21/46 of 9 August 2012).

[14] Padraig McAuliffe, 'From Molehills to Mountains (and Myths?): A Critical History of Transitional Justice Advocacy' (2011) 22 *Finnish Yearbook of International Law* 85.

[15] Dustin Sharp, 'Interrogating the Peripheries: The Preoccupations of Fourth Generation Transitional Justice' (2013) 26 *Harvard Human Rights Journal* 149, 177.

[16] Ruti Teitel, 'Transitional Justice Genealogy' (2003) 16 *Harvard Human Rights Journal* 69.

1. DEFINING 'POST-CONFLICT'

'Post-conflict' is a highly imprecise concept, but it generally refers to the situation pertaining when an armed conflict comes to an end. There are three main ways armed conflicts reach this point: (1) a negotiated settlement among the main protagonists in the absence of an outright victor, (2) victory by one side, or (3) the petering out of conflict without agreement or victory for any side. Only negotiated settlements are examined in this book, for reasons which are described below. The most common feature of a negotiated end to conflict is a peace agreement. Peace agreements are examined in greater detail in Chapter 3, but for now it will suffice to note that the typical agreement will, *inter alia*, reform or create *ab initio* the previously contested political rules by which society will be governed, provide rules for demobilization and security sector reform, deal with return of internally displaced persons, refugees and land, and elaborate forms of transitional accountability or reconciliation. Of course, even in this context the term 'post-conflict' is problematic, suggesting as it does an uncomplicated trajectory from violent insecurity to pacific stability that is belied by residual violence and spikes in criminal activity. There are no fixed boundaries between conflict and post-conflict, though there is a psychological element to it insofar as a consensus exists among antagonists, society at large and peacebuilders that there is peace, or at least that a new, non-violent political dispensation prevails.

Certainly, a settlement alone cannot be equated with 'post-conflict'. Significantly more peace agreements are signed than are ever put into practice. Depending on how and when war and recurrence are codified, anything from a quarter to a half to over four-fifths of intrastate peace settlements break down in the following five to ten years.[17] There are many reasons for this. In some cases, negotiations and even agreements may not be directed towards ending a conflict as belligerents conceal 'devious objectives' whereby they use the settlement process as a breathing space to regroup and prepare to resume fighting. They may do

---

[17] For example, Astri Suhrke and Ingrid Samset, 'What's in a Figure? Estimating Recurrence of Civil War' (2007) 14 *International Peacekeeping* 195, citing around 23 per cent; Philip Martin, 'Coming Together: Power-Sharing and the Durability of Negotiated Settlements' (2013) 15 *Civil Wars* 332, 334 citing one-half; Michael Brown and Marie-Joëlle Zahar, 'Social Cohesion as Peacebuilding in the Central African Republic and Beyond' (2015) 10 *Journal of Peacebuilding and Development* 10, 10 citing 85 per cent not lasting beyond the five-year mark.

this to enhance their status domestically before their own constituents, to legitimize themselves in the international area as legitimate recipients of the resources peace processes bring, or as a means of testing each other's will.[18]

The problem of domestic insincerity is compounded by that of international callowness. Widely reported civil wars present the international community with the choice of walking away and allowing antagonists to fight it out to the bitter end, or mediating between the warring sides to bring it to a close. In an era where the established norm is to resolve violent conflict through negotiation rather than through military force, the UN and third-party states face strong incentives to mediate – and to have something to show for it. In such an environment, there is a perception that a bad agreement may be better than none at all. As Weinstein argues, this leads to premature settlements that 'freeze unstable distributions of power and to provide a respite from hostilities for groups that are intent on continuing the conflict when the international community departs'.[19] In such circumstances, glorified truces that temporarily end conflict but omit authoritative stipulations regarding the future exercise of political power or quick-and-easy false peaces based on good faith that eschew tough choices like disarmament or genuine power-sharing, are the norm. A good example is Liberia after 1989, which ran through eleven peace agreements and approximately twenty ceasefires before the Accra Comprehensive Peace Agreement in 2003. Agreements such as those before Accra are replicated in many conflicted states and either neglect to establish credible minimum conditions for peace or leave ample space for opportunistic interpretation by either side, accounting for a large proportion of failed peaces. Some parties sign agreements not for short-term mutual security but in the strategic belief they can out-manoeuvre opponents and secure war aims within the context of the agreement. If this fails, or indeed if it succeeds, one of the parties may return to war. Some agreements are entered into with greater goodwill but fail because they are vague, leave key matters relating to the belligerents' war aims or identity undecided (e.g. Angola's Lusaka Protocol, which left military issues to be decided after signing) or

---

[18] Oliver Richmond, 'Devious Objectives and the Disputants' View of International Mediation: A Theoretical Framework' (1998) 35 *Journal of Peace Research* 707.

[19] Jeremy Weinstein, 'Autonomous Recovery and International Intervention Comparative Perspective' (Center for Global Development Working Paper 57, 2005) 9 <http://www.cgdev.org/files/2731_file_WP57.pdf> accessed 20 July 2016.

have faulty implementation mechanisms due to state weakness (e.g. Mali's Tamanrasset Accords). Others are signed while fighting still continues in largely undiminished form (e.g. DR Congo's 2003 peace agreement), see incomplete fulfilment of undertakings (e.g. the Linas-Marcoussis Peace Accord in Côte d'Ivoire) or are jeopardized by spoilers who use violence to undermine the peace or force their way into it (e.g. Jonas Savimbi in Angola or Foday Sankoh in Liberia). It is for these reasons that multiple bites of the cherry may be needed for an enduring peace.

It is to contexts where these pitfalls are avoided or where that final bite of the cherry has been taken that the titular phrase 'post-conflict' refers. The context for this book is the aftermath of reasonably successful settlements where military circumstances are ripe for resolution, where the peace agreement comprehensively addresses key grievances, initiates some form of inclusive power-sharing, and where the parties can credibly commit to abide by the terms. This includes ostensibly bad or incomplete peace agreements whose problems can be mitigated by peacebuilders or implemented forcefully by adversaries as their relationship grows more trustful. A good example of the type of context to which this book refers would be El Salvador's 1992 peace agreement, which provided for rebel disarmament and integration into the national military, land redistribution, dissolution of military intelligence and new elections. While by no means a solution to the roots of conflict, it provided a platform for sustainable peace and *could* potentially have opened the door to wider transformation. The sorts of post-conflict state this book refers to are the likes of Liberia, Nicaragua, Mozambique, El Salvador, Namibia, Sierra Leone, Nepal, post-Ta'if Accord Lebanon and Guatemala, where protagonists agree to pursue a definitive settlement. If peace is ever to occur in states like Libya, Yemen or even areas of Nigeria over-run by Boko Haram, then settlements of this sort will be indispensable in the absence of victories for one side. Of course, mere signing of an agreement would be an unacceptably short-term definition of 'post-conflict'. Even apparently comprehensive agreements break down due to state weakness and spoiler problems in the years following an agreement. Some even argue that ten-to-fifteen years need to pass in order to determine if a peace will last, but this is too long-term a view for the purposes of this book. Consequently, this book adopts Ingrid Samset's conventional understanding that a state is post-conflict if no new conflict emerges in the aftermath of a war for two-to-three years afterwards.[20] Of course,

[20] Ingrid Samset, 'Building a Repressive Peace: The Case of Post-Genocide Rwanda' (2011) 5 *Journal of Intervention and Statebuilding* 265, 268.

peacebuilding and transitional justice activities will generally begin before this time has elapsed, so in a sense there is an unavoidable element of retrospective validation to this approach.

This generic definition of post-conflict is open to the valid complaint that there is no singular, homogenous post-conflict ecology, but rather many different types. This vacuous empiricism would exclude any possibility of categorization. However, as Chapters 3 and 4 go on to argue, there are some standard dilemmas and opportunities that face peacebuilders and transitional justice practitioners in the aftermath of conflict. Though not all states emerging from war face the same challenges, enough of them share a threshold similarity in the nexus among context, opportunity and strategies to justify the classification of 'post-conflict'. Above all, the antinomy of war to peace manifests the traditional transition paradigm of a 'normative shift in the principles underlying and legitimating the exercise of power',[21] plus at least some redistribution of that power. The transition from war to this type of negotiated peace is one that at least in theory offers opportunities 'not only for returning to a previous state of order but for deeply reforming it and dismantling old structures of economic crime, structural violence, and oppression',[22] albeit tempered with a judicious concern for stability.

Thus, this book does not address states where the end of conflict was the product of victory by one side or the petering out of conflict without agreement or victory for any side. As regards victories, around one-third of civil wars since 1945 have ended in military victory for one side.[23] The peace that results from settlements imposed by the victor lasts 170 per cent longer than negotiated peace,[24] largely because the victors gain full control of the state while the defeated side lacks the strength to fight back or is aware of the likelihood of repeated defeat if they did. Although this coerced stability would in theory allow the government the power to undertake thoroughgoing justice, a government (re)established via raw power generated through military ascendancy has little incentive to

---

[21] Ruti Teitel, *Transitional Justice* (Oxford University Press 2000) 213.

[22] Kora Andrieu, 'Dealing with a "New" Grievance: Should Anticorruption Be Part of the Transitional Justice Agenda?' (2012) 11 *Journal of Human Rights* 537, 538.

[23] Christoph Zürcher, Carrie Manning and Kristie Evenson, *Costly Democracy: Peacebuilding and Democratization after War* (Stanford University Press 2013) 38.

[24] Philip Roeder, 'Power Dividing as an Alternative to Ethnic Power Sharing' in Donald Rothchild and Philip Roeder (eds), *Sustainable Peace: Power and Democracy after Civil Wars* (Cornell University Press 2005) 51 at 80.

bargain over changing pre-war institutions or distributions of wealth/ opportunity or to accommodate differences. Few characteristics of the polity or society are altered, and exclusion rather than inclusion tends to be the norm, even if sometimes concessions – even a measure of power-sharing – are granted to losing sides if it means avoiding prosecuting war to the bitter end. In wars where the state emerges victorious like Sudan (Darfur), Uganda and Sri Lanka, nothing cognisable as transition occurs in any case. As Kurtenbach and Meyler put it, strong sitting governments after war 'avoid deep-cutting reforms enshrined in constitutions while those with limited bargaining power give in much more easily'.[25] Wars that ended in a one-sided military victory do not need the sort of international mediation that could incentivize reforms for governments, and they tend to have a much lighter peacebuilding footprint – if any. In addition, the nature of the polity differs from that which follows a peace agreement. Negotiated settlements tend to introduce some sort of democratic settlement premised on power-sharing (though the democratic nature of this dispensation should not be exaggerated), while military victory tends to be less supportive of representative government.[26] These states often gravitate towards what is called 'dominant-power politics' with limited political space and some contestation, but overall one political grouping dominates the system in a manner that makes alternation of power improbable.[27] Power-sharing governments after peace agreements, by contrast, offer potentially greater scope for revision of socio-economic structures. Victory for insurgent forces also results most usually in one form of autocracy being replaced by another.[28] As familiar examples like Ethiopia, Rwanda and Côte d'Ivoire make apparent, transitional justice is apt to reinforce the power of the stronger party – victors' justice and purges directed at the loser of the conflict tends to trump reconciliation or toleration (to say nothing of economic transformation), while the victor's ability to impose their narrative of the conflict obviates the need for truth commissions to consider cause, responsibility

---

[25] Sabine Kurtenbach and Andreas Mehler, 'Introduction: Institutions for Sustainable Peace? Determinants and Effects of Institutional Choices in Divided Societies' (2013) 15 *Civil Wars* 1, 3.

[26] Mehmet Gurses and T. David Mason, 'Democracy Out of Anarchy: The Prospects for Post-Civil-War Democracy' (2008) 89 *Social Science Quarterly* 315.

[27] Thomas Carothers, 'The End of the Transition Paradigm' (2002) *Journal of Democracy* 5, 11–12.

[28] Larry Diamond, 'Promoting Democracy in Post-Conflict and Failed States: Lessons and Challenges' (2006) 2 *Taiwan Journal of Democracy* 93, 96.

or reform. It is not, of course, beyond the realm of possibility that the government or rebel winners might pursue genuine transitional justice or transformation of structures that benefit them in a more egalitarian manner, but the context in which it would happen is so different from the paradigm of a negotiated peace that this book cannot presume to speak to it.

The same applies to those wars that peter out. Depending on how wars are coded, as many as 40 per cent of civil wars simply ebb away, dropping below the threshold at which an armed conflict is classified, perhaps reflecting a mutual acceptance that a conflict has ended that may be surmised from the simple fact that hostilities are no longer occurring.[29] A good example is the Peruvian civil war, which ended not by negotiations but by the gradual decrease of conflict-related deaths to a literal handful by 2001.[30] Indeed, in states with low levels of formal institutionalization where war, political violence and displacement are the norm, the concept of 'post-conflict' may not even be that useful.[31] Consequently, these 'no war, no peace' situations are also excluded from the book.

2. THE IMPACT OF STRUCTURAL AND POST-CONFLICT VARIABLES

As Bhuta argues, the humanitarian urge to better the world fosters a propensity to see the world as 'limitlessly malleable' through political effort.[32] This propensity is exaggerated in the context of post-conflict transition, which tends to be viewed as a 'brief, but significant window for substantial institutional change … and in that short-lived post-conflict moment, a new equitable political and economic order seems entirely possible. … that privileges public interests and aims for a more equitable

---

[29] See generally Joakim Kreutz, 'How and When Armed Conflicts End: Introducing the UCDP Conflict Termination Dataset' (2010) 47 *Journal of Peace Research* 243.

[30] Charles Call, *Why Peace Fails: The Causes and Prevention of Civil War Recurrence* (Georgetown University Press 2012) 178.

[31] Charles Call and Susan Cook, 'On Democratization and Peacebuilding' (2003) 9 *Global Governance* 233, 240–41.

[32] Nehal Bhuta, 'Democratization, State-Building and Politics as Technology' in Brett Bowden, Hillary Charlesworth and Jeremy Farrall (eds), *The Role of International Law in Rebuilding Societies after Conflict: Great Expectations* (Cambridge University Press 2009) 38 at 60.

distribution of resources'.[33] The transformative turn in transitional justice is similarly guided by the belief that with superior knowledge, more openness to the views of ordinary people and deeper engagement, transitional justice can and should achieve more comprehensive and extensive transformation of the domestic structures of distribution. It is assumed that a transition from violence offers a rare period of rupture that affords opportunities to 'reconceive the social meaning of past conflicts in an attempt to reconstruct their present and future effects'.[34] Transitional justice scholars and policy-makers who share and urge this transformative impulse display an optimism that transitional justice can 'transcend' political conflict or that it enjoys a form of 'performative force' to impose new boundaries on the meaning of political reform.[35] In effect, this assumes or at least risks assuming that there are virtually no preconditions that preclude the possibility of societal transformation. There is an apparent conviction that the same aspirations for transformation are realizable through transitional justice in any number of states, even if not to the same extent. This type of logic has been applied to truth commissions and trials, which are understood to produce the same effects in wildly varying contexts, even where the most cursory glance at their historical record shows they are critically shaped by the ecology they apply to. As De Greiff puts it:

> New contexts of application generate *new* needs, yet the capacity to satisfy those needs in these novel contexts is simply attributed to the *same* measures, abstracting from institutional and other kinds of preconditions for their successful implementation, and without any careful analysis of their *functional adequacy* for the satisfaction of those needs.[36]

The problem with undifferentiated treatments of post-conflict states is that dilemmas are presented as generic and solutions as open-ended. The

---

[33] Christine Cheng, 'Private and Public Interests: Informal Actors, Informal Influence and Economic Order after War' in Mats Berdal and Dominik Zaum (eds), *Political Economy of Statebuilding: Power after Peace* (Routledge 2013) 63 at 63.

[34] Daniel Aguirre and Irene Pietropaoli, 'Gender Equality, Development and Transitional Justice: The Case of Nepal' (2008) 2 *International Journal of Transitional Justice* 356, 357.

[35] Catherine Turner, 'Deconstructing Transitional Justice' (2013) 24 *Law and Critique* 193, 201 and 200.

[36] Pablo de Greiff, 'Transitional Justice Gets Its Own Encyclopedia: Vitamins or Steroids for a Developing Field?' (2013) 7 *International Journal of Transitional Justice* 547, 552.

answer is always a better conceptualization of issues, more resources, improved attention, with the attendant risk of tautology – if transitional justice actors and domestic constituencies are willing to do everything that is necessary in the interests of transformative justice, then justice will be transformative. Advocates of a transformative approach make no attempt to calibrate justice interventions to the most salient political conditions, nor do they question whether there are any preconditions that preclude transformation in any real sense.

An all-embracing transformative theory of justice that encompasses a generic aspiration for post-conflict Liberia, Colombia and Syria is obviously susceptible to the criticism that it paints with a broad brush. Underlying political and economic configurations define likely trajectories of reform, transformation or stagnation. Some environments are simply more conducive to transformation (or sustainable peace, or democracy, or relapse into conflict, for that matter) than others. It matters a great deal if transitional justice actors are trying to catalyse transformative change in a state like Sri Lanka or Colombia, where the state controls the overwhelming majority of the country's territory and political and economic systems retained functionality (this is not to say either state has actually addressed the root causes of their conflicts, but they *could*) or in a state like the Democratic Republic of Congo or parts of Syria where the writ of the state does not extend beyond the capital and/or sectarian heartlands. For example, civil wars ended in Central America in a region with a history of liberal norms, integrated into the world economy and surrounded by developed states, which obviously offered more potential for sustainable peace, if not transformation, than those in the Horn of Africa.[37] Efforts at transformation in widely different states after wildly different conflicts are not analogous, or even comparable in most ways. Theories premised on a generic transformative potential cannot disaggregate different benign or malign situations or provide discriminating concepts for how a given state can achieve more equal opportunities or guarantee the provision of social minima. For transformative theories to be credible, they would need to at least minimally understand the differences between various types of post-war state, outline what variables matter to transformation in predictable ways or what common relationships exist between given justice approaches and socio-economic outcomes. Above all, to assess (rather than assume)

[37] Mark Peceny and William Stanley, 'The Resolution of Civil Wars in Central America' (2001) 55 *International Organization* 149.

transitional justice's effectiveness at catalysing socio-economic transformation, there needs to be some gauge to appraise the degree of difficulty, which will be differentially weighted in different contexts. This has been done elsewhere. For example, UN rule of law promoters acknowledge that in some post-conflict conditions where institutions are weak, resources negligible and the state is dominated by clientelism, neither historical developments nor economic incentives have produced the conditions that would allow 'thick' conceptions of the rule of law to emerge. Thus, any such ambitions should be jettisoned in favour of thinner versions that merely embed initial mechanisms that might or might not lead to the rule of law over time.[38] However, there is no such willingness in transitional justice's transformative literature to identify how ambition might be adjusted to conditions.

It should be uncontroversial to state that some characteristics of post-conflict ecologies impinge decisively on justice. There are two main types of variable that condition opportunities for transformative justice, namely generic structural conditions and particular conflict legacies. However, given the scope of socio-economic and political factors at play and the tendency of structures and conflict legacies to mutually undermine each other, there will of course be multiple causality – distinguishing the contribution of one from the other verges on the impossible. To begin with the generic conditions, while advocates of transformative justice are adept at identifying the need for structural alterations, they pay strikingly little attention to structural variables that explain the lack of prior and current transformation. The main such variables are state functionality, domestic politics and economics.

2.1 State Functionality

The degree of stateness affects a country's ability to provide services effectively, to be accountable to citizens and to respond to needs or changes in expectations, even if a transformative agenda were accepted by key stakeholders. The basic conditions of an effective political order must be in place in order to generate public goods like welfare or education, to redistribute wealth and resources from powerful groups reluctant to part from them in a bid to redress inequalities or to intervene in markets for beneficial development outcomes. The primary condition is the existence of governmental institutions capable of at least minimally

---

[38] Camino Kavanagh and Bruce Jones, *Shaky Foundations: An Assessment of the UN's Rule of Law Support Agenda* (Center on International Cooperation 2011) 7 and 9.

exercising authority, formulating and executing policies, appropriating and using revenue in effective budget plans, regulating social relationships and monopolizing violence. Transitional justice must frequently be administered in areas of limited statehood where these conditions do not obtain, though there is a spectrum of declining performance from merely recovering and weak states (characterized by weak authority, social divisions, some breakdown of law and order) on the one hand, to failed states (non-performance of core duties) and collapsed states (dissolution of state institutions) on the other.[39] De Greiff describes such societies as 'very imperfect worlds'; societies characterized not just by the massive and systematic violation of norms, but by the fact that there are enormous disadvantages implicated in any attempt to enforce compliance against the vested interests of powerful groups in society.[40] Weak and narrow tax collection, corruption in public services and lack of human resources are typical features of post-conflict states, most notably in Africa, that preclude the immediate realization of basic needs. Many of the transformative ambitions for transitional justice have questionable short- to medium-term applicability to post-conflict states like Angola, that had only one administrator in regions outside the capital[41] or South Sudan, where nearly half of its civil servants have only a primary-school education.[42] As Grindle argues, 'Weak or nonexistent institutions, unresponsive decision-making structures, inefficient organizations, and poorly developed human resources are likely to be overwhelmed by all the things that "must be done".'[43]

Given the chronic logistical difficulties in operating trials, truth commissions and reparations in the developing world (e.g. Liberia, Rwanda, Cambodia) without international transfusions of assistance for a much more limited set of tasks, these difficulties should be readily apparent to transitional justice theorists, but they have largely been glossed over. By

---

39 Thomas Risse, 'Governance in Areas of Limited Statehood' in Thomas Risse (ed.), *Governance Without a State: Policies and Politics in Areas of Limited Statehood* (Columbia University Press 2013) 1.

40 Pablo de Greiff, 'Theorizing Transitional Justice' in Melissa Williams, Rosemary Nagy and Jon Elster (eds), *Transitional Justice* (New York University Press 2012) 31 at 35.

41 Dorina Bekoe, *Implementing Peace Agreements: Lessons from Mozambique, Angola and Liberia* (Palgrave Macmillan 2008) 68.

42 Jago Salmon and Catherine Anderson, 'Elites and Statebuilding' in David Chandler and Timothy Sisk (eds), *Routledge Handbook of International Statebuilding* (Routledge 2013) 42 at 46.

43 Merilee Grindle, 'Good Enough Governance: Poverty Reduction and Reform in Developing Countries' (2004) 17 *Governance* 525, 543.

contrast, in more functional states that retain governing capabilities of extraction (taxation) and redistribution (welfare) even in the midst of war, it should be easier to rebuild the state and implement transformative agendas *if* such a commitment exists. One of the main challenges for transformative theories of transitional justice is to establish an equilibrium between the expectations for change and state capacity to either meet these expectations itself or secure the conditions where private, traditional or informal actors can do so sustainably. Attempts to reduce poverty, provide services and redistribute wealth have failed in far less challenging non-conflict environments.

2.2 Domestic Politics

The prospects for transformation will crucially be conditioned by whether the post-conflict government is pacted, revolutionary or externally imposed, or whether the new leader is an incumbent who seeks to conserve the status quo or the reformist heir of a rebel victory. Beyond this, crucial structural issues will shape the likelihood of social reform. If there has been no fundamental alteration in the allocation of power, then that society will prove of limited malleability. The existence of multiparty polyarchy, residual authoritarianism, loose or tightly regulated power-sharing, presidentialism or parliamentarism will all condition prospects for redistribution or positive discrimination.

The breadth and fragmentation of the government or ruling coalition and the characteristics of the state's revenue base are probably the most important determinants of transformability. For example, if the ruling coalition enjoys a narrow base of support and unrestricted access to revenue from natural resources, international capital flows or foreign aid, then this inevitably rent-seeking state has less need to respond to citizen demands or to build state-based infrastructure to collect taxes and develop services. By contrast, where revenue is dependent on collection from broad segments of society, the state needs to (re)develop administrative strength and is more likely to respond to citizen demands.[44] Transformation of society will obviously be affected by whether the state is mediated (where the state rules indirectly through alliance with local elites, often equated with patrimonialism) or unmediated (where state institutions, not local elites, govern the central features of the state and

---

[44] Louis-Alexandre Berg, 'Guns, Laws and Politics: The Political Foundations of Rule of Law and Security Sector Reform' (2012) 4 *Hague Journal on the Rule of Law* 4, 10–11.

provide public goods),[45] but the transitional justice literature has yet to acknowledge this issue, let alone address it. Transformation will also be affected by whether society is divided into well-defined blocs, is ethnically or religiously diverse and whether there is a strong or weak sense of a national public – transitional justice activities that can mobilize support across sectoral groupings of society are more likely to enjoy sub-state legitimacy and government responsiveness.

2.3 Economics

The state's economy will inevitably determine prospects for transformation, particularly if, like many post-conflict countries, the country is clustered around the bottom rungs of development indices. The damage war does to economic infrastructure, the contraction of the legal economy and destruction of human and material resources will of course be important, but they interact with existing economic conditions. Opportunities for states that historically can produce surpluses provide a very different arena for transformation than those that have never enjoyed internally generated change that compels greater state social organization.[46] The institutionalization of any policy requires a significant level of development in order to be effectively implemented. Countries with a per capita income of less than US$7,000–8,000 have great difficulty in maintaining a state framework to provide services or collect taxes.[47]

Transitional justice will obviously interact differently with states suffering chronic poverty than it will with states with high horizontal inequalities or with states with high-value natural resources, but no-one within the literature has begun to grapple with the difference between these ecologies. It will matter a great deal whether the state suffers from underdevelopment (suggesting inability to reform) or uneven development (suggesting unwillingness to reform). The extent of patrimonialism as manifested in revenue flows to elites will obviously curb the redirection of wealth and opportunity. Inherited debt is a burden neither the state

---

[45] Michael Barnett and Christoph Zürcher, 'The Peacebuilder's Contract: How External Statebuilding Reinforces Weak Statehood' in Roland Paris and Timothy Sisk (eds), *The Dilemmas of Statebuilding: Confronting the Contradictions of Postwar Peace Operations* (Routledge 2009) 23 at 27.

[46] Rod Nixon, 'The Crisis of Governance in New Subsistence States' (2006) 36 *Journal of Contemporary Asia* 75.

[47] Michael Ignatieff, 'Human Rights, Power and the State' in Simon Chesterman, Michael Ignatieff and Ramesh Thakur (eds), *Making States Work: State Failure and the Crisis of Governance* (UN University Press 2005) 59 at 69.

nor transitional justice actors has any control over. Conditionalities for repayments to – or relief from – international financial institutions depend on highly regressive poverty reduction strategies that commit states to reforms that might directly contradict transformative agendas. The transformative transitional justice literature has nothing to say about these barriers to transformation, bar an admirable but undifferentiated opposition to global liberalism (see Chapter 4). Finally, states with higher income levels and growing economies enjoy longer peace durations that may allow transformation to be sustained. Higher levels of economic development are consistently associated with greater probability of peace agreement implementation.[48]

2.4 Specific Post-conflict Variables

These semi-permanent structural features interact with more proximate conflict-related ones like war legacy, the peace agreement and the presence of peacebuilders. The nature of the war (i.e. conventional, guerrilla, international) is probably less significant than the peace agreement that ends it. The transformative transitional justice literature's neglect of this factor is notable, given that any agenda for reform would inevitably be a product of conflict variables. The intensity, fractionalization and duration of war and the asymmetries of power after it will influence factors like the state's revenue base, the willingness of factions to compromise and all issues of peace agreement implementation in states variously described as 'divided', 'less divided' or 'deeply divided'. So too will the motivations for war, as they influence what the factions believe the state should and should not do. Is the ideology group-based or universal and society-wide? Is it a successful or unsuccessful war for access to existing power structures or secession from them? Is it a war of identity or a war for resources? Prospects for transformation also depend on whether there is a sustainable peace or merely one that is frozen by the presence of peacekeepers. Any endurance of violence challenges the very presuppositions on which theories of justice are predicated. However, such variables find no place in the fourth generation transitional justice literature. Lack of appropriate differentiation inhibits a good understanding of prospects for social change.

Peace agreements are complex arrangements that can be designed through various combinations of possible post-conflict arrangements and

---

[48] Caroline Hartzell and Matthew Hoddie, 'Institutionalizing Peace: Power-sharing and Post-Civil War Conflict Management' (2003) 47 *American Journal of Political Science* 318, 326–30.

trade-offs. They are probably the most fundamental variable affecting the prospects for transformative transitional justice as they determine the scope and endurance of the peace that is *conditio sine qua non* for structural change across society. This element is so important that Chapter 3 of this book is dedicated to peace agreements. For now, it will suffice to point out some key conditioning factors they import. Peace will usually be a pacted agreement, but it matters a great deal whether the agreement is merely pacificatory ('conflict settlement' – for example ceasefire, separation of forces, DDR, power-sharing) or is a genuine attempt to deal with root causes ('conflict transformation'). The latter obviously opens more possibilities for transitional justice to work within and emerge from, as does constitutional review to address fundamental questions relating to the constitutive principles of the new order if it accompanies the peace agreements. The specificity of the agreement is important – those that are broad, ambiguous or insufficiently tailored to the context may impose limits on transformation by making every issue a recurrent source of contestation in the long-term, even if they are necessary to protect the positions of leaders within their factions in the short-term. It also matters, of course, whether the agreement is interim or final, whether provisions are implemented or not, and whether or not the potential spoilers have to be coerced by external actors into compliance. Power-sharing is probably the most important element of the peace agreement (again, examined in detail in Chapter 3). It places limits on subsequent political opportunities by privileging some political actors and marginalizing others, providing a stimulus to pursue certain social objectives over others, and making it less costly to pursue those objectives in some ways rather than others.[49] To the extent that it divides power politically, territorially and economically, the bargain will delineate opportunities for transformative transitional justice, a factor that is compounded by whether power-sharing is a transitional phase or a permanent regime type. The longer-term prospects for transformation depend on whether the agreement allows peace to endure or the main war-time cleavages to remain salient in the post-conflict political arena.

The peacebuilding mission which transitional justice will operate within or alongside (see Chapter 4) is a key element of the local ecology given that it will often assume a direct role in governing or rebuilding the state. Most often this role will be assumed by the UN as primary implementer or formal monitor, but NATO, the OSCE, the African

---

[49] Donald Rothchild and Philip Roeder, 'Power Sharing as an Impediment to Peace and Democracy' in Rothchild and Roeder (eds) (n 24) 29 at 29.

Union, European Union, regional coalitions or lead states increasingly play significant roles in creating incentives for peace. Though much is made later in this book of the impact of ideology on peacebuilding, it has organizational as well as conceptual foundations. Transitional justice's impact at anything but the most local level will be limited to the extent that the broader peacebuilding missions they are embedded within, or dependent on, have the right mandate and the requisite capacities to implement post-peace reforms. Peacebuilding operations run a spectrum of functional progression from passive observation and inter-positional missions that permit national actors to pursue their own peace unaided through to more coercive peace enforcement missions, more intrusive multidimensional state-building (over half of UN missions do this) and international territorial administration vested with administrative control and/or executive authority. Key factors affecting the success of peacebuilding missions include the degree of financial and political commitment of the international community, the balance between international authority and effective sovereignty of the state in areas like policy, legislation and constitution-drafting, the presence of boots on the ground that can compel spoilers to desist from challenging peace, the mission's time-frame, and the size of the mission relative to the state's population and geographic size. Light footprints almost guarantee light impacts. Above all, a mission's success will depend on the extent to which local leaders are dependent on them to achieve their political aims or for the country to survive. It is in conditions of dependence that international actors will most successfully encourage difficult choices to be made, but where the paradigmatically opposed situation applies in which the international community is wholly dependent on domestic actors to fulfil their mandates, there is a regrettable tendency to kick the reform can down the road indefinitely. A credible theory of transformative transitional justice would need to outline how these dynamics can be harnessed to the extent they are helpful, or mitigated to the extent they are not.

These variables, most of which cannot be manipulated by international or domestic actors who assume responsibility for transitional justice, are not prerequisites whose absence will doom transformative justice. They are, however, facilitative or non-facilitative, severally and in combination making transformative justice more or less feasible. Though most transitional justice theories begin with ringing affirmations that policies must be tailored to local context, almost no effort has been made to systematize the types of context they will confront when they seek to catalyse socio-economic transformation in post-conflict states. Thoms, Ron and Paris argue that '[c]ausal arguments about TJ should be carefully delimited by region, time, transition type, level of democracy, institutional capacity and other characteristics',[50] but it is clear that transformative theories of justice have engaged little with these variables. While it is axiomatic that the opportunity for transformation exists on a continuum on which these variables are arranged, Chapter 2 demonstrates that in the literature of the transformative turn all post-conflict ecologies appear as equivalent, flattening the empirical complexity of situations that need to be carefully parsed if key local actors are to be incentivized to participate. This is troubling, given that most qualitative and quantitative studies of where, when and how transitional justice is applied demonstrate that it continues to be shaped less by its own normative influence than by the political context in which it applies, an agent of change but one which is cabined by transitional politics.[51] Of course, one can argue that a transformative theory is a necessary prelude to more effectively reckoning with individual states, but that transformative theory itself must be shallow and misleading to the extent that it neglects even generic appreciations of how historical contexts, the shape of war and domestic political economies may limit potential for socio-economic transformation. The standard criticisms of the field, i.e. that policy and implementation are too reliant on ahistorical and decontextualized abstract principles[52] or that its intellectual and normative frame 'floats above in the realm of the transcendent', are never more apparent than in its transformative turn.[53]

3. OUTLINE OF THE BOOK

Transformative justice, to the extent it can be achieved, will be an intermestic product of the complex relationships among these general structural variables and particular post-conflict ones. While this book

---

[50] Oskar Thoms, James Ron and Roland Paris, 'State-Level Effects of Transitional Justice: What Do We Know?' (2010) 4 *International Journal of Transitional Justice* 329, 353.

[51] Padraig McAuliffe, 'The Roots of Transitional Accountability: Interrogating the Justice Cascade' (2013) 9 *International Journal of Law in Context* 106.

[52] Laurel Fletcher, Harvey M. Weinstein and Jamie Rowen, 'Context, Timing and the Dynamics of Transitional Justice: A Historical Perspective' (2009) 31 *Human Rights Quarterly* 163, 208.

[53] Rosalind Shaw and Lars Waldorf, 'Introduction: Localizing Transitional Justice' in Rosalind Shaw, Lars Waldorf with Pierre Hazan (eds), *Localizing Transitional Justice: Interventions and Priorities After Mass Violence* (Stanford University Press 2010) 3 at 4.

concentrates more on the post-conflict factors than the structural ones, it argues that states vary so much in terms of economics, politics and socio-cultural qualities that it is unwise and infeasible to assume *a priori* that transitional justice can have even minimal transformative effect. Instead, policy-makers and actors within the field should systematically analyse the conditions under which different approaches can succeed. This is not to argue that only context-specific empirical analysis is useful or that there is no place for theory. However, there needs to be a less scattergun assessment of the relationship between transformative norms and the politics, economics or culture of the state, and careful attention to war-time legacies, the parameters of the peace agreement and the degree of international involvement as the points of departure.

In exploring how this might be done, the book departs from a trend visible in most transitional justice theorization, which is to start from the position *our* (theorists, policy-makers, practitioners) implicit politics of justice – be they liberal-legalist, restorative, entirely deferential to local preference or transformative. Instead, it adopts an 'inside–out' approach, eschewing a focus on the values, biases and motivations of transitional justice actors and how this leads to the prioritization or marginalization of certain values in order to concentrate on the social and political power relationships and structures within the state that these actors must interact with – and must be shaped by. The 'inside–out, outside–in' language is adapted from Shahar Hameiri's *Regulating Statehood*.[54] While Hameiri's focus and conclusions differ in many critical respects to those of this book, I share his concern that the outside–in perspectives so common in critical peacebuilding discourse (not to mention transitional justice) mean that intervention is always seen as the imposition of external actors on essentially passive locals and explained in ideological/ideational terms. The resulting scholarly debate creates the misleading impression that intervention 'is essentially a struggle between competing and generally coherent paradigms of "liberal" and "non-liberal" peace, institutions and values', when the reality is much messier and more contested.[55] Outside–in analysis, by contrast, is directed less towards actual post-conflict or statebuilding ecologies than towards the static dichotomies that obsess theorists of transitional justice: international – local, state –

---

[54] Shahar Hameiri, *Regulating Statehood: State Building and the Transformation of the Global Order* (Palgrave Macmillan 2010) 26.

[55] Shahar Hameiri, 'A Reality Check for the Critique of the Liberal Peace' (2011) in Susanna Campbell and David Chandler (eds), *A Liberal Peace? The Problems and Practices of Peacebuilding* (Zed Books 2011) 191 at 197.

society, formal – informal, liberal – transformative.[56] It is more productive to look at interventions like transitional justice in terms of other regimes within the state that it interacts with and that have their own sources of power and legitimacy. These are factors worthy of explanation in their own right, as distinct from a focus on transitional justice as an avatar of a liberal-legalist ideology that in practice is mediated beyond recognition by its interaction with the post-conflict ecology. Transitional justice theorizing is so busy imagining where justice should go that it neglects to consider where it begins – an inside–out view means starting from the point of transition within the state, and not with our own conceptions of justice from outside it. As such, it requires the state to be considered as a site of social and political conflict.

Chapter 2 explores transitional justice's transformative turn. It examines the social constructivist notion that the discourse adopted within transitional justice establishes the bounds of what projects can be pursued. Policy-makers focus more on the end-goal of transformation ('the why') than they do on the policy-making and implementation aspects of this aspiration ('the how'). After this, this book examines these policy-making and implementation aspects under three distinct concepts:

1. It considers the prospects for transformative transitional justice within the political economy of a post-conflict peace agreement (Chapter 3).
2. It considers the prospects for transformative transitional justice within the context of a peacebuilding mission (Chapter 4).
3. It considers the prospects for transformative transitional justice within the geography of the post-conflict ecology – to what extent can top–down and bottom–up conceptions of transformation be reconciled? (Chapter 5)

3.1 Transitional Justice within the Political Economy of a Post-conflict Peace Agreement

As Chapter 2 goes on to argue in greater detail, peace, like any other significant political transition, is seen within the transitional justice literature as a window of opportunity. As the OHCHR notes, transitional justice 'is built on the assumption that social, economic and political changes are possible when significant negotiations of power are taking

[56] Hameiri, *Regulating Statehood* (n 54) 11 and 31.

place in a state'.[57] Peace agreements are seen as progressive, problem-solving institutions concerned with achieving normative goals. Peace agreements typically include human rights provisions, which open up the potential for a 'just peace' where humanitarian law, international law and human rights law create ideal demands. However, this vision of the normatively-infused just peace is but one normative frame. The other is a conflict management imperative which sees the onus to end conflict as the essential, and sometimes exclusive, objective of peace. For reasons that Chapter 3 examines in depth, the tension between conflict management in the short-term and more long-term normative objectives indispensable for a 'just' sustainable peace is generally resolved in favour of the former, largely as a result of internal dynamics but with the acquiescence of peacebuilders. Peace agreements are only ever concluded between belligerents with strong contrasting views as to what norms are important and what the content of those norms should be. The self-interest of those who wish to consolidate the gains of war-time economies and general concern for security often precludes detailed schemes for human rights, constitutionalization of structural reform or the participation of the voices of civil society or the most marginalized citizens. There is also a strong element of dividing the spoils, sometimes as a necessary adjunct to security but sometimes from more acquisitive motivations, which tends to preclude the use of those resources for social inclusion or equitable development. Power-sharing often transmutes military stalemate into political stalemate. Groups who did not take up arms – such as women, the urban poor and other minority groups – seldom have a voice in shaping agreements. Consequently, peace agreements revolve around give-and-take bargains struck by antagonists instead of shared holistic, rational political visions.

It is in this environment that transitional justice must be considered. Strategic options that are theoretically available to transitional justice implementers may not be 'incentive compatible' in as much as they are not in the rational self-interest of critical, politically effective groups (the government, faction leaders and other elites, for the most part) to adopt, as they may contradict the bargains reached to agree the peace, or appear entirely tangential to them. For this reason, much of the critique of liberal peace interventions is premised on the argument that they are 'so heavily biased towards institutions and the elites that control, hijack, or co-opt

---

57 Office of the High Commissioner for Human Rights 'Transitional Justice and Economic, Social and Cultural Rights' (2014) 6 <http://www.ohchr.org/Documents/Publications/HR-PUB-13-05.pdf> accessed 20 July 2016.

them that it undermines the very capacity of individuals in political, social, and economic spheres of life that it is supposed to promote'.[58] This has fed the transformative critique of transitional justice, which is seen to be actively perpetuating the position of existing economic elites instead of empowering the marginalized.[59] This position assumes that there is an alternative to dealing with elites, but it is one which a greater familiarity with the means by which peace is negotiated would call into question. Chapter 3 argues that transitional justice can only ever be the product of the dynamic interaction between internal and external transitional justice actors, on the one hand, and critical internal political actors whose commitment to these outcomes is indispensable and who retain capacity to resist or 'spoil' them, on the other. Transitional justice actors attempt to deliver broadly understood concepts of justice, while political elites accept, acquiesce or reject various outcomes depending on their own post-conflict interests and identities. The peace agreement, therefore, should be treated as a 'hard constraint' on transformation – without significant domestic impetus to alter the structures of society, we should be extremely cautious about expecting internal or external transitional justice actors to catalyse reform. The question is not what type of justice we wish to achieve, but rather what kind of generally acceptable structural transformation can occur in a particular country, based on present power distribution, countervailing forces that may arise with some encouragement and help, and the level of external support that can be mobilized for the particular country.[60]

3.2 Transformative Transitional Justice within the Context of a Peacebuilding Mission

Beyond the peace agreement, transitional justice in any post-conflict state will generally occur within, alongside or in the shadow of parallel peacebuilding missions. Even to the extent that transitional justice activities occur independently of peacebuilding missions (a rarity given how embedded transitional justice is within such missions and the

---

58 Roger Mac Ginty and Oliver Richmond, 'Myth or Reality: Opposing Views on the Liberal Peace and Post-war Reconstruction' (2007) 21 *Global Society* 491, 493.

59 Aguirre and Pietropaoli (n 34) 367.

60 To paraphrase Marina Ottaway, 'Promoting Democracy After Conflict: The Difficult Choices' (2003) 4 *International Studies Perspectives* 314, 321.

evident difficulty of conducting trials, truth commissions, vetting, constitutional reform or reparations without international donors or supranational help), its prospects and sustainability will be conditioned by the success of peacebuilding. However, theorization about the capacity of transitional justice to transform socio-economic arrangements has proceeded largely without any reference to peacebuilding, or any of the factors that condition the malleability of the structures of the state peacebuilders work with – military balances, spoilers, the state's administrative capacity, and so forth. As both Lambourne and Andrieu note, the research focus of transitional justice is rarely situated in a peacebuilding context.[61] This neglect is not entirely surprising. Observers note a tendency in transitional justice 'to reinvent the wheel – to believe that transitional moments require new or exceptional responses when more established disciplines have long wrestled with similar problems … [it] has often paid insufficient attention to what has already been written on these recurrent themes'.[62]

Even the elementary work of distinguishing transitional justice in the peacebuilding context from that of post-authoritarian democracy-building has yet to be done,[63] though it is hoped that this book will make such a contribution. Much has been made of the way transitional justice has embraced, and been embraced by, other disciplines like anthropology, development studies, feminist studies and sociology. As Chapter 2 goes on to explore, the increasingly interdisciplinary nature of transitional justice has led to an expansion of the claims made regarding how society can be transformed. It is unfortunate that peacebuilding, a field of study that is profoundly more pessimistic about the malleability of post-conflict societies and with expectations that are much narrower than the basket of goods associated with the transformative turn, has not been embraced with the same alacrity. Indeed, one explanation offered for transitional justice's failure to penetrate the dominant logics of peacebuilding in any

[61] Wendy Lambourne, 'Transformative Justice, Reconciliation and Peacebuilding' in Susanne Buckley-Zistel et al. (eds), *Transitional Justice Theories* (Routledge 2013) 19 at 19; Kora Andrieu, 'Civilizing Peacebuilding: Transitional Justice, Civil Society and the Liberal Paradigm' (2010) 41 *Security Dialogue* 537, 539.

[62] Phil Clark and Nicola Palmer, 'Challenging Transitional Justice' in Nicola Palmer, Phil Clark and Danielle Granville (eds), *Critical Perspectives in Transitional Justice* (Intersentia 2012) 1 at 4.

[63] Paige Arthur, 'How "Transitions" Reshaped Human Rights: A Conceptual History of Transitional Justice' (2009) 31 *Human Rights Quarterly* 321, 360; Dustin Sharp, 'Emancipating Transitional Justice from the Bonds of the Paradigmatic Transition' (2014) 9 *International Journal of Transitional Justice* 150, 151.

meaningful way is that considerations of stability that lie at the root of peacebuilding are more often considered to be at odds with justice, and not a necessary complement to it.[64]

Better understanding of peacebuilding is crucial because it guides all thinking and activity by other intervening actors. The manner in which peacebuilders try to augment and capitalize upon domestic processes of transition to alter the incentives of post-conflict elites to address basic human needs is something the transformative turn can learn from, particularly when we consider that some of the more expansive conceptions of transformative transitional justice replicate peacebuilding in a one-to-one facsimile.[65] Some generalization about the prospects for wide-ranging transitional justice is possible from within the peacebuilding literature as it attempts to reduce the mismatch between the domestic context and the hopes that are attached to it internationally. For example, Doyle and Sambanis differentiate among post-conflict ecologies and find that external interventions are more likely to be successful where local capacities are reasonably high and post-conflict context is less hostile, and less so where these conditions are reversed, but that international assistance can compensate for weak capacity and deep hostility.[66] Zurcher, Manning and Everson argue that all post-conflict projects depend significantly, though not exclusively, on the incentives facing domestic actors. That is, any co-operative peace process (like transitional justice, though the authors' focus is democratization) is most likely to succeed when interveners exercise a high degree of leverage over domestic political actors and when these actors perceive the costs of prescribed reforms to be low.[67] Reychsler and Langer outline a four-fold framework for understanding the potential for successful peacebuilding around four variables: difficulty of the conflict ecology, internal and external peacebuilding willingness and capacity, the architecture of the peace process overall and the success of the parallel peace process.[68]

---

64 Chandra Lekha Sriram, 'Justice as Peace? Liberal Peacebuilding and Strategies of Transitional Justice' (2007) 21 *Global Society* 579, 583.

65 See for example the 'thick' conception of transitional justice in Sarah Maddison and Laura Shepherd, 'Peacebuilding and the Postcolonial Politics of Transitional Justice' (2014) 2 *Peacebuilding* 253, 259.

66 Michael Doyle and Nicholas Sambanis, *Making War and Building Peace: United Nations Peace Operations* (Princeton University Press 2006) 4.

67 Zürcher, Manning and Evenson (n 23) 28.

68 Luc Reychler and Arnim Langer, *Researching Peace Building Architecture* (Centrum voor Vredesonderzoek en Strategische 2006) 48.

However, transitional justice theory takes place devoid of any such generalized analysis of opportunity structures.

If the transitional justice literature was more aware of peacebuilding, it would become apparent that few within the field share transitional justice's transformative optimism. Though much is made of the inherent liberalism of peacebuilding, it is clear that the UN's ultimate purpose in all peace missions is what it labels 'sustainable peace' (defined as the capacity of conflict parties to move political or economic struggles from the battlefield and into an institutional framework where disputes can be resolved),[69] a goal which falls a good deal short of the ambitions of the transformative turn. Though the UN's rhetoric of democracy and human rights is condemned in the critical peacebuilding and transitional justice literatures as insufficiently ambitious, a quarter-century of modern peacebuilding in the likes of East Timor, Bosnia, Rwanda and Libya make clear that international interveners are seldom capable of achieving any ambition beyond negative peace in anywhere but the most benign conditions. There has been a significant lowering of expectations that peacebuilders can socially engineer any outcome that is not already supported by domestic power elites who generally tend to benefit from systematically unequal structures. Some concede that elite dominance of society is unavoidable, and that the best that may be hoped for is that the elites prefer long-term stability and state-building to short-term partisan advantage.[70] Others counsel that the idea of reconstructing society is unrealistic and recommend a more minimalist 'security-keeping' approach that ends fighting and restores basic security rather than attempting to build any kind of political or economic metamorphosis.[71] Even those who argue that governance should be directed primarily towards development and poverty reduction accept a need for honest acknowledgement of how institutional capabilities evolve and the trade-offs that inevitably must be made. The best that can be achieved may merely amount to 'good enough governance', a minimally acceptable government performance that does not dramatically hinder development and allows poverty reduction initiatives to proceed even if more

---

69 UN Secretary-General, *No Exit without Strategy: Security Council Decision-making and the Closure or Transaction of United Nations Peacekeeping Operations,* Security Council UN Doc. S/2001/39 of 20 April 2001, para. 10.

70 Andrew Reynolds, 'Constitutional Medicine' (2005) 16 *Journal of Democracy* 54, 65.

71 Kimberly Zisk Marten, *Enforcing the Peace: Learning from the Imperial Past* (Columbia University Press 2004) 19.

ambitious output benchmarks go unrealized.[72] Similarly, state-building theorists remind us that the weaker and more fragile the country, the less sense it makes to evaluate governance services with reference to benchmarks derived from more developed states.[73] A country like El Salvador, where there is chronic criminal violence and widespread horizontal inequalities between the 'haves' and the 'have-nots', would appear the epitome of injustice in the transformative transitional justice literature, but is regarded as a success among peacebuilders.[74]

One of the key questions this book addresses is whether this attitude is the product of a liberal unconcern for structural injustice or a sober recognition of the limited malleability of such states. This brings us to the one exception to transitional justice's overall lack of awareness of peacebuilding, namely the general incorporation of a liberal peacebuilding critique into transformative theorizing. This critique argues that liberal peacebuilding's standard package of elections, rule of law and state-building, in which liberal democracy and market economics represent the most efficacious route to peace, excludes the key problems of redistribution and equality. As such, liberal intervention typically discounts (implicitly or explicitly) wider conceptions of democracy that would incorporate greater socio-economic participation premised less on individual freedom than on collective goods and reducing extant inequalities. Modern peacebuilding is seen as *alien* to the extent it attempts to impose democratic and market-based solutions, *securitized* to the extent that it merely attempts to contain conflict in the interests of the Global North's ease of exploitation, and *conservative* to the extent that these approaches preclude transforming conflicts by critically examining their basis. Transitional justice, rooted in post-authoritarian transitions to Westernized liberal market democracy, remains trapped in this liberal paradigm.[75] Transitional justice's neglect of maldistribution and poverty, therefore, is regarded as a deliberate choice, a 'constructed invisibility'

72 Grindle (n 43).

73 Risse (n 39) 17.

74 Chandra Lekha Sriram, *Peace as Governance: Power-sharing, Armed Groups, and Contemporary Peace Negotiations* (Palgrave Macmillan 2008) 45–47.

75 Kris Brown and Fionnuala Ní Aoláin, 'Through the Looking Glass: Transitional Justice Futures through the Lens of Nationalism, Feminism and Transformative Change' (2015) 9 *International Journal of Transitional Justice* 127, 137.

within the liberal-legalist schema of modern human rights discourse.[76] Sharp, for example, argues that transitional justice is so enmeshed in liberal peacebuilding schematics of democracy and the market economy that the issues of social justice that cause, exacerbate and flow from conflict go unnoticed. With this invisibility removed, he argues, transitional justice's emancipatory potential can be realized – a more holistic analysis of the drivers of conflict and capital can be marshalled to effect positive peace in the wake of conflict.[77]

Chapter 4 examines the impact of the liberalizing imperatives of transitional justice, but questions the taken-for-granted assumptions which underlie much of this critique. Above all, it asks the key question of how much influence exogenous transitional actors who are based temporarily in the state with limited resources and relatively shallow commitment actually exercise on post-conflict outcomes against endogenous actors, permanently based and, as the sheer fact of conflict demonstrates, keenly motivated. The success of transitional justice, no less than peacebuilding as a whole, is defined by the strategic interactions of international and domestic justice actors with critical domestic elites who largely dictate political and economic decision-making.[78] The resulting bargaining process is the best indicator of the prospects for peace. The international community is, at best, the facilitator of peace, but certainly not the engineer of it. As Torjesen argues, reflecting on the historical record of liberal post-conflict interventions, 'It is unlikely that outside initiatives can "impose" themselves on post-war societies and autonomously direct the process of transformation from war to peace'.[79]

3.3 Transitional Justice at Micro and Macro Levels

Of course, not all transitional justice is externally directed by the international community or those international NGOs that import comparative knowledge and mobile expertise to transitional states, and not all of it is located at state level. As Chapter 5 examines, transitional justice scholars increasingly emphasize the indispensability of what is variously

---

[76] Zinaida Miller, 'Effects of Invisibility: In Search of the "Economic" in Transitional Justice' (2008) 2 *International Journal of Transitional Justice* 266.

[77] Dustin Sharp, 'Introduction: Addressing Economic Violence in Transition' in Sharp (ed.) (n 6) 1 at 19.

[78] Barnett and Zürcher (n 45).

[79] Stina Torjesen, 'Transition from War to Peace: Stratification, Inequality and Post-war Economic Reconstruction' in Berdal and Zaum (eds) (n 33) 48 at 60.

described as local, bottom–up, micro-level and grassroots forms of justice that emerge from indigenous/traditional conceptions of justice or ad hoc forms of civil society-derived justice. Some even argue that bottom–up forms of justice should replace top–down, statist iterations of transitional justice like trials, truth commissions and national reparations programmes. Much of this emphasis stems from the normative propositions that localized forms of justice are more legitimate, more participatory and accord better with prevailing social norms in the locale. As such, they consciously depart from a previous preference for formal, national and international institutions at the expense of communities and individuals who actually engage in the everyday practices of peace and justice. This emphasis also stems from a transformative impulse flowing from an apparently widely shared faith that fruitful local initiatives can inculcate principles of peace, development and harmony beyond the immediate community and so contribute to restructuring broader social arrangements.[80] An emergent literature posits links between local justice and transformation on the basis that the former can outline the co-existence and legitimacy of multiple social meanings or can open critical space to redefine the social meaning of the good. Because grassroots approaches are informed by the local and particular needs of survivor communities, they increase the legitimacy of the demands of those involved and encourage micro-level actors to be more proactive in the process of social reconstruction.[81] It is assumed that localized justice projects will promote needs-based agendas and welfare, and that this feeds upwards into wider demand for reform by substantiating or catalysing civil society movements.[82] Localized forms of justice operated by non-state actors and civil society are presented as resistant to hegemonic social, political and economic forces that underpin poverty and structural inequality.[83]

The book examines the potential and limitations of grassroots approaches to justice to deal with underdevelopment and distributive

---

[80] Kora Andrieu, 'Civilizing Peacebuilding: Transitional Justice, Civil Society and the Liberal Paradigm' (2010) 41 *Security Dialogue* 537, 545 and 547.

[81] Patricia Lundy and Mark McGovern, 'Community, Truth-Recovery and Conflict Transformation "From Below"' in Libby Chapman et al. (eds), *A Sustainable Peace? Research as a Contribution to Peace-Building in Northern Ireland* (Community Relations Council 2008) 155.

[82] Paul Gready and Simon Robins, 'From Transitional to Transformative Justice: A New Agenda for Practice' (2014) 8 *International Journal of Transitional Justice* 339, 349.

[83] Chandra Lekha Sriram, 'Post-Conflict Justice and Hybridity in Peacebuilding' in Oliver Richmond and Audra Mitchell (eds), *Hybrid Forms of Peace: From Everyday Agency to Post-Liberalism* (Palgrave Macmillan 2012) 58.

injustices both within the community and in the post-conflict state at large. It argues that prevailing theories about the merits of bottom–up justice, which again take their starting point as *our* views of justice and *our* blindspots, are insufficiently grounded in analysis of how these communities are positioned within a post-conflict state. Though scholars in the area are commendably supportive of grassroots initiatives, the discourse has been far more about advocacy of community-led and participatory projects than establishment of causal relationships between these approaches and broader socio-economic structures. Little effort has been expended in the transitional justice literature to unpack the interactions between bottom–up processes centred on small-scale communities and individual relationships, on the one hand, and top–down dynamics that revolve around major, state-wide institutions and relationships. The assumption that changes in individual or small-group attitudes or behaviours induced by localized justice processes can eventually impact on surrounding socio-economic structures ignores a consensus among peacebuilding scholars that while citizen-driven, community-based processes can bridge social divides in communities, they seldom move beyond the local level. As one of the more forceful advocates of deference to local solutions to issues of peace and justice admits, '[i]n many cases the indigenous and traditional approaches are merely containment strategies that, while local and sustainable, do not have the potential to transform conflicts by critically examining their basis'.[84] Most scholars and practitioners of peacebuilding are therefore agreed that local approaches to peace and development cannot succeed without the state (and vice versa). If we take structural inequality and poverty seriously as collective action problems, the legitimate use of the state's administrative capacity and coercive power to extract taxes and resources is needed to lead social allies like rural or urban communities to execute an effective development or redistributive project.

While most peacebuilding theorists welcome grassroots processes, they consistently maintain that prospects for peace or justice cannot be fully understood by analysing the local alone, and so promote systematic approaches that understand localized processes as elements of an interrelated whole.[85] However, the bottom–up discourse in what I call transitional justice's 'local turn' evinces little interest in exploring systematic approaches. The emphasis on reconciliation within and between

---

[84] Roger Mac Ginty, *International Peacebuilding and Local Resistance: Hybrid Forms of Peace* (Palgrave Macmillan 2011) 52.

[85] Andries Odendaal, *A Crucial Link: Local Peace Committees and National Peacebuilding* (US Institute of Peace Press 2013).

communities cannot incorporate wider, state-driven geographies of inequality. The often anti-statist discourse of bottom–up justice rhetorically and organizationally pulls in distinctly different directions to top–down generation of public goods like welfare or education, the redistribution of wealth from powerful groups, or state intervention in markets to promote beneficial development outcomes.

4. CONCLUSION

The book essentially argues something simple – that domestic structural conditions and the domestic vicissitudes of peace-making weigh heavily in shaping justice outcomes to a degree that transformative theories of transitional justice have insufficiently acknowledged. The substantive commitments and institutional forms of socio-economic justice cannot simply be dropped into a given post-conflict state; they must be imbricated in its political, economic and social frameworks. In post-conflict states these networks are contested, and the means by which these contests occur tend to be less authoritative and more fragmented than the transformative turn appears to appreciate. The malleability of post-conflict society will be conditioned by fundamental characteristics of culture, history, agency, *fortuna* and intervention that do not depend on – and can only be minimally affected by – transitional justice projects. The book starts, therefore, from the position of transition, not justice. This book argues that transitional justice scholars should begin not from what the ideal transformative end-goal would look like, but from what can realistically be achieved over time based on the post-conflict distribution of power, the capacity of the state concerned, the resources available to transitional justice actors and other interveners, and the likely opposition of forces who stand to lose from redistribution, equality or structural reform. Prescriptions for what transitional justice should achieve in a given context would be more helpful if they were based on a clear understanding that these societies are not blank canvases awaiting the introduction of more holistic or transformative conceptions of justice than hitherto practised, but political systems with distinct dynamics which may or may not militate in favour of transformation. The direction of transitional justice energies should be determined by attainable objectives, not pre-fabricated goals. The book outlines the scope conditions for success or failure of transformative approaches to transitional justice. It squarely faces the likelihood that any attempt to catalyse transformation by building on domestic social forces, even where substantial, is unlikely to follow a linear trajectory. I do not argue that transitional justice is subsumed in its entirety into politics as usual, but it cannot be wholly abstracted from them. In all probability, any attempted transformation is instead likely to generate opposition that transitional justice actors cannot face down, and dilemmas they cannot resolve but (perhaps) only manage. In many cases, no more than minimal improvement is likely to follow.

The linkage between transitional justice and socio-economic outcomes is inevitably complex. For donors, NGOs and actors on the ground, a deeper understanding of how their programmes are affected by broader political and economic currents is necessary as our knowledge of why transformative outcomes are so difficult to achieve is underdeveloped. Though extremely ambitious in its aspirations, theorization in transitional justice is seldom able to answer basic policy-related questions regarding 'what works'. This means that the contribution of scholarship in the field to programmes on the ground that attempt to revise structural inequalities may be limited. It needs to develop more contingent and context-specific understandings if it is to more capably contribute to transformation of social structures. This book proposes that transitional justice needs to be seen in the broader context of the contingent, dynamic and historically-informed process of peacebuilding. In so doing, it purposefully integrates pertinent literatures like war studies, conflict settlement, peacebuilding and war recurrence that rarely serve as building blocks for policy reflection in the field's analytic mainstream.

Above all, the inside–out approach shifts the analytical focus from one that concentrates primarily on the ideology and behaviour of transitional justice actors (i.e. the liberalism that supposedly contaminates theory and practice) to the agency, interests and power of national actors elevated to key positions by the vagaries of conflict and its resolution. In a field characterized like so much of human rights-based scholarship by 'faith-based' over 'fact-based' prescriptions,[86] this book can therefore be seen as a path-clearing exercise to make a constantly expanding and inchoate realm of theory more manageable. It may help to refine our ability to comprehend transitional justice developments in post-conflict states. Although this chapter has drawn attention to the many variables that will affect the prospects for transformative peace, it cannot address them all in sufficient depth. Greater attention is given to proximate post-conflict variables than permanent features of the state's functionality and economy, where only the surfaces of these phenomena can be scratched. Nevertheless, understanding this post-conflict paradigm may permit more focused analysis than a generalized transitional justice discourse on

---

[86] Clark and Palmer (n 62) 5.

socio-economic transformation which eschews any effort to define what types of transition it refers to, and it might also permit wider generalizations beyond a particular state. Much of the learning experience in transitional justice is derived from *sui generis* individual states or localities, but there are obvious advantages to complementing this with general, transferable knowledge about the properties of post-conflict states and their interaction with other factors.

Transformative justice is inspirational as a transcendent abstraction, but identifying its implications in terms of the production, distribution and reproduction of power within the polity renders it more fallible than the rhetoric would suggest. The record of transitional justice in catalysing even minor change to socio-economic conditions is patchy at best, calling for greater humility and realism than is evident in Chapter 2's survey of the literature. Even if we accept that external actors can shape some outcomes in post-conflict states, there are pre-constituted, historical relations of political power and state capacity that interact with more proximate realities stemming from conflict that cannot be presumed to be more than minimally malleable. This book broadens the analytical focus of the transformative transitional justice literature from needs to opportunity to help appreciate the complexity and messiness of possible transformation. The approach is descriptive in attempting to recognize the processes that generate different outcomes, as opposed to normative in prescribing outcomes. The aspiration is not a general theory of transformative justice, but rather some mid-level theories that can explore how post-conflict ecologies emerge, what political economies they typically generate, and why these might or might not conduce to structural transformation. Some things are worth studying in order to understand how they can be overcome; other things are worth studying to understand how difficult they are to change.

2. Transitional justice's transformative turn: how we got here, what we know and what we don't

> What would be the point in knowing who chopped off your child's hands, when you can't afford to feed her breakfast, cure her boils, or send her to school … if locals have experienced infringements they understand as social, economic or cultural, then transitional justice mechanisms must respond with relevant forms of address.[1]

> There has been plenty of wishful thinking with respect to what transitional justice processes can and should achieve. Claims are made regarding the expected impact of individual [transitional justice mechanisms] … some of these claims are purely normative. Some are philosophical. Only a few are empirically grounded … the scholarly literature remains largely dominated by unsubstantiated claims about the positive consequences of various processes.[2]

1. THE AMBITION OF TRANSFORMATION

Two aspects are worth noting about the more expansive demands for welfare, redistribution, socio-economic rights or radical structural change made of transitional justice in the transformative turn, beyond the obvious point that the expansion of these claims currently outpaces their implementation. Firstly, they represent a dramatic change from the aspirations that historically dominated the field. Secondly, they are extraordinarily ambitious.

What we know as transitional justice began with a very narrow sphere of inquiry. The origins of the concept have been exhaustively quarried in

---

1 Gearoid Millar, 'Local Evaluations of Justice through Truth Telling in Sierra Leone: Postwar Needs and Transitional Justice' (2011) 12 *Human Rights Review* 515, 530–31.

2 Elin Skaar and Camila Gianella Malca, 'Transitional Justice Alternatives: Claims and Counterclaims' in Elin Skaar, Camila Gianella Malca and Trine Eide (eds), *After Violence: Transitional Justice, Peace and Democracy* (Routledge 2015) 1 at 2 and 3.

the literature and so will be recapped cursorily. The global human rights community has long believed in the desirability of accountability or acknowledgement as goods in themselves, as opposed to contingently good for consequentialist reasons, notwithstanding the obvious inadequacy of legal redress for mass atrocity. Accountability and acknowledgement were rarely realized, given the stasis of Cold War politics, but as authoritarian regimes began to give way to liberal democratic regimes in the 1980s and early 1990s, opportunities arose to test these propositions. State, non-state and international actors used the opportunities afforded by regime change to press for justice, invoking international law and soft law. Responsive new governments in Latin America and Eastern Europe began idiosyncratic, bargain-based attempts to pursue accountability for human rights abuses of the *anciens regimes* without aggravating instability in what remained potentially reversible transitions. The pursuit of justice was attenuated by these antecedent conditions. The first iterations of well-worn debates between idealists, who posited the beneficial effect justice processes could have on the overall health of the polity, and realists, who emphasized the constraints imposed by the residual power of old elites, were given their first airing. Though good faith attempts were made to mediate the tensions between order and accountability, justice was more tempered by realism than catalysed by the influence of norms. Criminal punishment, truth, lustration and reparation were generally pursued only to the extent that they did not imperil political liberalization, and if any larger goal could be discerned beyond the desire for retribution against wrongdoers or succour for victims, it was to legitimize the new order. Debates about transitional justice were 'generally framed by the normative proposition that various legal responses should be evaluated on their prospects for democracy'.[3] This democracy was conceived as tolerant, rights-based and protective of economic and political freedoms, and transitional justice was believed to help usher it in by drawing a line in the sand between regimes.

Because the conception of transition was typically a limited one implying a progression from authoritarianism to liberal democracy, this understanding of transition defined the types of justice measures that would be considered legitimate by scholars in the period of flux – prosecutions, truth-telling, restitution and institutional reform – while other measures of justice, most notably distributive justice, would not.[4]

---

[3] Ruti Teitel, *Transitional Justice* (Oxford University Press 2001) 3.

[4] Paige Arthur, 'How "Transitions" Reshaped Human Rights: A Conceptual History of Transitional Justice' (2009) 31 *Human Rights Quarterly* 321, 326;

The emphasis on elite and inter-elite bargaining relations fostered an 'indifference to underlying conditions' such as those of wealth, class division, and pre-existing political culture.[5] Because the transition was understood as one to liberal democracy, fairness would be gauged by adherence to its procedural rules and not by outcomes – transition centred on rule-of-law issues, as opposed to wider conceptions of democracy that would address socio-economic inequality or effect socio-economic transformation.[6] The most pernicious consequence of this was the colonization of justice by law and legalism, which narrowed the scope of justice to judicial and truth commission responses to human rights violations. This tended to isolate the most exceptional, physical manifestations of the conflict from the wider social dynamics that caused it.[7] Victims were encouraged to express themselves in an individual manner as part of this process of closure, as opposed to within a framework of collective mobilization,[8] and to cede any claims to more substantive redress beyond that which the trial or inquiry provided.[9] As Turner argues, 'The desire to achieve closure on past events, to reach a solution in the present that will safeguard the future place[d] boundaries or limits on the possibility of justice' by excluding broader understandings of it.[10] Social democracy was not disdained by all political actors, but it was consciously postponed in this conception of democracy. Social justice was seen as germane to the quality and perfectibility of the

---

Hannah Franzki and Maria Carolina Olarte, 'Understanding the Political Economy of Transitional Justice: A Critical Theory Perspective' in Susanne Buckley-Zistel et al. (eds), *Transitional Justice Theories* (Routledge 2013) 201 at 203.

[5] Thomas Carothers, 'The End of the Transition Paradigm' (2002) 13 *Journal of Democracy* 5, 7.

[6] Rosemary Nagy, 'The Scope and Bounds of Transitional Justice and the Canadian Truth and Reconciliation Commission' (2013) 7 *International Journal of Transitional Justice* 52, 54–55.

[7] Catherine Turner, 'Deconstructing Transitional Justice' (2013) 24 *Law and Critique* 193, 203–206.

[8] Sandrine Lefranc and Frederic Vairel, 'The Emergence of Transitional Justice as a Professional International Practice' in Liora Israël and Guillaume Mouralis (eds), *Dealing with Wars and Dictatorships* (T.M.C. Asser Press 2014) 235 at 240.

[9] Robert Meister, *After Evil: A Politics of Human Rights* (Columbia University Press 2011) 216.

[10] Turner (n 7) 206.

democracy achieved, but it was to be contested in the course of 'normal' democratic policy debates.[11]

Consequently, the early transitional justice literature had a strong influence on the parameters of the field as it developed *after* the Latin American experience inasmuch as it confirmed liberal democracy as the natural endpoint and defined the types of claim that would be considered legitimate, even as it moved geographically and circumstantially far beyond the distinctive context of Latin America and Eastern Europe. The conceptual and philosophical dimensions of economic injustice so evident in the likes of Bosnia, Rwanda, East Timor and Cambodia were not explored in any meaningful way. The over-riding concerns remained establishing political governance, reforming state institutions and securing civic involvement in politics. There remained an obvious orientation more towards negative peace (the absence of renewed social division as manifested in violence) than positive peace (the elimination of social injustices). The wrongs pursued were those gross human rights violations committed against individuals or collectivities (e.g. crimes against humanity, torture, murder) which were motivated by gaining or retaining political control, as opposed to social or economic abuses.[12] Likewise, the targets of transitional justice were perpetrators for whom criminal justice was the appropriate response, as opposed to beneficiaries of a systematically unfair economy where a more distributive conception of justice would be more opportune.[13] Criminal trial tended to cast conflict in terms of identifiable criminal acts against the victim's bodily integrity, formalizing an attitude that the conflict revolved more around physical violence than unequal social structures.[14] Truth commissions focused initially on a narrow range of extreme forms of human rights abuse, as opposed to more mundane socio-economic deprivations like land dispossession or ethnic/religious/gendered discriminations in access to

---

[11] Cath Collins, 'The End of Impunity? Late Justice and Post-transitional Prosecutions in Latin America' in Nicola Palmer, Phil Clark and Danielle Granville (eds), *Critical Perspectives in Transitional Justice* (Intersentia 2012) 399 at 405.

[12] Hugo van der Merwe, Victoria Baxter and Audrey Chapman, 'Introduction' in Hugo van der Merwe, Victoria Baxter and Audrey Chapman (eds), *Assessing the Impact of Transitional Justice: Challenges for Empirical Research* (US Institute of Peace Press 2009) 1 at 8.

[13] John Torpey, 'Introduction: Politics and the Past' in John Torpey (ed.), *Politics and the Past: On Repairing Historical Injustices* (Rowman and Littlefield 2003) 1 at 1, 7–8 and 10.

[14] Colm Campbell and Catherine Turner, 'Utopia and the Doubters: Truth, Transition and the Law' (2008) 28 *Legal Studies* 374, 376.

resources or opportunity. As van der Merwe put it, transitional justice remained a concept that could 'be criticized as superficial for addressing only the excessive use of oppressive power or the ravages of collective violence rather than the basic nature of an exploitative system'.[15] By contrast, in the literature of the transformative turn, the traditional focus on civil and political rights is as likely to be presented as a deviation from real transitional justice as a crucial foundation for it.

None of this is to argue that transitional justice was devoid of ambition – establishing a consensus about the past, ending impunity and reinforcing the relevance of human rights norms were significant macro-social processes and transformative of the context in which politics would take place. Nevertheless, they were effects extrapolated from accounting for particular wrongdoing by particular actors against particular victims, as opposed to agentless, all-encompassing society-wide structures.[16] Remedies were located very much within the constitutive domains of the state (its political settlement, the rule of law and its monopoly of violence) as opposed to its output domains (the range of public services the state provides).[17]

1.1 The Inflation of Ambition

The expansion in the scope of transitional justice from circumscribed liberal-legalist accountability to the state's output domain and macro-economic distribution is due to the convergence of a number of theoretical and policy-related trends. Thinking on transitional justice has developed less in terms of a linear progression than on an episodic basis. Like many fields of study, transitional justice developed inductively (some might, with justification, say intuitively) as new contexts and new insights led to the refining of its theoretical and empirical characteristics. As the field's familiar mechanisms were planned in new contexts and re-assessed in old ones, transitional justice was compelled to incorporate more moving parts because existing theories and practice were revealed

---

[15] Hugo van der Merwe, 'Delivering Justice During Transition: Research Challenges' in Hugo van der Merwe, Victoria Baxter and Audrey Chapman (eds) (n 12) 115 at 117.

[16] Arthur (n 4) 338–39, building on Nicolas Guilhot, '"The Transition to the Human World of Democracy": Notes for a History of the Concept of Transition, from Early Marxism to 1989' (2002) 5 *European Journal of Social Theory* 219, 235.

[17] Verena Fritz and Alina Rocha Menocal, *Understanding State-Building from a Political Economy Perspective* (Overseas Development Institute 2007) 5.

to have failed to fully capture real world complexities. While trials could single out the instigators and actual perpetrators of violence, it became apparent that they could achieve less for reconciliation than more tangible economic and social programmes.[18] Even the widely valorized Latin American and South African truth commissions have been criticized for merely revealing a 'diminished truth', defining victimhood too narrowly, ignoring the political economies of repression and obscuring ethnic relationships of dominance.[19] Supposedly restorative processes of reconciliation and reparation, while occasionally effective on individual levels, restored an unjust status quo ante. As victimization was studied in greater depth, the realization that it occurs on the level of gender, wealth and class emerged, paving the way for a greater insistence on the indivisibility of rights in the literature that was not always appreciated in the hitherto predominant liberal-legalist paradigm.[20]

In attempting to remedy these blind spots, transitional justice adopted new mechanisms, perspectives and goals. As hackneyed truth versus justice debates diminished and transitional justice as a policy option moved from the exception to the norm, there was an observable willingness to consider the various mechanisms of transitional justice as complementary. Trials, truth commissions, reparations and other forms of justice began to be used in combination. These holistic approaches did not simply compensate for the individual limitations of each measure, but were seen as inherently allowing 'deeper, richer and broader visions of justice' that merely required clarification.[21] At the same time, transitional justice became involved in a number of peacebuilding activities only tangentially related to accountability for past crimes, such as rule of law reconstruction, security sector reform (SSR), disarmament, demobilization and reintegration (DDR) and history education reforms that further compelled its holistic imaginary to expand. Above all, a root cause approach to justice reflected general assumptions about how certain

---

[18] Sampie Terreblanche, 'Dealing with Systematic Injustice' in Charles Villa-Vicencio and Wilhelm Verwoerd (eds), *Looking Back, Reaching Forward: Reflections on the Truth and Reconciliation Commission in South Africa* (Zed Books 2000) 265.

[19] Mahmood Mamdani, 'A Diminished Truth' in Wilmot James and Linda Van de Vijer (eds), *After the TRC: Reflections on Truth and Reconciliation in South Africa* (Ohio University Press 2001) 58 at 58.

[20] Lisa Laplante, 'Transitional Justice and Peace Building: Diagnosing and Addressing the Socioeconomic Roots of Violence through a Human Rights Framework' (2008) 2 *International Journal of Transitional Justice* 331, 346.

[21] Alex Boraine, 'Transitional Justice: A Holistic Interpretation' (2006) 60 *Journal of International Affairs* 17, 18.

factors – like wealth distribution, social injustice and systematic discrimination – relate to a conception of 'the good' in what is an overwhelmingly left-wing, progressive field of inquiry. Over time, it became clear that truly responsive transitional justice would need to be conceptualized in terms of a holistic approach, 'one that treats all rights as universal, interdependent and indivisible and situates violence on a continuum that spans interpersonal and structural violence, rather than simply focusing on acts of political violence'.[22]

There are many ways of characterizing this shift – justice as retrospective rectification to justice as prospective human security, justice as possibility to justice as desirability, justice as corrective to justice as distributive, justice as rights to justice as needs. What is striking is how much more expansive this focus is compared with what went before. As Ames Cobián and Reátegui put it, any significant developmental or redistributive project:

> operates in the arena of massive and anonymous policies directed to whole categories of the population and is aimed at designing a general institutional framework, [while] transitional justice usually takes as its starting point the domain of the particular and the concrete: bringing justice to bear in relation to serious human rights violations suffered by specific individuals.[23]

Though the argument is that transitional justice can unleash transformative dynamics, as opposed to create transformation all by itself,[24] what is equally striking about these claims is how ambitious these transformative dynamics are imagined. It is not enough to foster demand within the post-conflict society, to apply positive pressure to the government to redress structural inequalities, or to change expectations in ways that support redistributive or egalitarian norms. Though some suggest modestly that development and transitional justice should be linked even if we acknowledge their distinct bailiwicks,[25] for a growing number of

---

22 Paul Gready and Simon Robins, 'From Transitional to Transformative Justice: A New Agenda for Practice' (2014) 8 *International Journal of Transitional Justice* 339, 344.

23 Rolando Ames Cobián and Felix Reátegui, 'Toward Systemic Social Transformation: Truth Commissions and Development' in Pablo de Greiff and Roger Duthie (eds), *Transitional Justice and Development: Making Connections* (Social Science Research Council 2009) 142 at 147.

24 Gready and Robins (n 22) 355.

25 Markus Lenzen, 'Roads Less Travelled: Conceptual Pathways (and Stumbling Blocks) for Development and Transitional Justice and Development' in de Greiff and Duthie (eds) (n 23) 76 at 84.

scholars mere reform of social and economic structures is insufficient to satisfy an explicitly transformative paradigm implying long-term, sustainable processes embedded in society's social, economic and political structures.[26] The purpose is no longer to mediate political transition but the 'regeneration' of a whole society.[27] Positions in this area mix the top–down and state–centric (for example, Thomason outlines a conception of transitional justice as structural justice that revises or abolishes the institutions that contributed to violence and their replacement with institutions that prevent economic, social and political disenfranchisement)[28] with the individualized and everyday (Selim and Murithi assume transitional justice 'should be about expanding not only the choices, but also the options and blueprint for society and individuals to improve their livelihoods and wellbeing.')[29] Many of these plans are totalizing in their anticipated effect – for example, Gready and Robins outline a 'transformative' conception of justice that seeks to integrate macro-economic and macro–social policies with grassroots-driven approaches.[30] Muvingi argues that the mechanisms of transitional justice should be applied to transforming oppressive economic arrangements that disenfranchise and exclude vulnerable and resentful segments of society.[31] Some theorists outline a relatively wide form of 'socio-economic justice' divided into historical justice (compensation, restitution, reparation) for past abuses and prospective distributive justice to minimize structural violence in future.[32] Others, like Pillay, Mani and Alexander, argue for specifically redistributive approaches that would redress the material discrepancies and psychological legacies of conflict.[33] Sankey argues that transitional

---

26 Wendy Lambourne, 'Transformative Justice, Reconciliation, and Peacebuilding' in Buckley-Zistel et al. (eds) (n 4) 19 at 19–20.

27 Kora Andrieu, 'Civilizing Peacebuilding: Transitional Justice, Civil Society and the Liberal Paradigm' (2010) 41 *Security Dialogue* 537, 540.

28 Krista Thomason, 'Transitional Justice as Structural Justice' in Claudio Corradetti, Nir Eisikovits and Jack Volpe Rotondi (eds), *Theorizing Transitional Justice* (Ashgate 2015) 71 at 71.

29 Yvette Selim and Tim Murithi, 'Transitional Justice and Development: Partners for Sustainable Peace in Africa?' (2011) 6 *Journal of Peacebuilding and Development* 58, 64.

30 Gready and Robins (n 22) 345.

31 Ismael Muvingi, 'Sitting on Powder Kegs: Socio-Economic Rights in Transitional Societies' (2009) 3 *International Journal of Transitional Justice* 163, 181.

32 Lambourne (n 26) 41.

33 Suren Pillay, 'Conclusion' in Chandra Lekha Sriram and Suren Pillay (eds), *Peace Versus Justice?: The Dilemma of Transitional Justice in Africa*

justice *can* and *should* comprehensively address subsistence harms, defined as deprivations falling below the threshold where human life is severely impoverished.[34] Implicit within these arguments is the assertion that transitional justice can be an effective causal agent to achieve the outcomes identified.

Much like a comprehensive peacebuilding strategy 'becomes a synonym for all the positive things we would want to include in development in order to reduce any and all of societies' ills',[35] the most aspirational visions of transformative transitional justice resemble something of a Borgesian map of desired outcomes so multi-dimensional that they reproduce the entire scope of peacebuilding and development in one-to-one facsimile. For example, it has been proposed that transitional justice should be manifested in bills of rights, rights-based development and institutions to monitor ESC rights on an ongoing basis, admitting a large degree of cross-over with the ordinary concerns of these parallel fields of endeavour.[36] Maddison and Shepherd summarize the 'thicker' conceptions of transformative transitional justice thusly:

> We conceive of 'thick' [transitional] justice as the formulation of democratic governance strategies and mechanisms, the creation of functional economic, political, juridical and security institutions, socioeconomic redistribution and the cessation of armed conflict alongside or as well as the implementation of mechanisms to ensure accountability for war crimes.[37]

Similarly, Stover and Weinstein attempt to ground discussions about justice in the everyday life of citizens in ethnically divided states, but

---

(James Currey 2010) 347 at 353; Rama Mani, *Beyond Retribution – Seeking Justice in the Shadows of War* (Polity Press 2002) 10; Jane Alexander, *A Scoping Study of Transitional Justice and Poverty Reduction* (DFID 2003) 48.

[34] Diana Sankey, 'Towards Recognition of Subsistence Harms: Reassessing Approaches to Socioeconomic Forms of Violence in Transitional Justice' (2013) 8 *International Journal of Transitional Justice* 121, 121, 122 and 125.

[35] Michael Lund, 'What Kind of Peace is Being Built? Taking Stock of Post-conflict Peacebuilding and Charting Future Directions' (paper presented on the 10th Anniversary of Agenda for Peace, International Development Research Centre, Ottawa, Canada, 2003) 28 <http://web.idrc.ca/uploads/user-S/10527469720lund_final_mar_20.pdf> accessed 20 July 2016.

[36] Amanda Cahill-Ripley, 'Foregrounding Socio-Economic Rights in Transitional Justice: Realising Justice for Violations of Economic and Social Rights' (2014) 32 *Netherlands Quarterly of Human Rights* 183, 193.

[37] Sarah Maddison and Laura Shepherd, 'Peacebuilding and the Postcolonial Politics of Transitional Justice' (2014) 2 *Peacebuilding* 253, 259.

conflate it with a form of social reconstruction that incorporates education, security and economic development at all levels of society.[38] The more ambitious forms of reparation usually proposed (ranging from employment and property guarantees to compensation and guarantees of non-repetition) 'could easily be read as the stuff of modern governance in its entirety, rather than as a special case of the requirements of governance in transitional societies'.[39] What was once a ship steering a course across the ocean of political transition via ad hoc reparations, truth commissions and tribunals now appears to have become the ocean itself.[40]

1.2 The Co-existence of Doubt

However, transitional justice in its third decade as a self-conscious field of study and practice reveals a contradiction – the vast expansion in its ambition has accompanied increasing doubt about its efficacy and core premises, which calls into question the confident assertions of its potency to reverse structures of inequality. After a period of rapid growth, scholars are now attempting to systematize what is understood about the causal relationships between transitional justice and its overarching aspirations (peace, democracy, socio-economic justice, human rights, rule of law) and the micro-goals which contribute to them (retribution, restoration, redistribution, deterrence, reconciliation, social pedagogy). Regarding efficacy, it is impossible to point to any country that can with justification claim to have significantly achieved a widespread, consistent transitional justice. Trials and truth commissions are invariably selective given the scope of past atrocity or repression, while accountability and truth are at best partial due to matters of jurisdiction and scale. Vetting invariably strikes a balance between punishing complicity and abuse in the past and administrative sustainability in the future. The meagerness and scope of reparations compound each other in a vicious circle, while restorative justice often either fails on its own terms or merely succeeds in returning one to an adverse status quo. At times, it appears that to

---

[38] Harvey M. Weinstein and Eric Stover, 'Introduction: Conflict, Justice and Reclamation' in Harvey M. Weinstein and Eric Stover (eds), *My Neighbor, My Enemy: Justice and Community in the Aftermath of Mass Atrocity* (Cambridge University Press 2004) 1 at 5.

[39] Kader Asmal, 'Truth, Reconciliation and Justice: The South African Experience in Perspective' (2000) 63 *Modern Law Review* 1, 16.

[40] To adapt the metaphor presented by the economist Yann Moulier-Boutang in *Cognitive Capitalism* (Polity Press 2011).

pursue justice one must resign oneself to a paradoxical form of injustice. Warmongers who commit heinous crimes are seen not only to benefit from de jure or de facto amnesty, but they are rewarded with public office as peacemakers. Truth commissions may re-traumatize victims who testify while those who inflicted the trauma evade confession. Reparations programmes for survivors tend to be dwarfed by rewards of cash, access to training, employment or micro-credit extended to the soldiers who might have victimized them. Popular attitudes to transitional justice consistently make plain a perception of 'hollowness', a disappointment exacerbated by unrealistic expectations of what given mechanisms can be expected to achieve.[41]

Compounding the doubt caused by the shortcomings of transitional justice in practice are those that stem from its manner of theorization. Academics and policy-makers agree that transitional justice is dramatically under-theorized, insufficiently systematized and lacking in agreed-upon or proven strategies for how to work effectively towards even the most traditional of its goals.[42] There is little consensus on the roles to be fulfilled – or repercussions that might flow – from its mechanisms. The variety of disciplines incorporated into the scholarly literature is so wide that no single viewpoint has ever succeeded in imposing a singular framework on it, notwithstanding regular assertions that the field is overly legalistic. This tends to promote highly disparate and often antithetical approaches to transitional justice, which confound attempts to determine where its province lies, where its energies are most appropriately directed – or even what precisely it is. A 2010 survey of empirical knowledge within the field found it limited, questionable, contradictory and based more on faith than analysis, a state of affairs that has not changed to any significant extent in subsequent years.[43] Of course, empirically based theorization is problematic on account of the difficulty in assessing the impact of transitional justice projects on outcomes like rights or peace on a macro-social level, given the wide number of

---

[41] Rama Mani, 'Editorial: Dilemmas of Expanding Transitional Justice, or Forging the Nexus between Transitional Justice and Development' (2008) 2 *International Journal of Transitional Justice* 253, 255.

[42] See, for example, Pablo de Greiff, 'Theorizing Transitional Justice' in Melissa Williams, Rosemary Nagy and Jon Elster (eds), *Transitional Justice* (New York University Press 2012) 31.

[43] Oskar Thoms, James Ron and Roland Paris, 'State-Level Effects of Transitional Justice: What Do We Know?' (2010) 4 *International Journal of Transitional Justice* 329, 331. For a more recent iteration of this argument, see Skaar and Malca (n 2).

variables at play, even if these intangibles were susceptible to such analysis.[44] The impermeability of individual psyches prevents us from knowing whether goals like reconciliation, healing or deterrence have actually been achieved or, if achieved, whether they lead to wider relational transformation.

Buckley-Zistel et al. put it best when they argue that in the few attempts to theorize the field, discourse is based on implicit assumptions about justice that appear commonsensical to Western thinking, suggesting a failure to contextualize theory.[45] Clark and Palmer similarly worry that transitional justice lacks theoretical or conceptual clarity, positing that it may have developed too rapidly since its initial elaboration to fully think through some of the more fundamental questions.[46] They argue that the tendency of scholars in the field to engage in zealous advocacy for certain policy responses to human rights violations has eclipsed the type of empirical analysis that could ground more fine-grained theory.[47] The literature reveals a commitment to expanding transitional justice that generally foregoes or downplays any misgivings or doubts about its potential competence. Some acknowledge that transitional justice's empirical tradition is rooted in normative idealism or largely descriptive approaches instead of research that employs observation to build theory.[48] This echoes other findings that claims by advocates represent more their hopes for a 'happy ending' than evidence-based policies that the international community can rely upon.[49] 'Vague statements' and 'received wisdom' have historically supplanted empirically-derived theory about transitional justice and its prospects for achieving any goal.[50]

The dangers of such an approach should be apparent from the history of under-theorized propositions that have come and gone within the field. For example, the widespread belief that transitional justice would positively benefit the rule of law was arrived at without any real engagement

---

[44] See, generally, van der Merwe, Baxter and Chapman (eds) (n 12).

[45] Suzanne Buckley-Zistel et al., 'Transitional Justice Theories: An Introduction' in Buckley-Zistel et al. (eds) (n 4) 1 at 2.

[46] Phil Clark and Nicola Palmer, 'Challenging Transitional Justice' in Palmer, Clark and Granville (eds) (n 11) 1 at 1.

[47] ibid 5.

[48] Gready and Robins (n 22) 5–6.

[49] Laurel Fletcher, Harvey Weinstein and Jamie Rowen, 'Context, Timing and the Dynamics of Transitional Justice: A Historical Perspective' (2009) 31 *Human Rights Quarterly* 163, 169.

[50] Sandra Rubli, *Transitional Justice: Justice by Bureaucratic Means?* (SwissPeace 2012) 9.

with – or even awareness of – rule of law reconstruction missions.[51] Strong advocacy for indigenous justice mechanisms took no account of how pluralist legal systems integrate or co-exist with them.[52] Restorative justice was championed as a more necessary and context-specific approach to justice than existing legalistic models, but superficially drew on literatures that were less supportive than assumed. Though there were confident prognostications about how the 'festering wounds' of individuals and societies could be 'healed' by official acknowledgement and localized accountability, the biomedical model of trauma and therapeutic language used to describe restorative processes of justice betray simplistic views of how psychotherapy works.[53] The emphasis on breaking unhealthy silences revealed varied and legitimate reticence to speak,[54] while state-level truth-telling processes have been criticized for their assumption that societies can suffer post-traumatic disorders like individuals.[55] Enthusiasm for new directions in the field tends to trump careful analysis. Even today, it appears that exuberant claims within transitional justice in relation to social, economic and cultural rights are based on elementary misconceptions about the legal framework and scholarship in the area.[56]

Even where there are empirically-based theory or policy proposals, they may be insufficiently broad. Much of the literature in transitional justice from which theory is extrapolated or which is explicitly theoretical is derived from practitioners who base their knowledge and broader hopes for transitional justice on personal experience in the field. This has resulted in a literature reliant on ideographic case-studies (describing mechanisms and actors in a given time and place) that are inherently context-specific and not necessarily transferable or generalizable beyond tentative dos and don'ts. One becomes an expert or consultant on transitional justice by virtue of knowing about a specific country or

---

51 Padraig McAuliffe, *Rule of Law and Transitional Justice: A Contentious Relationship* (Routledge 2013) 83–114.

52 ibid 239–74.

53 Laurel Fletcher and Harvey M. Weinstein, 'Violence and Social Repair: Rethinking the Contribution of Justice to Reconciliation' (2002) 24 *Human Rights Quarterly* 573, 593–94.

54 Kimberley Theidon, 'Editorial Note' (2009) 3 *International Journal of Transitional Justice* 295, 295–96.

55 David Mendeloff, 'Truth-Seeking, Truth-Telling, and Postconflict Peacebuilding: Curb the Enthusiasm?' (2004) 6 *International Studies Review* 355, 364.

56 A claim made by Evelyne Schmid and Aoife Nolan, '"Do No Harm"? Exploring the Scope of Economic and Social Rights in Transitional Justice' (2014) 8 *International Journal of Transitional Justice* 362, 364.

specific mechanism without necessarily having any specific competence in areas like development, peacebuilding or comparative politics that give crucial insights into the factors that condition the prospects for any preferred justice outcome. This approach inevitably elevates anecdotal use of evidence over falsifiable methodologies or in-depth engagement with literatures that might demonstrate the plausibility or otherwise of the larger claims for the field's potential. Systematic research capable of assessing macro-level costs and benefits of transitional justice still needs to be prioritized.[57] The literature in the area is simply not mature enough to provide definite answers about transitional justice's efficacy in even its most minimal sense, let alone to substantiate more recently asserted assumptions about its maximal transformative potential.

A fear has developed among practitioners and theorists about the damage to the credibility of transitional justice from insufficiently substantiated claims, and apprehensions have emerged that theory 'claims too much'.[58] The expected inclination might be to backtrack on claims that have been made, but as the opening section of this chapter demonstrates, the intellectual energy is running in the opposite direction. It has been observed that the failures of particular humanitarian initiatives are usually interpreted as warnings to do more or to intensify effort[59] – every reflection on the disappointments and uncertainties of the field leads less towards sober reflection on means and ends than a determined doubling down. The best exemplar of this thinking is Nickson and Braithwaite, who begin by acknowledging the widely shared opinion that transitional justice has an expectation management problem stemming from the gap between hopes and expectation, but they go on to argue that 'one step towards narrowing this gap could be to broaden our conception of justice, then deepen it, then lengthen it'.[60] Others argue that the failure of transitional justice to catalyse substantial change is not, as one might assume, because it is a limited series of tools in an inhospitable context, but rather because it has not delved deeply enough into the roots of

---

[57] Geoff Dancy, 'Choice and Consequence in Strategies of Transitional Justice' in Christopher Coyne and Rachel Mathers (eds), *The Handbook on the Political Economy of War* (Edward Elgar 2011) 397 at 413.

[58] Fletcher and Weinstein (n 53) 601.

[59] David Kennedy, *The Dark Sides of Virtue: Reassessing International Humanitarianism* (Princeton University Press 2005) 143.

[60] Ray Nickson and John Braithwaite, 'Deeper, Broader, Longer Transitional Justice' (2014) 11 *European Journal of Criminology* 445, 445.

conflict.[61] As Balasco argues, the field 'is facing a kind of inverted "paradox of success": The less effective its mechanisms seem to be in their efforts to build democracy and peace, the more we are demanding from them'.[62] When transitional justice is troubled, the impulse is to keep digging. The problem is that the analytical spade very quickly hits the bedrock.

2. THE QUESTION OF CAPACITY, THE PROBLEM OF VAGUENESS

2.1 Capacity of the Transitional Justice 'Industry'

Contemporary scholarship in the field is characterized by the demand that transitional justice 'must' or 'should' address poverty or change the logic of systemic processes that underpin poverty, as if transitional justice is a construct that somehow enjoys its own volition. It does not. It needs support by individuals and organizations, both domestic and international, to be realized, as well as political will. When we talk about the potential of transitional justice to effect transition or transformation in a given state or type of state, we speak not merely of a normative theory in its own right or a corpus of knowledge/theory about the impact of justice measures on processes of large-scale social change. What we are really talking about is transitional justice *in action*, where those international and domestic individuals and organizations concerned with transitional justice consult populations, propagate principles, develop institutions and engage in outreach. It has become a commonplace to refer to this not-entirely-pejoratively as the transitional justice 'industry', a sprawling network of (1) advocates, donors and experts, (2) journals, think-tanks and university programmes, and (3) the practices and applied beliefs of cross-fertilized academic and non-governmental circuits.[63] Transitional justice in action combines a collection of practices, a base of knowledge

---

[61] Natalia Szablewska and Sascha-Dominik Baumann, 'Current Issues and Future Challenges in Transitional Justice' in Natalia Szabalewska and Sascha-Dominik Baumann (eds), *Current Issues in Transitional Justice: Towards a More Holistic Approach* (Springer 2014) 339 at 342.

[62] Lauren Marie Balasco, 'The Transitions of Transitional Justice: Mapping the Waves from Promise to Practice' (2013) 12 *Journal of Human Rights* 198, 198.

[63] E.g. Anna Macdonald, 'From the Ground Up: What Does the Evidence Tell Us about Local Experiences of Transitional Justice?' (2015) 3 *Transitional*

and activist endeavour among actors from the internationalized social worlds of academia, international institutions and human rights NGOs, individuals who move fluidly between different organizations and hotspots.[64] It has been professionalized and bureaucratized through the employment of experts who apply lessons from other transitional states, codify these lessons in best-practice manuals and institutionalize them via permanent or temporary institutions at the international and domestic levels to develop and implement policies.[65] They establish mechanisms, staff them, lobby for them and act as their direct agents, while also working in collaboration with local activists to augment their voice. Consultations, workshops, polls, surveys and outreach have been mainstreamed as enduring features of any deployment. Typically serving as both participant and observer in the states in which it sets up, the International Center for Transitional Justice, for example, is regarded as a highly influential reference point in terms of technical expertise, providing relevant knowledge and respected 'how to' literature. Rubli argues that this professionalization 'implies that a handful of (mainly international) experts decide upon a local transitional justice process and the normative conceptualization of justice, reconciliation and peace'.[66] Similarly, Subotic argues that the supply of specific models both creates its own demand, given limited or mixed domestic interest, and allows international experts to 'frame' the justice choices of the states.[67] The ways in which scholars, advocates and practitioners comprehend transitional justice undoubtedly influences how it is practised given that the framing process strongly influences what international donors at supranational, bilateral or INGO levels are willing to pay for.[68]

The situation on the ground, however, is more nuanced. While transitional justice organizations rapidly descend upon states via consultation, expertise, steering and follow-up,[69] they generally do so with permission of the host state. This is so in relation to UN missions outside the

---

Justice Review 72, 73; Theidon (n 54) 96; Richard Ashby Wilson, 'Anthropological Studies of National Reconciliation Processes' (2003) 3 *Anthropological Theory* 367, 383.

[64] Lefranc and Vairel (n 8) 237 and 241.

[65] Rubli (n 50) 3 and 7.

[66] ibid 7.

[67] Jelena Subotic, 'Bargaining Justice' in Suzanne Buckley-Zistel et al. (eds) (n 4) 127 at 129–30.

[68] Barbara Oomen, 'Donor-Driven Justice and its Discontents' (2005) 36 *Development and Change* 887.

[69] See, for example, descriptions of transitional justice's technocratic entries into Morocco by Lefranc and Vairel (n 8) at 241 or Burundi by Rubli (n 50) at 7.

exceptional case of transitional administration. It is also the case with European and North American donor states and apparently influential regional organizations like the Arab League, OSCE, Council of Europe, the EU and the Organization of African States, which have all advocated for, funded or supported transitional justice projects. Though Nesiah argues that Western-supported NGOs can punch above their weight in defining local justice policy,[70] without the assent or permission of government, the impact of transitional justice is generally limited. Even with this assent there is a long tradition of bad faith transitional justice where domestic governments pay lip-service to transitional justice with truncated trials, paltry reparations and truth commission reports that go ignored (see Chapter 4). A globalized, professional and highly prescriptive transitional justice network may frame the choices for justice, but the long and frustrating history of the field in action demonstrates that it exerts little leverage over the seriousness with which justice is pursued by the bureaucracy of the state or local power-brokers which is necessary to give meaningful effect to it. Critical scholars may argue that if transitional justice processes were anchored to an agenda that combatted broad structures of impunity (as opposed to a more traditional 'governance' agenda), 'they could help tilt the scales in favour of vulnerable groups and civil society activists rather than elite groups and state officials during transition'.[71] However, there is little evidence to suggest they enjoy this degree of leverage. As one group of observers laments, transitional justice interventions are usually 'delegated to institutions that matter least in transitional decision-making', i.e. ad hoc bodies with the power to make recommendations but not to enforce them.[72] 'We have no influence' is the cry of more than one policy-maker on the ground.[73] As Chapters 3 and 4 argue, compromise is the main characteristic of most forms of intervention in transitional states. In the aftermath of their experiences with Peru's truth and reconciliation commission between

---

70 Vasuki Nesiah, *Transitional Justice Practice: Looking Back, Moving Forward* (Impunity Watch 2016) 16.

71 ibid 48.

72 Paul Gready, Jelke Boesten, Gordon Crawford and Polly Wilding, 'Transformative Justice – A Concept Note' (Unpublished manuscript, October 2010) 12 <http://www.wun.ac.uk/files/transformative_justice_-_concept_note_web_version.pdf> accessed 20 July 2016.

73 David Taylor, '"We Have No Influence": International Discourse and the Instrumentalisation of Transitional Justice in Burundi' (2013) 2 *Stability: International Journal of Stability and Development* 1, 5. Taylor is sceptical of this claim, but exaggerates the influence of the leverage donors exercise due to budgetary support. This issue is addressed in Chapters 3 and 4.

2001 and 2003, Ames Cobián and Reátegui argued that 'truth commissions often exist in a sort of tension between, on the one hand, their objectives and results and, on the other hand a reality external to them over which they exercise no direct control'.[74] This is equally the case with other transitional justice mechanisms, and almost always has been – transitional justice is a practice that manipulates influence, not one that authorizes authority.

Nevertheless, this amorphous 'industry' is variously tasked with advocating, catalysing, establishing or implementing a transformative instantiation of transitional justice in conjunction with domestic change agents. Most of this chapter examines how transformative approaches would represent a significant normative departure from transitional justice as practised heretofore, but less remarked upon in the literature is how much of a departure it is in technical and organizational terms. Historically, transitional justice is deployed in the form of projects characterized by discrete tasks and predefined goals that are planned and managed by professionals over a limited time-frame.[75] At most, it singles out the instigators and actual perpetrators of violence, 'while leaving to broader initiatives in rule of law, humanitarian assistance, democracy building, and economic development the task of resuscitating a "sick society".'[76] Projects in the form of tribunals, commissions, memorialization activities or reparation programmes and the traditional concentration on consequences of conflict appeared to leave it ill-equipped to influence or inform any broader structural reform project.[77] Though the transformative turn is premised on reversing this circumspection, those who have more recently considered the strengths of the field's traditional mechanisms of truth, criminal justice and reparations are deeply sceptical of any widely transformative impact they can generate, given the preference for clearly defined, mutually coherent and projectizable objectives.[78] The traditional reliance on exercising influence (the mobilization of shame) as distinct from defining policy (which needs wide-ranging expertise, enforcement capacity and democratic legitimacy) would also appear to offer obvious

---

[74] Ames Cobián and Reátegui (n 23) 153.

[75] Christopher Colvin, 'Purity and Planning: Shared Logics of Transitional Justice and Development' (2008) 2 *International Journal of Transitional Justice* 412, 421.

[76] Fletcher and Weinstein (n 53) 580.

[77] Ruti Teitel, 'Transitional Justice in a New Era' (2002) 26 *Fordham International Law Journal* 893, 894.

[78] Alexander (n 33) 55; Lenzen (n 25) 83.

limitations. Scholars like Duthie or Hecht and Michalowski have suggested that the relative neglect of economic justice might owe to the complex nature of socio-economic deprivation which the mechanisms of transitional justice might not be able to reckon with adequately on account of their limited resources, expertise, size or capacity.[79] As suggested above, the lack of social and political power enjoyed by transitional justice mechanisms to veto actions of domestic actors, draft laws or constitutions or to bypass governments to enforce proposed measures, as evidenced by the prevalence of impunity and disregard of truth commission recommendations, is the most obvious limitation. The open-ended and contested nature of distributive justice is felt by many to be more properly the province of a more representative state structure than ad hoc transitional justice bodies.[80] Reparations, though valuable, are limited in terms of amount and so are 'unlikely to fundamentally alter the structural situation of discrimination'.[81] Recommended reparations programmes are rarely implemented fully (or at all) on account of lack of public will. Indeed, the consistent preference of transitional states has been to use finite resources for general development rather than particularized reparations,[82] which in itself testifies to the limitations of reparations in addressing structural issues.

Truth commissions are seen as possible routes to economic justice as the best 'spokesperson' for changes sought, possessing an ability to diagnose the state's failure to provide core minimum socio-economic conditions as rights violations.[83] However, truth commissions are felt to lack the size, capacity, resources, expertise and/or time to adequately

---

79 Roger Duthie, 'Toward a Development-Sensitive Approach to Transitional Justice' (2008) 2 *International Journal of Transitional Justice* 292, 306; Lisa Hecht and Sabine Michalowski, 'The Economic Dimensions of Transitional Justice' (University of Essex, Transitional Justice Network Concept Paper 2012), 5 <www.essex.ac.uk/tjn/documents/TheeconomicandsocialdimensionsofTJ.pdf> accessed 20 July 2016.

80 Jeremy Webber, 'Forms of Transitional Justice' in Williams, Nagy and Elster (eds) (n 42) 98 at 119 and Lars Waldorf, 'Anticipating the Past: Transitional Justice and Socio-Economic Wrongs' (2012) 21 *Social and Legal Studies* 1, 179.

81 UN Office of the High Commissioner for Human Rights, *Transitional Justice and Economic, Social and Cultural Rights* (United Nations Publications 2014) 56.

82 Naomi Roht-Arriaza and Katherine Orlovsky, 'A Complementary Relationship: Reparations and Development' in de Greiff and Duthie (eds) (n 23) 170 at 192.

83 Ames Cobián and Reátegui (n 23) 148 and 151; Laplante (n 20) 352.

grapple with policy formulation in relation to economic issues. A lack of real power to enact law in a governance world of painful budgetary choices, prioritization, and macro-economic stability has tended to undermine executive commitment to implement truth commission recommendations.[84] Space precludes a more detailed engagement with the shortcomings of the individual trial, truth and reparation mechanisms as the catalysts of structural change or agents of economic redistribution, which in any case have been dealt with in detail elsewhere.[85] At least in respect of the traditional mechanisms it employs there is little reason to demur from the UN Office of the High Commissioner's conclusion that 'even if transitional justice measures deal with root causes and violations of economic, social and cultural rights, their contribution to social change will continue to be modest'.[86] However willing may be the spirit, the flesh, interpreted in terms of power, organizational capacity and know-how, is weak.

However, little of the transformative justice literature precisely spells out how traditional mechanisms outlined above can generate structural change. Though some, like Pasipanodya, remain sanguine about the possibilities for using truth commissions to air socio-economic grievances or using reparations to redress collective injustices like land inequality,[87] few of the most forceful advocates for transitional justice examined in this book explicitly place their faith in trials, reparations or truth commissions. This can, in some cases, be attributed to a strikingly muted acceptance that the more familiar mechanisms are unconducive to transformation. However, it might also be explained by the concern among critics that because the transitional justice industry that has propagated and implemented these mechanisms comes from the West, transitional justice as traditionally understood is too strongly influenced and dominated by liberal values.[88]

---

[84] Rama Mani, 'Rebuilding an Inclusive Political Community after War' (2005) 36 *Security Dialogue* 511, 518.

[85] Waldorf (n 80); Matthew Evans, 'Structural Violence, Socioeconomic Rights and Transformative Justice' (2016) 15 *Journal of Human Rights* 1; Padraig McAuliffe, 'Rhetoric and Realpolitik: Interrogating the Relationship between Transitional Justice and Socio-Economic Justice' (2012/13) 23 *Finnish Yearbook of International Law* 239.

[86] UN Office of the High Commissioner for Human Rights (n 81) 57.

[87] Tafadzwa Pasipanodya, 'A Deeper Justice: Economic and Social Justice as Transitional Justice in Nepal' (2008) 2 *International Journal of Transitional Justice* 378, 392–95.

[88] Rubli (n 50) 7; Gready and Robins (n 22) 342–43.

Where then do transitional justice scholars see the potential for transformation of unjust socio-economic structures? The state, peacebuilding and civil society are the most obvious channels, but, perhaps surprisingly, only civil society is strongly emphasized. The main explanation for this lies in the fact that much of the transformative turn originates in a critical approach that takes as its starting point the problematization of the dominant frameworks (the state and international peacebuilding) and instead seeks to find transformative alternatives that shift the basis on which the meaning of justice is constituted (most notably civil society broadly understood). Given its ability to pass laws, raise revenue and potentially solve the largest collective action problems, one would assume transformative theories of transitional justice would have something to say about the generic possibilities or potentials for transitional justice actors to guide or influence post-conflict governments. Scholars like Sharp and Andrieu have argued that transitional justice could embrace or be connected to broader social justice and development projects like nationalization, special or redistributive taxation, expropriation, anti-corruption commissions, special developmental assistance to regions and affirmative action as the most likely avenues for socio-economic reform.[89] However, as Chapter 4 goes on to describe, for many critics of traditional transitional justice, the post-conflict state is too inherently conservative and elite-driven to serve as a vehicle for change. For those with a less jaundiced view of the state, its weakness (examined below in section 2.2) precludes it from being the vehicle for transformation. Contemporary transitional justice discourses 'perceive the State as only one among several actors with the ability to shape and implement transitional justice'.[90] The UN (and other peacebuilding agents) would appear to offer another avenue, given its record in assisting in the design and implementation of transitional justice mechanisms, providing technical and logistical support, facilitating national consultations and supporting capacity-building.[91] Though many critics of transitional justice see liberal peacebuilding as something with a near-hegemonic potential

[89] Andrieu (n 27) 544; Dustin Sharp, 'Interrogating the Peripheries: The Preoccupations of Fourth Generation Transitional Justice' (2013) 26 *Harvard Human Rights Journal* 149, 171.

[90] Thomas Obel Hansen, 'The Vertical and Horizontal Expansion of Transitional Justice' in Buckley-Zistel et al. (eds) (n 4) 105 at 107.

[91] UN Secretary-General, 'Guidance Note of the Secretary-General: United Nations Approach to Transitional Justice' (2010) 3 and 9 <https://www.un.org/ruleoflaw/files/TJ_Guidance_Note_March_2010FINAL.pdf> accessed 20 July 2016.

to alter domestic political and economic structures, it too has extreme limitations to its transformative potential. As Chapter 4 further illustrates, peacebuilding is seen as an inherently liberal undertaking which the elite international and donor network of transitional justice is inseparable from. Peacebuilders are rejected as transitional justice change agents on account of their liberal-legalist inclinations to elevate freedom and liberty over equality or structural transformation.

This explains why locally rooted social movements are explicitly preferred to internationally exported models of transitional justice. Advocates of transformative transitional justice assume that civil society is an advocate for radical social change, and it may lose this ability if it is co-opted as a key actor in peacebuilding and statebuilding.[92] Civil society empowerment programmes are invariably part of transitional justice activities as they are seen to spring organically from the agency of the citizenry and therefore are sensitive to the needs, culture, ideas and norms of those affected by past harms.[93] The UN's *Rule of Law and Transitional Justice Report* calls for the active and meaningful participation of national stakeholders like civil society and key groups representing women, minorities, displaced persons and refugees in the expectation that they can foreground needs that might otherwise be passed over.[94] The impact of constructivist thinking on transitional justice is examined later in this chapter, but one of its core tenets is that civil society can employ soft power, persuading governments to adopt ideas or change behaviours through attraction, exhortation and example. Gready and Robins, for example, argue that civil society and victim mobilization can effect shifts in agency and power relations over time even in the face of official opposition due to long-term participation, constituency building and new patterns of engagement.[95] Transitional justice and civil society often enjoy mutually beneficial relationships. Civil society is usually the most avid advocate of transitional justice and often plays a role in designing, monitoring and assisting it. Transitional justice reciprocates by offering normative support and an institutional platform for non-state actors to campaign and propagate principles like those in the

---

[92] See Chapter 5, Section 7.

[93] Aaron Boesenecker and Leslie Vinjamuri, 'Lost in Translation? Civil Society, Faith-Based Organizations and the Negotiation of International Norms' (2011) 5 *International Journal of Transitional Justice* 345, 363.

[94] UN Secretary-General, *The Rule of Law and Transitional Justice in Conflict and Post-Conflict Societies*, UN Doc. S/2004/616 of 3 August 2004, para. 15.

[95] Gready and Robins (n 22) 358.

International Covenant on Economic, Social and Cultural Rights. It also often fosters an upswing in the numbers and activity of civil society. While most advocates of a role for transitional justice assiduously warn against the dangers of idealizing or romanticizing civil society,[96] the greater danger may in fact be to exaggerate the potential of civil society networks that advocate radical change and mobilize particular agendas to this end to exercise strong influence on policy-making in post-conflict societies. For example, Hovil and Okello argue:

> Civil society actors, with control of vast resources (in aggregate), are proliferating in postconflict and postauthoritarian contexts, settings in which they are often able to exert disproportionate influence relative to the fragility of the state. Their ability to influence decision-making processes within governments (as well as the UN) has made these entities indispensable patrons in contemporary politics … civil society (which includes social movements) have the potential – and, indeed, the imperative – to ensure that any transition is genuinely transformational.[97]

Civil society undoubtedly becomes more important in post-conflict contexts, often taking over the role of the state in welfare and monitoring reformed state institutions. However, civil society and social movements will still manifest many of the same weaknesses as traditional transitional justice mechanisms. Firstly, and most obviously, they share the same lack of coercive power. While civil society and social movements can affect the more intangible factors underlying conflict like public attitudes and relationships among groups (though it is difficult to measure their contribution to social change in the post-conflict environment), non-governmental organizations 'generally do not have the capacity to change political incentives', as they lack either carrots or sticks.[98] Little or no attention is paid to potential links between transitional justice-based social movements and the largest civil society organizations like political parties and trade unions with the greatest potential to mediate and leverage demand from below. Hovil and Okello are correct that civil society can check and dilute the power of the state, but for transformation the key must surely be to harness the state instead. However, civil society

---

96 For example, Lucy Hovil and Moses Okello, 'Editorial Note' (2011) 5 *International Journal of Transitional Justice* 333, 337.

97 ibid 333.

98 Diana Chigas, 'Capacities and Limits of NGOs as Conflict Managers' in Chester A. Crocker, Fen Osler Hampson and Pamela Aall (eds), *Leashing the Dogs of War: Conflict Management in a Divided World* (US Institute of Peace Press 2007) 553 at 562–63 and 575.

can rarely do so on a macro-level commensurate with transformative change. Again echoing the problems of traditional transitional justice mechanisms, the types of consultation post-conflict states engage in with civil society 'tends to be project centered, and not provide the sort of broad participation and accountability that are useful to reduce exclusionary governance … It is rare that civil society groups are formally part of state decision-making about funding priorities or about resource management and allocation in ways that affect specific regions and ethnic groups'.[99] The ability of civil society and social movements to articulate interests is assumed, not proven – given the multiplicity of agendas, the lack of accountability and tendencies to divide across the lines of the prior conflict that typically blight post-conflict civil society, some of the enthusiasm about the efficacy of civil society in catalysing structural change may have to be curbed. As Lutz argues, while civil society can keep issues of accountability alive, it still 'takes a certain level of government political will to decisively move forward'.[100] Even scholars who are sanguine about a role for civil society in transitional justice admit that it may be weak, disorganized and lacking in independence in post-conflict situations contexts.[101] Typically, efforts to negotiate peace and implement the settlements agreed fail to assign a role for civil society.[102]

It is perhaps for these reasons that no advocate of a transformative role for transitional justice has sketched how civil society can do so beyond vague intimations that bottom-up movements facilitate social justice through targeted advocacy campaigns, lobbying and government monitoring, media attention and support from international networks. Even the very obvious balance between civil society as a partner of transformation and a critical evaluator of progress in this regard has yet to be problematized. There is no consensus in the transformative turn over whether the role of civil society is to be consultative (having an

---

[99] Charles Call, *Why Peace Fails: The Causes and Prevention of Civil War Recurrence* (Georgetown University Press 2012) 269.

[100] Ellen Lutz, 'Transitional Justice: Lessons Learned and the Road Ahead' in Naomi Roht-Arriaza and Javier Mariezcurrena (eds), *Transitional Justice in the Twenty-First Century: Beyond Truth Versus Justice* (Cambridge University Press 2006) 325 at 338.

[101] Andrieu (n 27) 550; Eric Wielbelhaus-Brahm, 'Transitional Justice, Civil Society, and the Development of the Rule of Law in Post-Conflict Societies' (2007) 9 *International Journal of Not-For-Profit Law* 1, 1.

[102] See Chapter 3, Section 3.1 on the failure to include civil society voices during and after peace negotiations.

opportunity to formally voice opinion and formulate policy) or direct (where it has a role in developing and implementing policy). By comparison, the means by which civil society can catalyse truth commissions and criminal accountability are well understood. Fischer has argued that when discussing civil society organizations in the context of post-conflict recovery it is often unclear whether the term is linked to a normative notion (i.e. the belief that civil society is good and should be fostered) or used as an analytic concept (i.e. assessing the uses to which it can concretely be put).[103] The blind but under-specified faith that civil society can affect transformative change to structures of inequality and poverty suggests that the advocacy of a leading role for civil society in transitional justice is as much about comprehending our own participation in these discourses as it is about understanding how civil society can concretely impact society in the context of a given post-conflict ecology. The questionable potential for bottom-up justice to effect meaningful transformation is examined in much greater detail in Chapter 5.

2.2 Capacity of the State

If the mechanisms of transitional justice are weak, so too is the state they attempt to influence. The transformative transitional justice literature concerns itself more with the *kind* of transitional state it observes or desires (i.e. the organizing principles that inform the rules of society, such as liberalism, welfarism, redistributivism) than the *degree* of state (the organizational apparatus to regulate, control, extract from and develop society). This is a matter of some concern as the transformative ambitions assigned to transitional justice at times imply social contract-type expectations for service delivery. Even if we do not go that far, to serve everyday lives or restructure relations of wealth would appear to assume the existence of an at least minimally functioning developmental state 'whose politics have concentrated sufficient power, autonomy and capacity at the centre to shape, pursue and encourage the achievement of explicit developmental objectives, whether by establishing and promoting the conditions and direction of economic growth, or by organizing it directly, or a varying combination of both'.[104] This should not be interpreted as relating solely to the capacity of state institutions to

---

[103] Martina Fischer, *Civil Society in Conflict Transformation: Ambivalence, Potentials and Challenges* (Berghof Research Center for Constructive Conflict Management 2006) 21.

[104] Adrian Leftwich, 'Bringing Politics Back in: Towards a Model of the Developmental State' (1995) 31 *Journal of Development Studies* 400, 401.

manage the affairs of state, but rather to ensure that certain political goods like security, adjudication of disputes, education, infrastructure or healthcare can be delivered with some degree of generality across the polity by private, indigenous or informal non-state actors if necessary.

Transformative justice must frequently be pursued in states that are socio-politically weak inasmuch as they lack the ability to govern, maintain a monopoly of violence, extract revenue or maintain social cohesiveness and identification of its citizens with the polity.[105] Weak policy formulation, ineffective bureaucratic administration and corruption blight the pursuit of any development or poverty alleviation strategy, regardless of how well it is articulated. Some states, particularly those in Africa, may never have enjoyed Weberian rational-legal bureaucracy or even other less demanding metrics of institutional effectiveness, and instead depend on patrimonial networks for minimal, and often exclusionary, governance. In particular, in African states that enjoy juridical statehood but none of the infrastructural capacity or control of citizenry that would make it a reality, 'state failure is less an objective condition than a permanent mode of political operation'.[106] This weak state capacity is further debased by conflict.

In this respect, advocates of transformative transitional justice risk replicating the traditional failures of international human rights organizations and democracy promoters to realize that certain basic preconditions need to be established before the chasm that exists between what societies are supposed to do and what they can reasonably be expected to achieve is bridged. Humanitarian outcomes in post-conflict settings need radically different strategies than those brought to bear on stable societies due to the lack of anything resembling domestic planning and enforcement capacity. However, human rights scholars tend to focus more on recipients and rights holders than the nuts and bolts of realization, leading to the 'free-floating rhetoric' identified by O'Neill that blandly overlooks the need for realistic accounts of how and why agents should carry out their obligations.[107] These, after all, are states that have recently failed to fulfil their most basic function – securing internal peace – and

[105] Boaz Atzili, 'When Good Fences Make Bad Neighbors: Fixed Borders, State Weakness and International Conflict' (2006–2007) 31 *International Security* 139, 146.

[106] Pierre Englebert and Denis Tull, 'Postconflict Reconstruction in Africa: Flawed Ideas about Failed States' (2008) 32 *International Security* 106, 110.

[107] Onora O'Neill, 'Agents of Justice' (2001) 32 *Metaphilosophy* 180, 183 and 186.

that are frequently subject to processes of state reconstruction. Transitional justice, like most post-conflict human rights advocacy, essentially assumes the functionality of the very institutions contemporaneous peacebuilding missions are attempting to resurrect or originate.[108] Moreover, state-building of necessity emphasizes the development of security, governance and rule of law functions before responsiveness to the longer-term socio-economic needs of the people, for reasons that are explored in Chapters 3 and 4. Without a state apparatus to translate decisions into authoritative rules applicable to society overall, the state will be reliant on bargaining with powerful class and identity group elites to achieve policy goals. Institutions and policies that do respond to structural inequalities and welfare needs may need to be created from square one, imposing enormous one-time start-up costs that transformative justice wish-lists seldom consider. Even where state-building occurs, power-sharing may have the effect of paralyzing the state as an autonomous, non-partisan deliverer of social goods, a danger that is examined in detail in Chapter 4. Capacity in most states is measured in terms of its distance from Weberian ideal types. However, in view of problems of post-conflict political economy and the extreme reluctance of governments, faction leaders and elites to relinquish control of economic assets, the most appropriate measurement might be that of Arnold, who defines it as 'a state's ability to devise and implement policies *even against the will of major social actors*'.[109]

Transitional justice scholars are already familiar with over-promising. The mandate given to the DR Congo's abortive truth commission to 'decide the fate of the victims of … crimes, for hearing them, and taking all the necessary measures to compensate them and completely restore their dignity' or the Sierra Leone Truth and Reconciliation Commission's recommendation that reparations be awarded in 'social service packages' encompassing medical care, psychological support, education and skills training were beyond anything that could reasonably be expected of those states or, indeed, of most states that have been ravaged by war, even with international assistance.[110] If any transitional justice scholar advocating a

---

[108] Tonya Putnam, 'Human Rights and Sustainable Peace' in Stephen John Stedman and Donald Rothchild (eds), *Ending Civil Wars: The Implementation of Peace Agreements* (Lynne Rienner 2002) 237 at 238.

[109] Walter Arnold, 'Bureaucratic Politics, State Capacity, and Taiwan's Automobile Industrial Policy' (1989) 15 *Modern China* 178, 179.

[110] Inter-Congolese Dialogue, Resolution DIC/CPR/04 and Truth and Reconciliation Commission, *Witness to Truth: Report of the Sierra Leone Truth and Reconciliation Commission* (Freetown 2004), Chapter 4, 245–47.

transformative role for transitional justice had been asked whether even these more limited goals were achievable in the DR Congo or Sierra Leone at the time, they presumably would have expressed significant doubts. Nevertheless, when we move from the particular context of a state like the DR Congo or Sierra Leone to general theorization, the obvious limitations that characterize the typical post-conflict state are apparently discarded. Little attention is paid in human rights frameworks as to how they should be assured in the absence of a functional and committed state. Haldeman and Kouassi note the inattention to the special challenges generated by the poverty and resource scarcity of transitional states. They contend that if the thesis that transitional justice can improve economic, social and cultural rights 'is not to be merely an ideal without practical import, it must provide a realistic view of how to make it "work" in the world as it is'; something it has demonstrably failed to do.[111] In the African context, less optimistic scholars warn of the need to thoroughly assess the institutional basis of transitional states before embarking on justice projects, and to cultivate 'extremely modest expectations about what can be delivered'.[112]

2.3 The Problem of Vagueness

The unreflective, all-encompassing approach to theorizing transitional justice has encouraged an extreme conceptual imprecision when it comes to elaborating how abstract desires can be converted to practical activity, bearing in mind the weakness of transitional justice's traditional mechanisms, the civil society actors they rely on and the state in which they will operate. The various transformative or socio-economic conceptions of transitional justice outlined at the start of this chapter are more a nodal cluster of egalitarian principles than anything resembling a coherent programme. Any type of socio-economic transformation within a state must potentially comprehend all relations between the state's delivery of services and society's articulation of need, plus the alignment of socially powerful groups who enjoy the power to resist or legitimate re-ordered socio-economic relations. At even the most basic blueprint level, a

---

[111] Frank Haldeman and Rachelle Kouassi, 'Transitional Justice without Economic, Social and Cultural Rights?' in Eibe Riedel, Gilles Giacca and Christophe Golay (eds), *Economic, Social and Cultural Rights: Contemporary Issues and Challenges* (Oxford University Press 2014) 498 at 509.

[112] Lydiah Bosire, *Overpromised, Underdelivered: Transitional Justice in Sub-Saharan Africa* (International Center for Transitional Justice 2006) 34–35.

relationship between transitional justice and factors like growth, redistribution, the market and the state must be canvassed. Economic relationships between state and society, and within society, must be conceptualized across diverse areas of economic and political activity to restrain, accommodate and utilize power.

However, because much of the 'transformative turn' implicitly or explicitly departs from the familiar transitional justice mechanisms while at the same time under-elaborating the role of other agents like the state, peacebuilders or civil society, it instead mostly consists of vague assertions that transitional justice as a field can and must 'elaborate remedial actions that comprehensively address grievances in societies emerging from conflict', without ever suggesting what those actions should be.[113] Far from specifying how these mechanisms could be reformed to advance a transformative vision of transition, scholars in the area have taken refuge in a form of positive ambiguity in which the revelatory or participatory nature of transformative transitional justice has an inherently catalytic or beneficial effect on domestic change processes. For example, reconceiving the social meaning of past conflicts may allow for the reconstruction of their present and future effects,[114] exposing violations of ESC rights may assist in transforming oppressed societies,[115] transitional justice can expand the normative parameters of human rights debates and so expand the range of claims validated as rights.[116] Advocates of a role for transitional justice in fundamentally altering the structures of divided societies acknowledge that thus far all we have are a series of hypothetical connections to be further researched,[117] 'points of

---

[113] Japan International Co-operation Society and International Center for Transitional Justice, 'Workshop on Transitional Justice and Development in Africa: Enhancing Socio-Economic Justice in Societies in Transition: Case Studies on the African Continent' (2008) 7 <http://ictj.org/sites/default/files/ICTJ-JICA-Africa-Justice-Development-2008-English.pdf> accessed 20 July 2016.

[114] Daniel Aguirre and Irene Pietropaoli, 'Gender Equality, Development and Transitional Justice: The Case of Nepal' (2008) 2 *International Journal of Transitional Justice* 356, 357.

[115] Louise Arbour, 'Economic and Social Justice for Societies in Transition' (2007) 40 *NYU Journal of International Law and Policy* 1, 3–4.

[116] Gready and Robins (n 22) 354.

[117] Colvin (n 75) 414.

possible interconnection',[118] 'a starting point for a broader conversation'[119] and underdeveloped concepts and boundaries.[120] There is minimal understanding of the relationship between proposed outcomes and even the most general policy and programme interventions. Suggested activities ('recovery of the deeper politics of transitional justice',[121] 'reframings of socio-economic rights and continuities of conflict',[122] 'promot[ing] more coherent and comprehensive recognition')[123] are more an incitement to further reflection than anything resembling a broadly supportable policy agenda. The assumption instead in most transitional justice theorization is that if sufficient planning and technique can be brought to bear on the ground, any goal can effectively be realized, obviating the need to elaborate in theory even a minimal set of priorities or acceptable trade-offs or to outline sequences of actions.[124]

Chapter 4, Section 5 examines precisely how vague these injunctions tend to be. For now, it will suffice to note that while the transformative turn is adept at explaining the shortcomings of transitional justice *ex posteriori*, little or no theory within it is oriented towards developing *ex ante* knowledge of how to accumulate sufficient authority and capability to define what constitutes the public wealth that is to be redistributed, how it is to be collected or used to provide services. Sequenced, organizationally competent and sustainable pathways to economic justice with a level of coherence needed to mobilize elites or activate grassroots social support, and that anticipate predictable barriers to progress like state bureaucratic weakness, patrimonial economics or elite control of the economy's levers, are conspicuous by their absence. There is also a noticeable lack of anything resembling what development actors call a 'theory of change' that would articulate how and why a transitional justice intervention would effect a specific change. Theories of change emerged within international development studies to both explore change in a manner that plausibly reflected complex and systemic understandings of intervention in a given society and to demonstrate impact as part of the emergent results agenda. They outline the 'set of assumptions that

---

118 ibid.

119 Zinaida Miller, 'Effects of Invisibility: In Search of the "Economic" in Transitional Justice' (2008) 2 *International Journal of Transitional Justice* 266, 291.

120 Hecht and Michalowski (n 79) 1.

121 Sharp (n 89) 157.

122 Gready and Robins (n 22) 355.

123 Sankey (n 34) 121 (Preamble).

124 Colvin (n 75).

explain both the mini-steps that lead to a long term goal and the connections between these activities and the outcomes of an intervention or programme', connecting activities to outcomes and describing a basic organization or programme pathway to the latter.[125] Even the most basic or generic theory of change in the transformative transitional justice literature would explicitly outline a link between a transitional justice intervention, a change process and ultimate goals, the inputs needed, the actors involved, internal or external risks, obstacles to success and potential knock-on effects.[126] Such thinking, however, has rarely been present in a literature that assumes better insight, participatory ethics or broader articulation of socio-economic rights have an inherent potency to transform structures and behaviours within the tumult of the inherently metamorphic process of transition. Though some suggest the technocratic approach to transitional justice impedes political analysis of the opportunities or constraints of a given transitional ecology,[127] the greater impediment is the field's enduring impulse towards wishful thinking. As Jones et al. note, those practitioners who assume their interventions automatically lead to political change are those least likely to formulate theories of change.[128] This is particularly problematic in the context of transitional justice, given that even in relation to its traditional goals like stability or democracy, the existing literature on transitional justice 'cannot sufficiently explain the relationship between specific mechanisms and processes and the broader, long-term social and political change which is necessary for a peaceful future'.[129] Transitional justice has long proven capable of highlighting injustices, defining the discourse of violation and proposing general outlines for reform. However, this traditional remit is quite distinct from the inherently conflictive, deeply technical and expertise-based processes by which macro-economic or structural proposals are budgeted, designed and implemented.

Of course, one can argue that it is unrealistic or unfair to demand blueprints for action in the theoretical literature, given the heterogeneity of states and the complexity of the task. This argument is entirely

---

[125] Danielle Stein and Craig Valters, *Understanding Theory of Change in International Development* (Justice and Security Research Programme and Asia Foundation 2012) 3.

[126] ibid 14.

[127] E.g. Nesiah (n 70) 20. See also Chapter 4, Section 2.3 on the supposed technicism of transitional justice.

[128] Briony Jones, Elisabeth Baumgartner and Sidonia Gabriel, *A Transformative Approach to Dealing with the Past* (SwissPeace 2015) 4.

[129] ibid 4.

reasonable, but incorporates an inevitable corollary, namely that a generalized transformative efficacy for transitional justice cannot be universally assumed.

Appealing as the idea of transformative transitional justice is, it can only be based more on hope than experience, given the paucity of examples of transformative justice that have projectized recommendations for structural reform.

3. CONSTRUCTIVISM, DECONTEXTUALIZATION, OPTIMISM: HOW WE THINK ABOUT TRANSITIONAL JUSTICE

Why then, if the record of transformative achievement is so limited, if the policy proposals are so nebulous, if the mechanisms are so unsuited, and if the context is so unconducive, is there such confidence in the transformative efficacy of transitional justice? The explanation lies in how the modern transitional justice discourse discusses its composite elements of *transition* and *justice*. It is important to remember that transitional justice is not just a bundle of practices applied on the ground, but a form of theorization that exists as a realm of often decontextualized academic knowledge. The latter is expected to guide the former, and insofar as it addresses transformative justice, has had three impacts:

1. Transitional justice demonstrates the impact of constructivist theorizing, which in this case is directed more at the international transitional justice community's internal debates about its own values than any realistic estimation of what transitional societies can achieve or cope with. This means that
2. Much theorizing relates very little to the paradigmatic transitions from authoritarianism and/or war to democracy and/or peace, and so assumes much more favourable (but hardly transferable) opportunities for emancipatory change, while
3. On those occasions where the paradigmatic transitions from conflict or authoritarianism are addressed, an idealized vision of transition is abstracted from the likely context of application.

3.1 The Impact of Constructivism

As Koskenniemi argues, political intervention (like transitional justice) is often a 'politics of redefinition'; that is, the strategic interpretation of a situation (like post-conflict) by reference to a technical idiom (such as transitional justice) which allows for the application of expertise related to that idiom. This expertise incorporates its own biases, vocabularies and narratives in searching for solutions which highlight some solutions while backgrounding others.[130] Because transitional justice is an essentially open-ended concept (it is not, after all, a distinct legal regime or political programme in itself, but rather an amorphous bundle of practices idiosyncratically conditioned by transitional bargains and directed towards diverse visions of the good), there is always a struggle over how it should be framed. Frames are the collective, inter-subjective perceptions that individuals employ in constructing roles and interpreting objects.[131] Frames illustrate how knowledge is organized and interpreted, and they are embedded in discourses that influence ideologies, paradigms, operating procedures and shared definitions of an environment.[132] They shape how people such as transitional justice actors understand the world, and these understandings are used to rationalize and justify what courses of action are seen as possible, natural, legitimate or illegitimate.[133]

This process of framing has been particularly important in transitional justice. All debates in its advocacy-cum-policy-oriented literature concern both the conceptual terrain for intervention and the field's self-identity. This identity has become contested, a site for moral and political struggle. As noted earlier, the argument that legalism narrowed the possibilities for transitional justice's development and that it needed to give space to other forms of knowledge became mainstream.[134] A broad interdisciplinary space emerged spanning fields as diverse as anthropology, the arts, development studies, economics, education, gender studies, healthcare, history, psychology, sociology and theology. These new transdisciplinary mindsets coalesced around the imaginary of 'justice' and represented an even broader medium than law through which to conceptualize the social world as we would like it to be –

---

[130] Martti Koskenniemi, 'The Politics of International Law – 20 Years Later' (2009) 20 *European Journal of International Law* 7, 11.

[131] Karl Weick, *Sensemaking in Organizations* (Sage Publications 1995) 109.

[132] Séverine Autesserre, 'Hobbes and the Congo: Frames, Local Violence and International Intervention' (2009) 63 *International Organization* 249, 252.

[133] ibid 254–55, 272 and 275.

[134] Kieran McEvoy, 'Letting Go of Legalism: Developing a "Thicker" Version of Transitional Justice' in Kieran McEvoy and Lorna McGregor (eds), *Transitional Justice from Below: Grassroots Activism and the Struggle for Change* (Hart Publishing 2008) 15 at 20.

transitional justice's symbolic capital led to increased claims for inclusion and pressure to 'reframe' the field to include the broader agendas canvassed at the start of this chapter.[135] Disputes over the goals of transitional justice tend to reflect the philosophical and conceptual propensities of those making the claims. The glut of different transformative visions for transitional justice are largely the product of different theorists and practitioners outlining revised models that explore new possibilities for what a transformative agenda might look like. Once scholars accept that transitional justice should have a role in socio-economic transformation, there is a natural floodgates tendency to invoke any social good positively valued, given that it is difficult to identify an attractive policy that is *not* conducive to reducing inequality – arguments can be made for why any desirable policy goal (redistribution, education, progressive taxation, welfare) is indispensable for real structural transformation. As suggested by the totalizing possibilities for transitional justice's extension, there is a risk that it may become an analogue for all the beneficial things a society could incorporate to mitigate inequalities. However, while scholars often acknowledge the dangers of over-expanding the concept to the point where it becomes too fragmented to remain a coherent field,[136] there is a countervailing tendency to argue that the range of challenges and problems societies in transition face cannot be navigated if practice is limited by anything that smacks of disciplinary isolationism.[137]

This ostensibly academic debate is extremely important given the aforementioned cross-fertilization between the scholarly and policy worlds in transitional justice. Academics are often employed as consultants (though they might have originally established their credentials on the ground in the first place) and sometimes research is purchased or employed by donors and INGOs as governments lack capacity or awareness in the area. These consultants and INGOs often serve as outside experts advising states and peacebuilding missions on policy options.[138] Indeed, the frameworks for transitional justice on the ground

---

[135] Christine Bell, 'Transitional Justice, Interdisciplinarity and the State of the "Field" or "Non-Field"' (2009) 3 *International Journal of Transitional Justice* 5, 13.

[136] Kora Andrieu, 'Dealing with a "New" Grievance: Should Anticorruption Be Part of the Transitional Justice Agenda?' (2012)11 *Journal of Human Rights* 537.

[137] For example, Szablewska and Baumann (n 61) 341–42.

[138] Priscilla Hayner, *Negotiating Justice: Guidance for Mediators* (HD Centre for Humanitarian Dialogue 2009) 7.

are increasingly influenced by professionalized and specialized international bodies that provide (or at least advise upon) the models national actors employ.[139] How the field views the acceptable/potential limits of transitional justice can have a significant impact in practice. As Franzki and Olarte put it, 'We hold the specific significance of transitional justice scholarship to lie in its efforts to provide legal, political, philosophical or moral concepts that back the practice of transitional justice … In doing so, scholars contribute to the production and reproduction of transitional justice interventions'.[140] The reframing agenda was initially presented in contrast to the more circumscribed ambitions of early transitional justice, and more recently in a highly critical contradistinction to a liberal peacebuilding model the field is believed to be complicit in (see Chapter 4). Transitional justice is thus subject to a constant meta-conflict over its direction, aspirations and conceptualization, a battlefield occupied by academics and practitioners fighting over what it is and should be.[141] At times, this framing process is explicit, a site of purposive struggle familiar from other forms of norm entrepreneurship:

> Issues are framed so as to resonate with already accepted norms, attract funding, consolidate partnerships and networks, and encourage action. Frames enable activists to 'create' an issue and insert it onto the transitional agenda. For transitional justice to become more transformative will require a reframing of both the problem it seeks to address and related responses and interventions.[142]

One obvious risk of such a motivated bias is that it may foster a reluctance to acknowledge the limitations of one's preferred approaches.

The core aspect of this reframing process is a strong constructivist belief that inter-subjectively constructed norms shared among the relevant agents in transition can be a decisive causal factor in shaping outcomes. In the literature of the transformative turn, equality, redistribution and attention to structures of poverty are the most common of these norms. Constructivism is generally understood in opposition to realist and rational choice approaches that see material constraints, vested interests and strategic calculations in relation to political, economic and social resources as the key factors determining the impact of norms. Constructivists, by contrast, focus on the influence of the beliefs, discourses, ideology and, above all, norms of interveners in forming collective

---

139 Subotic (n 67) 129.
140 Franzki and Olarte (n 4) 203.
141 Bell (n 135) 6 and 27.
142 Gready and Robins (n 22) 355.

understandings that guide action.[143] They share the view that while these collective understandings do not absolutely determine action in causal terms, behavioural norms serve as prescriptions for policy more so than the actual economic, political and social contexts or the interests on which realists focus.[144] As Risse and Sikkink put it:

> We do not mean to ignore material conditions. Rather, the causal relationship between material and ideational factors is at stake. While materialist theories emphasize economic or military conditions or interests as determining the impact of ideas in international and domestic politics, social constructivists emphasize that ideas and communicative processes define in the first place which material factors are perceived as relevant and how they influence understandings of interests, preferences, and political decisions.[145]

Social constructivist thought holds that cultural, normative and ideological frameworks can shape the interpretation of context and constraints.[146] Normative goals like transformation or equitable development may not emerge via a 'rational input/output formula, but rather from the value that impacted populations put on both the process and outcome of change'.[147] In this view, material interests become mere secondary concerns to ideas and identity, and they lose the causal agency included in more realist accounts.[148] Ideas become more relevant than military or political power, giving interventionary actors major (and possibly decisive) influence through the power of persuasion.[149] Constructivists tend to disregard the potential limitations of humanitarian action – failure is

---

143 Séverine Autesserre, 'Construire la Paix: Conceptions Collectives de son Etablissement, de son Maintien et de sa Consolidation' (2011) 51 *Critique Internationale* 153, 154.

144 ibid 156.

145 Thomas Risse and Kathryn Sikkink, 'The Socialization of International Human Rights Norms into Domestic Practices: Introduction' in Thomas Risse, Stephen Ropp and Kathryn Sikkink (eds), *The Power of Human Rights: International Norms and Domestic Change* (Cambridge University Press 1999) 1 at 6–7.

146 Autesserre (n 143) 156.

147 Shahrbanou Tadjbakhsh and Oliver Richmond, 'Conclusion: Typologies and Modifications Proposed by Critical Approaches' in Shahrbanou Tadjbakhsh (ed.), *Rethinking the Liberal Peace: External Models and Local Alternatives* (Routledge 2011) 221 at 224.

148 David Chandler, 'Hollow Hegemony: Theorising the Shift from Interest-Based to Value-Based International Policy-Making' (2007) 35 *Millennium: Journal of International Studies* 703, 709.

149 ibid 710.

instead attributed to collective lack of will on the part of the international community and domestic actors.[150] On this view, anything can be accomplished if we understand the problem correctly and want to accomplish it badly enough.

These constructivist and realist debates have always been at the core of transitional justice theory. Rights, of course, are always conceived in a pre-political manner in forms of Western theorization premised on universality, but in the explicitly political arena of transition they could not avoid instrumentalization and compromise. As noted above, the earliest debates about transitional justice concerned the extent to which it fostered stability or catalysed change – both constituted by, and constitutive of, transition. As such, justice in periods of political change was extraordinary, maintaining order to the extent it deferred to political interest in stability while enabling transformation to the extent its norms infused society.[151]

There was an appreciation that norms could not be advanced independently of power. Choices over accountability were framed as an instrumental/pragmatic logic of consequences versus a legalist/normative logic of appropriateness. It followed that the conception of justice that emerged would be contextualized and partial, and veered more towards realist stability than idealist accountability in its earliest days. However, over time, and as transitional justice became normalized and mainstreamed as a policy option, there emerged a belief that clearly defined international human rights obligations could transcend the grubby bargaining of early Cold War transitions and displace politics as the basis for decisions on accountability. With this internationalization and the parallel growth of global NGOs with mobile expertise, the 'centre of gravity' of transitional justice processes switched from their domestic context to the international public sphere, and as a result 'scaling' up the lessons and models of the 90s onto the global stage with a gradual shift away from endogenously-defined, ad hoc approaches to justice issues.[152] As international criminal courts, regional human rights bodies, soft law and advocacy networks proactively articulated, developed and diffused justice norms, it became possible to conceive of transitional justice in a deterritorialized manner as a shared obligation of the international community that deprecated trade-offs between peace and justice and

---

150 Christopher Coyne, *Doing Bad by Doing Good: Why Humanitarian Action Fails* (Stanford University Press 2013) 14–15.

151 Teitel (n 3) 6.

152 Nesiah (n 70) 10.

posited only positive synergies.[153] Indeed, it became possible to argue that old causal arguments about transitional justice have been reversed – whereas once transition was a precondition for justice (and limited its possibilities), 'the contemporary field increasingly seems to expect that transitional justice is what will bring about such political transformation or other forms of fundamental and progressive change'.[154] Old arguments relating to stability versus justice have given way to those over different values of justice, manifesting the tendency in constructivist accounts for political interests and power to lose their ontological centrality as ideas become discussed in their own terms, ascribed an agency that was previously associated with interest-bearing state actors.[155]

One sees in the transformative transitional justice literature great optimism that the social world within states can be changed – the main barriers to justice exist not in context, state capacity or the efficacy of transitional justice's mechanisms, but at the cognitive or ideational level. The faith that transitional justice can significantly impact the distribution of wealth and opportunity in an economy if only practitioners understand justice in a more holistic sense betrays what Colvin describes as a technocratic and utopian imperative in which the right combination of technique and planning will accomplish the goals set for any given mechanism.[156] This remains the case even if, as argued earlier, technique and planning are underspecified – there is a strong belief that once holistic, transformative conceptions of transitional justice are adopted, these will serve as a guide for the actions of governments, international interveners, civil society and vaguely articulated local agents. It assumes that the open-ended solutions outlined earlier ('exposing' discriminatory practices, 'reframing of socio-economic rights and continuities of conflict', 'promot[ing] more coherent and comprehensive recognition') will generate the desired political dynamics to make emancipatory outcomes a reality. For example, Arbour contends that highlighting economic and social rights deprivations can serve as a 'springboard' for systematically embedding economic, social and cultural rights in the political, legal, and

---

153 Ruti Teitel, 'Rethinking *Jus Post Bellum* in an Age of Global Transitional Justice: Engaging with Michael Walzer and Larry May' (2013) 24 *European Journal of International Law* 335, 340–42.

154 Thomas Obel Hansen, 'Kenya's Power-Sharing Arrangement and its Implications for Transitional Justice' (2013) 17 *International Journal of Human Rights* 307, 310.

155 Chandler (n 148) 710–11.

156 Colvin (n 75).

social structures of societies in transition.[157] Gready and Robins argue that a coherent theoretical or practical framework for justice interventions that emphasizes local agency and that challenges unequal and intersecting power relations and exclusion will unleash transformative dynamics.[158] This approach, no less than the most traditionalist 'toolbox' thinking that characterizes more traditional approaches, tends to assume the universality of the norms underlying a revised transitional justice as applicable in all contexts. Such an optimism inevitably disregards national political, social, cultural and historical contexts and purports to operate immune to local power struggles and political instrumentalization.[159] It assumes that all societies are capable of transformation regardless of initial conditions – the effectiveness of transitional justice is less a function of its mechanisms, strengths or the contexts they deploy to, but rather of how comprehensively it conceptualizes injustice.[160]

There is a strongly romantic quality to the idea that just as law can legitimately regulate politics in old-style transitional justice, the more holistic, post-legalist conceptions of transformative justice can reduce poverty or inequality or improve a critical mass of everyday lives. Notwithstanding its roots in the observation of a world of gross structural deprivation, the redistributive, egalitarian conceptualizations of transformative justice tend to be informed more by pristine concepts (those that outline 'what, ideally, the world should be like with respect to justice … unsullied by the world in which we actually live') than by rectificatory ones (those applied in the 'real' flawed context of application with particular specifications of what should be done).[161] The reasons for this have been outlined already. Firstly, the argument is pitched at the international ideational-cognitive level where the norms to guide post-conflict interventions are decided. At least at this level of theorization, the most demanding ideals of justice may naturally seem more appealing than circumspect attention to the likely materialist-realist context. Secondly, there is a conscious conceptual battle over the future of transitional justice which does not encourage the moderation of claims. Most transitional justice scholarship ignores the justifiable doubts that have been expressed about the manner in which transitional justice is

---

157 Arbour (n 115) 26.

158 Gready and Robins (n 22) 17–19.

159 Rubli (n 50) 9.

160 E.g. Cahill-Ripley (n 36) 213; Thomason (n 28) 79.

161 Mark Evans, 'At War's End: Time to Turn to *Jus Post Bellum*?' in Carsten Stahn, Jennifer Easterday and Jens Iverson (eds), *Jus Post Bellum: Mapping the Normative Foundations* (Oxford University Press 2014) 26 at 31.

theorized. In a recent survey of scholarship in the 2003–2008 period, Fletcher and Weinstein conclude that 'those researching in this area were largely sympathetic to the transitional justice project … their work aimed to strengthen the efficacy of the established transitional justice mechanisms'.[162] Though the period they survey ends just before the time when transformative conceptions of transitional justice became more mainstream, there is little reason to suspect this supportive orientation has changed. The danger Miller notes – that the cross-fertilization of ideas by veterans of past transitional justice institutions could conceivably result in over-stating the success of an institution advocating a certain approach to justice – is familiar to most people who have attended conferences on the topic.[163] Because transitional justice is presented in very idealistic terms, scholars in the field have begun to acknowledge that its virtuous effects are more easily presumed than proven.[164] As Thomason argues, even if there are doubts over its achievability, it still serves the normative aims of theory.[165] The warning that the 'expectations of truth commissions have tended to be exaggerated, and their challenges minimised' is one that applies across the board in transitional justice.[166] As in many areas of human rights, the norms in question are so fundamental that commitment to equality and poverty alleviation might attenuate an appropriately sceptical attitude to what transitional justice can realistically do.[167]

The constructivist theorizing that characterizes the transformative turn speaks more to a world at large where it aspires to norm convergence than to any individual state. It is expected that the inherent superiority of a global human rights norm and its propagation in the international arena by global norm entrepreneurs will lead a critical mass of states to embrace it either willingly or through international peer pressure. It should then become internalized domestically and thereafter guide

---

162 Laurel Fletcher and Harvey M. Weinstein, 'Writing Transitional Justice: An Empirical Evaluation of Transitional Justice Scholarship in Academic Journals' (2015) 7 *Journal of Human Rights Practice* 177, 191.

163 Miller (n 119) 271–72.

164 Van der Merwe (n 15) 121.

165 Thomason (n 28) 76.

166 Eirin Mobekk, *Transitional Justice and Security Sector Reform: Enabling Sustainable Peace* (Geneva Centre for the Democratic Control of Armed Forces 2006) 77.

167 To lightly adapt Andreas Follesdal, 'Methods of Philosophical Research on Human Rights' in Fons Coomans, Fred Grunfeld and Menno Kamminga (eds), *Methods of Human Rights Research* (Intersentia 2009) 233 at 233.

government behaviour consistent with that norm.[168] However, this focus on the international realm and universal norms of socio-economic justice risks abstracting justice from anything even generically recognizable as post-conflict transition.

3.2 The Abstraction of Transition from Context

Though initially transitional justice was conceived of as a response to processes of authoritarian transition in the Southern Cone and, later, Eastern Europe, with the increasing frequency in the 1990s of civil war, the field quite rapidly assimilated the exigencies of post-conflict transition in states like El Salvador, those emerging from the former Yugoslavia, Guatemala and Rwanda to a peace settlement which in most cases reaffirms, modifies or creates democratic governance. Post-conflict movements towards peace and democracy became one of the paradigmatic transitions in the discipline. They were different in origin and endpoint from the Southern Cone and Eastern European precedents, but shared the characteristics of dramatic political change formally identified in pacts, agreements, elections, referenda, constitutions or peace treaties, and superficial but definite temporal limits at the undemocratic/war-torn and democratic/peaceable ends of the interregnum.[169] Transitional justice would capitalize on, but crucially be limited by, these political transitions. What made it distinctive was the fact that it occurred in times of heightened, epiphenomenal opportunity when a state is re-evaluating or re-establishing the norms on which it is based.

However, the inherently imprecise term 'transition' has proven susceptible to extreme conceptual stretching, encompassing any transformation in social, economic or political life. 'Transition' as a concept has become a homogenized abstraction enveloping all conceivable political projects, flattening out contingent and heterogeneous national histories. In part, this stems from the fact that the transitional paradigm is itself grossly reductive inasmuch as it implies a routine teleology from one form of state to another in political milieus of invariably deceptive complexity. The appreciation that socio-economic reform in unchanging daily life typically fails to keep track of political progress (and may even be retarded by it) led transitional justice to gradually abandon the unidirectional 'before and after' conception of transition as the herald of

---

[168] Martha Finnemore and Kathryn Sikkink, 'International Norm Dynamics and Political Change' (1998) 52 *International Organization* 887.

[169] Fionnuala Ní Aoláin and Colm Campbell, 'The Paradox of Transition in Conflicted Democracies' (2005) 27 *Human Rights Quarterly* 172.

emancipatory new beginnings. The related influx of other disciplines to transitional justice tended to muddy and distend the concept of transition. By demanding and promoting ever-more original and comprehensive forms of transitional justice, justice, not transition, became the ontological starting point for assessing the possibilities of the field. The relationship between subfield and field has been inverted – 'transition is constituted as a subfield of transitional justice rather than vice versa'.[170] The distinctiveness of transitional justice has gradually, but almost totally, been sacrificed for inclusiveness.[171] Consequently, the concept of the transition as the site of justice action has become more fungible and less essential – some wonder if any substantial transition is needed for the term 'transitional justice' to be applied.[172] In contemporary debates, transitional justice represents a hopelessly capacious norm that can justify almost any form of intervention in any context.

The most prevalent example of this is its routine proposal as a solution to problems in states in the developing world where there has been no progress towards war termination or even partial democratization,[173] or where any such progress has been reversed, most notably the Arab Spring.[174] This has perhaps had less influence on the transformative turn than might be expected – while any examination of these states makes apparent the need to redress the roots of conflict in these societies, context-specific examinations of these states are generally couched with appreciations of the difficulties presented by the societies in question. Perhaps more influential is theorizing about transitional justice in the context of long-consolidated Western democracies as they address historic injustices against their own marginalized groups, their subalterns and the developing world. Transitional justice provided a fashionable, academically legitimate rallying point for advocacy in redressing past injustices of all types. Initially, this was manifested in the use of truth commissions, restoration projects, historical inquiries and trials in mature democracies attempting to repair instances of past abrogation of the

---

170 Bell (n 135) 24.

171 Undine Kayser-Whande and Stephanie Schell-Faucon, 'Transitional Justice and Conflict Transformation in Conversation' (2010) 50 *Politorbis* 97, 102.

172 Jens Iverson, 'Transitional Justice, Ius Post Bellum and International Criminal Law: Differentiating the Usages, History and Dynamics' (2013) 7 *International Journal of Transitional Justice* 413, 413.

173 For example, around 30 states in David Backer, 'Cross-national Comparative Analysis' in van der Merwe, Baxter and Chapman (eds) (n 12) 23 at 73–82.

174 Kirsten Fisher and Robert Stewart (eds) *Transitional Justice and the Arab Spring* (Routledge 2014).

universalistic ideas on which they claim legitimacy.[175] Transitional justice language was gradually applied to enduring legacies of oppression in settler colonies with indigenous groups like Australia and Canada.[176] Soon, even these moorings slipped. Scholars argue that transitional justice (or at least its techniques) can be employed unproblematically to developed, Western societies to correct the contemporary deficiencies of liberal societies (one example is Fourlas's examination of the US prison system).[177] Indeed, the editors of one recent volume argue that transitional justice is 'applicable to *all* political and societal arrangements in need of change'.[178] Some even suggest the notion of 'transition' may eventually be dismissed as a mere syntactical error and a specifically transitional framework dispensed with entirely.[179] There is much fretting within the literature that its enlargement to encompass an infinite variety of contexts makes transitional justice normatively meaningless – too inclusive to be useful, too centrifugal to retain coherence.[180]

The broader issue of whether the centre of transitional justice has collapsed under an excessive load of meanings is beyond the scope of this work. However, it is relevant that applying the term 'transition' so broadly tends to preclude any form of disaggregation of contexts and potentialities when talking about what transitional justice can or should aspire towards. This, in turn, impedes focused theorization when we come to specifically discuss post-conflict states. A progressively amorphous and diffuse transitional justice has no core substantive concern that could unify all modes of usage. It is increasingly apparent that when scholars talk about what transitional justice must, can or should do, they are not talking solely about the paradigmatic transitions that anchored the

---

[175] Torpey (n 13) 9.

[176] Rosemary Nagy, 'The Scope and Bounds of Transitional Justice and the Canadian Truth and Reconciliation Commission' (2013) 7 *International Journal of Transitional Justice* 52; Jennifer Balint, Julie Evans and Nesam McMillan, 'Rethinking Transitional Justice, Redressing Indigenous Harm: A New Conceptual Approach' (2014) 8 *International Journal of Transitional Justice* 194.

[177] George Fourlas, 'No Future Without Transition: A Critique of Liberal Peace' (2015) 9 *International Journal of Transitional Justice* 109.

[178] Szablewska and Bachmann (n 61) 339.

[179] Arthur (n 4) 325 and 363.

[180] See, for example, David Restrepo Amariles, 'Reassessing the Boundaries of Transitional Justice: An Inquiry on Political Transitions, Armed Conflicts, and Human Rights Violations' in Israël and Mouralis (eds) (n 8) 209 at 230; Pablo de Greiff, 'Transitional Justice Gets its Own Encyclopaedia: Vitamins or Steroids for a Developing Field?' (2013) 7 *International Journal of Transitional Justice* 547, 553.

field before the turn towards holistic approaches and interdisciplinarity, but rather an aspirational global project. This global project is one that could, for example, engage with climate change and indeed 'all justice-related matters pertinent to equity' between developed and developing nations,[181] and so at this level of generality need not distinguish between Mexico and Mozambique, Canada or Cambodia. There is an epistemic predilection towards universalist approaches that standardize complex and idiosyncratic circumstances, which are invariably more attractive rhetorically than narrowly specified intervention proposals. However, this predilection exacerbates the ever-present danger that responses advocated in transitional justice to massive violations of human rights diverge from the context-specific needs and capabilities of any given society.[182] Transitional justice addresses what a pristine ideal post-conflict justice would look like, not what a rectificatory conception of justice derived from a given context would approximate. The critical focus no longer analyses the limited but policy-relevant internal reasons why aspects of justice are more or less feasible in a given state, but rather the theoretical, externally driven reasons why the international community does or does not propound this or that (expansive) vision of transitional justice.

3.3 Transitional Optimism

Of that apparently dwindling number of scholars who specialize in post-conflict transitions, the democratization, peacebuilding and transitology literatures that they draw on take the malleability of post-conflict states as an article of faith. The sheer event of peace is deemed to make politics, economics and culture tractable. Events, particularly the most momentous ones like the end of conflict, are among the most prominent epistemological types for understanding societies. They are located at the intersection of intentions, actions and consequences, and appear pregnant with agency and advancement, serving as reference points for future action and change.[183] Ordinarily, the design of states and their power structures are historically so well entrenched that they appear impervious to any significant type of reform. Marginalized groups are excluded, or only included once they signal a willingness to play by the rules of dominant group, which precludes anything but gradual reform. However,

---

181 Szablewska and Bachmann (n 61) 355.

182 Fletcher, Weinstein and Rowen (n 49) 209; Clark and Palmer (n 46) 5, 6 and 8.

183 Gëzim Visoka, 'Peace is What We Make of It? Peace-shaping Events and "Non-Events"' (2016) 4 *Peacebuilding* 54, 56–7.

the tumult of conflict and the signing of peace treaties provide opportunities for revisiting these arrangements as static concentrations of power that suppressed group demands are removed and politics become more plastic.[184] The peacebuilding and development literatures are replete with references to 'special opportunities for political, legal, economic and administrative reforms',[185] 'windows of opportunity for fundamental change'[186] and even 'blank slates'.[187]

This optimism has translated to transitional justice and, in some ways, it is justified. Bell and O'Rourke are among the most prominent of those who argue that peace agreements often function as a constitutional 'big bang', allowing for the sort of radical overhaul of societal structures rarely achievable under politics as usual.[188] The hope, if not the expectation, is that they will go beyond merely specifying the modalities for ending hostilities to address power structures and allocation of resources within a rights-based framework that rectifies previous discriminations and exclusions. Implicit in this argument is the assumption there has been a large-scale migration of power from those concerned purely with administering repression or prosecuting warfare to more normatively guided actors. A second source of optimism is the presence of peacebuilding missions. There is an assumption that by virtue of their international mandate, the resources they can mobilize to manipulate local partners and their freedom to choose among those partners, that peacebuilders enjoy a large power imbalance over any national or local form of authority. Indeed, some argue the liberal peace framework 'has

---

184 As Lazar puts it, moral reasoning is polarized and telescoped in war, but once it is over, a 'broader palette' of moral reasons can be drawn on (Seth Lazar, 'Skepticism about Jus Post Bellum' in Larry May and Andrew Forcehimes (eds), *Morality, Jus Post Bellum, and International Law* (Cambridge University Press 2012) 204 at 218).

185 Andreas Mehler and Claude Ribaux, *Crisis Prevention and Conflict Management in Technical Cooperation* (Deutsche Gesellschaft Technische Zusammenarbeit 2000) 37.

186 Sabine Kurtenbach, 'Why is Liberal Peacebuilding So Difficult? Some lessons from Central America' (2007) 88 *European Review of Latin American and Caribbean Studies* 95, 95 (Abstract).

187 As noted, but not endorsed, in Timothy Donais, 'Empowerment or Imposition? Dilemmas of Local Ownership in Post-Conflict Peacebuilding Processes' (2009) 34 *Peace and Change* 3, 15.

188 Christine Bell and Catherine O'Rourke, 'The People's Peace? Peace Agreements, Civil Society, and Participatory Democracy' (2007) 28 *International Political Science Review* 293, 295–96.

the power to alter the very nature of society'.[189] This is assumed to give peacebuilders the power to 'leverage the transition' to spread values, address root causes and formulate new rules of the game, if they are so minded.[190] Transitional justice, assumed to form a core part of liberal peacebuilding, stands to benefit from the influence of peacebuilders as surrogate enforcers, particularly if it can catalyse a move away from the liberal institutionalism that dominates it. The UN, most notably, had decisive involvement in establishing more thoroughgoing accountability than would otherwise have been the case in the likes of Timor-Leste, Cambodia, Guatemala, and Sierra Leone.

This belief in the malleability of states in transition infuses the transformative transitional justice literature. Previously subject to conservative stasis, the fabric of society has now become contestable in an open-ended way with no options foreclosed.[191] Ames Cobián and Reátegui argue that transitions are

> On the one hand, instances of strategic action and negotiation; on the other hand, acute awareness of the crisis to be overcome and the enthusiasm of the democratic restoration generate a climate in which certain executive or legislative decisions become possible, along with certain agreements among various sectors of society that would not be possible in routine situations.[192]

Bergsmo et al. go further, seeing transition as a transformative constitutional moment where the distribution of poverty and wealth, land reform and the economy may be publicly addressed.[193] Others present transition as a 'unique opportunity for social change' in which justice projects can gain democratic traction to foster transformation.[194] For example, truth commissions may have greater purchase because they take place in times when significant decisions about the future course of the state will be

---

189 Roger Mac Ginty and Oliver Richmond, 'Myth or Reality? Opposing Views on the Liberal Peace and Post-War Reconstruction' (2007) 21 *Global Society* 491, 497.

190 Alexandra Gheciu and Jennifer Welsh, 'The Imperative to Rebuild: Assessing the Normative Case for Postconflict Reconstruction' (2009) 23 *Ethics and International Affairs* 121, 127.

191 Francois DuBois and Adam Czarnota, 'The Transitional Rule of Law' (1999) 24 *Alternative Law Review* 9, 10.

192 Ames Cobián and Reátegui (n 23) 154.

193 Morten Bergsmo et al., 'Introduction' in Morten Bergsmo et al. (eds), *Distributive Justice in Transitions* (Torkel Opsahl 2010) 1 at 2.

194 Nesiah (n 70) 44.

adopted.[195] States should feel a greater compulsion to redress conditions of socio-economic deprivation in the transitional period, especially if they are presented as rights violations.[196] This optimism endures notwithstanding the reality that numerous single-case studies and comparative analysis of transitional justice mechanisms across countries have generated little reliable evidence that they have beneficial (or indeed harmful) impacts.[197]

4. THE POLITICAL ECONOMY OF POST-CONFLICT TRANSITION

The previous chapter noted that this book would adopt an 'inside–out' approach in contradistinction to an 'outside–in' one, abjuring a focus on the values, biases and motivations of transitional justice actors to concentrate on the social and political power relationships and structures within the state that these actors must interact with and be shaped by. This approach is a departure from the transformative transitional justice literature, which is the product of a constructivist view that policy and practice can and should be shaped primarily by shared ideas about justice rather than material forces, and that the goals of purposive actors in transition are *constructed* by these shared ideas, rather than *given* by vested interests. This position was directed more at the international transitional justice community's internal debates than any specific state, conceived of transition generically for the most part, and when it considered post-conflict transition specifically was relatively optimistic about the prospects for transformation after internal conflict. The transformative literature posits that normative change can alter political will, but fudges the question of whose political will (international interveners? the government? domestic elites? civil society?) this refers to. This literature is always written in imperative language – transitional justice 'must' or 'should' or 'can' catalyse domestic forces, but it is never specified who the active agents of transformation should be. Few specify to what extent transformation must be generated internally and autonomously. Fewer still deal with the related question of whether they see transitional justice as capitalizing on autonomous developments for transformation or resisting internal tendencies towards unequal status quo.

---

195 Ames Cobián and Reátegui (n 23) 145.
196 Laplante (n 20) 331 (Preamble) and 341.
197 Skaar and Malca (n 2) 17.

This language also implies that transitional justice has autonomy as an actor in its own right independent of social forces. However, transitional justice actors in and of themselves are strong neither in political influence (see Chapter 3) nor in terms of the mechanisms traditionally employed. Transitional justice as practice, as opposed to theory, cannot be comprehended or assessed in such abstract or disembodied terms. Prospects for transformation can be assessed only with an historically informed understanding of the loci of effective political power in a given post-conflict state in terms of the balance of social divisions after war, the institutions and sites where power is contested, and the means through which political will is formed and employed. Nesiah is correct in arguing that the failure to open up their hierarchies of power in transitional states to accountability lies at the root of social justice concerns, but identifying this need is not the same as meeting it.[198] The extent to which theories of transitional justice do not grapple with these profound complexities of elite power and wealth retention suggests the limits of the field's utility for catalysing emancipatory change. The example of the enormous conferences in Tunis and Cairo in 2011 to initiate post-Arab Spring transitional justice without any significant analysis of whether political conditions were in any way conducive to it is pertinent in this respect.[199] The notable lack of researchers from the Global South in overall theorization of the field (though many have proven strongly influential within individual states) may have impaired reflection on the general possibilities (as opposed to needs) for justice in post-conflict areas of limited statehood.

The assumption that the event of transition to a post-conflict society automatically conduces to permitting existing social forces, either independently or in conjunction with transitional justice actors at domestic or international level, to transform how collective benefits, opportunities and burdens are allocated, is questionable. Transformation, after all, is something which the existing constellation of forces has heretofore not permitted, even if there is no overt resistance – if it were otherwise, transformation would largely be self-enforcing without needing significant stimulus from transitional justice activities. Transitional justice does not happen in a political vacuum, and it always challenges an existing order that did not permit such progress to develop organically. Systemic, structural violence that disenfranchises distinct sectors of society must be deliberately sustained by a political system that distributes power and

[198] Nesiah (n 70) 5.
[199] ibid 34–35.

resources unequally. As Bell notes, there is often an asymmetry in the demand for human rights protections, which most vociferously emerge from the weaker party and their analysis of the causes of conflict, and which is directed at a status quo.[200]

These asymmetries are difficult to change, particularly if war may have done as much to compound as to subvert them. While it has become commonplace to argue that the most disenfranchising institutions need to be addressed, these institutions and the practices they compel will also tend to be the most entrenched by virtue of myriad antecedent conditions. We may assume that in a period of transition from conflict to post-conflict this order has been left somewhat in flux. It is something of a cliché that there is more than one (political) transition occurring and that there are simultaneous, often deeper, transitions in the social, cultural and economic spheres. However, it is by no means certain that this turbulence might facilitate fundamental revision of these structures. Civil war needs some type of political resolution in the absence of military victory, but this political transformation usually outpaces any deeper transformation of the socio-economic structures on which it is superimposed. In post-conflict states we are familiar with, like Sierra Leone, Bosnia, East Timor or Cambodia, neither historical developments nor economic incentives catalysed the types of structural change desired by the most marginalized groups in society. Transitional justice, when viewed as either a domestic phenomenon supplemented by international normative change, or an alliance between some domestic social forces and the transnational transitional justice community, is effectively trying to expedite or substitute for organic domestic processes that never emerged or, even if they emerged, did not succeed.

Consequently, there is a certain political naiveté to the discourse as it implicitly assumes that in the post-conflict context former antagonists represent a new coalition of social forces altruistically intent on fulfilling the general interests of society through compromise, and that the settlement they agree represents both a shared vision of the future and a capacious architecture for its realization that transitional justice can inform or steer. Where the literature does not take so rosy a view of top–down political settlements (as Chapter 4 goes on to argue, much of the critical literature that the transformative turn relies on is explicitly suspicious of elite bargaining), it relies on domestic coalitions of social

---

200 Christine Bell, 'Negotiating Human Rights' in John Darby and Roger Mac Ginty (eds), *Contemporary Peacemaking: Conflict, Violence and Peacemaking* (Palgrave Macmillan 2003) 210 at 215.

forces to realize these aims from the bottom-up, but elides the question of why these groups have failed to catalyse such progress in the past. As Subotic notes, much of what she labels the transnational activism literature 'oversimplifies' the domestic elite's impact on compliance by giving those 'true believers' (the civil society and political groups that accept internationally propagated transitional justice models) more agency than resisters who are ideologically, politically or pragmatically opposed to transitional justice.[201] Empirically, she notes that what instead happens is competition and contestation between different coalitions over justice and how it redounds to their political advantage.[202] Along similar lines, Thoms Ron and Paris note that

> TJ advocates may mistake broad public support for TJ with feasibility. If warlords, political leaders or other key figures are virulently opposed to TJ, it may not matter if the broader public is in favour of it. Some groups have more leverage than others, and well-organized, funded or armed groups can derail peace deals and TJ efforts despite favourable public opinion.[203]

If we bear this in mind, plus the aforementioned tendency to elide any discussion of key structural and post-conflict variables, it is clear that constructivist theory has its limitations as a means of explaining the gap between intended and actual justice outcomes. The interests of local actors, particularly political elites, cannot be passed over. Neither can the legitimacy of transformative norms be assumed, as they clearly implicate balances of power and resources between social groups, which need to be examined. Any such analysis necessarily takes us out of constructivist theorizing and into the realms of rational choice and realism. By this, I do not mean a synonym for defeatism in the face of antagonism, nor what has memorably been called the 'bastardised conception of political realism' by which a proposal is realistic only to the extent that it approaches what already exists.[204] Instead, it refers to the incorporation of deep conflict among contending social forces at the core of transitional justice, in addition to abstract values – as Bhuta puts it, an 'insistence on the material dimensions of power' that emphasizes human finitude and

---

201 Subotic (n 67) 138.
202 ibid.
203 Thoms Ron and Paris (n 43) 351.
204 Roberto Mangabeira Unger, *False Necessity: Anti-necessitarian Social Theory in the Service of Radical Democracy* (Cambridge University Press 1987) 350.

the finite nature of the political in the face of lofty norms and values.[205] Too much of the transformative theorization relies on subordinating domestic politics to the norms of transitional justice. It is not enough to ask the normative question of what societies should do when this implicitly disregards the positive question of what post-conflict societies actually tend to do. Transitional justice attempts to remove or alter barriers to transformation, but it cannot do so without acknowledging them and the limits they impose on structural change. As Coyne argues, 'Normative considerations absent positive analysis result in a disconnect between what should be done and what can be done given real and existing constraints. What is morally appealing in an ideal world may not be as appealing when constraints are taken into account'.[206]

Taking due account of constraints does not mean the post-conflict ecology should be treated as immutable. It does, however, require taking seriously the self-evident fact that peacebuilding and transitional justice are sites of contestation, as opposed to neutral grounds for theorization or the guarantors of defined political outcomes. Any revised social contract, however loosely conceived, stems from first the expectations of society within the state (which the transitional justice literature is extremely attentive to), secondly the state's resources and capacity to provide services (which it largely ignores), and thirdly elite will to direct these resources and services towards the fulfilment of those expectations (which again, it ignores).[207] These factors are mediated by the political processes through which bargains between the state and society are agreed and institutionalized.[208] The most obviously underanalysed determinant of transitional justice's transformative capacity is political will. Critical transitional justice theory seldom addresses the political basis for why an actor who benefits from the status quo and enjoys the ability to maintain it might be motivated to shift from it to his economic detriment.

Accounting for this takes us into the realm of political economy analysis, which concentrates on how power and wealth are apportioned and disputed in a given society. It may allow for a more informed, pragmatic estimation of how malleable these structures are. Political

---

[205] Nehal Bhuta, 'New Modes and Orders: The Difficulties of a *Jus Post Bellum* of Constitutional Transformation' (2010) 60 *University of Toronto Law Journal* 799, 848.

[206] Coyne (n 150) 26.

[207] Organisation for Economic Co-operation and Development, *From Fragility to Resilience: Concepts and Dilemmas of State Building in Fragile States* (Organisation for Economic Co-operation and Development 2008) 17.

[208] ibid.

economy analysis 'is concerned with the interaction of political and economic processes in a society: the distribution of power and wealth between different groups and individuals, and the processes that create, sustain and transform these relationships over time'.[209] Political economy analysis has not been factored into the transformative transitional justice literature. One exception is the work of Franzki and Olarte, who quite rightly assert the importance of such an approach, but conclude that the political economy of transitional justice is rooted in the separation by interveners of the economic and the political fostered by liberal political rationality.[210] This is echoed in a number of other critiques of transitional justice which are premised on a rejection of liberal peacebuilding and see adverse outcomes as flowing from its diversion from emancipatory transformation to the securitized and neo-liberal discourses of the international community. The problem with such critiques is that they address only one of the three dimensions of a post-conflict state's political economy, namely the international actors who participate in the affairs of state. As a result, they ignore or downplay the institutions and structures of the formal state which antagonists have fought expressly to control, not to mention those informal structures central to the organization and exercise of power.[211] The presence of peacebuilders is unlikely by itself to transform the strategic interests or power of major domestic political forces, and above all of those opposed to peace, and may in fact remain hostage to their strategies and behaviours.[212] As Chapter 4 argues in greater detail, external actors (the 'liberal peacebuilders') enjoy little capacity to fundamentally alter historically constituted political relations between elite groups and between elites and their own constituencies. Political economy analysis reminds us that 'no matter how international

---

[209] OECD, 'Political Economy Analysis' (2009) as cited in DFID, 'Political Economy Analysis How to Note' (2009) 4 <https://www.odi.org/sites/odi.org.uk/files/odi-assets/events-documents/3797.pdf> accessed 21 July 2016.

[210] Franzki and Olarte (n 4) 208.

[211] Mats Berdal and Dominik Zaum, 'Power After Peace' in Mats Berdal and Dominik Zaum (eds), *Political Economy of Statebuilding: Power after Peace* (Routledge 2013) 1 at 5.

[212] Katarina Ammitzboll and Stina Torjesen, *Maximum or Minimum? Policy Options for Democratisation Initiatives in UN Peace Operations* (Norsk Utenrikspolitisk Institutt 2006) 17.

actors wish to reshape and reform the domestic political economy, it is the primacy of domestic politics that is a major theme of … statebuilding efforts'.[213]

Taking as given the conflictual nature of society, a political economy approach assesses political opportunity in terms of how class-, religion- or ethnic-based groups bargain over power and economic resources. It views economics in terms of how resources are produced and how competing political claims determine how they are allocated. It incorporates both formal and informal actors and structures. The normative agenda of transformative transitional justice, no less than any other peacebuilding activity, affects patterns of exclusion, accumulation and other socio-cultural realities, which will create incentives for potential 'losers' to resist. A political economy approach allows policy-makers to comprehend political behaviour in unfamiliar political milieus and how it affects policy. Above all, it helps observers to comprehend the incentives of those critical internal political actors whose commitment to macro-level outcomes is indispensable and who retain capacity to resist or 'spoil' them. It takes seriously materialist state theories that present the state as particular expressions of power that privilege certain interests and marginalize others as the outcome of historically specific (if often haphazard) contests between (semi)organized, dynamic constellations of vested interests embedded in its political economy.[214] Political economy analysis allows for a better understanding of the post-conflict context and the means by which it shapes overall transitional justice strategies, and it can diagnose critical challenges that drive or impede structural change. Elites, conflict protagonists, change agents and transitional justice actors never exist alone, but only in relation to each other. A form of power analysis that scrutinizes these co-constitutive relationships and identifies the incentives of protagonists, the marginalization or empowerment of change agents relative to established structures or the critical junctures where change is more or less possible is of obvious use to transitional justice theorization and policy-making. Above all, political economy analysis helps explain (1) why the interests of certain domestic actors can coalesce around outcomes that are sub-optimal for marginalized groups like women, the indigent and minorities and (2) why advocacy, norm diffusion and dialogue with power-brokers have limited effect absent compelling political leverage. Power analysis helps us better understand

---

[213] Oisín Tansey, 'Statebuilding and the Limits of Constitutional Design' in Berdal and Zaum (eds) (n 211) 17 at 18.

[214] Bob Jessop, *State Theory: Putting the Capitalist State in its Place* (Penn State Press 1990); Nicos Poulantzas, *State, Power, Socialism* (Verso 1978).

why resistance to seemingly necessary and progressive processes of social change that might otherwise appear as irrational or even nihilistic can have its own rationalism or functional utility. As such, it provides at the very least a realistic picture of the patterns of political life within post-conflict states and a threshold competence to anticipate cycles of action and response. Contrary to the transformative justice literature, it concentrates not on pathological descriptions of what is wrong or what is not in place, but rather addresses what is there – what coalitions promote reform, what actions can produce results efficiently, under what conditions can transformative projects take place. Only a political economy approach can enable the sort of 'paradoxical rationality' that can mix idealist views of the possible with realist views of the situation presented.[215]

A political economy approach takes seriously the possibility that transition to peace not only creates opportunity but also produces its own limits, and so draws attention to the possible path dependency of transitional justice. Path dependency means that the array of outcomes and available policy options in any given circumstance is significantly limited by prior decisions which can become self-reinforcing. Once a polity starts on a certain trajectory, certain institutions or patterns of distribution are established that continue to propel it along that trajectory, becoming so resilient that they can be defended by those who benefit from them and constrain what can be done subsequently by would-be social engineers. Possible elements of the path-dependent nature of different starting-points were suggested in Chapter 1's examination of structural variables (weak state institutions, underdevelopment, illegitimate governance) and post-conflict variables (legacy of war, peace agreement, international intervention) that might limit or increase the malleability of the state. The most pertinent are probably the compromises made during the negotiation of the agreement which embodies and defines the peace and interacts with the other variables. Much of the optimism examined earlier about the prospects for transformation in post-conflict states flows from the supposition that peace agreements are binding commitments entered into by antagonists that set out common visions of the future where the root causes of the earlier war are addressed. The hope is that peace reflects the aspirations of society at large and not merely those of the antagonists, and responds to the needs of all citizens as revealed in public discourses and dialogues about peace.

---

215 John Paul Lederach, 'Cultivating Peace: A Practitioner's View of Deadly Conflict and Negotiations' in Darby and Mac Ginty (eds) (n 200) 36 at 39.

To the (increasing) extent that international organizations are involved in peace negotiations, the expectation is that any agreement would be governed by international human rights law even where it runs against the grain of local balances of power.

However, this view of peace does not tally with observable trends in post-conflict peace-making. As Chapter 3 goes on to argue in detail, civil war rarely nurtures the sense of compromise and generosity between factions that might facilitate a fundamental revision of social structures. Peace agreements are therefore seldom objective rational-choice determinations for redressing the root causes of conflicts on which transitional justice projects might capitalize. Instead, they are keenly bargained products of contestations between opposing elites. The primary impulse of all external and internal actors is to respond to the pressing emergency of war by constructing forms of political organization that end the conflict and ensure future conflicts can be handled routinely without large-scale violence. Policies necessary to achieve goals like security or power-sharing may require the deferral or repudiation of others, like structural reform or equality agendas, and so may in fact solidify inequalities in the post-conflict period. In divided and developing states (even those not subject to war) political settlements are best understood as the distribution of benefits and privileges by powerful cohorts that must be at least minimally acceptable to them lest they be overturned.[216] Settlements, and the institutions they establish, both reflect and organize power. Those who typically exert the most influence over politics or the distribution of resources in a given state are those well-organized interests able (and, crucially, willing) to defend themselves and achieve their goals by extra-legal means – in practice, such groups typically achieve their goals without recourse to this undoubted potential for force and can avail of legal means.[217] These elites can be contrasted with less organized, marginalized groups like women, minorities and the indigent who have strong interests in the outcome of peace negotiations but negligible capacity to either spoil the peace or bind antagonists to it. While the benefits of redistribution and welfarism are spread widely among the population at large, most citizens have a relatively weak

---

[216] Mushtaq Khan, 'Political Settlements and the Governance of Growth-Enhancing Institutions' (unpublished monograph, School of Oriental and African Studies, 2010) 4 <http://core.ac.uk/download/files/103/2792198.pdf> accessed 20 July 2016.

[217] Stephen Holmes, 'Lineages of the Rule of Law' in Jose Maria Maravall and Adam Przeworski (eds), *Democracy and the Rule of Law* (Cambridge University Press 2003) 19 at 21.

personal incentive to actively seek improvements in the system, in contradistinction to the relatively few powerful individuals who may have a strong incentive to oppose any such policies. The influence of international human rights law might mitigate this weakness, particularly if enshrined in the peace agreement. However, as Putnam notes, 'formal enumeration of human rights provisions correlates only weakly, if at all, with the quantity and quality of human rights protection during and after peace implementation'.[218] This tendency is explored in greater detail in the next chapter.

[218] Putnam (n 108) 238.

3. Transitional opportunity? How peace negotiations and power-sharing impede root cause approaches

> [P]eace processes are inter-elite political accommodations whose aim is often not so much 'peace' as the reconfiguration of domestic hegemony and/or international legitimacy; peace processes are reformist, conservative and far from revolutionary phenomena, and often therefore do not provide a basis for the social transformations necessary for sustainable peace.[1]

> Contrary to commonsensical assumptions, negotiation does not occur between co-equal parties or in an inclusive manner. Rather it engages heterogeneous groups with highly differentiated assets, entitlements, legitimacy and styles of expression. Not everything is or can be negotiated and not everyone takes part in negotiating statehood. But the political configurations and institutional arrangements that result from such negotiation processes must be seen as imprints of domination by the more powerful over weaker groups.[2]

Since at least the time of the Bosnian and Rwandan conflicts, the post-conflict ecology has been considered as one of the two paradigmatic transitions that define the field alongside post-authoritarian regime alteration. Though few transitional justice scholars pinpoint the stage in a peace process where the field's activities can inform processes of social change, given the realities of how peace is negotiated, the implementation phase would seem to offer the most potential. However, it is rare for any treatment of transitional justice's potential to catalyse socio-economic change in this context to specifically engage with war, its ontological and epistemological underpinnings, and how it alters the political economy of states. This is unfortunate as the nature of war, and

[1] Jan Selby, 'The Political Economy of Peace Processes' in Michael Pugh, Neil Cooper and Mandy Turner (eds), *Whose Peace? Critical Perspectives on the Political Economy of Peacebuilding* (Palgrave Macmillan 2008) 13 at 15.

[2] Tobias Hagmann and Didier Péclard, 'Negotiating Statehood: Dynamics of Power and Domination in Africa' (2010) 41 *Development and Change* 539, 545.

in particular war termination, significantly influences the motivational calculus of political leaders afterwards, to say nothing of the leverage peacebuilders, donors, civil society or the transitional justice industry can exert on them. Chinkin is correct to argue that while explicit guarantees within peace agreements for economic, social and cultural (ESC) rights may not be required for their realization, their provision 'facilitates their being taken into account during policy and planning post-conflict and may minimize the likelihood of their being relegated to a subsequent phase of development'.[3] The key question, therefore, is whether the process of agreeing peace is conducive to ESC rights promotion or any other forms of economic justice.

Civil wars are ultimately acutely competitive conflicts over the organizing principles and paramount rules of the polity. All militarized conflicts between historically specific coalitions of interest are grounded in the political economy of the state in question. Every institution that emerges from it gives expression to that conflict and must of necessity promote or marginalize certain interests. Given the primacy of conflict elites and the tendency for peace negotiations to degenerate into conservative bargaining over political and economic power, there is rarely that window of opportunity 'not only for returning to a previous state of order but for deeply reforming it and dismantling old structures of economic crime, structural violence, and oppression' so commonly assumed in the transitional justice literature.[4] Before examining the impact of peace negotiation on opportunities for revising economic structures, it is necessary to examine (in an admittedly generic sense) how present-day wars begin and end.

1. MODERN INTRA-STATE WAR: CAUSES, ASYMMETRIES AND STALEMATES

Defining what war is is difficult. Conflict is a universal and endemic feature of political society, and only becomes war through the formation

---

[3] Christine Chinkin, 'The Protection of Economic, Social and Cultural rights in Post-Conflict (United Nations High Commissioner for Human Rights Women's Human Rights and Gender Unit, 2008) 5 <http://www2.ohchr.org/english/issues/women/docs/Paper_Protection_ESCR.pdf> accessed 21 July 2016.

[4] Kora Andrieu, 'Dealing with a "New" Grievance: Should Anticorruption Be Part of the Transitional Justice Agenda?' (2012) 11 *Journal of Human Rights* 537, 538.

of militarized conflict parties. Non-international armed conflict seldom occurs between standing armies. Instead, it typically sees a government and national army face off against one or more opposition groups capable of mounting effective resistance. Deciding when these parties or their activities depart from transient intensifications of constant and casual friction to cross the threshold of something recognizable as war is a basic task of conflict studies. One common definition comes from the Political Instability Task Force, which employs both a mobilization threshold (each party must mobilize 1,000 or more people) and a conflict intensity threshold (where there must be at least 1,000 deaths over the duration of the conflict and at least one year where the death toll exceeds 100).[5] Some seriously destabilizing 'conflicts' (with quantitative thresholds as low as a minimum of twenty-five battle-related deaths) may fall short of these benchmarks in weak states.[6]

The sheer complexity of war makes it challenging to generalize about its key determinants. There is an almost limitless array of theories on the spectrum from rational choice to endemic savagery to explain the commencement of war, though this work excludes the savagery end of this spectrum. There are common patterns to many of the wars seen since the end of the Cold War, particularly in the contemporary Middle East and Africa. State weakness or collapse is often seen as the cause or indispensable background condition for war. As the state, its social institutions and markets prove unable to deliver justice, economic opportunities and services to the entire citizenry or a definable portion thereof, loyalties are withdrawn from the state and redirected elsewhere. Because the institutions for generating the power, authority and monopoly of violence necessary to regulate latent conflict cease to function, power vacuums emerge. Defensive incentives flowing from the resulting security dilemma (fear of being attacked or dominated) lead groups to seek to arm themselves to be protected from anarchy, which then leads other groups to arm. This becomes mixed with incentives to gain state power or to impose an ideology or form of rule dominated by the group.[7]

Competing ethnonational, ethnoreligious or ethnolinguistic claims over the state are often seen as the driving force of civil wars – the more

---

[5] Political Instability Task Force, *Problem Set Codebook* (2014) 5 <http://www.systemicpeace.org/inscr/PITFProbSetCodebook2013.pdf> accessed 21 July 2016.

[6] Lotta Themnér and Peter Wallensteen, 'Armed Conflicts, 1946–2012' (2013) 50 *Journal of Peace Research* 509, 509 (abstract).

[7] Michael Doyle and Nicholas Sambanis, *Making War and Building Peace: United Nations Peace Operations* (Princeton University Press 2006) 28.

ethnic groups are excluded from state power, the higher their mobilization capacity, and the more they experienced conflict in the past, the more likely conflict with the state is likely to be initiated.[8] Explanations of war rooted in this sort of rationality can be attributed to the 'grievance' theory of war, i.e. that groups rebel over issues of identity and exclusion from power. Other explanations emphasize a 'greed' thesis. They posit that war is started by rebels seeking economic gain from the opportunities war provides to loot natural resources or to control them. Resource dependency both weakens the state to provide the opportunity for armed rebellion, and, if captured, generates the means by which war can be funded. Where once resources were the means for warfare, in these 'new wars' examined by the greed thesis resources are the object of it. Few are absolutist in their attribution of war to greed or grievance – monocausal explanations belie inevitably multiple and shifting causalities. Though wars like those in Syria, Côte d'Ivoire or Sri Lanka were clearly driven by the rejection of systematized exclusion, in other less ideologically driven conflicts the dynamics of greed and grievance are often found in operation simultaneously, each reinforcing the other.[9] Strong statistical association between any factors like poverty, ethnic fractionalization, governance type or resource availability are hard to draw. Ultimately, many of the supposed causes of war are best conceptualized as factors that merely increase the risks that catalyse warfare when combined in different ways in given contexts. These retrospectively look like 'powder kegs' that explode but often share characteristics with societies that experience no war at all. Elite manipulation of identity groups is perhaps the most unpredictable variable determining which societies go to war and which do not. Fundamentally, war occurs where the preferences of belligerents are mutually incompatible, where none of them can credibly commit to peaceful settlement and the parties believe their aims are best secured through coercion.

1.1 Starting War, Fighting War

Though the origins of civil wars are (very) roughly generalizable, the conduct of them is not. Wars can be majoritarian (fought on behalf of an excluded population as a whole) or minoritarian (fought by an

[8] Lars-Erik Cederman, Andreas Wimmer and Brian Min, 'Why Do Ethnic Groups Rebel? New Data and Analysis' (2010) 62 *World Politics* 87.

[9] See generally David Keen, 'Incentives and Disincentives for Violence' in Mats Berdal and David Malone (eds), *Greed and Grievance: Economic Agendas in Civil Wars* (Lynne Rienner 2000) 19.

excluded group for inclusion or secession). They come in three main types: (1) conventional civil wars where two sides can deploy heavy weaponry against each other, (2) irregular civil wars where the state military fights lightly armed rebels and (3) symmetric non-conventional war where both government and rebels share low levels of military sophistication.[10] Not all conflicts present a dyadic division between regular state forces and rebels. As Kalyvas reminds us, 'Civil wars are not binary conflicts, but complex and ambiguous processes that foster an apparently massive, though variable, mix of identities and actions'.[11] There can be long-term wars (e.g. 34 years in Guatemala, over 50 years in Colombia) or short-term ones (e.g. three months in Croatia in the mid-1990s).

The most intractable wars are those that are not only long but produce significant numbers of casualties and endure repeated cycles of violence. These may be mortal combats (where belligerents try to kill each other), counterforce duels (where combatants try to forcibly disarm the other) or 'contests of punishment' (where one belligerent tries to bend the other to its will).[12] Civil wars will manifest recurrent periods of escalation, dormancy, stalemate, failed negotiation, recurrence and intensification. In modern warfare, distinctions between civilians and soldiers are blurred, often meaning that civilians make up the vast majority of casualties, though direct battlefield deaths are dwarfed by indirect poverty, destruction of basic services and disease. El Salvador's civil war resulted in approximately 75,000 deaths, 200,000 died in Guatemala, while in the DR Congo some estimates go as high as over five million deaths once disease and starvation are included. Human rights abuses typically abound both as a tactic of war and a means of suppressing opposition – ethnic cleansing, rape, displacement, massacres, forcible recruitment, torture. Civil wars are developmentally ruinous as lives are lost, homes are abandoned and infrastructure is destroyed, while government spending shifts from development to the military and foreign aid becomes logistically far more difficult to administer.

---

[10] Laia Balcells and Stathis Kalyvas, 'Does Warfare Matter? Severity, Duration and Outcomes of Civil Wars' (2014) 58 *Journal of Conflict Resolution* 1390, 1391.

[11] Stathis Kalyvas, 'The Ontology of "Political Violence": Action and Identity in Civil Wars' (2003) 1 *Perspectives on Politics* 475, 475.

[12] Robert Harrison Wagner, 'The Causes of Peace' in Roy Licklider (ed.), *Stopping the Killing: How Civil Wars End* (New York University Press 1993) 235 at 238.

Civil war has famously been described as development in reverse. Macroeconomic effects include depression, collapse of economic regulation, falling exports, black markets, hyperinflation and unemployment. For example, Guatemala's poverty levels would have been 12 per cent lower without war; Sierra Leone became one of the poorest countries in the world in terms of life expectancy (34 years) and GDP per capita (US$142) after its civil war; while Liberia endured much the same while its mining, agriculture and service industries collapsed completely.[13] Uganda's per capita GDP fell by 40 per cent in fifteen years of warfare.[14] Infrastructure for public administration like the civil service, judiciary and police are severely diminished. Exacerbating the realities of radically uneven income distribution and high levels of absolute poverty are the routinization of violence, division and mistrust in the public sphere even after warfare has officially ended. Post-conflict is a context where each faction expects the other to behave opportunistically when circumstances allow.[15]

Civil wars arise because of incompatibilities between the socio-economic interests or values held by groups and the distribution of political, social and economic goods within that state. However, as war goes on over months and then years, it usually becomes clear that 'violence is an inherently interactive and dynamic process: the violence of one side impacts on the violence of the other side, while the war evolves and changes as the political actors strategize in response to evolving constraints and their rivals' strategy'.[16] Conflict endurance owes less to the original and underlying goal incompatibility, and more to the tendency of belligerents to become trapped in extended action–reaction sequences, in which the conflict behaviour of one antagonist today is a response to that of the other yesterday.[17] This produces relational

---

[13] Astri Suhrke, Torunn Wimpelmann and Marcia Dawes, *Peace Processes and Statebuilding: Economic and Institutional Provisions of Peace Agreements* (Chr. Michelsen Institute 2007) 32–34.

[14] Paul Collier, *The Challenge of Ugandan Reconstruction, 1986–98* (World Bank Development Research Group 1999) 1.

[15] Chrissie Steenkamp, 'The Legacy of War: Conceptualizing a "Culture of Violence" to Explain Violence after Peace Accords' (2005) 94 *The Round Table* 253.

[16] Stathis Kalyvas, 'Promises and Pitfalls of an Emerging Research Program: The Microdynamics of Civil War' in Stathis Kalyvas and Ian Shapiro (eds), *Order, Conflict, and Violence* (Cambridge University Press 2008) 397 at 405.

[17] Dennis Sandole, *Capturing the Complexity of Conflict: Dealing with Violent Ethnic Conflicts in the Post-Cold War Era* (Pinter 1999).

dynamics that reduce the salience of initial conflict root causes when it comes to negotiating peace. These relational dynamics also impose path dependencies and structural constraints for policy-making in any sphere, most notably transitional justice, giving the lie to the insistence by critics of peacebuilding that peace processes are 'creatures of the international community' that reflects its interests.[18] Strategic choices supposedly characteristic of liberal peacebuilding, most notably power-sharing, security sector reform and elections, are not solely international impositions but endogenous responses to intractable civil wars, albeit with international guidance. As such, they are inherently bargained processes. The bargaining process is conditioned by the relative strengths of the parties and the way the conflict ultimately terminates.

An asymmetry of one strong party (usually the government) and one weaker party (a rebel group or groups) is a near-constant feature of civil war. The government can call upon its national military to prosecute warfare. Typically, it is better trained and equipped as well as more experienced and organized than any domestic adversary. It can take advantage of a longer-term source of revenue in the national tax-base and the freedom to import weaponry and other materiel. Rebels, by contrast, are less organized and enjoy less systematic training, have far fewer weapons and more difficult supply chains. Most conventional wars thus favour incumbent governments, but they also win most irregular wars as well, albeit in a more prolonged fashion.[19]

However, asymmetric war allows weak rebels to pursue indirect attacks via guerrilla warfare instead of direct defence, permitting them to forestall defeat indefinitely (though extreme asymmetry will usually permit government to win, while occasionally asymmetries can be reversed as governments wane and rebels wax). This is made easier where there is civilian support, where mountainous terrain and/or many borders permit rebels to endure as moving targets, where arms and explosives are plentiful and where they can secure outside military assistance or even intervention. As Holl notes, the ability to wage war is dependent on two factors – resources available and the strength of the commitment to apply available resources to securing conflict goals.[20]

---

[18] As argued in John Darby and Roger Mac Ginty, 'Introduction: What Peace? What Process?' in John Darby and Roger Mac Ginty (eds), *Contemporary Peacemaking* (Palgrave Macmillan 2008) 1 at 4.

[19] Balcells and Kalyvas (n 10) 1393.

[20] Jane Holl, 'When War Doesn't Work: Understanding the Relationship between the Battlefield and the Negotiating Table' in Licklider (ed.) (n 12) 269 at 279.

Asymmetry of commitment can significantly offset asymmetry of power. Even where governments are militarily much stronger in terms of resources available, rebels can compensate for lack of numbers and power with an unwavering commitment to bear costs in pursuit of the conflict objectives, a belief in ideological or moral superiority of their position and use of violence that creates disproportionate amounts of disruption.[21] Even where rebels cannot win a war, they can escalate the costs to their state adversary by increasing the costs of failure to come to a settlement. As the cliché goes, rebels win by not losing. Attrition of will, as opposed to destruction of power, is the main goal of rebels. Most contemporary civil wars therefore become 'contests of punishment' where one belligerent tries to bend the other to its will, but generally fails to do so fully. Once this becomes apparent, much warfare becomes less about victory than about extracting a better deal in negotiation, a process that makes war 'indistinguishable from bargaining'.[22]

Statistical studies of civil war demonstrate that when rebels are strong, when they can impose significant casualties on government forces and when conflict is long and drawn-out, negotiated settlement is most likely.[23] In particular, rebel strength relative to that of the government increases the likelihood of at least one power-sharing provision in a peace settlement.[24] Prolonged war induces fatigue among combatants and formerly supportive civilian populations. It also resolves previous uncertainties about military strength and willingness to prosecute war, allowing both sides to better understand the limitations and potential of existing strength. Prolonged wars generate the most fatigue and the most information, and they are more likely to end in durable peace settlements, better known as the 'war weariness' theory where military impasse compels re-evaluation of rivalry policy.[25] In many African states, cyclical processes of violence, negotiation and new elections are at work as rebels become aware that inflicting casualties can compel governments to

---

[21] I. William Zartman, 'Dynamics and Constraints in Negotiations in International Conflicts' in I. William Zartman (ed.), *Elusive Peace: Negotiating an End to Civil Wars* (Brookings Institution 1995) 3.

[22] Wagner (n 12) 238 and 260.

[23] Jeffrey Dixon, 'Emerging Consensus: Results from the Second Wave of Statistical Studies on Civil War Termination' (2009) 11 *Civil Wars* 121, 123–24.

[24] Stephen Gent, 'Relative Rebel Strength and Power Sharing in Intrastate Conflicts' (2011) 37 *International Interactions* 215, 221.

[25] Christoph Zürcher, Carrie Manning and Kristie Evenson, *Costly Democracy: Peacebuilding and Democratization After War* (Stanford University Press 2013) 37.

engage in dialogue.[26] This is particularly the case where international actors can be manipulated by militarily effective insurgencies to pressure domestic government to undergo negotiations – violence 'creates incentive structures which turn the rebel path into an appealing option in the pursuit of otherwise blocked political aspirations'.[27] Groups in repressive or exclusionary states strategize and organize on the basis that a sufficiently interminable conflict can attract international attention, a reality that increases the damage military impasse does to the government.[28] Negotiation can even be the rule after apparent government victory on the battlefield. Relatively few rebels are so thoroughly defeated that they are incapable of asserting influence over a potential peace. In these situations, governments may decide that the gains from the escalation that would guarantee final victory may be slight compared to a compromise peace, particularly if the difference between acceptable settlements proposed by both sides is narrow.[29]

1.2 Mutually Hurting Stalemates

Usually it takes one antagonist to kick-start the process by proposing negotiations, but getting to a point where negotiation is preferred to victory is difficult. The initiator will appear weak (encouraging the other to continue with war), because agreeing to talk legitimizes the other side as of equal standing and because psychologically it calls into question past sacrifices of blood and treasure expended in pursuit of victory. Peace proposals usually have a pendulum effect where one side proposes peace talks but the other rejects it in the belief that unilateral means can achieve a more satisfactory result.[30] This can even occur in periods of obvious stalemate as military impasses can be advantageous for governments that can justify internal repression or for rebels that can exploit land and territory they control. Consequently, those windows of opportunity are relatively rare where all parties (1) acknowledge the impossibility of

---

26 Ian Spears, 'Africa's Informal Power-Sharing and the Prospects for Peace' (2013) 15 *Civil Wars* 37, 49.

27 Denis Tull and Andreas Mehler, 'The Hidden Costs of Power-sharing: Reproducing Insurgent Violence in Africa' (2005) 104 *African Affairs* 375, 376.

28 Andreas Mehler, *Not Always in the People's Interest: Power-Sharing Arrangements in African Peace Agreements* (German Institute of Global and Area Studies 2008) 4 and 10.

29 Holl (n 20) 276.

30 John Darby and Roger Mac Ginty, 'Conclusion: Peace Processes, Present, and Future' in Darby and Mac Ginty (eds) (n 18) 352 at 353.

decisive military victory, (2) recognize the other side can effectively veto their own preferred outcomes, and so (3) are ready to negotiate. Those moments where commitments to peace are based on a reasonable expectation that the other side have negotiated in good faith, will reciprocate commitments in the future and behave predictably can only ever arise where both sides realize the utility of settling or institutional accommodation is greater than the utility of fighting to (potential) victory regardless of the objectives that led them into war in the first place. At these points the status quo is intolerable for both sides, overturning it is impossible or not worth the effort and second-best solutions become bearable. These 'ripe moments' are best known as those 'mutually hurting stalemates' briefly sketched in Chapter 1, though it often takes a long time for this convergence of expectations to occur. They are based 'on the notion that when the parties find themselves locked in a conflict from which they cannot escalate to victory and this deadlock is painful to both of them (although not necessarily in equal degree or for the same reasons), they seek an alternative policy or way out'.[31] The main theorist in the area is Zartman, who focuses on the relationship or division of power between the antagonists and how it shapes perceptions of the future. Zartman deepens his analysis by suggesting that this mutually hurting stalemate can be influenced by the existence of either a looming disaster that threatens to further exacerbate the costs of continuing war for one or both parties[32] and/or a 'way out' (not necessarily a specific solution, but rather a confidence that a just and satisfactory solution is negotiable for both parties).[33] Others extend this notion of a 'way out' with reference to his discussion of an 'enticing opportunity' model where new options become feasible that offer more gains (or at least more certain gains) as belligerents focus more on the benefits of negotiation than existing or anticipated costs.[34] These opportunities will usually have

---

[31] I. William Zartman, 'The Timing of Peace Initiatives: Hurting Stalemates and Ripe Moments' in Darby and Mac Ginty (eds) (n 18) 22 at 22.

[32] Though this element is somewhat neglected elsewhere in the conflict studies literature – it is not fundamental to the definition or existence of a mutually hurting stalemate.

[33] Two particularly useful works that show the evolution of his idea are *Ripe for Resolution: Conflict Resolution in Africa* (Oxford University Press 1989) and 'Ripeness: The Hurting Stalemate and Beyond' in Paul Stern and Daniel Druckman (eds), *International Conflict Resolution after the Cold War* (National Academy Press 2000) 225.

[34] Christopher Mitchell, 'The Right Moment: Notes on Four Models of "Ripeness"' (1995) 9 *Paradigms* 38, 44–46.

'been in the air for a long time' but only now appear attractive.[35] Others focus less on divisions of power between antagonists to concentrate on the internal politics of the parties. Haas argues that a conflict is ripe when four conditions are satisfied: there is a shared perception of the desirability/necessity of a compromise; the leaders have sufficient internal leverage to force compromise upon their side or are so weak that it appears unavoidable; the compromise is 'rich' enough to make it palatable to the leaders' own constituencies (particularly hard-liners and true believers); and finally, a procedure can be assented to that deals with other elements of the conflict.[36]

There are many examples of mutually hurting stalemates that preceded peace. In Mozambique's apparently interminable conflict, internal military stalemate meant victory seemed impossible, while the withdrawal of international support for both sides in the war meant the costs were no longer worth bearing. The government could no longer pay army salaries and risked mutiny, while the Mozambican National Resistance (RENAMO) realized that participation in legitimate politics would generate more benefits than continued attacks.[37] Similarly, in El Salvador, the national army stalled at the foothills of the mountains and understood it had reached an impasse with the Farabundo Martí National Liberation Front (FMLN), which could field 2,000 combatants in the capital but were outnumbered 5:1. It became apparent that neither side could achieve their objectives through military victory and so meaningful peace negotiations commenced.[38] In Guatemala, the National Revolutionary Unity (URNG) guerrillas were essentially beaten militarily but politics created stalemate conditions as international pressure (sanctions and diplomatic isolation) meant military advantage could not be pressed, resulting in a bargained transition which allowed the rebels to wrest concessions from the government at the negotiation table, albeit fewer than their counterparts in El Salvador.[39] Military setbacks for Hutu rebels in Burundi were

---

35 Zartman (n 31) 22.

36 Richard Haas, *Conflicts Unending* (Yale University Press 1990).

37 Shanna Kirschner and Jana Von Stein, 'The Pieces of Peacemaking: Understanding Implementation of Civil War Settlements' (2009) 11 *Civil Wars* 279, 295.

38 Doyle and Sambanis (n 7) 305.

39 Susan Burgerman, 'Building the Peace by Mandating Reform: United Nations-mediated Human Rights Agreements in El Salvador and Guatemala' (2000) 27 *Latin American Perspectives* 63, 74–75.

paralleled by the political enfeeblement of the Tutsi political establishment, and this mutual weakness positively affected the peace process.[40] In Bosnia, 'the costs of continued conflict … had reached a sufficiently painful level for both sides that the status quo could no longer be maintained', though international military intervention played a much larger role than usual in compelling this realization.[41] The June 2016 peace agreement between the Colombian government and the Revolutionary Armed Forces of Colombia (FARC) acknowledged that, despite fifty years of warfare, neither part could secure its combat goals at an acceptable cost.

Though Aggestam, for example, argues that most peace processes are initiated after heavy international pressures of the sort suggested above, as opposed to mutually hurting stalemates or enticing opportunities, international pressure alone is insufficient to compel a meaningful, sustainable peace.[42] Unless both sides believe victory is impossible or only possible with unconscionable costs, international pressure alone is likely to generate only those premature, volatile settlements that merely distribute power temporarily between belligerents who remain intent on continuing the conflict once international attention switches elsewhere.[43] As suggested in Chapter 1, in these instances of temporary, internationally-pressured peace definite provisions regarding the future exercise of political power and economic opportunity, to say nothing of tough choices like disarmament or genuine power-sharing, are unlikely to be authoritatively established. That said, there is a general consensus that the presence of peacekeepers makes the failure of temporary peace far less likely to occur and peace agreements more likely.[44]

---

[40] Mehler (n 28) 16.

[41] Michael Greig, 'Moments of Opportunity Recognizing Conditions of Ripeness for International Mediation between Enduring Rivals' (2001) 45 *Journal of Conflict Resolution* 691, 691.

[42] Karin Aggestam, 'Internal and External Dynamics of Spoiling: A Negotiation Approach' in Edward Newman and Oliver Richmond (eds), *Challenges to Peacebuilding: Managing Spoilers During Conflict Resolution* (United Nations University Press 2006) 23 at 29.

[43] Jeremy Weinstein, 'Autonomous Recovery and International Intervention Comparative Perspective' (Center for Global Development Working Paper 57, 2005) 9 <http://www.cgdev.org/files/2731_file_WP57.pdf> accessed 21 July 2016.

[44] For example, Michael Tiernay, 'Which Comes First? Unpacking the Relationship Between Peace Agreements and Peacekeeping Missions' (2015) 32 *Conflict Management and Peace Science* 135.

Stalemated ceasefires and temporary peaces cannot simply be declared as parties fear the other side will take advantage if they put down weapons or abandon positions. In these cases, the deployment of international actors protects one party from being 'suckered' by aggressors by operating as a buffer. It is by now a cliché to note that traditional Cold War peacekeeping has evolved into an entirely new set of functions like the peacebuilding examined in the next chapter, but before an agreement this classical model of interposition between belligerent armies is probably the most important. This blue helmet role may also mean there is a credible threat of retaliation against intentionally destabilizing or spoiling violence and that recalcitrant elements can be forcibly disarmed. Given the weakness of peacekeeping numbers and policing capacity, this potential is still dependent on local acquiescence of larger armies that, as the examples of Angola, Bosnia and modern Libya demonstrate, can return to war if they are determined to do so. Notwithstanding UN intervention, local capacities (quality of peace agreement and commitment to it are obvious factors, but factors like levels of income, economic growth and resource dependency are also significant) remain the critical factor determining recurrence of war.[45] Domestic politics condition all policy options.

The metaphor of 'ripeness' usefully presents both objective indictors (military stalemate, some power parity or at least parity of futility) and subjective ones (conflict mindsets, strategic visions, perceived counterfactual risks, willingness to compromise) of when mediation for peace can succeed, though it is more useful as a retrospective explanatory tool than as a predictive heuristic to manage the likely denouement of conflict.[46] Usually, mutually hurting stalemates point more to ripeness for negotiations to start than to ripeness for them to actually succeed. Being a metaphor, ripeness should not be taken too literally – peace does not fall like an apple from a tree into waiting hands.[47] It requires keen internal and external negotiation by conflict principals and, as will be seen in the next section, may need to be carefully cultivated by international mediators using incentives and disincentives that raise the costs of war or benefits of agreement. At all points, the belligerents retain significant military capability and have the power to reject the settlement

---

[45] Nicholas Sambanis, 'How Strategic is UN Peacebuilding?' in Daniel Philpott and Gerard Powers (eds), *Strategies of Peace: Transforming Conflict in a Violent World* (Oxford University Press 2010) 141 at 158.

[46] Marieke Kleiboer, 'Ripeness of Conflict: A Fruitful Notion?' (1994) 31 *Journal of Peace Research* 109, 111 and 114.

[47] ibid 111.

if they so wish. In Colombia, Northern Ireland and Nicaragua negotiations occurred at times that objectively appeared ripe but mediation still failed on numerous occasions. In Angola and Cambodia conditions 'unripened' even after settlements were negotiated when one or both parties reneged on terms, notwithstanding undiminished military gridlock.[48] Ripeness, therefore, is best conceptualized not as a single optimum opportunity but as part of a continuum – less ripe periods are less likely to result in rewarding mediation while riper junctions in the conflict cycle potentially conduce to conflict resolution.[49]

The mutually hurting stalemate theory provides little certainty and is rarely disaggregated by conflict type or country context. In particular, it is questionable how relevant it is to the more 'greed'-driven new wars characterized by the proliferation of factions and militias as in Liberia (which had eight factions at one point in 1994) or the Second Congo War (with as many as twenty) where small armies operate on limited geographical bases beyond the control of any larger faction fighting in a more traditional binary, grievance-driven conflict. However, the observable reality of mutually hurting stalemates is the primary domestic explanation of the sharp increase in negotiated settlements after the Cold War. This trend towards negotiated peace is widely accepted, although there are disparities in measuring it depending on how war and termination are codified and the year the research starts and concludes. For example, Wallensteen and Sollenberg found that of 74 conflicts concluded by 1998, 21 ended by peace agreements versus 24 via victory,[50] while in 2006 the Uppsala Conflict Data Programme found that 34 per cent of conflicts between 1990 and 2005 ended in negotiated settlement.[51] Between 2000 and 2005, there were almost four times as many civil wars that ended in negotiated settlements than by battlefield victory.[52] Though the years between 2009 and 2012 saw a decrease in the number of negotiated peaces,[53] ten peace agreements were concluded and

---

48 Hugh Miall, Oliver Ramsbotham and Tom Woodhouse, *Contemporary Conflict Resolution* (Polity Press 2011) 179–80.

49 Greig (n 41) 692.

50 Peter Wallensteen and Margareta Sollenberg, 'Armed Conflict, 1989–98' (1999) 36 *Journal of Peace Research* 593, 597.

51 Cited in Timothy Sisk, 'Power Sharing after Civil Wars: Matching Problems to Solutions' in Darby and Mac Ginty (eds) (n 18) 195 at 195.

52 Human Security Centre, 'Human Security Brief' (2006) 19 <http://www.hsrgroup.org/docs/Publications/HSB2006/2006HumanSecurityBrief-FullText.pdf> accessed 21 July 2016.

53 Themnér and Wallensteen (n 6) 509 (abstract).

signed in 2014, representing an increase of four from the previous year and solidifying the enduring trend towards peace negotiation.[54] In addition to this domestic explanation for negotiated settlement, the growing international normative shift towards peaceful settlement of civil war and the increased tendency for supranational organizations and third-party states to get involved in mediation have increased the incentives for domestic parties to negotiate and raised the costs of refusal to engage. Even bearing this in mind, the existential uncertainty underpinning mutually hurting stalemates demonstrates that peace must nevertheless be a keenly bargained process between sides that can credibly threaten a return to warfare and where factional interest may trump considerations of general well-being. It is to this that attention now turns.

2. NEGOTIATING PEACE

Much of the optimism examined in Chapter 2 about the prospects for transformation in post-conflict states flows from the supposition that peace agreements provide an opportunity for revisiting oppressive structural arrangements as the static concentrations of power that suppressed the demands of the marginalized are in flux. Peace agreements bring antagonists together to outline a future vision of the state that enjoys legitimacy and wide ownership, and reflects values and norms that function as public goods for the national community as a whole.[55] The assumption on the part of those within the transitional justice literature who share this optimism is that at least sometimes peace agreements are binding commitments entered into by antagonists that set out common visions of the future where the root causes of the earlier war are addressed, permitting a sweeping overhaul of societal structures rarely achievable under politics as usual.[56]

---

[54] Therése Pettersson and Peter Wallensteen, 'Armed Conflicts, 1946–2014' (2015) 52 *Journal of Peace Research* 536, 544.

[55] E.g., Kirsti Samuels, 'Postwar Constitution Building: Opportunities and Challenges' in Roland Paris and Timothy Sisk (eds), *The Dilemmas of Statebuilding: Confronting the Contradictions of Postwar Peace Operations* (Taylor and Francis 2009) 173; Miall, Ramsbotham and Woodhouse (n 48) 188.

[56] Christine Bell and Catherine O'Rourke, 'The People's Peace? Peace Agreements, Civil Society, and Participatory Democracy' (2007) 28 *International Political Science Review* 293, 295–96; Rolando Ames Cobián and Felix Reátegui, 'Toward Systemic Social Transformation: Truth Commissions and Development' in Pablo de Greiff and Roger Duthie (eds), *Transitional Justice and Development: Making Connections* (Social Science Research Council 2009)

However, nothing about contemporary peace negotiations reflects the non-hierarchical, progressive, integrative solutions flowing from analytic problem-solving that this optimism appears to be founded on. Though the burdens of military stalemate are borne more by the general population than conflict leaders, neither the compulsion to negotiate nor the provisions that are ultimately reached result from social pressure from below.[57] Instead, peace negotiations begin when conflict elites realize that their goals can no longer be secured at acceptable cost by prosecuting war. Peace terms must of necessity fit the expectations of conflict principals who judge what they secure at the negotiating table by comparing the settlement with what they might still potentially anticipate from the theatre of operations. The conflict-driven nature of negotiated peace agreements means that they are more usually the result of political trade-offs over power rather than deliberated in the interest of – or with the input of – the general public.[58] Though mediators and interveners may present objective rational-choice options for improving society

> [i]f the terms are considered wrong or out of step with what local actors think they need to be secure, or what they think they might be able to achieve, they will not support the terms no matter how fair others may consider them. Effective peacemaking and peacebuilding are thus only partially connected to equity and right. Being fair is not so much the challenge; instead, the task is to address the cognitive and perceptual issues that will make groups feel both satisfied and secure.[59]

Bargaining involves a competitive exchange of preferences, and so is inherently inimical to the realization of win–win solutions or mutually attractive peace design. The goals and aspirations of all antagonists, even those most committed to a vision of social justice or a more equitable society, may need to be scaled down because without concessions, there

---

142 at 154; Morten Bergsmo et al., 'Introduction' in Morten Bergsmo et al. (eds), *Distributive Justice in Transitions* (Torkel Opsahl 2010) 1 at 2.

[57] Sahla Aroussi and Stef Vandeginste, 'When Interests Meet Norms: The Relevance of Human Rights for Power-sharing' (2013) 17 *International Journal of Human Rights* 183, 190.

[58] Jennifer Easterday, 'Peace Agreements as a Framework for Jus Post Bellum' in Carsten Stahn, Jennifer Easterday and Jens Iverson (eds), *Jus Post Bellum: Mapping the Normative Foundations* (Oxford University Press 2014) 380 at 387.

[59] Andrea Kathryn Talentino, 'Perceptions of Peacebuilding: The Dynamic of Imposer and Imposed Upon' (2007) 8 *International Studies Perspectives* 152, 158.

can be no agreement, particularly with those parties who do not necessarily aspire to a protective role over the population as a whole. The greater the degree of insecurity parties feel, the more they draw inward to their own communities at the expense of broader national interests. As Doyle and Sambanis argue, even if a purely co-operative solution to conflict were imaginable, the confusion, violence and hardening identities that result from war do not conduce to rational co-operation among factions.[60] Where a range of peace compromises exist, successful settlement instead involves working out a distribution of dissatisfactory aspects until a mutually agreeable position is reached.[61] Windows of opportunity and constitutional big bangs cannot be assumed. Schemes for addressing root causes and past failures to provide equally for all groups are rarely indispensable for securing a mutually acceptable deal. As the next chapter examines in detail, because of the reality of mediation by consent and the weakness of under-resourced peacebuilding missions, international interveners acquiesce to the over-arching goal of these agreements to avoid the recurrence of conflict on the basis that this aspiration can garner the most agreement between them and stalemated antagonists. Even then, supposedly definitive solutions are envisaged not as permanent dispensations, but rather as a state of affairs that can be sustained long enough for domestic institutions to emerge that can process antagonisms on a normal basis and resolve incipient disputes. Signing a peace agreement does not end political bargaining as parties continue to compete for advantage. The agreement may at best be an agreement to struggle in more constitutional ways.[62]

Of course, settlements that have no normative foundations beyond pure power considerations are unlikely to endure, and so peace agreements finalized by negotiations will reflect a balance between normative principles and the power differential between the parties.[63] However, human rights considerations in either their most conservative liberal guise or in socio-economic form rarely function as a 'lever' in reaching settlements.[64] Antagonists place more faith in more straightforward (and,

---

[60] Doyle and Sambanis (n 7) 28.

[61] Holl (n 20) 276.

[62] Michael Doyle, *UN Peacekeeping in Cambodia: UNTAC's Civil Mandate* (Lynne Rienner 1995) 66.

[63] Adrian Guelke, 'Negotiations and Peace Processes' in Darby and Mac Ginty (eds) (n 18) 63 at 67.

[64] Tonya Putnam, 'Human Rights and Sustainable Peace' in Stephen John Stedman, Donald Rothchild and Elizabeth Cousens (eds), *Ending Civil Wars: The Implementation of Peace Agreements* (Lynne Rienner 2002) 237 at 242.

in the short-term, easier-to-verify) signals like endurance of ceasefires, demobilization, disarmament and reintegration, third-party guarantees, elections and dispute resolution procedures than more complicated, longer and harder-to-authenticate positive processes of socio-economic change. As Alex de Waal puts it:

> In a weakly institutionalized country in which patrimony rules, any attempts to address supposed root causes such as injustice, lack of liberal democracy and unequal development may not help – or may even hinder – the achievement of more modest but realizable goals based on elite bargains … [T]hree components to success are necessary – a normative agreement, improvement in human security, and an elite bargain. The main conclusion … is that the elite bargain is the first and most essential component. It follows that any mediator, peacekeeper or peacebuilder should frame other activities accordingly.[65]

2.1 The Modalities of Peacemaking

The validity of De Waal's argument becomes clear when we examine how negotiations take place. Peace agreements are subject to some familiar stations of the cross, though there is seldom an unproblematic sequence as rote as the rest of this paragraph suggests. The usual first stage is an inchoate process of pre-negotiation once stalemated parties begin to relinquish self-help solutions. This stage may or may not be preceded by de-escalation, and international actors may or may not man the back-channels before face-to-face meetings take place. Back-channel, unofficial pre-negotiation (a pre-talks phase of informal sounding out and then secret talks) serves as a non-committal testing ground where belligerents resolve who is to negotiate, how the conduct of warfare is or is not to be tempered during pre-negotiations, and what the agenda for broader talks might resemble. Once they take place, these communications offer distinct advantages over formal negotiations as controversial test-balloon 'what if' hypotheticals can be floated at minimal risk and without public commitment. If productive, the existence of these talks can be revealed, often via public announcement and usually coupled with a ceasefire. Indeed, after ceasefire successful preliminary talks may see further de-escalation/disengagement and bargaining as mutually-reinforcing or overlapping processes. More public and formalized talks can then take place.

---

[65] Alex De Waal, 'Mission Without End? Peacekeeping in the African Political Marketplace' (2009) 85 *International Affairs* 99, 112 and 113.

However, notwithstanding de-escalation and preliminary agreement, there is a crisis of credibility on the part of disputants to uphold past and future undertakings. As noted above, the pacific bona fides of each side are untested, and all sides have legitimate fears that the other side will opportunistically exploit the peace to pursue victory. Peacekeeping buffers and forcible disarmament are one solution to the problem, but need to be complemented by peacemaking. Because trust and institutional capacity are so diminished and because the ultimate end-points of a peace agreement are so unpredictable, reaching a settlement may prove impossible without external assistance, and so third-party intervention is voluntarily sought. International actors, most notably the UN but also third-party states, increasingly play a substantial role in brokering peace, though this involvement can vary significantly. International intervention at this point is usually labelled mediation, defined by Bercovitch as 'a process of conflict management, related to, but distinct from the parties' own negotiations, where those in conflict seek the assistance of, or accept an offer of help from, an outsider to change their perceptions or behavior and to do so without resorting to physical force or invoking the authority of law'.[66] The expectation is that third parties can flesh out the apparent general sense of eirenic opportunity into a concrete formula for settlement. While sitting at the negotiation table, international actors can help one side understand the other's aspirations and fears, may help reconcile ostensibly irreconcilable positions and overcome obstacles to communication imposed by the incentives peace creates for misinformation and secrecy. External mediators can reassure antagonists that the other side is abiding by what it agreed in good faith and can monitor progress in implementation. They can also serve as a convenient scapegoat for national or local leaders who wish to excuse their acceptance of unpopular settlement terms to their own constituents. Aside from neutralizing the peace environment like this, mediators attempt to steer the peace in a manner that consolidates insider loyalty to the process.[67] This is particularly important in the case of the weaker party. Though mediation implies that both sides are equal in standing to negotiate (even where unequal in power or military success), the weaker party generally fears the consequences of defection more than the

---

[66] Jacob Bercovitch, 'Mediation and Conflict Resolution' in Jacob Bercovitch, Victor Kremenyuk and I. William Zartman (eds), *The SAGE Handbook of Conflict Resolution* (Sage 2008) 340 at 343.

[67] Marie-Joëlle Zahar, 'Understanding the Violence of Insiders: Loyalty, Custodians of Peace and the Sustainability of Conflict Settlement' in Newman and Richmond (eds) (n 42) 40 at 41.

stronger one. To the extent that rebels are the weaker party, they fear non-implementation the most as the majority of peace reforms lie within the province of the government. It is for this reason that belligerents have different expectations of mediation. As Aggestam argues, stronger parties prefer impartial and less-active intervention, while weaker parties tend to favour active and full engagement of mediators as a means of compensating for the asymmetry of forces.[68]

Much of the faith underpinning the notion that external actors can catalyse substantial structural change comes from the faith that once third-party states or international organizations involve themselves in the mediation process, peace negotiations depart from an exclusively domestic political logic to become amenable to international norms and values, notwithstanding the language of scrupulous neutrality they employ.[69] It is hoped that mediators can exercise 'directive' influence, shaping the substance of the agreement by wielding the stick of deadlines and ultimatums and proffering material or political inducements to introduce human rights concerns into the negotiation agenda.[70] However, because they are selected for impartiality and not the leverage they might enjoy to control the process, third party actors are rarely those 'mediators with muscle' that can force antagonists to the negotiating table or dictate terms. Most peacemaking by invitation will mimic the Sudanese experience of merely brokering a peace agreement on terms fundamentally determined by local actors which formed the basis for subsequent constitutional review.[71] Here, the Sudanese were procedurally and substantively independent to reach internally agreeable solutions – international mediators had little power to impose solutions and enjoyed influence primarily in an advisory capacity.[72] Mediators instead may employ more procedural strategies which give them much influence over the logistics and process of peace talks, but rarely afford determinative control over the substance of the process. As Hayner points out, the mediator's role in peace processes and the paramount necessity of reaching a settlement 'will not permit the forceful advocacy of particular

---

[68] Aggestam (n 42) 30–31.

[69] On this expectation, see David Lanz, 'Who Gets a Seat at the Table? A Framework for Understanding the Dynamics of Inclusion and Exclusion in Peace Negotiations' (2011) 16 *International Negotiation* 275, 280–81.

[70] Aroussi and Vandeginste (n 57) 192.

[71] Philipp Dann and Zaid Al-Ali, 'The Internationalized *Pouvoir Constituant*: Constitution-making under External Influence in Iraq, Sudan and East Timor' (2006) 10 *Max Planck Yearbook of United Nations Law* 423.

[72] ibid 442–49.

options; this may be especially so on sensitive matters including the question of justice'.[73] Mediators at all points straddle a line between what is normatively desirable and what the parties are realistically willing to assent to. The latter usually exercises the greater influence on the shape of agreements. In many contemporary peace processes, mediators are at most undertaking a very narrow process of identifying a finite set of possible solutions amongst a plethora of unsatisfactory alternatives.[74]

2.2 Hard Bargaining

Generalizating about peace negotiation imposes difficulties because every individual conflict incorporates different issues, intensities, actors, duration and coherence of the antagonists. Three assertions can confidently be made, however; that (1) it is a fundamentally rationalistic processes, (2) starting positions are viewed through a veil of confusion over antagonist commitment and intentions that gradually come into focus through discussion and mediation, and (3) the most important judgement of their quality is made subjectively by the parties and not objectively by peacemakers or peacebuilders. Peace negotiations are an admixture of principle and tactics, though the lines between the two are blurred. This blurring is due to the paradox of peace – by negotiating, it is apparent that the belligerents have given up their maximalist war aims (stalemate clearly demonstrates that certain objectives simply cannot be imposed at an acceptable cost), but short of this protagonists seek as far as possible to reproduce their own model of a peace settlement. Disputants attempt to maximize their political, security and economic interests while conceding the minimum consistent with pacification. As Licklider notes, peace itself is not the primary goal of the parries. 'On the contrary', he argues, 'the violence arose precisely because both sides felt there were other issues more important, things that were worth dying for and killing for'.[75] Turning Clausewitz on his head, negotiations become a way of continuing the conflict by other means. As a result, mistrust typifies

---

[73] Priscilla Hayner, *Negotiating Justice: Guidance for Mediators* (Centre for Humanitarian Dialogue and International Center for Transitional Justice 2009) 5–6.

[74] Michael Greig and Patrick Regan, 'When Do They Say Yes? An Analysis of the Willingness to Offer and Accept Mediation in Civil Wars' (2008) 52 *International Studies Quarterly* 759, 761.

[75] Roy Licklider, 'Obstacles to Peace Settlements' in Chester Crocker and Fen Osler Hampson (eds), *Turbulent Peace: The Challenges of Managing International Conflict* (US Institute of Peace Press 2001) 697 at 697.

negotiations. While peace can only be reached when both parties expect concessions will be reciprocated by the other disputant(s) and then honoured, promises made even on the most explicit *pacta sunt servanda* basis lack credibility owing to fear and mistrust. There is a fear that concessions made will be 'banked' by the other side with no corresponding recompense. Negotiation strategies therefore are competitive, emphasizing self-interest, wealth and autonomy that advance or decline relative to those of the other conflict principals. Negotiations are rarely about objectively identifying and remedying definable structural injustice that underpins or exacerbates conflict, but are instead about reconciling different conceptions of justice. As a result, negotiations are characterized by 'diffuse reciprocity' in which there is a reasonably balanced exchange of concessions. Disputants are expected to reciprocate 'enough' relative to the concessions of the other party and their own capacity to afford adjustments to pre-conflict objectives.[76]

Bearing these limitations in mind, the literature on negotiating peace contains endless laundry-lists of criteria necessary for a successful accord. One of the most comprehensive is that of Hampson, who argued that successful peace needs:

1. inclusion of as many parties as possible,
2. precision in spelling out necessary undertakings (e.g. demobilization, voting, ceasefires),
3. a sensitive equilibrium between firm commitments and flexibility,
4. incentives to sustain the process and to participate in politics,
5. ongoing media for dispute settlement, mediation and renegotiation, and
6. comprehensive treatment of the core issues of the conflict.[77]

Few contemporary peace processes display all of these characteristics, however. Negotiations are extended learning processes as the views of the principals are stretched, tested and moderated in the ebb and flow of mediation. Negotiations may advance in surges, as opposed to gradual increments, interspersed with prolonged stretches of inertia and stasis. These surges are distinguished by brinkmanship which hazards the loss or reversal of peace but which can confirm to a community that its

---

[76] Cecilia Albin, 'Peace vs. Justice – and Beyond' in Bercovitch, Kremenyuk and Zartman (eds) (n 66) 580 at 585.

[77] Fen Osler Hampson, *Nurturing Peace: Why Peace Settlements Succeed or Fail* (US Institute of Peace Press 1996) 217–21.

leaders are fighting against tough opposition.[78] Adversaries may initially concentrate on peripheral issues on which early progress can be made to reduce tensions, while costly early concessions like recognition or disarmament signal vulnerability and reveal meaningful information about conciliatory intent and may build trust. Early accords deal with procedure for further talks and contain looser statements of principles and confidence-building measures. Later ones tend to be more specific, addressing more contentious issues unresolved by earlier negotiations and specifying details of implementation.[79]

As they move towards more essential matters, parties employ 'red lines' to mark points beyond which concession is impossible, impose time-frames to maintain momentum and provide critical junctures at which to judge the other's commitment. Calculations are always made with reference to how an antagonist behaved at similar junctures in any past peace negotiations. Violence and negotiation are not discrete phenomena. Most peaces operate on the basis of sufficient inclusion, not necessarily incorporating all actors who threaten or employ violence but encompassing those actors who represent a significant proportion of the population represented by a faction and who enjoy the military, economic or political potential to destroy an argument.[80] Negotiators will always be conscious that there is little point in agreeing matters with the opposition if they lead to, or exacerbate, divisions within their own side. Consequently, the mainstream of each party needs to reach out and build sufficient support to ensure the move from war to peace has wide acceptance among the armed. The more organized, motivated and well-resourced rejectionists are, the broader the coalition of the willing must be. The success of negotiations can often depend on something as random as the personalities of the principal parties. For example, Jonas Savimbi's monomaniacal determination to rule all of Angola precluded the necessary compromises needed to build a settlement there, but with his death the process of securing a ceasefire, credible negotiations and the consolidation of peace accelerated dramatically.[81]

If successful, different forms of accord can be reached progressively. Framework agreements are those that establish a schema for resolving the substantive issues of the conflict. They typically deal with consequences of the conflict (e.g. prisoner release/swaps, accountability, emergency legislation), the exercise of power, elections, security sector reform and

---

78 Darby and Mac Ginty (n 30) 356.
79 Selby (n 1) 14–15.
80 Darby and Mac Ginty (n 30) 363.
81 Mats Berdal, *Building Peace After War* (Routledge 2009) 34.

reconstruction.[82] These settlements reflect the post-war constellation of forces and essentially constitute 'convergence points' among the preferences of the belligerents for new institutions and principles of governance to define a post-war peace.[83] Agreements that lack political will or a domestic consensus are unlikely to be adequately implemented and will have little impact. As long as one side does not suffer wholesale and unequivocal defeat, agreement is possible even if there are differing degrees of benefits accruing to the parties. Some peace agreements are, in fact, bundles of agreements – for example, there were seven and fourteen, respectively, in El Salvador and Guatemala. Specific agreements are preferable to vague ones if the basic incompatibilities of the parties are to be regulated or resolved. The clearer the obligations of the agreement, the easier it is for each side to distinguish compliance from non-compliance. However, fudging and constructive ambiguity are sometimes unavoidable to finesse some incompatibilities and to allow certain factions to save face in front of the constituencies they must sell their positions to. Nevertheless, as Bell argues, successful peaces tend to a lesser or greater extent do three things – state redefinition (responding to the dissenters' complaints), disaggregation of power (state governance and jurisdiction are 'aggregated into a wide variety of territorial, functional, and identity-based institutional innovations, so as to accommodate competing group demands for effective participation, and the dislocation of power') and dislocation of power (disturbing the notion that a state enjoys automatic sovereignty over a unitary people bound within its territorial integrity).[84]

2.3 Towards Implementation

By this point, the focus has shifted from removing the barriers to agreement to ensuring that one or all parties do not renege on their obligations. It is credible to speak of 'partners for peace', as opposed to warring parties. Beyond this point come implementation agreements where the framework is elaborated on in detail in terms of timelines, phases, numbers, necessary legislation and so on. Full implementation is rarely necessary for a peace agreement to endure, provided systems are in place to ensure any failures can be coped with. This will sometimes be done by domestic or hybrid supervisory bodies like Colombia's initial

[82] Christine Bell, 'Negotiating Human Rights' in Darby and Mac Ginty (eds) (n 18) 210 at 215–16.

[83] Sisk (n 51) 198.

[84] Christine Bell, *On the Law of Peace: Peace Agreements and the Lex Pacificatoria* (Oxford University Press 2008).

tripartite monitoring and verification mechanism made up of government, FARC and a UN mission or El Salvador's National Commission for the Consolidation of Peace (made up of two representatives from the government and FMLN, plus one from each party in the legislative assembly). Implementation might also be accelerated if peacebuilding missions are involved in assisting in the process, building public confidence and developing institutions. Missions like ONUSAL in El Salvador, ONUMOZ in Mozambique or UNTAET in East Timor were indispensable to processes of disarmament and demobilization, conversion of factions into parties, elections and humanitarian activities. Sometimes they will even need to engage in peacekeeping, for example when UNMIL had to bring to an end violent post-election contestation by the defeated candidate in Liberia's 2005 elections. In fact, peace *enforcement*, not the peace settlement itself, may have been the key to short- to medium-term success in places like Sierra Leone and post-Dayton Bosnia.[85] Once peace agreements are concluded, Hartzell and Hoddie find that the presence of a third-party enforcer reduces the risk of settlement failure by as much as 87 per cent,[86] though some parties do reach self-enforcing peace agreements that did not need external enforcement or surveillance to overcome commitment problems. Power-sharing in particular serves a similar purpose to third-party guarantees by assuaging suspicions that their security, territory or other interests could be harmed once arms are relinquished. Its success is highly correlated with the presence of peacekeeping missions.[87] It should be apparent that even those peace settlements that offer clear benefits to various factions and enjoy widespread support may terminate conflict but may not necessarily resolve the issues that led to it. Peacebuilding agendas will be pursued via other institutional arrangements beyond the negotiation table. Future reform or transformation designed either as conscious responses to the post-conflict ecology or merely as politics as usual will require further negotiation among competing interests.[88]

---

85 Mehler (n 28) 22.

86 Caroline Hartzell and Matthew Hoddie, 'Institutionalizing Peace: Power-Sharing and Post-Civil War Conflict Management' (2003) 47 *American Journal of Political Science* 318, 328.

87 Caroline Hartzell and Matthew Hoddie, *Crafting Peace: Power-Sharing Institutions and the Negotiated Settlement of Civil Wars* (Pennsylvania State University Press 2007) 43–63.

88 Aliza Belman Inbal and Hanna Lerner, 'Constitutional Design, Identity, and Legitimacy in Post-Conflict Reconstruction' in Derick Brinkerhoff (ed.),

However, peace agreements that look perfectly adequate sometimes fail. Elements of implementation may turn out to have been badly designed, while constructive ambiguities negotiators relied upon may prove to be unbridgeable in practice. Settlements that are signed under pressure to reach a ceasefire and end humanitarian suffering will leave out many issues that cannot be settled and may gloss over key areas of contention. Even well-designed settlements can fail. As Baker reminds us, the duration of peace agreements ultimately rests primarily on the goodwill of the disputants, not on the legal authority of the settlement or the institutions it created.[89] Commitment is as likely to be instrumental (because it generates valuable benefits, of which peace is only one) as intrinsic (i.e. the parties consider it morally and legally binding).

After international peacebuilders leave or the benefits of institutional guarantees like power-sharing or elections prove less beneficial than imagined, what appears to be wholehearted commitment to peace may be revealed as temporary acquiescence to a more pacific politics, a strategic manoeuvre which did not entail a fundamental commitment to the terms. In particular, governments may later attempt to renegotiate terms they conceded when they were militarily weak. As their strategic situation improves in conditions of peace, they may wish to renege on the settlement or not fully implement their side of the bargain.[90] The previous chapter illustrated a number of peace agreements that were not fully implemented like those in Guatemala, El Salvador and Kenya. These settlements ultimately endured, but post-Cold War peacemaking is replete with examples of failed settlements like those in Central African Republic (the 2008 Global Peace Accord), Rwanda (1993 Arusha Accords), Angola (the Bicesse and Lusaka accords in 1991 and 1994), Sierra Leone (the Lomé Peace Accord), Côte d'Ivoire (the 2003 Linas-Marcoussis Accords), Liberia (too numerous to mention) and Somalia (ditto), though some later saw successful peace processes. Failed peace processes lie outside the scope of this book, but the risks of spoilers, failure and non-implementation are ever-present in the calculations of

---

Governance in Post-Conflict Societies: Rebuilding Fragile States (Routledge 2012) 45 at 57–60.

[89] Pauline Baker, 'Conflict Resolution Versus Democratic Governance: Divergent Paths to Peace' in Chester A. Crocker and Fen Osler Hampson (eds) with Pamela Aall, *Managing Global Chaos: Sources of and Responses to International Conflict* (US Institute of Peace 1996) 753 at 760.

[90] Karl DeRouen, Jenna Lea and Peter Wallensteen, 'The Duration of Civil War Peace Agreements' (2009) 26 *Conflict Management and Peace Science* 367, 369.

those who mediate or negotiate peace. This risk of failure explains why security and institutionalization tend to trump socio-economic justice in the calculations of domestic and international peacemakers.

3. THE MARGINALITY OF SOCIO-ECONOMIC ISSUES IN PEACE NEGOTIATION

Peace agreements can do one or all of three things to secure peace – they can remedy the root causes of conflict, they can (negatively) reassure the acute security concerns of the disputants, and/or they can (positively) distribute certain power- or wealth-sharing arrangements. At the core of the transformative turn is the notion that peace negotiations are a propitious time to address root causes. The most obvious way this can be achieved is by the disputants agreeing on what the root causes are and what needs to be done to address them, a debate transitional justice is expected to be able to inform in its implementation stage. This level of agreement, however, is quite rare. One of the most pertinent features of contemporary civil war is that conflict politics tends to be more about identity (religious, ethnic, other) than it is about a politics of national interest or ideology (such as principles of democracy, socialism or Islam or any other overarching principle for dealing with the society's key problems), making clear strategic goals and shared negotiating formulas hard to identify.[91] As observers of the Darfur peace process concluded, if the negotiators 'had common aspirations, it would have been a done deal months ago. It is their lack of common aspirations and conflicting political agendas that have meant they have to fight tooth and nail for every gain they make or loss they concede'.[92] It may be difficult to find compatible notions of justice. The notion of mutually hurting stalemates might render futile militarized conflict behaviour, but does not negate the motivations behind it, nor the parties' perception of the issues in conflict. One of the reasons why it often proves difficult to confirm that addressing the root causes of conflict leads to long-lasting peace settlements is that most peace agreements do not attempt to do so –

---

91 Aggestam (n 42) 25.

92 Integrated Regional Information Networks, 'Peace Unsustainable Without Democratization – Think-tank' (2004) <http://www.irinnews.org/report/50200/sudan-peace-unsustainable-without-democratisation-think-tank> accessed 21 July 2016.

agreements that holistically address the incompatibilities between antagonists may be those that run the greatest risk of abrogation.[93] Therefore, economic root cause approaches are far less common in peace agreements than measures to reassure security concerns or to distribute political power. The very real sense of civil-political possibility that transitions from war or authoritarianism to peace and democracy occasion is rarely accompanied by a redistribution of economic power.

Outside of consensus between conflict principals, there are three main ways to address root causes in peace negotiations. The first is the involvement in peace negotiations of civil society actors outside the conflict principals who emphasize root-cause approaches. The second is the introduction of international economic, social and cultural human rights law into the agreement to accompany the bargaining positions of the conflict principals. The third is wholesale reform of the structures that led to conflict through constitutionalization beyond the peace agreement.

3.1 The Lack of Civil Society Involvement

In theory, peace negotiations attempt to design a blueprint for a more peaceful future by putting in place rules and institutions to deal with the root causes of conflict. However, the issues and interests that are considered in peace talks depend largely on who gets a seat at the negotiating table, what stage they get involved in and in what capacity they negotiate. As Lanz argues, there are two sets of factors that affect inclusion of individuals or organizations in peace negotiations. The first are practical requirements (does the participation of an actor improve the chance of reaching an acceptable peace?) and the second are normative (is participation of a given actor consistent with the norms and values the parties to the negotiation wish to promote?).[94] The common assumption is that civil society involvement is necessary in the latter respect, making peace more sustainable and inclusive than it would be if confined to the perspectives and needs assessments of the conflict principals. There is an assumption in the transitional justice literature that not only does civil society naturally represent the population's demands and concerns, but its inclusion broadens the policy options available for justice.[95] There is a confidence in the literature that civil society can serve effectively as an

---

93 DeRouen, Lea and Wallensteen (n 90) 382.
94 Lanz (n 69) 277.
95 Hayner (n 73) 12.

advocate for radical social change.[96] As Berdal notes, civil society organizations are almost always understood in comparison to more conservative state or elite interests; they have a role to play in post-conflict environments that is inherently helpful, constructive and representative of grassroots wishes.[97] The competence of NGOs and social movements in terms of human rights make them fundamental to the realization of change in the socio-economic structures of society to the extent that they advocate for the inclusion of relevant issues into peace agreements. Civil society is 'often seen to carry the best hopes for a genuine democratic counterweight to the power-brokers, economic exploiters, and warlords who tend to predominate in conflict-ridden, weak, or failed states'.[98] Inclusive peace processes are the only way the perspectives of politically marginalized groups like women, minorities, displaced persons and the indigent are included. Furthermore, the legitimacy of peace agreements, particularly those that take the form of, or culminate in, a post-conflict constitution, needs the open-ended participation and empowerment of voices from the broader public if they are to be seen as legitimate and a sense of ownership fostered.[99] There is a consensus that peace negotiations incorporating direct participation by civil society generate the most durable agreements.[100]

International and domestic civil society and NGOs have always been involved in mediation *during* conflict as they enjoy a level of trustworthiness that encourages factions to place confidence in them for facilitating contacts, building confidence between antagonists, fostering cross-cultural understanding and probing possibilities for compromise in so-called Track II diplomacy initiatives. However, civil society organizations have also been included as separate parties in their own right in official, governmental Track I negotiations between governments, rebels and international mediators at the apparent *end* of conflict. For example, in Sierra Leone, civil society had an official role in peace talks as

---

[96] Lucy Hovil and Moses Okello, 'Editorial Note' (2011) 5 *International Journal of Transitional Justice* 333, 333.

[97] Berdal (n 81) 146.

[98] Béatrice Pouligny, 'Civil Society and Post-Conflict Peacebuilding: Ambiguities of International Programmes Aimed at Building "New" Societies' (2005) 36 *Security Dialogue* 495, 496.

[99] Vivien Hart, 'Constitution-making and the Transformation of Conflict' (2001) 26 *Peace and Change* 153, 160.

[100] Anthony Wanis-St. John and Darren Kew, 'Civil Society and Peace Negotiations: Confronting Exclusion' (2008) 13 *International Negotiation* 11, 26–32.

observers, rather than as delegates, but nevertheless took part in the formal meetings and was influential in outlining core elements of the accord through policy proposals and advocacy.[101] The 2003 Accra Agreement in Liberia saw civil society representatives granted official delegate status in formal talks. They were influential in affecting the justice and security sector provisions that were included in the agreement.[102] In Guatemala bilateral negotiations mediated by the UN were paralleled by a Civil Society Assembly tasked with discussing the substantive issues and root causes of the conflict, culminating in proposals which were included in the final accords, even if civil society was not a direct participant in this case.[103] Some peace agreements stipulate that civil society be formally included in subsequent constitution-drafting activities, as occurred in Sudan, Bougainville and Afghanistan.[104] The National Unification Commission in the Philippines hosted a nationwide consultation process with civil society organizations that generated a set of principles that guided subsequent peace processes.[105] Some of these examples resembled weaker consultative participation (where civil society had the chance to voice opinions and make proposals) more than strong representative participation (where civil society exercises influence as a direct participant in negotiation), and others undoubtedly resemble cosmetic co-option of NGOs by conflict principals and international mediators as fig-leaves for exclusionary peaces. Provisions generated by broad inclusion at the negotiation stage could be watered down at the implementation stage due to vagueness of the agreed terms (the 'broad participation, diffuse responsibility' problem) and the need for assent through popular referenda, most notably in Guatemala.[106] The inclusion of a wide spectrum of society in formal peace talks in the likes of DR Congo (2002), Côte d'Ivoire (2003) and Liberia (2003) did not guarantee thoroughgoing commitment to socio-economic structural reform. Nevertheless, a model whereby civil society establishes a role in negotiations

---

[101] Hayner (n 73) 12.

[102] ibid.

[103] Enrique Alvarez with Tania Palencia Prado, 'Guatemala's Peace Process: Context, Analysis and Evaluation' in Catherine Barnes (ed.), *Owning the Process: Public Participation in Peacemaking* (Accord 2002) 38.

[104] Bell and O'Rourke (n 56) 302.

[105] Miriam Coronel Ferrer, 'Philippines National Unification Commission: National Consultation and the "Six Paths to Peace"' in Barnes (ed.) (n 103) 82 at 82–85.

[106] William Stanley and David Holiday, 'Broad Participation, Diffuse Responsibility: Peace Implementation in Guatemala' in Stedman, Rothchild and Cousens (eds) (n 64) 421.

between antagonists and forms a collaborative relationship with conflict principals in which their proposals can be incorporated formally at the negotiating table does highlight the model by which civil society can potentially assure a 'people-focused peace agenda'.[107]

However, while normative requirements may demand civil society inclusion because they lead to a better quality peace, these are more often than not over-ridden by practical requirements that a participant improve the chance of reaching a peace in the first place. As noted earlier, peace negotiations tend to operate on the basis of 'sufficient inclusion', encompassing those factions or groups with an effective veto power to end the peace process by recourse to violence. Armed groups actively involved in conflict 'will always play an oversized role' in deciding who the legitimate representatives of a national community or particular ethnic, religious or social group are.[108] Those who do not take up arms seldom have a voice in shaping agreements even where they enjoy a stronger social base than the government or armed groups. While they may be able to propose solutions to society's most intractable problems, civil society groups have little ability to apply pressure or coercion to recalcitrant or equivocating parties to come to an agreement, given their lack of coercive tools like arms, blockades or control of funds, nor can they offer security guarantees that might convince parties to make large compromises.[109] Peace movements seldom succeed in ending conflict or encouraging peace talks, and once they begin mere enumeration of human rights provisions civil society 'offers little in the way of leverage in the absence of institutions or actors willing and able to implement them'.[110] Contemporary peace negotiations are defined by *realpolitik* – only those who both add value to the process and improve the likelihood of reaching a sustainable settlement are given meaningful participation at the table, regardless of normative factors.[111] While civil society may be valuable in opening up communication between antagonists or pressuring the international community into mediation, they tend to be superseded at

---

107 Malin Brenk and Hans van de Veen, 'Development: No Development Without Peace, No Peace Without Development' in Paul van Tongeren et al. (eds), *People Building Peace II: Successful Stories of Civil Society* (Lynne Rienner 2005) 399 at 399.

108 Charles Call, *Why Peace Fails: The Causes and Prevention of Civil War Recurrence* (Georgetown University Press 2012) 246.

109 Pamela Aall, 'The Power of Non-Official Actors in Conflict Management' in Crocker, Hampson with Aall (eds) (n 89) 477 at 486.

110 Putnam (n 64) 241.

111 Lanz (n 69) 281.

the most critical period of peace negotiations, which is often based on the explicit exclusion of civil society and social movements from direct participation. Though some scholars argue that this is the deliberate choice of international mediators,[112] this may exaggerate the degree of influence they actually enjoy. Peace negotiations grow out of existing balances of forces, their expectations, the bargaining style of their leaders and the capacity of non-combatants to influence belligerent decision-making. If the disputants wanted civil society involvement, they could insist upon it at relatively low cost to the mediators (after all, consultation by peacemakers with civil society and other excluded voices has long been UN policy in peace negotiations).[113] International mediators may acquiesce to civil society exclusion, but there can be little doubt that the exclusionary impetus comes internally.

Beyond pure *realpolitik*, there are legitimate practical reasons why social movements and civil society might be excluded. The need for a high degree of confidentiality is often argued to preclude any aspiration to open the process to actors outside the conflict principals.[114] More convincing is the argument that the more parties that are involved in a peace agreement, the more difficult it becomes to reach a settlement because multiple actors reduce the range of acceptable settlements, destabilize alliances and increase the numbers of potentially non-co-operative parties.[115] The presence of numerous parties may lead each to exaggerate their preferences to the extent that an optimal, mutually agreed settlement becomes impossible, pre-emptively negating the value of wider 'buy-in' broad participation is designed to foster.[116] Bearing in mind the familiar peace versus justice debates of the 1990s and 2000s, Putnam notes that international human rights organizations in particular have been known to 'overplay their hand', superimposing their own priorities in sensitive negotiations, insufficiently cognizant of the precariousness and complexity of the process as a whole.[117] This risk might

---

112 E.g., Roberto Belloni, 'Civil Society in War-to-Democracy Transitions' in Anna Jarstad and Timothy Sisk (eds), *From War to Democracy: Dilemmas of Peacebuilding* (Cambridge University Press 2008) 182 at 194.

113 UN Secretary-General's High Level Panel on Threats, Challenges and Change, *A More Secure World: Our Shared Responsibility*, UN Doc. A/59/565 of 2 December 2004, para. 103.

114 Belloni (n 112) 194.

115 David Cunningham, 'Veto Players and Civil War Duration' (2006) 50 *American Journal of Political Science* 875.

116 Wanis-St. John and Kew (n 100) 22–23.

117 Putnam (n 64) 240.

logically extend to purely domestic social movements. Though these priorities may seem imperative for a meaningful peace, negotiations that are restricted to elites with a narrow social base might accord entirely with ordinary patterns of political decision-making in many states outside the Global North. Even in the extraordinary context of conflict, peace-making may still be seen as a classic governmental activity to be jealously guarded. The forms of legitimacy claimed by NGOs may be inappropriate to the forms of legitimacy at work among the conflict principals and dysfunctional in the context of the dispute to be resolved. The types of progressive civil society imagined in the transformative transitional justice literature of an economic justice-inclined social movement with a broad-based constituency of the marginalized may have shallow roots. They also may be mistrusted by disputants who, with greater or lesser disingenuousness, 'often dismiss local civic groups as either instruments of improper international interference, or political dissidents on the payroll of the opposition'.[118]

Examples are legion of peace processes that are exclusionary in the sense of disdaining any significant role for civil society. A prime example is the Dayton Accords, where the chief negotiator consciously opted not to meet with any party who did not directly control the means of violence.[119] Haiti's NGOs were excluded by governmental and international negotiators when its Interim Cooperation Framework was agreed in 2004 after a prolonged period of political conflict and natural disasters.[120] National civil society organizations were similarly excluded from peace talks in places as diverse as the Aceh peace talks in Indonesia and the ZANU PF/MDC talks in Zimbabwe. Sriram offers the telling example of a proposal by women in the Sudanese People's Liberation Movement/Army for a 25 per cent quota for participation in peace talks being first reduced by an all-male SPLM/A preliminary drafting committee, and then eliminated entirely by the Khartoum government on the basis that they were not fighters.[121]

The consequences of such exclusion are predictable. Most obviously, the parties are less accountable in peace processes without meaningful public participation, and are more likely to adopt temporary expedients which leave underlying causes of conflict unaddressed, while their

---

118 Belloni (n 112) 194.

119 ibid 195.

120 Call (n 108) 269.

121 Chandra Lekha Sriram, 'Making Rights Real? Minority and Gender Provisions and Power-Sharing Arrangements' (2013) 17 *International Journal of Human Rights* 275, 277.

settlement will enjoy less public legitimacy. However, it remains the case that identifiable groups are marginalized in negotiations. Despite the dramatic increase in references to women's rights after UN Security Council Resolution 1325 on women, peace and security, it nevertheless has had far less impact on the inclusion of women in peace negotiations than was hoped, with the predictable effect that governments do not deliver on the commitments they espouse in the National Action Plans.[122] Exclusion of women is not an insuperable barrier to addressing their needs after the agreement, but it does make it more difficult to do so, to say nothing of attracting the support and funding of international organizations.[123] Groups like minorities and indigenous peoples[124] or refugees and internally displaced persons (IDPs) are at best viewed as passive recipients of outcomes that are negotiated in distant arenas of power,[125] significantly increasing the probability that the agreement will contain little by way of justice language and that the terms of a settlement will reflect the demands of conflict principals and their constituencies. As it goes for these groups, so it can be said for disenfranchised, indigent and marginal groups within societies who do not fit within the binary conflict metanarrative. As Section 4 examines in greater detail, models of power-sharing that approximate a division of the spoils between belligerents willing to employ violence to access wealth and power are predictably antagonistic to inclusion of organized elements advocating structural reform, equitable development and ESC rights regimes. The means by which civil society is excluded from substantive peace negotiations can also limit their future ability to advocate for causes like redistributive or welfarist policies. Easterday finds that only 13 per cent of peace agreements include provisions related to civil society,[126] while Bell and O'Rourke find that 139 peace agreements out

---

[122] A good overview is Barbara Miller, Milad Pournik and Aisling Swaine, 'Women in Peace and Security through United Nations Security Resolution 1325: Literature Review, Content Analysis of National Action Plans and Implementation' (Institute for Global and International Studies 2014) <https://ggp.elliott.gwu.edu/sites/ggp.elliott.gwu.edu/files/downloads/igis_wp13_ggp_wp09.pdf> accessed 21 July 2016.

[123] Christine Chinkin, *Peace Agreements as a Means for Promoting Gender Equality and Ensuring Participation of Women* (UN Division for the Advancement of Women 2003) 12.

[124] Sriram (n 121).

[125] Karen Jacobsen, Helen Young and Abdalmonim Osman, 'Refugees and IDPs in Peacemaking Processes' in Darby and Mac Ginty (eds) (n 18) 313.

[126] Easterday (n 58) 399.

of 389 examined contained explicit provisions for civil society involvement.[127] Many of these provisions are merely tepid commitments to develop or strengthen civil society.[128]

3.2 The Peripheral Nature of Human Rights in Peace Negotiations

Much, but by no means all, of the academic and policy arguments that transitional justice can and should transform economic opportunity and structures of poverty are premised on the idea that transitional justice should employ the human rights 'respect, protect, fulfil' framework to address breaches of economic and social rights.[129] That it does not is seen as the product of three long-standing and damaging liberal-legalist assumptions in the wider human rights literature, namely (1) that the transitioning government's obligations to positively secure economic rights will inevitably fall foul of the state's lack of resources or capacity and therefore should not be pursued;[130] (2) that deprivations of economic, social or cultural rights are less egregious than violations of civil and political rights;[131] and/or (3) that socio-economic rights violations are non-justiciable and therefore better addressed by development actors.[132] By contrast, it is clear to critics that civil and political rights constitute the core norms promoted by international actors in peace agreements.

In the classic treatment of human rights in peace negotiations, Bell argues that human rights law has become the primary normative framework governing the peace agreement regime. As the demand for civil war peace agreements grew and involvement of international mediators increased, so did the demand to affix human rights norms to them, most notably transitional justice, as part of an emerging international *lex pacificatoria*.[133] This external impetus towards inclusion of human rights raises an interesting question – whether human rights impose unnecessary additional burdens on the bargaining process or whether they

---

[127] Bell and O'Rourke (n 56) 297.

[128] ibid 302.

[129] E.g. Sam Szoke-Burke, 'Not Only Context: Why Transitional Justice Programs Can No Longer Ignore Violations of Economic and Social Rights' (2015) 50 *Texas International Law Journal* 465.

[130] Rama Mani, *Beyond Retribution – Seeking Justice in the Shadows of War* (Polity Press 2002) 41.

[131] Andrieu (n 4) 543.

[132] Ruben Carranza, 'Plunder and Pain: Should Transitional Justice Engage with Corruption and Economic Crimes?' (2008) 2 *International Journal of Transitional Justice* 310, 315.

[133] Bell (n 84) 184.

are crucial to achieving a durable, positive peace 'characterised by the removal of structural violence and of systemic patterns of discrimination and oppression'.[134] Answers to this question may differ between external analysts and the parties themselves. Aroussi and Vandeginste conclude, like the present author, that addressing root causes of conflict and the human rights dimensions of underlying grievances are imperative if peace is to be sustainable.[135] Such judgements, however, are not made in the endogenous context of commitment problems, competitive bargaining and existential dilemmas that characterize actual peace negotiations. Here, weakened governments and inherently vulnerable rebels elevate short-term reassurance over long-term and ultimately highly conditional and administratively difficult aspirations for transformation. It is well established that the higher the intensity of the war (usually a matter of deaths and duration), the number of factions and the greater the salience of identity all tend towards the diminution of mutual confidence and lead disputants to emphasize security over other goals.[136] Furthermore, to the extent that there is pressure for a human rights component, it generally comes from the weaker side's analysis of the causes of the conflict. This pressure is seen to challenge a status quo against which they are fighting.[137] Though human rights are premised on universalism, there is therefore a perception that one side to the peace stands to benefit from their inclusion, while the other (and usually the stronger of the two) stands to be the net loser.

This is evident in the treatment of human rights in both their civil-political and socio-economic guises. In a survey of 82 peace agreements in 20 sub-Saharan African states concluded between 1989 and 2011, Aroussi and Vandeginste note a consistent trend of human rights increasingly being incorporated in peace agreements as substantive issues, either as cross-cutting themes when dealing with other matters, as provisions in designated sections as guarantees in themselves, or as blueprints for future bills of rights or constitutional provisions.[138] While these agreements contain commitments to ratify human rights conventions, to fight discrimination and inequality and to a raft of substantive civil and political rights, not one agreement they assessed made these commitments an integral element of the implementation, monitoring or

---

[134] Aroussi and Vandeginste (n 57) 184.

[135] ibid.

[136] Zürcher, Manning and Evenson (n 25) 44.

[137] Bell (n 82) 215.

[138] Aroussi and Vandeginste (n 57) 185.

evaluation of the agreement.[139] This is particularly the case with ESC rights. In a survey of their specific inclusion in peace agreements in states like Guatemala, Bosnia and Nepal, Chinkin observes that 'where peace agreements have explicitly incorporated economic and social rights ... they have not however generated the national legal frameworks for their implementation'.[140]

This fits with a general trend whereby peace agreements become more comprehensive in terms of the provisions included but less specific in terms of mechanisms to ensure implementation.[141] The explanations for this may lie in the way peace is negotiated. As Bell argues, political peace processes tend to be legalized, and legal substance to be politicized, at different junctures in peace processes. The sort of legalization that would underpin a meaningful human rights regime in peace is more and less productive at different stages of the peace process. Initial peace process matters such as the implementation of a ceasefire or the demobilization of armed forces tend to exhibit precisely defined rights and obligations. However, because addressing human rights needs a complex package of measures, agreement about what the conflict was about and what human rights are, they tend not to be addressed at the pre-negotiation stage.[142]

At later stages, where framework or substantive agreements are hammered out, precision and clarity are often deemed unconducive to a successful transition over the longer term. Instead, it is thought that norms, legal forms and rules of substance or implementation should be able to evolve with the process. As a result, at the most crucial stage in peace negotiations 'human rights terms are framed in general, abstract, and impartial terms as internationally applicable means that both sides may come to frame their claims using human rights language as the process progresses'.[143] Though Bell argues that individual human rights guarantees can address fears of annihilation, abuse and discrimination and can serve as an integral part of how power is exercised and controlled, more often human rights institutions 'can end up almost hastily tacked on to an agreement without the institutional detail which would make them effective ... This can produce institutions with serious gaps which leave them largely rhetorical and symbolic, rather than

139 ibid.
140 Chinkin (n 3) 7.
141 Suhrke, Wimpelmann and Dawes (n 13) 28.
142 Bell (n 82) 215.
143 ibid 217.

capable of effecting real change'.[144] It is for this reason that the formal enumeration of human rights provisions in peace agreements 'correlates only weakly, if at all' with the quality of human rights protections citizens enjoy in their aftermath.[145] Though there has been an increase in the inclusion of criminal justice provisions in peace agreements in the years since the Rome Statute was agreed and accountability is included as part of the by-now standard holistic mix of justice mechanisms, peace treaties like the Arusha Accord in Burundi, the Linas Marcoussis agreement in Côte d'Ivoire or the DR Congo's Global Accord never delivered on the extensive justice provisions agreed therein. Though mediators are advised that accountability measures in peace agreements should include explicit steps, a clear timeline for implementation and a logistics plan spelling out how these can be achieved, few peace agreements come close to this level of detail.[146] There is a discernible trend of states apparently adopting transitional justice norms to obtain aid, improve their international profile or discredit other domestic actors without ever implementing the measures necessary to give effect to them lest they cast an unforgiving light on past atrocities of peace partners.[147] This is symptomatic of the wider trend of rhetorical incorporation of liberal human rights norms in peace settlements. This incorporation incurs zero short-term costs due to the absence of sanctioning mechanisms for non-compliance but awards much in the way of reputational benefit. Much of the so-called human rights liberalism of peace agreements in fact resembles what Meyer and Rowan term 'ceremonial conformity', where a belligerent pays lip-service to principles to preserve a supply of material and normative benefits that are required in the short-term for survival and legitimacy without substantive change to existing practices.[148]

The failure to include socio-economic rights in peace agreements has been attributed to the liberal bias of negotiators, a point with which the author does not quibble. The impact of liberal bias is examined in greater detail in Chapter 4. However, given the weakness of commitment to civil and political rights commitments, this may misunderstand the problem.

---

[144] Christine Bell, *Peace Agreements and Human Rights* (Oxford University Press 2003) 231.

[145] Putnam (n 64) 238.

[146] Hayner (n 73) 10.

[147] Jelena Subotic, 'Bargaining Justice' in Suzanne Buckley-Zistel et al. (eds) *Transitional Justice Theories* (Routledge 2013) 127.

[148] John Meyer and Brian Rowan, 'Institutionalized Organizations: Formal Structure as Myth and Ceremony' (1977) *American Journal of Sociology* 340.

International mediators may attribute lesser juridical status to ESC rights for the reasons outlined above, and this may explain failure of the international community to promote them in peace talks. However, this evades the key question of why domestic and rebel negotiators also neglect them. The problem may be less that economic and social rights are neglected relative to civil and political rights, but rather that human rights as a whole and in any form are neglected relative to other issues. An assessment of the UN peace agreement database reveals that notwithstanding the increased emphasis on human rights in peace agreements, the most common substantive issues included are security arrangements (69 per cent), rule of law (53 per cent), military issues (47 per cent) and statehood, territory and identity (40 per cent).[149] Human rights, by contrast, were included in 31 per cent of agreements and transitional justice in 22 per cent (interestingly, 'socio-economic and development issues' were included in 50 per cent of agreements, but this rubric is too vague to lend much analytical purchase).[150] These figures vindicate Mehler's argument that human rights of any type are perceived by disputants as of secondary importance in divided societies to issues of representation, power-sharing and regulation of identity group demands.[151] Much of the debate on human rights and peace revolves around the question of whether human rights measures facilitate or jeopardize conflict resolution. Contemporary trends indicate that they do neither. What is clear is that a wide system for human rights protection, be it civil and political rights and/or socio-economic rights, is not fundamental to the indispensable reassurance antagonists seek for their security fears when entering a peace agreement and transition to revised modes of social ordering.

3.3 A Role for Constitutionalization?

Because commitments to human rights in peace treaties have proven so unreliable, there is increasing focus on the possibility that post-conflict constitutional processes provide an alternative to these narrow bargains and could pave the way for more thoroughgoing reform of the structures that lead to conflict. It should be pointed out that this is more a feature of

---

149 Easterday (n 58) 388–89.

150 ibid.

151 Andreas Mehler, 'Peace Through Constitutional Amendment? Opportunities and Tendencies' (German Institute of Global and Area Studies 2011) 2 <https://giga.hamburg/en/system/files/publications/gf_international_1102.pdf> accessed 21 July 2016.

the peacebuilding literature than transitional justice's transformative turn, which has shown surprisingly little interest in the issue. As they become more complicated, peace agreements often incorporate constitutional frameworks, or approximate temporary constitutions inasmuch as they set rules over the exercise of power.[152] Alternatively, constitution drafting is used as a peacemaking tool with the resulting constitution serving as a peace treaty.[153] Because constitutional peace agreements aspire to transform conflicted societies by altering social norms, renegotiating the underlying causes of social dissensus and establishing new institutions, they raise the obvious possibility that integrated processes of peace negotiation and constitutionalization can legally anchor provisions for socio-economic justice matters beyond the exceptional exigencies of peacemaking. After all, constitutional blueprints require more broad-based participation to achieve legitimacy than the narrower restriction to warring group leaders seen in peace agreements. Furthermore, constitutions are designed to serve more forward-looking roles by developing permanent frameworks for governing and anticipating the long-term needs of the citizenry they serve, while peace agreements attend to more short-term purposes in bridging war and peace.[154]

However, constitutionalization is unlikely to resolve the problem of a conservative peace. While post-conflict constitutions can enshrine normative change and institutional transformation, they also have a paramount role as 'power maps' delineating the power relationships among groups, society and the economy. Processes of constitutionalization cannot be considered in isolation from existing structures of power, dominance and possession.[155] As Bhuta argues, constitution-making undertaken simultaneously with the formation of new political orders is characterized more by hard-bargaining over interests than by disputes over the public good.[156] In highly divided societies, even conspicuous good-faith attempts may have to rely on constructive ambiguity and the marked avoidance of controversial issues if a constitution is to be agreed.[157] It

---

[152] Bell (n 84).

[153] Hallie Ludsin, 'Peacemaking and Constitution-Drafting: A Dysfunctional Marriage' (2011) 33 *University of Pennsylvania Journal of International Law* 239, 239.

[154] ibid 277 and 245–46.

[155] Hart (n 99) 158.

[156] Nehal Bhuta, 'New Modes and Orders: The Difficulties of a Jus Post Bellum of Constitutional Transformation' (2010) 60 *University of Toronto Law Journal* 799, 845.

[157] Inbal and Lerner (n 88).

should be noted that simultaneous processes of establishing a new constitution (or an important amendment thereto) and an important peace agreement are relatively rare. A study of approximately 110 divided societies between 2001 and 2010 revealed that only around 10 per cent of those states combined both.[158] Though the study does not relate to socio-economic transformation (most constitutional changes examined were about institutional overhauls and reform of the executive, which of course in itself is indicative of the typical goals of such constitutions), it undermines the notion that post-conflict transition is ordinarily or as a matter of course conducive to the type of constitutional 'big bangs' raised as a possibility in Chapter 2. The more usual course of events sees a multi-stage process in which interim constitutions merge peacemaking and constitutionalization, but typically more permanent constitutions 'must wait for more peaceful, secure and stable times'.[159] The transitional period between the signing of peace agreements and new constitutions is often in the region of three years, though this says nothing about how transformative the latter ultimately is.[160] The infrequency of radical constitutional reform in and around peacemaking suggests 'that strong sitting governments avoid deep-cutting reforms enshrined in constitutions while those with limited bargaining power give in much more easily'.[161]

3.4 The Emphasis on Security over Root-Cause Approaches

If consensus on root causes is seldom discoverable and if neither civil society involvement, nor the inclusion of human rights provisions in peace, nor constitutionalization are deemed fundamentally imperative to most settlements, what makes peace agreements stick? In answering this question, it is instructive to recap the model of conflict and peace presented in this chapter and which is present to a greater or lesser extent in most contemporary civil wars. War in essence is a situation where the

---

158 Andreas Mehler, 'Consociationalism for Weaklings, Autocracy for Muscle Men? Determinants of Constitutional Reform in Divided Societies' (2013) 15 *Civil Wars* 21, 25.

159 Ludsin (n 153) 242.

160 Katia Papagianni, 'Political Transitions after Peace Agreements: The Importance of Consultative and Inclusive Political Processes' (2009) 3 *Journal of Intervention and Statebuilding* 47, 47.

161 Sabine Kurtenbach and Andreas Mehler, 'Introduction: Institutions for Sustainable Peace? Determinants and Effects of Institutional Choices in Divided Societies' (2013) 15 *Civil Wars* 1, 3.

belligerents have incompatible objectives that motivate conflict. In undertaking military struggle, in the absence of victory for one side it often results in a mutually hurting stalemate, which compels the sides to negotiate. However, because the belligerents differ so fundamentally in terms of their identities, beliefs and post-conflict aspirations, major disagreement is inevitable regarding the perception of the issues at play in the conflict and the resolution to them. This is why mediation is often necessary, but it highlights the importance of the disputants' perceptions. Existential questions of group survival will dominate the thinking of weaker parties, while fundamental questions about the nature of the state, territory or power will be key in the mind of the stronger. This balance between weak and strong parties is significant. All civil war peace processes pit power-holders (usually those who historically control political, economic and social arrangements, and benefit from them) against power-seekers (those who seek to amend the prevailing arrangements).[162] As noted above, the inclusion of human rights guarantees may be perceived internally to stand to benefit the weaker of the two parties while the stronger benefiting from the currents rights dispensation stands to be the net loser. This complicates the search for mutually satisfactory principles of peace. As Albin argues

> If both or all parties regard negotiation as the only reasonable hope to reduce injustice, this obviously facilitates. If only one party is dependent on negotiation to restore justice for itself, or even to survive in any form, this creates an inequality which makes justice difficult to combine with peacemaking.[163]

While most peaces represent the compulsion of the stronger party by the weaker one to negotiate and agreements are premised on everyone having something to show to their constituency, peace nevertheless tends to be reformist and rarely brings revolutionary transformation as a result.[164]

Though some peace negotiations will contain some common interests, some issues at least will be understood as a zero-sum game, a position that flows from each party's claim to some positions, ownership and resources where a gain for one side automatically involves a loss to the

162 John Darby, *The Effects of Violence on Peace Processes* (US Institute of Peace Press 2001) 120.

163 Albin (n 76) 583.

164 See the quotes from Selby (n 1) and Hagmann and Péclard (n 2) at the opening of this chapter.

other.[165] The redistribution of wealth or opportunity from one faction (usually the stronger) to another is the most obvious zero-sum issue. Even limited schemes for welfare or structural reform are inherently redistributive. They might enshrine universal norms and provide entry points for later reforms, but they might equally endanger the agreement by imposing costs deemed unacceptable to the stronger party. It is for this reason, and contrary to the assumption in the Western scholarly mindset that peace agreements would address these types of root causes, that the parties tend to leave issues as divisive as this unresolved. As Darby and Mac Ginty note, 'In order to secure the agreement, it is tempting for negotiators to defer some sensitive issues for post-accord attention, laying minefields for the future in the interests of long-term gain'.[166] Economic injustice and development are the most sensitive of these issues, while security and political status are deemed the most imperative. For example, observers agree that if the FMLN had pressed for exhaustive socio-economic transformation in negotiating El Salvador's Chapultepec Peace Accord with the right-wing ARENA government, there is little doubt the process would have collapsed. Only approximately 10 per cent of the final agreement was dedicated to social and economic issues, while most of the text was dedicated to the details of the military ceasefire and to military and police reforms.[167] Peace agreements therefore only carry 'what the traffic can bear', deliberately leaving seemingly indispensable ESC rights issues unresolved.[168] A survey conducted for the World Bank and UN Development Programme of the frequency of provisions in peace agreements demonstrates that security issues like security reform, civilian oversight and DDR are present more than twice as often as issues like women's rights, minority rights, social welfare and land reform.[169] The average specificity of these provisions is also illustrative – provisions relating to security issues, power-sharing, elections and property rights (the latter tellingly has by far the greatest specificity) are far more specific in terms of benchmarks and timetables for implementation than ESC rights issues.[170] While the

165 Jacob Bercovitch, Victor Kremenyuk and I. William Zartman, 'Introduction: The Nature of Conflict and Conflict Resolution' in Bercovitch, Kremenyuk and Zartman (eds) (n 66) 1 at 6.

166 Darby and Mac Ginty (n 30) 359–60.

167 Charles Call, 'Assessing El Salvador's Transition from Civil War to Peace' in Stedman, Rothchild and Cousens (eds) (n 64) 383.

168 Suhrke, Wimpelmann and Dawes (n 13) 14.

169 ibid 21.

170 ibid 22.

peace accords in El Salvador contained sweeping measures for socio-economic justice, the provisions were lacking almost entirely in specificity. Instead of outlining defined benchmarks or a consensus for economic policy, it merely devolved future responsibility to commissions and forums.[171] The 2006 Darfur Peace Agreement committed the parties to achieve economic development, eradicate poverty, distribute wealth equitably and secure health and education, but again it was characterized by vague objectives and devolution of future responsibility to commissions. Mediators faced with the choice of a flawed agreement or the continuation of violence generally acquiesce to this process of fudging.

By contrast to the perceived all-or-nothing nature of economic resources and opportunities, political power is an endlessly divisible good, one that can be divided at any point along a continuum or in discrete units without destroying its value.[172] Presidencies can be split, cabinets expanded, parliaments reformed, provinces given increased autonomy. This diminishes the power of those who enjoy the present dispensation but not as irrevocably as the transfer of land, the increase of taxes or the expansion of welfare. By contrast to almost all other factors influencing conflict, political institutions are the most easily altered to increase the likelihood of managing conflict democratically.[173] It has long been the case that even in relatively benign transitions, of the four sources of power typically contested in war to peace transitions, namely military, political, ideological and economic, the last of these will generally see the least change.[174] Agreement to alter political institutions or territorial arrangements between conflict elites can be enacted with the stroke of a pen and mutually enforced. The governance norms that underpin such alteration are akin to public goods as they are non-rivalrous and non-exclusive, susceptible to appropriation and interpretation by either side of the agreement to promote their aspirations. Economic redistribution, provision of welfare and regulation of land and

---

[171] Cynthia Arnson and Dinorah Azpuru, 'From Peace to Democratization: Lessons from Central America' in Darby and Mac Ginty (eds) (n 18) 271 at 283.

[172] To paraphrase Steven Brams and Alan Taylor, *Fair Division: From Cake-cutting to Dispute Resolution* (Cambridge University Press 1996) 240.

[173] Katharine Belmont, Scott Mainwaring and Andrew Reynolds, 'Introduction: Institutional Design, Conflict Management, and Democracy in Divided Societies' in Andrew Reynolds (ed.), *The Architecture of Democracy: Institutional Design, Conflict Management and Democracy in the Late Twentieth Century* (Oxford University Press 2002) 1.

[174] Christopher Cramer, 'Trajectories of Accumulation through War and Peace' in Paris and Sisk (eds) (n 55) 129 at 134.

natural resources can also be agreed at the stroke of a pen, but cannot be mutually enforced to anything like the same extent because numerous other elites, sub-elites and ordinary citizens control much of the necessary resources to be redistributed and there may exist little bureaucratic capacity to seize it, tax it or devolve it. As Cheng notes, there is a distinction between the open theatre of negotiations over the formal political order and the interactions of informal actors and networks. Clans, families, religions, secret societies, to say nothing of individuals, may have little control over state-level ceasefire or political design, but form comprehensive ecosystems that can undermine agreed economic rule, impose rents and skew the distribution of state resources. These loci of economic power are extremely difficult to penetrate.[175]

This is most apparent in the economic realm, where the business owner, exporter or multinational corporation who profits or suffers losses in war but essentially sits it out is a familiar figure, the 'bystander' so frequently referred to in transitional justice literature. While peace agreements represent some form of coalescence of rival political and military powers, in poorly institutionalized states economic power is not coterminous with political or military power. Instead, it may be dispersed among informal, deeply imbricated systems that to a significant extent interact far beyond the control of the state or non-state party. Human rights scholars accept that central state authority may have little authority over sub-state entities in relation to the delivery of ESC rights,[176] but this reality is especially pertinent in relation to informal economic elites and power-brokers in areas of limited statehood.

As noted earlier, in most internal armed conflicts rebels are effectively attempting to secure a share of power or alter its distribution. The distribution of political power is always the most important issue in any civil war settlement because power either constitutes the basic incompatibility of war or is the most malleable and available proxy for it. As Whaite puts it, '[i]n essence political settlements are in place wherever those with the power to threaten state-structures forego that option either for reward (which may simply be personal security), for the sake of belief, or to wait [for] an opportunity to become the government

---

[175] Christine Cheng, 'Private and Public Interests: Informal Actors, Informal Influence, and Economic Order after War' in Mats Berdal and Dominik Zaum (eds), *Political Economy of Statebuilding: Power after Peace* (Routledge 2013) 63 at 65–70.

[176] Chinkin (n 3) 9.

overseeing the existing structures'.[177] Far from trying to develop a coherent political vision to remedy the most destabilizing sources of injustice or structural inequality, peace agreements are best understood as keenly negotiated bargains to create a new constituent power or authority sufficient to 'create and maintain a concrete, collective condition of political unity and social order'.[178] New orders in post-conflict states bear the hallmarks of Russell Hardin's rational-choice presentation of constitutions – they are not a freely negotiated contract based on the consent of the people to justifiable principles for distributing rights, positions, and resources in society as they would behind a veil of ignorance, but instead are compacts to regulate and organize the interests of those elements within the polity powerful enough to significantly unsettle the emerging order.[179] This explains why issues of political representation and accountability are dealt with in almost every peace agreement.[180]

By contrast, there is little domestic political compulsion to respond to the interests of relatively marginal groups. Peace is negotiated solely amongst those with the power to bring it down. Even to the extent that other parties are included, peace is nevertheless dominated by these elite power-brokers. The potential in any peace agreement to placate these constituencies through rights and more responsive forms of governance (improved welfare, redistribution, gender equity) may be too long-term, too uncertain or too widely dispersed towards people who do not have the military-political power to undermine the settlement or to significantly improve the potential for the settlement to stick in the short- to medium-term. Those elements of society a transformative turn in transitional justice would address like women, the rural and urban poor and disregarded minorities rarely amass enough capabilities and authority to collectively undermine or sustain an emerging peace. Given the difficulties of starting rebellion from positions of complete marginalization, social science studies of the emergence of conflict illustrate that discrimination, abuses of socio-economic rights and subsistence crises are less clearly identifiable as conflict triggers than violations of civil and

---

[177] Alan Whaites, *States in Development: Understanding State-building* (DFID 2008) 7.

[178] Bhuta (n 156) 836.

[179] Russell Hardin, *Liberalism, Constitutionalism, and Democracy* (Oxford University Press 2003) 86–90 as cited in Bhuta (n 156) 841.

[180] In the study in Suhrke, Wimpelmann and Dawes (n 13), for example, all but one of the 27 peace agreements signed after 1989 that they study have provisions dealing with these issues with a high degree of specificity relative to other provisions (at 25).

political rights,[181] a particular danger in inherently precarious post-conflict governance agreements. As Chinkin notes

> Economic and social rights are perceived as appertaining to development rather than as being central to establishing political stability and security. Too often development is seen as subsidiary to political security and is addressed separately and subsequently through a donors' conference and the work of the International Financial Institutions (IFIs) rather than being integrated into a holistic approach to reconstruction.[182]

Though we speak of *peace agreements*, what we actually get are *political settlements*, a social order 'based on political compromises between powerful groups in society that sets the context for institutional and other policies'.[183] Settlements combine power and institutions in ways that are mutually compatible between powerful groups (who reap an acceptable distribution of benefits sufficient to obviate the desire to change it) and sustainable (capable of achieving at least minimum levels of economic performance and political stability) to form a social order based on political compromises that establishes the context for institutional reform and other policies.[184]

Though most peace settlements can be characterized as agreements between violent elites to form a dominant coalition prepared to allow institutionalized politics to take the place of violence, it would not be fair to simply assume that might simply makes right. Because peace agreements are born of mistrust (after all, an antagonist with a proven capability of engaging and matching one's forces in conflict probably retains the ability to inflict further harm), there is generally an attempt on the part of all sides to restrain power and to moderate political behaviour so as to diminish competition and extremist tendencies. Two overarching strategies have emerged to regulate security dilemmas in the peacebuilding model, namely (1) political and security guarantees resting on formal group right arrangements, most notably power-sharing, and (2) political and security guarantees based on individual rights. The limited willingness of antagonists to prioritize rights-based regimes has been addressed

---

[181] Oskar Thoms and James Ron, 'Do Human Rights Violations Cause Internal Conflict?' (2007) 29 *Human Rights Quarterly* 674.

[182] Chinkin (n 3) 8.

[183] Mushtaq Khan, 'Political Settlements and the Governance of Growth-Enhancing Institutions' (unpublished monograph, University of London School of Oriental and African Studies, 2010) 4 <http://core.ac.uk/download/files/103/2792198.pdf> accessed 21 July 2016.

[184] ibid 4.

already. Power-sharing, by contrast, has proven a much more attractive means than human rights guarantees to consolidate security, to the extent that it conditions future opportunities for justice even more than the peace agreement itself. It is to this that the rest of this chapter turns.

4. SLICING THE PIE: WHY POWER-SHARING IMPEDES TRANSFORMATION

Given that the exclusion of ethnic, religious and linguistic groups from representation and influence in the state is one of the root causes of conflict, it comes as no surprise that inclusiveness is a non-negotiable bottom-line for most civil war principals. In one count, since 1945 about 97 per cent of negotiated settlements at the end of civil wars have involved the promise, if not always the implemented reality, of at least one element of power-sharing.[185] Scholarship in the area is divided between those who are sceptical of power-sharing's conduciveness towards building sustainable peace and those who welcome it as a useful, temporary means of bridging the divide from conflict to non-conflict. Some are tentatively sanguine about its potential as a long-term institution that empowers states to build an effective, democratic state, while some are not. For the purposes of this chapter, Aroussi and Vandeginste's definition of power-sharing as agreements 'guaranteeing representation, control and/or influence in the government, the army, the national economy and resources or over a specific territory to the signatories' is adopted.[186] This definition includes improvised or unofficial arrangements and practices as well as formal law-based institutions and policies. It should be apparent, therefore, that power-sharing is neither a homogenous nor a consistent phenomenon in terms of the forms adopted. There are four dimensions to power-sharing, namely political, territorial, military and economic:

1. Political Power-Sharing: Political power-sharing is addressed in detail in Section 4.1.
2. Territorial Power-Sharing: In non-international armed conflicts fought by groups seeking independence or autonomy from the state

[185] Matthew Hoddie and Caroline Hartzell, 'Power Sharing in Peace Settlements: Initiating the Transition from Civil War' in Donald Rothchild and Philip Roeder (eds), *Sustainable Peace: Power and Democracy after Civil Wars* (Cornell University Press 2005) 83 at 85.

[186] Aroussi and Vandeginste (n 57) 184.

for their region, territorial power-sharing is a standard response to guarantee those regions greater control over their own political, economic and cultural affairs at a sub-national level. It is designed to reduce the potential for conflict by reducing opportunities and motivations for friction with a state characterized by the dominance of another group, most notably by limiting its authority. Examples of territorial power-sharing include ethnofederalism (where territorial governance units are explicitly designated as ethnic homelands but include other minorities), regional autonomy (the legal grant of specific responsibilities or powers to a regional authority), and non-territorial federalism (where distinct responsibilities and powers are devolved to a community in areas like traditional law, education, language or religion).

3. Military Power-Sharing: Most military power-sharing involves the integration of rebel armed forces into those of the state. This can take the form of a proportional share relative to population/size of faction (e.g. Mozambique, Philippines) or a definite 50/50 split (e.g. Burundi), though much will depend on the strength of the rebel bargaining position. Alternatively, or in addition, high-ranking positions within the reformed military can be allotted to certain factions (e.g. Sudan, Nicaragua). Military power-sharing is reassuring to both parties as it prevents unilateral use of force by either of the former belligerents and means the cession of strategic combat positions. It also provides jobs and incomes for rebels going forward and needs to be considered in the context of DDR and security reform.
4. Economic Power-Sharing: Economic power-sharing is examined in depth in Section 4.2.

As this chapter has argued, given the relatively short transition from war to post-conflict, radical change in inequality or ESC rights cannot be expected from peace agreements, from the rights guarantees they incorporate or from any simultaneous processes of constitutionalization they foster. As a result, there can be little doubt that power-sharing in the immediate post-conflict period and in the years following will exercise an inordinate influence on the prospects for economic justice, improved welfare or respect for ESC rights. The malleability of structures of oppression will be conditioned by the domestic political economy to the extent that it is obstructive, merely permissive or positively facilitative, and domestic politics will be conditioned by how power is shared. Power-sharing institutions 'constrain subsequent political processes by empowering some political actors rather than others, creating incentives to press some demands rather than others, and making it less costly to press these demands in some ways rather than others'.[187] Political power-sharing defines much of economic opportunity, economic power-sharing specifically redistributes resources, and both territorial and military power-sharing have significant resource and distributive implications. In short, power-sharing is a robust determinant of the potential for change, even if it is not the only one.

4.1 Principles of Power-sharing

Power-sharing as a concept has attracted little attention in the transitional justice literature beyond isolated case-studies[188] and some general treatments.[189] Though these works take an appropriately pessimistic view of the obstacles to thoroughgoing justice posed by power-sharing, they suffer from a tendency to view power-sharing as an imposition of liberal peacebuilders[190] and to assess its potential on the lines of the Lijphartian consociationalism familiar in Europe.[191] There is, by contrast, something of a consensus in the peacebuilding literature that power-sharing works in radically different ways.[192] Contrary to the notion that power-sharing is an exogenous imposition of peacebuilders, the phenomenon is generally embraced by factions in post-conflict ecologies for two main reasons. Firstly, domestic disputants accept that at the end of civil war conflicts no

---

[187] Donald Rothchild and Philip Roeder, 'Power Sharing as an Impediment to Peace and Democracy' in Rothchild and Roeder (eds) (n 185) 29 at 29.

[188] E.g., Laura Davis, 'Power Shared and Justice Shelved: The Democratic Republic of Congo' (2013) 17 *International Journal of Human Rights* 289.

[189] Most notably Stef Vandeginste and Chandra Lekha Sriram, 'Power Sharing and Transitional Justice: A Clash of Paradigms?' (2011) 17 *Global Governance* 489.

[190] Chandra Lekha Sriram, *Peace as Governance: Power-sharing, Armed Groups and Contemporary Peace Negotiations* (Palgrave Macmillan 2008) 1; Kris Brown and Fionnuala Ní Aoláin, 'Through the Looking Glass: Transitional Justice Futures through the Lens of Nationalism, Feminism and Transformative Change' (2015) 9 *International Journal of Transitional Justice* 125, 136.

[191] ibid 131–35; Paige Arthur, 'Identities in Transition: Developing Better Transitional Justice Initiatives in Divided Societies' (International Center for Transitional Justice, 2009) 20 <https://www.ictj.org/sites/default/files/ICTJ-Global-Divided-Societies-2009-English.pdf> accessed 21 July 2016; Vandeginste and Sriram (n 189) 492–93.

[192] Caroline Hartzell and Matthew Hoddie, 'The Art of the Possible: Power Sharing and Post-Civil War Democracy' (2015) 67 *World Politics* 37; Anna Jarstad, 'Power Sharing: Former Enemies in Joint Government' in Jarstad and Sisk (eds) (n 112) 105 at 108.

alternative set of rules can dependably bring about the reassurances demanded by antagonists in sharply conflicted polities to initiate the transition. Secondly, power-sharing may amount to a mere modification within the state of long-established, informal, but highly deliberate means of regulating diversity within divided societies. Historically, those states with little or no coercive ability to rebuff rebel attacks but who nevertheless enjoy prolonged periods of peace rely on the operation of effective systems of political accommodation and elite-level consultation to overcome internal divisions and the problems of diversity. In these areas, effective governance is secured primarily through bargaining and concessions between weak executives with finite capacity to effectively enforce policy and other sub-national elites who legitimately regulate social conduct of identifiable groups or territories.[193]

This is most apparent in patrimonial states where stability is underpinned by states that bring elites with their own clientelist bases within the political system. Often, these actors will of necessity be the leaders of ethnic, religious or linguistic groups. Rothchild and Foley describe how in African polities 'the political incorporation of all major social interests' is the primary 'rule of the game'.[194] On similar lines, other scholars describe the routinized alternation of power in states outside the Global North where opposition forces do not necessarily take up arms to redress obvious grievances but instead do so to reintegrate themselves within systems of shared political power from which they were previously removed.[195] They, like Spears, argue that many African wars are fought less by the people to address deep ethnic or social grievances than by elites to reintegrate themselves into a system of power rotation/bargaining from which they have been excluded.[196] Power-sharing in one form or another has been adopted in African states like Angola, the Comoros, Burundi, Central African Republic, Congo, Chad, Côte d'Ivoire, DR Congo, Djibouti, Kenya, Liberia, Mali, Senegal, Somalia,

---

[193] Thomas Risse, 'Governance in Areas of Limited Statehood' in Thomas Risse (ed.), *Governance Without a State: Policies and Politics in Areas of Limited Statehood* (Columbia University Press 2013) 1 at 2 and 11.

[194] Donald Rothchild and Michael Foley, 'African States and the Politics of Inclusive Coalitions' in Donald Rothchild and Naomi Chazan (eds), *The Precarious Balance: State and Society in Africa* (Westview 1988) 233 at 233.

[195] Pierre Englebert and Denis Tull, 'Postconflict Reconstruction in Africa: Flawed Ideas about Failed States' (2008) 32 *International Security* 106.

[196] Englebert and Tull (n 195) 122; Spears (n 26) 39.

South Africa, South Sudan and Zimbabwe, to say nothing of states like Colombia and Bosnia. Power-sharing, therefore, is best understood less as a novel liberal imposition than as an institutionalized way to re-establish old modes of managing social equilibrium in under-developed but ethnically or linguistically fractionalized states. Though power-sharing might be explicitly linked to democratic processes and representation by external peacebuilders who promote it, these are not the reasons it is embraced by those who adopt it. Democratic consociationalist theory therefore does not provide the model for how it is exercised.

There is an observable consensus in conflict resolution and peace-building scholarship that power-sharing provisions in peace agreements improve the immediate outlook for peace in the short-term, and that the success of power-sharing exercises decisive influence over the endurance of peace in the longer-term. The more positive explanations for this effect suggest that power-sharing may gradually accustom antagonists into moderation and compromise, while gratifying some pre-war aspirations of combatants through the opportunities produced within inclusive governance structures. More negative explanations, by contrast, foreground the ability of power-sharing to mitigate the greatest fears of disputants that the other side will defect or resile from the agreement. Most observers and participants in power-sharing would accept that power-sharing essentially represents a concession by the more powerful actor to the less powerful one in order to gain the latter's assent to a peace agreement in the absence of military victory.[197] Nevertheless, peace agreements usually provide explicitly that the weaker parties will disarm. This makes them vulnerable if we take into account the (re)centralization of power and the means of violence in the hands of the government with the cessation of hostilities. Armed groups will predictably refuse to demobilize or disarm if any agreement implies reinforcing the power of their rivals or the incumbent government as such reinforcement may ultimately permit them to evade obligations assumed in the prior accord. They therefore seek degrees of political, economic, military or territorial power that either reduce the danger of one side reneging or provides them with some security in the event that this occurs. In deeply divided societies, elections alone cannot induce rebels to implement a peace agreement. Groups who perceive themselves as permanent minorities may find it difficult to accept the incalculable uncertainty that comes

---

[197] Donald Rothchild, 'Reassuring Weaker Parties after Civil Wars: The Benefits and Costs of Executive Power-sharing Systems in Africa' (2005) 4 *Ethnopolitics* 247, 249.

with majoritarian democracy or proportional representation. Power-sharing, therefore, can be understood as an effort to address three categories of security concern for the weaker party that peace settlements naturally give rise to. Firstly, that one side assumes control of the state's coercive apparatus (army and police) and turns it against the weaker party; secondly, that one side dictates the allocation or employment of political influence and patronage; and/or thirdly, that one side achieves a predominant economic position that would reduce the flow of resources or opportunities to the communities the other side represents.[198]

Power-sharing is designed to guarantee the security and interests of weaker parties by ensuring that their interests cannot be disregarded or over-ridden by either majority vote or executive fiat. In so doing, it also provides some reassurance to the stronger party that their antagonists will not decide to resume warfare lightly. It is assumed that the diffusion of power between the disputants will channel conflict into institutions of governance, regulate competition between them and reduce the zero-sum nature of political contestation. The most effective forms of power-sharing are those that are transparent, predictable in their outcomes and that prevent one collectivity from capturing the state or dominating unilaterally to promote its interests to the prejudice of others. As such, power-sharing is essentially a matter of 'fear reduction', more about curtailing the risk that disputed claims can escalate from protests, demonstrations or even terrorism into renewed warfare than laying the foundation for democratic governance.[199] More positively, effective power-sharing signals a willingness to remedy discrimination, to acknowledge the need of groups for recognition and/or representation, and to maintain incentives for co-operation. The fundamental rationale is that if all antagonists are brought within the political fold, they are more likely to trust it and cultivate an interest in its stability and effectiveness.[200] In the longer-term, participants and observers hope that power-sharing leads to joint decision-making, mutual trust and a piecemeal inclusion of parties who have not yet committed to peace into the political process.[201]

---

[198] Caroline Hartzell, 'Explaining the Stability of Negotiated Settlements to Intrastate Wars' (1999) 43 *Journal of Conflict Resolution* 3, 6–7.

[199] Michaela Mattes and Burcu Savun, 'Fostering Peace after Civil War: Commitment Problems and Agreement Design' (2009) 53 *International Studies Quarterly* 737.

[200] Melani Cammett and Edmund Malesky, 'Power Sharing in Postconflict Societies Implications for Peace and Governance' (2012) 56 *Journal of Conflict Resolution* 982, 1016.

[201] Papagianni (n 160) 48.

As a result, power-sharing is better understood as a form of conflict management than as a holistic method of conflict resolution. Though it cannot address all post-conflict ills, the consensus among mediators at the international level is that it delivers a structured context within which some of the most divisive recurrent issues may be tackled. It is effective because the very act of giving up or pooling power mitigates commitment problems in a context of mistrust and vulnerability. It serves as a costly signal by those factions that enter into it that they renounce the possibility of securing their goals through extra-legal means and that they intend to respect the rights of others for as long as it lasts. The architects of a power-sharing compact must balance the imperative to reassure minorities that the state cannot renege on the powers awarded to them in the agreement with the obligation to ensure these powers are not so unlimited that the weaker party can use them to obtain ever more prerogatives.[202] It is assumed that because the antagonists become mutually vulnerable as they grow towards some form of power parity, they may therefore become more willing to fulfil their responsibilities and embrace self-restraint for as long as that parity holds.[203] Most studies of the phenomenon reach the conclusion that power-sharing reduces the risks of return to conflict, even if it cannot eliminate the risk completely.[204]

There is, however, a scholarly debate about which forms of power-sharing (i.e. political, military, economic and territorial) are most effective singularly and in combination. The leading contender is Hartzell and Hoddie's 'the more, the better' hypothesis. They argue that the more dimensions of power-sharing that are included in the agreement, the better the chance that peace endures in the longer-term, because each successive layer of power-sharing further institutionalizes the settlement. It borders on the truistic to suggest that sharing power along political military, territorial and economic lines provides parties with more reassurance and influence than one dimension alone. This dispersal and diversification of power ensures that even where one dimension is not fully implemented, vulnerable groups still retain sufficient power to

[202] Philip Roeder, 'Power Dividing as an Alternative to Ethnic Power Sharing' in Rothchild and Roeder (eds) (n 185) 51 at 58–59.

[203] Dorina Bekoe, 'Mutual Vulnerability and the Implementation of Peace Agreements: Examples from Mozambique, Angola and Liberia' (2005) 10 *International Journal of Peace Studies* 43.

[204] See Helga Malmin Binningsbø, 'Power Sharing, Peace and Democracy: Any Obvious Relationships?' (2013) 16 *International Area Studies Review* 89, 91–94 for a summary of the key works.

protect themselves.[205] Most negotiated settlements contain at least two forms of macro-level power-sharing (territorial, political, economic and military), while less than a third contain only one mechanism.[206]

None of this is to argue that power-sharing does not have disadvantages. The most obvious is its tendency to reward violence (or the threat thereof) with power. This policy has the potential to ingrain violence as a political tool, as the earlier examination of the ritualized use of warfare by parties to reintegrate themselves within systems of shared political power makes clear.[207] Scholars who are explicitly sceptical of the pacific potency of power-sharing and instead prefer more integrationist approaches argue that it further embeds ethnic, religious or linguistic divides. This may reinforce the distinctions between groups in society and weaken any motivation for the coalition of elites to moderate and co-operate on issues that cut across former conflict lines.[208] Because power-sharing builds conflict cleavages into post-war governance, it generates a strong incentive for former warring parties to seek political support primarily from their own constituent groups, which tends to reduce public confidence in newly established governmental institutions.[209] Though premised on careful balances of power, power-sharing is not self-reinforcing and depends on the moderation and goodwill of those whom it places in positions of responsibility. It can therefore break down, either because it is perceived by these individuals as impeding the implementation of the peace, because it is unresponsive to public needs, or because the resources needed to sustain the coalition run out. Rothchild and Roeder point out a 'second-generation problem' where the need for the majority group to make power-sharing concessions or reassure the weaker party decreases over time, reducing the need to act in a conciliatory manner or to maintain principles of proportional allocation.[210] Even in those states where power-sharing may guarantee some measure of stability, it may not meet the test of representativeness, accountability or effective governance. Though power-sharing institutions reduce fear, they also ultimately serve to institutionalize it – 'fear of each

---

205 Hartzell and Hoddie (n 87).

206 Cammett and Malesky (n 200) 992.

207 Andreas Mehler, 'Peace and Power Sharing in Africa: A Not So Obvious Relationship' (2009) 108 *African Affairs* 453.

208 Donald Horowitz, *Ethnic Groups in Conflict* (University of California Press 1985) 566–76.

209 Jai Kwan Jung, 'Power-Sharing and Democracy Promotion in Post-Civil War Peace-building' (2012) 19 *Democratization* 486.

210 Rothchild and Roeder (n 187) 38.

other (thus the need for hard-and-fast guarantees of minority rights, for example) and fear of the failure to conciliate (avoiding a worse alternative)'.[211] The institutionalization of fear limits the malleability of the structural roots of conflict.

4.2 Economic Power-sharing, Justice and the Politics of Oblivion

The most compelling objection to power-sharing is its elevation of pragmatism and power in the inclusion or exclusion of groups to cement alliances over any more principled search for the ideal peace. This reality is most evident in what has been identified as the 'clash of paradigms' between power-sharing and transitional justice, most notably in the areas of criminal justice and truth. As Sriram and Vandeginste contend, the emergence of power-sharing as a preferred policy tool for peacemakers and mediators has occurred simultaneously with the gradual clarification of norms outlining the state's duty to investigate, prosecute and punish crimes. What they observe as a result is a clash between norms of anti-impunity and the pressing interests of negotiating partners to avoid accountability for gross human rights abuses they or their power-sharing partners may have committed. Avoiding accountability is something power-sharing permits antagonists to do as control of the executive, the military or a defined territorial area allows the partners to resist accountability measures *de jure* through law or, most commonly, by the *de facto* amnesty that results from inactivity.[212] The reality of power-sharing in states like Kenya, Burundi and Mozambique is that of a 'coalition of oblivion' where accountability, reparation and truth-telling are consciously abandoned as policy options in the interests of facilitating the process of reallocating authority between conflict elites.[213]

The politics of oblivion are even more apparent in relation to socio-economic justice if we consider the modalities by which conflict elites undertake economic power-sharing. Economic power-sharing is a far less common phenomenon than its political, territorial or military equivalents. Studies show political power-sharing to be around three times as common as economic power-sharing.[214] One explanation is that former combatants 'tend to view economic concerns as secondary in importance

---

[211] Timothy Sisk, 'Power-Sharing in Civil War: Puzzles of Peacemaking and Peacebuilding' (2013) 15 *Civil Wars* 7, 13.

[212] Vandeginste and Sriram (n 189) 489–94.

[213] ibid 499.

[214] Aroussi and Vandeginste (n 57) 188, citing Anna Jarstad and Ralph Sundberg, 'Peace by Pact: Data on the Implementation of Peace Agreements' in

to establishing institutions and policies that they perceive to have a more immediate impact on providing for the security of the group'.[215] There are no studies in the peacebuilding literature solely dedicated to economic power-sharing. On those occasions when something cognizable as economic power-sharing occurs, it covers a gamut of options from informal consultations between the executive and former combatants in relation to the state's macro-economic trajectory to very precise agreements relating to shares or ownership of natural resources or nationalized industries. Though distinguishing between generic references to socio-economic rights and something distinctly identifiable as economic power-sharing is difficult, some peace agreements stipulate reformed patterns of resource allocation that merit the latter characterization. Conflict root causes like inequitable land allocation in Colombia and El Salvador and improper use of natural resources in Sudan, Liberia and Sierra Leone have been addressed directly in peace agreements through explicit stipulations that certain lands or resources should be redistributed or that the government should ensure specific ring-fencing of income on a group or territorial basis. There are grounds for hope, therefore, that economic power-sharing could become the vehicle through which horizontal inequalities between antagonistic groups could be tackled. An obvious potential exists to negotiate more equitable shares of resources, opportunities and income not only from one religious/ethnic/territorial group to another, but within groups as part of a revised national approach to economic redistribution. Economic power-sharing could enshrine competitive but holistic negotiation over social investment by the state, land reform or more redistributive taxation. However, while economic power-sharing is often understood by outside observers as 'aspiring to correct injustices present prior to or evolving during conflict',[216] resource sharing between post-conflict elites has typically been more in evidence than resource redistribution across society at large in most instances. As Brown and Ní Aoláin note, former antagonists may use power-sharing to divide spoils and split the polity in ways that maintain their own advantages vis-à-vis their own communities.[217] Three reasons for this may be proposed.

Ashok Swain, Ramses Amer and Joakim Ojendal (eds), *Globalization and Challenges to Building Peace* (Anthem Press 2007) 73–79.

[215] Hoddie and Hartzell (n 185) 103.

[216] Binningsbø (n 204) 97.

[217] Brown and Ní Aoláin (n 190) 31.

4.2.1 Difficulty and Risk

Power-sharing imposes costs on both sides. That both parties are willing to suffer an obvious detriment, concede certain principles or bind themselves to co-operative courses of action serves as a credible signal of intent to be bound by the peace agreement. However, while military and political power are fungible for reasons explored earlier (armies and cabinets can expand without necessarily damaging them) and while territorial autonomy may do little more than acknowledge a fact on the ground, there is good reason to believe that economic power-sharing is more difficult to achieve and offers more irreversible detriments for those who make economic concession. As noted earlier, one of the main concerns of factions after war is that the state or a faction could use economic resources to build its power base at their expense, and so the rivals seek a distribution of wealth and income that prevent such domination.[218] The parties in such instances are more likely to prefer the maximization of their economic security in preference to redistribution to other elements of society. Particularly in patrimonialist and clientelist regimes (examined in greater detail in Chapter 4), genuine sharing of resource wealth, industries or economic opportunities can reduce the ability of a government or faction to retain the support of key constituents on whom security, taxation or welfare provision may rely.

As long as economic power-sharing involves forcible redistribution from unwilling agents, it may prove too difficult to implement effectively given the fluidity of capital, lack of bureaucratic reach to tax it or the indivisibility of land and resources from the surrounding economy. In a study of peace settlement duration, Derouen, Lee and Wallensteen find that provisions that are both costly *and* difficult decrease the life span of peace agreements. This is because governments perceive themselves to be conceding too much and so drag their heels in implementation, while rebels respond by abandoning the agreement because of these delays in implementation and/or because the temptation to move pre-emptively is too strong.[219] There will always be spoilers 'who only accept peace and democratization on terms under which their investments and privileges are not severely threatened'.[220] Within the transitional justice literature, some accept that if expanding the scope of justice into areas like economic justice motivates entrenched economic elites to thwart or

---

[218] Hartzell (n 198) 5 and 10–11.

[219] DeRouen, Lea and Wallensteen (n 90) 367.

[220] Kristine Hoglund, 'Violence in War-to-Democracy Transitions' in Jarstad and Sisk (eds) (n 112) 80 at 96.

oppose transition to peace and/or democracy, then prudence may dictate a postponement in dealing with these issues until more favourable times.[221]

4.2.2 Informal Economic Power-sharing

Few transitional justice scholars have explicitly considered power-sharing as a subject in its own right, and none have specifically addressed economic power-sharing. There is, nevertheless, a reasonable supposition on the part of observers like Sriram and Bell that power-sharing in any guise tends to operate as a form of constitutionalization of self-interest over the greater good.[222] This is most evident in the demonstrable tendency for economic interests to be traded off against the original political goals of antagonists, most notably in the case of non-state militias who acquire interests in the war economy.[223] Sometimes this trade-off is explicit – Papagianni, for example, points to settlements in South Africa and El Salvador which were premised on the prevention of any redistribution of economic benefits from privileged economic classes to marginalized communities.[224] However, it is more usually the case that agreement to maintain or modify a conservative economic status quo is implicit. As Salomon and Anderson observe, those elite bargains visible in accords and public statements 'are only part of the story' – most peace settlements are accompanied by unspoken understandings among entrenched networks of power and predatory exclusive groups that their interests are best served by a particular way of organizing economic power.[225] This understanding is often tacit, surreptitiously negotiated or taken for granted as the natural way of doing things. Informal rules also emerge to exclude certain issues from government jurisdiction.[226] While in political settlements on government expenditure 'redistribution to the

---

[221] Pablo de Greiff, 'Articulating the Links Between Transitional Justice and Development: Justice and Social Integration' in de Greiff and Duthie (eds) (n 56) 28 at 41.

[222] Christine Bell, 'Transitional Justice, Interdisciplinarity and the State of the "Field" or "Non-Field"' (2009) 3 *International Journal of Transitional Justice* 5, 14; Sriram (n 121) 277.

[223] Licklider (n 75) 702.

[224] Katia Papagianni, 'Participation and State Legitimation' in Charles Call (ed.) with Vanessa Wyeth, *Building States to Build Peace* (Lynne Rienner 2008) 49 at 56.

[225] Jago Salmon and Catherine Anderson, 'Elites and Statebuilding' in David Chandler and Timothy Sisk (eds), *The Routledge Handbook of International Statebuilding* (Routledge 2013) 42 at 48.

[226] Donald Rothchild, 'Settlement Terms and Postagreement Stability' in Stedman, Rothchild and Cousens (eds) (n 64) 117 at 124.

not-so-poor would be difficult if not impossible to justify in terms of general public principles of welfare, [i]nformal arrangements are therefore used to enable powerful groups to have continued access to income through "political" accumulation'.[227] Davis's description of the DR Congo peace agreement is a good example of this largely tacit form of exclusionary governance that has generally been ignored in the transitional justice literature:

> The Global Accord did not address economic power-sharing in any meaningful way despite the fact that illegal resource extraction, if not a root cause of the conflicts in Congo, soon became a crucial motivating factor for domestic and foreign combatants. The Global Accord included an annex on state companies but the real economic issues were deliberately kept off the agenda of the peace process by both the Congolese actors and their foreign backers in order that they could continue their illegal and lucrative economic activity.[228]

4.2.3 Gathering at the Pork Barrel

Critics have long complained that power-sharing agreements 'reek … of rewards for crime coupled with pork-barrel politics'.[229] It is something of a commonplace that all civil war forces involve loose coalitions of moderates and extremists on both sides. While most peace settlements involve integrating the moderates of both sides, there is also a need to bring extremists and other elements less convinced of the need for peace into the fold. As Atlas and Licklider argue, one of the key guarantors of stability is the distribution of material and psychological resources between those individuals and groups who can undermine the settlement. In practice, of course, 'this often means responding to elites and ignoring the demands of the masses based on the pragmatic calculation that elites are cheaper and masses by themselves are unlikely to overthrow the system'.[230] A familiar example is of course the sharing of mineral wealth in West African post-conflict agreements, the paradigmatic example being the appointment of the Revolutionary United Front leader as chair of Sierra Leone's Commission for the Management of Strategic Resources in the Lomé Peace Agreement. A supplementary annex to

---

[227] Khan (n 183) 26.

[228] Davis (n 188) 292.

[229] Gérard Prunier, *From Genocide to Continental War: The Congolese Conflict and the Crisis of Contemporary Africa* (C. Hurst and Co. 2009) 277.

[230] Pierre Atlas and Roy Licklider, 'Conflict among Former Allies after Civil War Settlement: Sudan, Zimbabwe, Chad and Lebanon' (1999) 36 *Journal of Peace Research* 35, 50.

Liberia's Accra Agreement provided that ministerial postings, the leadership of the state's autonomous agencies, public corporations and national enterprises would be proportionately allocated in a ratio of two national agencies and four state corporations to each bloc.[231] Indeed, in African civil wars, negotiations make apparent that 'the most important spoils of factional struggle … are government and party offices'.[232] 'Managed inclusion' were the watchwords of the Naivasha peace agreement between Sudan and the (South) Sudan People's Liberation Movement (SPLM), but this principle in practice led to an extreme expansion in the latter's state payroll, cash transfers and government contracts to the degree that $4 billion disappeared over four years, mostly to SPLM cadres.[233] This is not a phenomenon limited to Africa. For example, the Paris Peace Accords for Cambodia called for elections, but this process was characterized by the rampant recompense of political supporters of the various factions with jobs in the administration.[234] It should be obvious that in grossly impoverished post-conflict circumstances, the redirection of public wealth, resources and job opportunities to combatants who may already have prospered in the war economy can have a deleterious impact on any plans by political leaders, donors or domestic reform constituencies to use state revenue for the realization of socio-economic rights. The self-evident irony of power-sharing is that it usually demands increased public spending on the most powerful actors in society when public funds are least available. Indeed, power-sharing can consume a considerable proportion of what little wealth there is available for development and welfare.

4.3 The Impact of Power-sharing on Cultures of Governance

While the exclusive and often corrupt means by which economic power-sharing operates can serve to limit the prospects for structural transformation, these problems are compounded by the culture of governance that political power-sharing tends to produce. In many post-conflict states political power-sharing means predetermined quotas of executive posts in over-size unity cabinets across the lines of the conflict in proportion to population size, ensuring all policy can be monitored or

---

231 Mehler (n 210) 12–13.

232 Robert Jackson and Carl Rosberg, *Personal Rule in Black Africa: Prince, Autocrat, Prophet, Tyrant* (University of California Press 1982) 52.

233 Salmon and Anderson (n 225) 48.

234 David Roberts, 'Hybrid Polities and Post-Conflict Policy' in Chandler and Sisk (eds) (n 225) 94 at 100.

blackballed. It might also incorporate partitioned authority over some aspects of politics and legal codes, mutual vetoes to allow minority groups to prevent potentially threatening legislation and proportional voting in the legislature. Softer guarantees that foster political inclusiveness in decision-making but do not provide pre-assigned allocation of power like open and closed-list proportional representation in legislative elections are also forms of political power-sharing. However, because the harder guarantees of a grand coalition, proportional voting in the legislature and mutual vetoes are more common in post-conflict states, they form the focus of this section.

Political power-sharing allows executive or legislative power to be divided among adversaries and serves a powerful incentive to renounce violent solutions. However, it also permits peace accords to be finalized without any agreement on how to address the structural causes of conflict. In some ways, power-sharing operates as a highly elaborate means of papering over these cracks, but the roots of conflict will have to be addressed within this divided executive. It is clear that some degree of governmental responsiveness to elections, social movements and protests is needed if socio-economic rights are to be met, if basic needs are to be provided for, or if wealth is to be redirected towards social minima within society. Non-partisan administrative competence is also essential. The assumption behind much power-sharing is that by providing conflict principals with guaranteed access to power, they will be inclined to moderate their stances, thereby facilitating effective institutional reform to diffuse the underlying roots of instability.[235] However, many post-conflict power-sharing governments are characterized by palsied policy formation and weak capacity for effective or responsive governance. This is because they are ultimately concerned more about the consolidation of a political coalition that will maintain security than a linear, goal-oriented policy to address root causes of conflict. What's more, to the extent that it builds war-time divisions into post-conflict political structures, a power-sharing government tends to foster the type of institutional rigidity that prevents it from addressing new or ongoing problems:

> Once power-sharing is agreed upon, it becomes difficult to make changes to the initial set-up. This is because power-sharing assumes a coherent leadership in each warring party and does not take into account potential within-group divisions in the implementation of the power-sharing deal. Should

[235] Nic Cheeseman and Blessing-Miles Tendi, 'Power-sharing in Comparative Perspective: The Dynamics of "Unity Government" in Kenya and Zimbabwe' (2010) 48 *Journal of Modern African Studies* 203, 204.

> dissatisfied factions within former warring parties threaten to derail the entire peace process, power-sharing institutions tend to be unable to adapt to the new political grievances.[236]

The goal of power-sharing is conflict management, not conflict transformation. Parties abide by power-sharing rules out of self-interest and to avoid recurrence of warfare they may no longer be prepared to wage. For three main reasons (explored below), few post-conflict power-sharing executives are either willing or able to constructively reconcile contending normative visions about what the ultimate remit of the state should be vis-à-vis its citizens.

4.3.1 Ineffective Governance and Paralysis of Policy

The raison d'être of power-sharing is to ensure stability by channelling patent and latent conflict down predictable, non-violent channels. This stabilization remit is the end in itself and so tends to take priority over the achievement of other specific goals. As Arnson and Azpuru put it, power-sharing 'is an accord on processes for discussing change, rather than an accord on specific results'.[237] While it can safeguard necessary balances between linguistic, ethnic, regional or racial collectivities, it may not guarantee co-operation between them given the simultaneous existence of hard guarantees like weighted majorities or the availability of absolute vetoes. As examples of deadlock in the likes of Northern Ireland, Iraq, Bosnia and Lebanon (to say nothing of Belgium's 541 days needed form a government after its 2007 election), these precautions run the obvious risk of fostering inactivity caused by equal but opposing forces –'[w]ith so many built-in opportunities to veto governmental decisions, the system encourages inefficiency and rigidity, leading to poor governance and inferior public goods provision'.[238] Even where the ritual brandishing of partisan vetoes and tit-for-tat bargaining are eschewed, the existence of qualified or concurrent majority voting procedures mean that governance comes to resemble a continuous form of relationship management through the rigid apparatus of power-sharing rather than a flexible, adaptive form of government capable of responding expediently to emerging social needs. In drafting global agreements on power-sharing, those who lead the government or factions have strong incentives to frame issues relating to common goods like healthcare, development, the environment or welfare in sectarian terms in order to

---

236 Jung (n 209) 490.
237 Arnson and Azpuru (n 171) 277.
238 Cammett and Malesky (n 200) 986.

secure concessions from the partners in governance, which has an inevitable tendency towards escalation of like-for-like demands.[239] Because of the size of large executive coalitions, their veto-driven unwieldiness and lack of provision for their own alteration, power-sharing governments tend to be inflexible and non-adaptive to significant changes in social conditions that follow peace. While political power-sharing can secure sufficient compromise to sustain the peace, it is more likely to inculcate a politics of procrastination and institutional deadlock than the co-operative solution of common problems.[240]

4.3.2 Harmful Inclusionary and Exclusionary Dynamics

Given the incentive structures at play in peace agreements, it is clear that transformative governance, be it in relation to recognizing ESC rights or reforming discriminatory economic patterns, can only occur where the government is forced to respond to public demands. The most common vehicles for the articulation of these demands are civil society agents with cross-cutting interests, most notably in the form of reformist political parties pressing for change within the institutions of governance or NGOs campaigning for change outside it. The power-sharing rhetoric found in the policy documents of peacebuilders suggests that power-sharing is adopted on account of its inherent ability to reconcile the principles of democracy with those of conflict management by tempering the excesses of the former and providing a structured machinery for the latter. However, for the reasons outlined earlier, in most instances of power-sharing, non-signatories are either not included in arrangements for grand coalition, proportionality or mutual vetoes, or given disproportionately small shares of power.[241] The institutionalization of group identities reduces the incentives of political leaders to become responsive to the interests of those who do not necessarily conceive of their identity along the same group lines like the indigent, immigrants, those of mixed heritage or women.[242] This is because spoiling capacity defines the 'inclusive enough' allocation of power and whose demands most need to be listened to:

---

239 Mehler (n 28) 37.

240 Matthias Basedau, 'Managing Ethnic Conflict: The Menu of Institutional Engineering' (German Institute for Global and Area Studies, 2011) 18 <https://www.giga-hamburg.de/en/system/files/publications/wp171_basedau.pdf> accessed 21 July 2016.

241 Mehler (n 207) 10.

242 Ian O'Flynn, 'Democratic Values and Power-Sharing' in Ian O'Flynn, David Russell and Donald Rothchild (eds), *Power Sharing: New Challenges for Divides Societies* (Pluto Press 2005) 15 at 23.

> A political order will successfully stabilize where the constitutional arrangements it guarantees are sufficiently advantageous to powerful or politically effective parts of the population for them to coordinate their interests in conformity with those arrangements; politically ineffective groups or parts of the population can be ignored as long as enough of those who are effective acquiesce in the 'coordination order'.[243]

This exclusion may become self-perpetuating. Once revised rules for allocating power are established, they are difficult to change – the tendency of power-sharing to generate rewards means that it creates an incentive to sustain the status quo of the initial institutional set-up.[244]

Though power-sharing is almost always accompanied by elections, introducing any form of responsive political system necessitates a fundamental change in the way political power is exercised. This is unlikely in a system where war-time identities remain the defining feature in deciding who gets access to it and what it must be used for. The political groupings that assume defined roles in power-sharing tend to reflect the military balance at negotiations as opposed to potential electoral or social support. As a result, they are more likely to be based on identity-based interests, as opposed to broad-ranging ideologies that appeal across the conflict divide. Aggregative, programmatic parties that integrate disparate groups, represent cross-cutting interests and craft alternative policy agendas to those of the government struggle to emerge in electoral systems dominated by ethnic/religious/linguistic-based parties that are guaranteed some access to power.[245] As in weak states and semi-authoritarian regimes, elections that do not incentivize the emergence of new parties or allow real competition for power are more likely to foster the perpetuation of existing power divisions via 'premature closure' of the transitional process.[246]

Even where new parties emerge, the prior incorporation of as many war-time groupings as possible within the executive and/or legislature prevents the emergence of vibrant opposition by numerically dwarfing it. This means governance can become unaccountable between elections. It also undermines the prospect that an alternative coalition might be elected at a later point. One of the characteristics of externally mediated

---

[243] Bhuta (n 156) 841.

[244] Jung (n 209) 490.

[245] Benjamin Reilly, 'Political Parties and Post-Conflict Peacebuilding' (2013) 15 *Civil Wars* 88.

[246] Marina Ottaway, 'From Political Opening to Democratisation' in Marina Ottaway (ed.), *Democracy in Africa: The Hard Road Ahead* (Lynne Rienner 1997) 1 at 3.

power-sharing is the use of 'sunset clauses', whereby the rigid strictures of power-sharing are limited to a period of months or years before giving way to the softer guarantees of multi-party elections. Though in theory these ballots should permit parties initially excluded from governance by the initial agreement to gain power, there is an observable tendency for power-sharing to endure in renewed or modified form even after open elections to choose a new government. This is because incumbents can manipulate the process though clientelism or cheating, or they can employ the threat of renewed violence when exit from power looks possible to justify mandatory re-inclusion in government.[247] Far from creating space for reform coalitions, therefore, power-sharing is more often 'manipulated by incumbents desperate to retain their positions in the face of electoral defeat'.[248] Both advocates and detractors of power-sharing acknowledge that it can significantly impede the consolidation of democracy.[249] As Chapter 4 argues, most post-conflict states that do not return to war become hybrid states, i.e. political regimes which contain elements of both an autocratic system and a democratic system.

4.3.3 Patterns of Neo-patrimonialism

Neopatrimonialism is a system of social hierarchy where elites employ state resources to secure the loyalty of clients and sub-elites in the general population via informal relationships that can reach from the highest state structures down to individuals and communities. In areas of limited statehood, the lack of cross-cutting parties or effective administration means that the primary methods of exercising influence are patron-client networks, corruption and clientelism. In neopatrimonial regimes the offices of state are used for personal uses and gains, subordinating the public interest to private accumulation of political power or wealth. Chapter 4 examines its deleterious impact on the prospects for transformative transitional justice. For now, it will suffice to note that power-sharing is one of the main vehicles through which traditional patrimonialism and rational-bureaucratic rule are interwoven.

[247] Larry Diamond, 'Promoting Democracy in Post-conflict and Failed States' (2006) 2 *Taiwan Journal of Democracy* 93, 99.

[248] Cheeseman and Tendi (n 235) 207.

[249] Hartzell and Hoddie (n 192) 44; Julia Strasheim and Hanne Fjelde, 'Pre-designing Democracy: Institutional Design of Interim Governments and Democratization in 15 Post-conflict Societies' (2014) 21 *Democratization* 335, 340. For a sobering perspective see Kåre Vollan, Nils Butenschøn and Øyvind Stiansen, *Power-sharing in Conflict-ridden Societies: Challenges for Building Peace and Democratic Stability* (Ashgate 2015).

It has this effect by constructing 'stable cartels' among the elites of the factions it aggregates. This enables patrimonial relations between these elites and the 'politically deferential and organizationally encapsulated following' they lead, ensuring that the former are predominant and that their demands are consistently fulfilled.[250] Economic power-sharing guarantees control of state resources to individuals who can create order and opportunities by limiting access to resources within the collectivities they represent.[251] As De Waal argues, peacebuilding effectively renovates a pre-existing 'patrimonial marketplace' that operates on the basis of socio-culturally established conventions in which the metropolitan centre 'buys in' the allegiance of sub-national elites who extract from the government the maximum price for their loyalty.[252] It defeats the long-term objective of peace by 'institutionalizing the predatory behavior of warlords into the body politic, giving them the cloak of state authority to prey on the state and its citizen'.[253]

5. CONCLUSION

As noted in Chapter 2, the transitional optimism that peace agreements present an optimum opportunity for addressing the root causes of conflict animates much of fourth generation theorizing about the prospects for socio-economic transformation. There is an assumption at play that post-conflict transition represents a change from a society based on insecurity and fear to one based on trust and co-operation. There is a further assumption that a rational response to conflict should compel a reckoning with its root causes. However, as this chapter has argued, the tendency for powerful groups to reach elitist, exclusionary bargains is magnified in peace agreements where the threat of war recurrence is patent and where certain facts have been created on the ground that

---

250 Rothchild and Roeder (n 187) 36, citing Adriano Pappalardo, 'The Conditions for Consociational Democracy: A Logical and Empirical Critique (1981) 9 *European Journal of Political Research* 365, 365.

251 Jonathan Di John, 'Conceptualizing the Causes and Consequences of Failed States: A Critical Review of the Literature' (Crisis States Research Centre Working Paper No. 25, 2010) 31 and 15 <http://www.lse.ac.uk/internationalDevelopment/research/crisisStates/download/wp/wpSeries2/wp252.pdf> accessed 21 July 2016.

252 De Waal (n 65).

253 Jeremy Levitt, 'Illegal Peace: An Inquiry into the Legality of Power-sharing with Warlords and Rebels in Africa' (2005) 27 *Michigan Journal of International Law* 495, 501.

belligerents and peace-makers are compelled to accept. War in itself is transformative of a society and economy in ways unrelated to the original motivations for the conflict as new structures of political order and economic production/predation emerge – a peace agreement must address the outcomes of the war before it addresses the root causes of it, because the outcomes have a more immediate causal connection to the renewal of warfare.[254] Contemporary civil war is not between defenders and abolishers of a status quo, but rather revolves around the inclusiveness of that status quo. Peace agreements typically organize the monopoly of violence, the allocation of political power and the distribution of resources among antagonists. The terms need to fit their expectations, which are largely defined by their perception of what they can gain via the peace process compared to what they can secure via the battlefield. Compromises in terms of political power and economic resources, usually but not exclusively encapsulated in power-sharing agreements, are usually required to persuade rebels and governments to refrain from renewed warfare. These compromises are typically manifest in elaborate divisions of governmental control as political power is endlessly fungible and can easily be divided and shared, as well as more amorphous divisions of economic power which tend to maintain the status quo.

This is the quandary of peace – the compromises needed to end war may contradict or impede the policies necessary to address root causes. The decisions made at each stage constrain the options available at the next, setting particular outcomes in motion, but foreclosing others to the degree that some iniquitous outcomes are irreversible.[255] If we return to the constructivist divide between norms and interests, it would appear that in terms of the internal politics of peace, interests are paramount. The reality of many peace processes is that they are more often than not elite political pacts whose aim in economic terms is less an holistic, inclusive, positive peace than a recalibration of a hidebound status quo. As Keen puts it, post-conflict transition involves 'a realignment of political interests and a readjustment of economic strategies rather than a clean break from violence to consent, from theft to production, or from

[254] Susan Woodward, 'Do the Root Causes of Civil War Matter? On Using Knowledge to Improve Peacebuilding Interventions' (2007) 1 *Journal of Intervention and Statebuilding* 143, 155.

[255] Roberto Belloni, 'Hybrid Peace Governance: Its Emergence and Significance' (2012) 18 *Global Governance* 21, 28–29.

repression to democracy'.[256] If a path to mere reconfiguration of pre-existing hegemony is established in a peace process (and even one that is sub-optimal), transitional justice will struggle to revise the terms – obstacles to change are built into political institutions established to secure the peace, and decisively shape what is later achievable.[257] As a result, failures of transitional justice may be locked-in or over-determined due to reasons no transitional justice schema could reasonably be expected to mitigate, like the allocation of power and resources in a peace agreement, like outright veto of transformation by political or military elites or opportunist sabotage of the peace, to say nothing of effects outside the peace agreement like economic or ecological crisis, or the indolence of the major international powers on whose support transitional justice actors were depending. This makes it self-defeating to assign blame to transitional justice. The literature so far has provided few answers to the question of how to avoid the predictable consequences of such pacts, but instead conflates transitional justice's failure with the pre-existing circumstances which caused it.

The nature of contemporary conflict resolution imposes no absolute barriers to transformation. Though this chapter has taken a pessimistic view of the limits peace agreements and power-sharing might impose on structural transformation, it is important to leave space for agency, adaptivity and goodwill. After all, if power-sharing achieves its primary purpose of sustainably managing conflict peacefully, it is entirely possible that the attention of the governing coalition can be diverted towards to those intractable issues that power-sharing was in part introduced in order to circumvent. As peace agreements are implemented, the emerging sense of security may give rise to opportunities that could not have been anticipated amidst the more circumspect political horizons of negotiations. Power-sharing parties might foster genuine co-operation and gradual adaptation of power and representation to respond to changes in society, especially if the governing coalition enjoys creative, sustained engagement with international peacebuilders and civil society groups that incentivize such reform. The consolidation of peace may build confidence and permit effective institutions of governance to emerge that gradually erode the fears of former belligerents that the other side might resume armed conflict, reducing the incentives for elites to make longer-term agendas for the common good secondary to security. As

---

[256] David Keen, *The Economic Functions of Violence in Civil Wars* (Oxford University Press 1998) 32.

[257] Belloni (n 255) 29.

Berdal argues, this period should not be understood 'in purely negative or risk-filled terms: it is better seen as a unique kind of political space, shaped by fatigue, uncertainty and war-weariness, but also by the hope that a new political dispensation will result in rapid improvements to quality of life'.[258] Post-conflict transitional justice will ultimately be realized in this space between uncertainty and hope. However, the experiences of post-conflict states as diverse as Bosnia, South Sudan, Sri Lanka, Rwanda and Peru, which all failed to address the structural causes of the conflicts they endured, tend to suggest that the pragmatic bargaining that comes with this uncertainty may exercise greater influence than the straightforward rule-following or the norm implementation that negotiators hoped it would foster. For most post-conflict antagonists, peace is crisis to be managed, not an opportunity to be seized.

[258] Berdal (n 81) 21.

4. Transitional justice, liberal peacebuilding and the endogenous determinants of transformation

> The fetishization of familiar terms, tropes and debates masks other projects which are neglected in the effort to describe and construct the new liberal state. Each trope stands in for an aspect of the liberal project: justice represents the struggle for a 'depoliticized', trustworthy rule of law; truth represents the rights of victims to tell their stories and thus to 'democratize history' and reconciliation represents the aspiration to a newly united citizenry in the postconflict state. The terms are played against one another, defining and redefining the ability to achieve the liberal democratic ideal. In the process, deeper challenges to the state-building project potentially disappear. The questions of inequality and structural violence are lost in the process of reconfiguring familiar debates.[1]

> Students of peacebuilding are not alone in fixing the analytical gaze on one set of actors in accounting for particular outcomes while ignoring or assuming as fixed the actions of others. Much of the literature on global governance is focussed on the role and power of different types of non-state actors, whose power is said to be on the increase. Whether these actors are transnational advocacy groups, epistemic communities or international organisations, these actors are said to be central in shaping policy outcomes. Typically, the analytical story starts with the identification of a group that shares some characteristic, whether labelled as an advocacy group or expert group, and then moves on to retrospectively tracing the processes through which a group influenced a policy outcome, concluding that the final outcome … can be traced to the agency of these actors. In basing their claims about global governance on the power of particular types of actors, these accounts make unduly strong assumptions about the lack of power of other groups, whether these are state or non-state.[2]

---

[1] Zinaida Miller, 'Effects of Invisibility: In Search of the "Economic" in Transitional Justice' (2008) 2 *International Journal of Transitional Justice* 266, 275.

[2] Ole Jacob Sending, 'The Effects of Peacebuilding: Sovereignty, Patronage and Power' in Susanna Campbell, David Chandler and Meera Sabaratnam (eds), *A Liberal Peace? The Problems and Practices of Peacebuilding* (Zed Books 2011) 55 at 65.

The previous chapter examined how processes that are predominantly controlled by domestic actors like the modalities of warfare and war conclusion, the means by which peace is negotiated, the terms of peace agreements and the use of power-sharing tend to obstruct the transformation of those structures which gave rise to conflict in the first place. However, even with a peace agreement and power-sharing firmly in place, third party or supranational guarantors may be needed to ensure they function and to undertake the indispensable task of rebuilding the state. There is an obvious potential for actors engaged in peacebuilding ('activities undertaken on the far side of conflict to reassemble the foundations of peace and provide the tools for building on those foundations something that is more than just the absence of war')[3] to modify the conservatism of post-conflict settlements. Similarly, most transitional justice interventions like trials, truth commissions, reparations and memory projects will deploy after peace agreements. The assumed potential of transitional justice to catalyse transformative change was canvassed in Chapter 2.

This chapter explores the potential of transitional justice actors, and the peacebuilding missions they are embedded in or function contemporaneously with, to transform structures of inequality and poverty. As will be seen, critics of transitional justice and peacebuilding are confident that these interventions could stimulate positive change, but insist that they are undermined by liberal biases that limit what projects can be pursued. This confidence is in part born of an assumed power differential between interventionary actors and the post-conflict state they operate in. Critics of peacebuilding assume that interveners enjoy almost untrammelled power to fundamentally alter the social structures of post-conflict societies. For example, Donais argues that 'peacebuilding is marked by a serious power imbalance between outsiders and insiders. Outsiders control all the resources and frame the decision-making structure concerning what types of capacity are to be constructed – where and how – and they enjoy considerable flexibility in choosing among local implementing partners'.[4] Others contend that peace cannot be built without the significant resources that international intervention brings, but the allocation and control of those resources becomes 'the new site of power and domination in post-conflict societies' that allows for the reordering of

---

[3] United Nations, *Report of the Panel on United Nations Peace Operations*, UN Doc. A/55/305-S/2000/809 of 21 August 2000, para. 13.

[4] Timothy Donais, 'Empowerment or Imposition? Dilemmas of Local Ownership in Post-Conflict Peacebuilding Processes' (2009) 34 *Peace and Change* 3, 15.

domestic power, prestige, rule and rights by peacebuilders.[5] Any national stakeholders who reject international prescriptions or conditionalities can be excluded politically and economically from the peace.[6] As a result, peacebuilding is not merely facilitative of domestic endeavours, but rather is directive – international peacebuilders are the dominant interventionary actors and mainly decide the nature of peace.[7] Consequently, almost all policy options supported by peacebuilders are seen as something imposed coercively without meaningful negotiations with national actors or their consent,[8] and so do not reflect any domestic impetus or consensus. Where liberal projects like democratization, rule of law or transitional justice are underway, it is clear that national elites, civil society and the media may play important roles. However, international statebuilders become the 'gravitational centre of politics' who can open up political opportunities to certain actors and close them to others, giving them a 'strong dynamizing effect' on local power constellations.[9]

A similar presumption of international omnipotence characterizes critiques of transitional justice. Much transitional justice activity arises as the result of campaigns by domestic NGOs, victim groups and reform constituencies, domestic activists and international human rights organizations. However, even the most dynamic of these tend to leverage their influence with domestic governments by allying with the transnational network of justice activists who magnify the pressure to comply with the norm of individual accountability.[10] Larger transitional justice projects like truth commissions and reparations often depend on international support, and standard formats and templates have emerged. Because the goals of the international community override local particularities, the largely legalistic repertoires for accountability that are adopted on the ground are invariably formulated and exported by the international

---

[5] Oliver Richmond and Jason Franks, *Liberal Peace Transitions: Between Statebuilding and Peacebuilding* (Edinburgh University Press 2009) 4 and 6.

[6] ibid 9.

[7] Oliver Richmond, 'Patterns of Peace' (2006) 20 *Global Society* 367, 378.

[8] Alejandro Bendaña, 'From Peacebuilding to Statebuilding: One Step Forward and Two Steps Back?' (2005) 48 *Development* 5, 6.

[9] Berit Bliesemann de Guevara, 'Introduction: The Limits of Statebuilding and the Analysis of State-Formation' (2010) 4 *Journal of Intervention and Statebuilding* 111, 115.

[10] Kathryn Sikkink, The Justice Cascade: How Human Rights Prosecutions Are Changing World Politics (W.W. Norton and Co. 2011) 1–28 and 96–125.

community.[11] The international community is seen to enjoy a neo-colonialist power to deny self-determination on justice issues[12] and a largely unfettered freedom to impose a definite vision of the society they wish to create.[13] Weak state governments limply accept the latest and best approaches for delivering justice proffered by the international community in a further echo of colonial intervention.[14] As Rubli puts it, the donors, international organizations and NGOs of the Global North 'defines and finances transitional justice projects, while the global south is supposed to absorb and implement them'.[15] The degree of justice sought and attained is essentially a function of the choices made by those tasked with formulating project policy – transitional justice is a matter of 'investments' 'allocated in some proportion between distributive development aims and a retributive rule of law', and the emphasis on the latter automatically detracts from the former.[16] To the extent that structures of inequality, discrimination and poverty endure after conflict, therefore, much of the blame is attached by critics to the unduly conservative visions of justice and peace inherent in the liberal projects of peace-building and transitional justice.

It is contended in this critical literature that transitional justice reflects a liberal-legalist worldview that precludes attention to the socio-economic roots of conflict. The liberalism of transitional justice is commonly cited as the reason for its lack of impact on socio-economic structures. In this way, much of this transitional justice critique replicates similar arguments within a larger liberal peacebuilding critique. Indeed, some argue that peacebuilding and transitional justice processes are too conjoined for any 'firewall' to be erected between them, and so the

---

[11] Chandra Lekha Sriram, 'Justice as Peace? Liberal Peacebuilding and Strategies of Transitional Justice' (2007) 21 *Global Society* 579, 589.

[12] Abdullahi Ahmed An-Na'im, 'Editorial Note: From the Neocolonial "Transitional" to Indigenous Formations of Justice' (2013) 7 *International Journal of Transitional Justice* 197, 198.

[13] Makau Mutua, 'What Is the Future of Transitional Justice?' (2015) 9 *International Journal of Transitional Justice* 1, 3.

[14] Laurel Fletcher, Harvey Weinstein and Jamie Rowen, 'Context, Timing and the Dynamics of Transitional Justice: A Historical Perspective' (2009) 31 *Human Rights Quarterly* 163, 214.

[15] Sandra Rubli, *Transitional Justice: Justice by Bureaucratic Means?* (SwissPeace 2012) 14.

[16] Topher McDougal, 'The Trilemma of Promoting Economic Justice at War's End' in Dustin Sharp (ed.), *Justice and Economic Violence in Transition* (Springer 2014) 51 at 67.

criticisms that apply to one naturally apply to the other.[17] However, the application of the liberal peacebuilding critique to transitional justice also reproduces some of the more questionable assumptions within the critique and offers little in the way of ideas as to how to transcend domestic obstacles to social change. This chapter argues that in the types of post-conflict state that this book examines, issues of politics and economic distribution remain largely controlled by domestic actors, both the state and the elites operating within it. An analysis rooted in liberal impositionism cannot fully grapple with the obstacles to structural justice. None of this is to deny the limitations of liberal projects like democracy, institution-building and the rule of law as agents of change. However, the degree to which ostensibly liberal prescriptions introduced or supported by external actors are mediated, bent or ignored by domestic actors calls into question the argument that the liberalism of peacebuilding and transitional justice outweigh incentives in the domestic political economy in restraining the prospects for structural transformation.

In contrast to the more traditional corrective or reparative approaches that characterized transitional justice (i.e. those that were delimited by past transactions or transgressions), the types of transformative transitional justice outlined in Chapter 2 require the reapportionment of specific economic and social goods and the elaboration of an appropriate theory of redistribution.[18] Transitional justice as structural justice is envisaged not only as revising or abolishing the systems that catalysed conflict, but also as implementing new systems that would prevent any such disenfranchisement in the future.[19] One would expect, therefore, that theories of transformative change would formulate approaches based on different combinations of public and private norms or legal measures (expropriation, (de)nationalization, investment, affirmative action, taxation policy) to the most fundamental questions of distribution of wealth, allocation of capital, control of production and standard of living. However, there is little coherence to the claims that transitional justice

---

[17] Kris Brown and Fionnuala Ní Aoláin, 'Through the Looking Glass: Transitional Justice Futures through the Lens of Nationalism, Feminism and Transformative Change' (2015) 9 *International Journal of Transitional Justice* 125, 137.

[18] Jeremy Webber, 'Forms of Transitional Justice' in Melissa Williams, Rosemary Nagy and Jon Elster (eds), *Transitional Justice* (New York University Press 2012) 98 at 103.

[19] Krista Thomason, 'Transitional Justice as Structural Justice' in Claudio Corradetti, Nir Eisikovits and Jack Volpe Rotondi (eds), *Theorizing Transitional Justice* (Ashgate 2015) 71 at 78.

should and can address the structural causes of conflict. Some approaches are top-down and state-centric while others are bottom-up and rooted in everyday experience. Some advocates of transformative transitional justice would prefer the field to prioritize social minima like education, nutrition, education and health for the survivor population,[20] while others stress affirmative action and land reform.[21] Some emphasize the redistribution of unjustly accumulated wealth,[22] while others contend that transitional justice should assure outcomes based on the third generation right to development.[23]

The only real coherence of vision or unity of purpose that transformative approaches to transitional justice achieve is a negative one in specifying that which they are opposed to, namely a 'liberal peace' that imports liberal justice solutions. The liberal peace thesis posits that peace is best secured by three main components: institutions, liberal democracy and securitization. These goods in and of themselves seldom succeed in tackling economic violence or poverty. Truth commissions, trials, reparations and the failures they manifest exemplify a trend towards globalization, where liberal democracy and market economics represent the most effective route to peace, to the exclusion of redistribution and equality. Transitional justice scholars argue that liberal peacebuilding's top-down imposition of external legal frameworks and institutional templates represent the 'foundational' limitations to a more transformative transitional justice.[24] While one might expect modest theories of change that would articulate how and why a transitional justice intervention could effect a specific structural reform (e.g. like land redistribution, poverty alleviation, welfare or gender discrimination) or empower specific actors to discharge these responsibilities, the general tendency

---

[20] Pablo Kalmanovitz, 'Corrective Justice versus Social Justice in the Aftermath of War' in Morten Bergsmo et al. (eds), *Distributive Justice in Transitions* (Torkel Opsahl 2010) 71 at 76–77.

[21] Kora Andrieu, 'Civilizing Peacebuilding: Transitional Justice, Civil Society and the Liberal Paradigm' (2010) 41 *Security Dialogue* 537, 544; Dustin Sharp, 'Interrogating the Peripheries: The Preoccupations of Fourth Generation Transitional Justice' (2013) 26 *Harvard Human Rights Journal* 149, 171.

[22] Paige Arthur, 'How "Transitions" Reshaped Human Rights: A Conceptual History of Transitional Justice' (2009) 31 *Human Rights Quarterly* 321, 359.

[23] Daniel Aguirre and Irene Pietropaoli, 'Gender Equality, Development and Transitional Justice: The Case of Nepal' (2008) 2 *International Journal of Transitional Justice* 356, 356.

[24] Paul Gready and Simon Robins, 'From Transitional to Transformative Justice: A New Agenda for Practice' (2014) 8 *International Journal of Transitional Justice* 339, 340.

has been to eschew templates and to instead assert a generalized need for alternatives to the field's foundational liberal paradigm.[25] Transformative justice is defined not by what it is but by what it is not, less an imaginary of structural reform or redistribution than a critical response to the field's inattention to wider systemic issues like the international political economy, poverty and the inherent conservatism of sovereignty. As noted in the Preface, a theory of change is needed because without concrete proposals for how transitional justice can achieve these aspirations, it is difficult to engage critically with, or build upon, the transformative turn as an intellectual endeavour. This problem is returned to in the final section of this chapter. In more general terms, defining transformative transitional justice in terms of what it is not is problematic because international ideational factors are not the only obstacle to fundamentally reforming domestic structures underpinning inequality. Any fundamental transformation of access to economic resources to favour redistribution or the use of the state for securing social minima in the post-transition phase will inevitably create winners among hitherto marginalized communities, but also potentially create losers among those personal or group interests who previously benefited from the status quo. As Chapter 3 suggested, many of these actors will enjoy power within the society and the means to resist, to say nothing of the diminished functionality of the state in the immediate post-conflict years when it is weak and its authority is contested.

At the root of the transformative critique of transitional justice is the notion that the concepts justice agents apply matter more than, or possess an inherent potency to overcome, the post-conflict context in which they apply. One obvious problem with such an approach is that it takes some or all of the elements of a reconfigured social economy as the model for successful transition, instead of reflecting on the vagaries of the transition, the limitations of the state or the impact of deep divisions between communities. The aspirations for transitional justice examined in Chapter 2 presume that transformative outcomes can be produced, legitimized and stabilized as matters of intention and design, and that transitional justice can catalyse desired economic dynamics and outcomes. However, there is good reason to believe that unless these aspirations stand in some way in relation to the interests of politically effective groups like conflict principals and societal elements who formally or informally contest

---

[25] See, for example, Simon Robins, 'Mapping a Future for Transitional Justice by Learning from its Past' (2015) 9 *International Journal of Transitional Justice* 181, 189.

control of the economy with the state, it is unlikely that transitional justice actors can co-ordinate sufficient political power to secure these outcomes.[26] For reasons largely related to the legacy of conflict and domestic political economy outlined in the previous chapter, the dominant norm in building peace is inclusion of elite military and political groups instead of justice for all, inevitably constraining options for transformation.

The bargaining over transitional governance arrangements that serve as the departure point for all post-conflict policy choices will reflect political institutions and economic allocations inherited from the past.[27] In subsequent conditions of peacebuilding and transitional justice, neither good intentions nor overwhelming popular support for reforms can displace these inherited circumstances unless war has done so already. Even if the normative emphasis of transitional justice changes to embrace socio-economic transformation, for domestic and international actors tasked with securing transformative transitional justice the relationship between these revised norms and actual results on the ground is far more mediated and compromised than critical scholars are willing to admit. It is something of a commonplace amongst reflective peacebuilders that policies can only be effective if they can discern from the post-conflict ecology how proposed measures might provoke spoilers or bolster rejectionists, on the one hand, or exceed the bureaucratic capability of the polity, on the other. The preoccupation of the transitional justice critique with the interests and mores of external interveners largely disregards any such contemplation. As this chapter goes on to argue, the ostensibly liberal priorities of peacebuilders are in fact predominantly shaped and then distorted by domestic political economy factors. There is little reason to believe that a re-orientation of these priorities towards socio-economic justice and structural transformation would not similarly be distorted. Transformative transitional justice must proceed from a penetrating assessment of the core opportunities and restraints that define the political life of the state in question and how justice interventions can capitalize on or alter these syndromes.

This chapter is not a defence of liberal peacebuilding. It accepts the well-established limits of legalism outlined by the critical transitional

---

[26] Nehal Bhuta, 'New Modes and Orders: The Difficulties of a *Jus Post Bellum* of Constitutional Transformation' (2010) 60 *University of Toronto Law Journal* 799, 843.

[27] Charles Call, *Why Peace Fails: The Causes and Prevention of Civil War Recurrence* (Georgetown University Press 2012) 247.

justice literature. It also accepts that democratic competition, institution-building and rule of law seldom resolve the root causes of conflict, and that economic liberalism may exacerbate them. The chapter does, however, examine how the influence of interveners is mediated by domestic factors of political economy in conditioning the opportunities for justice. Section 1 examines the role of transitional justice within liberal peacebuilding and the emerging argument that critiques of peacebuilding apply automatically to transitional justice. Section 2 examines the parallels and interaction between the liberal peacebuilding critique and transitional justice. Critics of transitional justice have both drawn on the liberal peacebuilding critique and independently arrived at conclusions that reveal the hegemonic, technicist, inherently conservative impulses behind intervention that maintain unjust economic conditions. Section 3 looks at the reality of peacebuilding and transitional justice on the ground, arguing that the critiques they are subject to radically overstate both the degree of influence international interveners have in post-conflict states and the liberalism of the post-conflict dispensation. It contends that the ultimate allocation of power and resources is largely determined endogenously, with attendant consequences for transformative prospects. Section 4 looks at some of the obvious domestic factors that would mediate between a revised approach to transitional justice and actual transformation, most obviously the administrative weakness of state institutions, the endurance of patrimonialism and the heightened influence of elites with support bases to satisfy in the aftermath of civil war. Section 5 argues that critiques of liberal intervention that engage only with the ontology, epistemology and prescriptions of interventionary actors are unsuited to the fundamentally reactive, highly bargained nature of transitional justice. Approaches that ignore the domestic impediments to transformation will struggle to develop policy-relevance not only in relation to peacebuilding projects overall, but also to many transitional justice projects on the ground.

1. TRANSITIONAL JUSTICE AND LIBERAL PEACEBUILDING

Peacebuilding by the United Nations and other international actors in post-conflict states is usually labelled 'liberal peacebuilding' because it is generally conducted by Western states and because its core tenet is that the surest foundation for peace, both within and between states, is a liberal democratic polity premised on functional state institutions and security. Post-conflict peacebuilding emphasizes security, rule of law, legitimate political processes and conflict management capacity, basic services and restoration of core government functionality.[28] It limits itself in terms of its economic remit to supporting employment generation and rehabilitation of basic infrastructure.[29] This is important because it helps us distinguish between the narrow concept of *liberal peacebuilding*, a reaction by the international community to a conflict within a certain state, from the broader concept of the *liberal peace* which refers to the more proactive and permanent process of intervention by the international community in the Global South, 'a universalizing modality in the wider architecture of a globally expansive liberal order'.[30] This broader liberal peace, most obviously evident in the securitization of the Global War on Terror and economic frameworks of international financial institutions (IFIs), has a deleterious impact on socio-economic conditions in post-conflict states. However, most critics of liberal peacebuilding disaggregate peacebuilding from the much wider liberal peace, both to allow critical distinctions between different forms of external intervention (after all, peacebuilding policies of democracy, stabilization, rule of law are often dramatically at odds with economic liberalization)[31] and because none of the core elements of peacebuilding like statebuilding, rule of law, human rights and power-sharing are solely a product of the economic dimensions of liberal ideology.[32] This distinction between the liberal peacebuilding and the liberal peace has been accepted in the transitional justice literature, and it is adopted here.[33]

Since at least the late 1990s, critics have assailed the liberal peacebuilding model on account of its origins, biases, contradictions and, above all, its empirical record. Depending on how and when war and recurrence are codified, anything from a quarter to a half of intrastate

---

[28] United Nations, 'UN Peacebuilding: An Orientation' (2010) 12 <http://www.un.org/en/peacebuilding/pbso/pdf/peacebuilding_orientation.pdf> accessed 21 July 2016.

[29] ibid.

[30] Suthaharan Nadarajah and David Rampton, 'The Limits of Hybridity and the Crisis of Liberal Peace' (2015) 41 *Review of International Studies* 49, 49.

[31] See for example Alvaro de Soto and Graciana del Castillo, 'Obstacles to Peace Building' (1994) 94 *Foreign Policy* 69, 74.

[32] Susan Woodward, 'The IFIs and Post-Conflict Political Economy' in Mats Berdal and Dominik Zaum (eds), *Political Economy of Statebuilding: Power after Peace* (Routledge 2013) 140 at 148.

[33] For example, Sriram (n 11) argues that transitional justice is complicit in the iniquities that flow from peacebuilding's emphasis on democratization but not those related to marketization strategies (at 580).

peace settlements collapse in the following five to ten years.[34] Liberal peacebuilding may contain conflict, but it rarely transforms it. It fails on its own terms to guarantee security, human rights, democracy and the rule of law. At various places and times missions have been accompanied by, or left a legacy of, increased crime and social unrest, corruption, distorted democratic practices, economic disarray and gender disparities. Post-conflict governments face challenges of legitimacy, competence and development. Poverty remains a feature of post-conflict societies even after significant international intervention. Socio-economic inequality is known to undermine the peace dividend by weakening, and sometimes rendering redundant, improvements in human rights, democracy and rule of law. As Belloni argues, '[i]t has become commonplace to state that liberal peacebuilding in war-torn states has, by and large, failed'.[35] Critics are sceptical as to whether statebuilding and liberal democratic structures with values and rationality embedded in Western culture can achieve sustainable peace in the aftermath of conflict. Many argue these supposed solutions may in fact catalyse a return to conflict instead. Modern peacebuilding's emphasis on stability, maintenance of elite pacts and construction of institutions tends toward conservatism, indicating a narrowing of aspirations from transforming unjust societies to merely regulating, managing or securitizing them.[36]

That transitional justice is a core element of peacebuilding is an article of faith among both advocates and critics of transitional justice. Since its earliest days, transitional justice has been associated with the construction of identity politics in nation-building in conflicted states.[37] Sriram was among the first to identify the inextricable links between transitional justice and liberal peacebuilding, arguing that it risked replicating the latter's agenda of unsuitable, destabilizing programmes and its tendency to respond to manifestations of conflict rather than its structural causes.[38] Andrieu argues that transitional justice is an 'essential' and 'extensive'

---

34 See, for example, Astri Suhrke and Ingrid Samset, 'What's in a Figure? Estimating Recurrence of Civil War' (2007) 14 *International Peacekeeping* 195, citing around 23 per cent.

35 Roberto Belloni, 'Hybrid Peace Governance: Its Emergence and Significance' (2012) 18 *Global Governance* 21, 21.

36 David Chandler, *International Statebuilding: The Rise of Post-Liberal Governance* (Routledge 2010) 32.

37 Ruti Teitel, 'Transitional Justice in a New Era' (2002) 26 *Fordham International Law Journal* 893, 901–905.

38 Sriram (n 11).

part of the liberal peacebuilding package,[39] while Dancy agrees that it lies at the 'strategic forefront' of peace operations.[40] In its most active form, transitional justice is so intimately involved in rule-of-law reconstruction, security-sector reform and demobilization that it may become indistinguishable from peacebuilding as a whole.[41] The field is perceived to 'dominate debates on the intersection between democratization, human rights protections and state reconstruction after conflict'.[42] The assumption that transitional justice forms part of peacebuilding is intuitively satisfying. Both stem from the compulsion Western governments and international institutions feel to 'do something' in the face of conflict by transposing measures from one country to another. Both appear to construct the relevant problems and the solutions thereto in similar ways. Liberal peacebuilding's promotion of democracy, rule of law and human rights and transitional justice's legalized understandings of harm are derived from Western liberalism's affinity for individual rights, choice and personal autonomy. Each field can be said to be oriented more towards civil and political rights than economic, social or cultural rights.

Transitional justice, no less than peacebuilding, represents the increasingly internationally accepted practice of solving problems though institutional and legal settings. Both peacebuilding and transitional justice emphasize state-driven, top-down, national-level initiatives. Transitional justice is oriented more towards strengthening or legitimizing the state peacebuilders attempt to reconstruct rather than towards challenging it.[43] Indeed, both transitional justice and liberal peacebuilding appear to enjoy a symbiotic relationship. Liberal peacebuilding not only delimits the scope of transitional justice in defining democracy as a certain state of

---

[39] Andrieu (n 21) 537, 538 and 541.

[40] Geoff Dancy, 'Choice and Consequence in Strategies of Transitional Justice' in Christopher Coyne and Rachel Mathers (eds), *The Handbook on the Political Economy of War* (Edward Elgar 2012) 397 at 397.

[41] Sriram (n 11) 584.

[42] Kieran McEvoy, 'Letting Go of Legalism: Developing a "Thicker" Version of Transitional Justice' in Kieran McEvoy and Lorna McGregor (eds), *Transitional Justice from Below: Grassroots Activism and the Struggle for Change* (Hart Publishing 2008) 15 at 15.

[43] Jennifer Balint, Julie Evans and Nesam McMillan, 'Rethinking Transitional Justice, Redressing Indigenous Harm: A New Conceptual Approach' (2014) 8 *International Journal of Transitional Justice* 194, 201.

social relationships in the political sphere, it also legitimizes it as such.[44] In return, transitional justice, accountability and human rights compliance form core elements of the recognition legitimacy of reconstructed post-conflict states.[45] In so doing, transitional justice initiatives are said to 'uncritically endorse' liberal peacebuilding.[46] It is because of these organizational complementarities and similarities that transitional justice is argued to automatically be subject to 'some of the same flaws and critiques' of the peacebuilding agenda within which it is subsumed.[47] The critique of liberal peacebuilding is argued to 'parallel' that of transitional justice – one in which Western liberal democracy, consisting of institutional guarantees of civil and political rights, dominates the conceptualization of possible change, and marginalizes concerns for economic violence and social justice.[48] Key works in the critical peacebuilding literature are routinely cited in the transformative transitional justice literature.[49]

This influence is significant because the more established and fully elaborated critique of peacebuilding is extremely potent. There are two main schools of peacebuilding critique, described variously as the critique *from* liberalism versus the critique *of* liberalism[50] or the policy-oriented ideas-based critique versus the radical power-based

---

[44] Hannah Franzki and Maria Carolina Olarte, 'Understanding the Political Economy of Transitional Justice: A Critical Theory Perspective' in Susanne Buckley-Zistel et al., *Transitional Justice Theories* (Routledge 2013) 201 at 204–7.

[45] Catherine Turner, 'Delivering Lasting Peace, Democracy and Human Rights in Times of Transition: The Role of International Law' (2008) 1 *International Journal of Transitional Justice* 126.

[46] Rubli (n 15) 16.

[47] Sriram (n 11) 586; Laura Davis, 'Power Shared and Justice Shelved: The Democratic Republic of Congo' (2013) 17 *International Journal of Human Rights* 289, 289.

[48] Dustin Sharp, 'Introduction: Addressing Economic Violence in Times of Transition' in Sharp (ed.) (n 16) 1 at 25.

[49] For example, Bell cites Mac Ginty (Christine Bell, 'Of Jus Post Bellum and Lex Pacificatoria: What's in a Name?' in Carsten Stahn, Jennifer Easterday and Jens Iverson (eds), *Jus Post Bellum: Mapping the Normative Foundations* (Oxford University Press 2014) 181 at 203); Gready and Robins (n 24) cite Richmond, Roberts and Mac Ginty (at 351); Sharp cites Mac Ginty and Richmond in 'Addressing Dilemmas of the Global and the Local in Transitional Justice' (2013) 29 *Emory International Law Review* 71, 84.

[50] Oliver Richmond and Audra Mitchell, 'Introduction: Towards a Post-Liberal Peace: Exploring Hybridity via Everyday Forms of Resistance, Agency

critique.[51] The fundamental, power-based critiques *of* liberal peacebuilding are sceptical of interventions and view the liberal peace discourse of free politics, free markets and free bodies as a veil behind which Western self-interest is obfuscated and exploitative global structures are legitimated. Liberal peacebuilding is seen to respond more to the needs of the Global North than those of conflicted states. The more policy-oriented, moderate, 'problem-solving' critiques *from* liberalism are less concerned with the possibility of hegemony or exploitation through unequal global power relations. They instead accept the legitimacy of liberal values and of intervention, but argue that liberal approaches need to be tempered or delayed on the basis that the prescriptive rationality underlying liberal peacebuilding is unsuitable to post-conflict and developing world ecologies.[52] Critiques *from* liberalism judge peacebuilding interventions for their failure to either live up to their own aspirations and norms or their failure to inculcate them domestically. Critiques *of* liberalism, by contrast, see these goals as 'ethically bankrupt, subject to double standards, coercive and conditional, acultural, unconcerned with social welfare, and unfeeling and insensitive towards its subjects'.[53] Problem-solvers deal with particular sources of trouble in a particular post-conflict state. They attempt to remedy the faults of peacebuilding generally through technical improvement to policies on the ground, but do not question the implicit value of liberalism, and so maintain an inherently conservative status quo. Radical critics, by contrast, resist the exploitative and hegemonic power of international interveners. They deny that peace can or should be achieved through liberal intervention and instead wish to fundamentally address structural issues.[54] They argue that the tendency of problem-solvers to 'work with what we've got' represents a missed opportunity 'to interrogate the order itself and, by accepting it as "reality" re-enforces its underlying values and structures'.[55] Fundamental critics of the liberal peace envision a more emancipatory peace project premised on culturally

---

and Autonomy' in Oliver Richmond and Audra Mitchell (eds), *Hybrid Forms of Peace* (Palgrave Macmillan 2011) 1 at 5.

[51] Chandler (n 36) 24.

[52] A prime example being Roland Paris, *At War's End: Building Peace After Civil Conflict* (Cambridge University Press 2004).

[53] Oliver Richmond, 'A Post-Liberal Peace: Eirinism and the Everyday' (2009) 35 *Review of International Studies* 557, 558.

[54] See for example Oliver Richmond, 'Peace During and After the Age of Intervention' (2014) 21 *International Peacekeeping* 509, 515.

[55] Michael Pugh, 'The Political Economy of Peacebuilding: A Critical Theory Perspective' in Alex Bellamy and Paul Williams (eds), *Peace Operations and Global Order* (Routledge 2005) 39 at 41.

adaptive provision of human security, everyday welfare and socio-economic rights that go beyond ambitions for security, rule of law and civil-political rights. This critique is so sustained and successful in terms of the scholarly discourse that it is by now credible to argue that it has become the new mainstream.[56]

The first two decades of transitional justice scholarship were characterized by critiques *from* liberalism, most evident in the debates about retroactivity, selectivity and justice versus peace. Today, the fundamental/radical critique *of* liberalism has the most discernible parallels in transitional justice scholarship. This critique is echoed in the general trend of criticism of traditional transitional justice for its liberal conservatism sketched in Chapter 1. Similarly, the emancipatory post-liberal visions of peace premised on empathy, care, social contracting and redistribution articulated within the critique bear affinities with the transformative aspirations for transitional justice examined in Chapter 2. Just over a decade ago, it was credible to argue that transitional justice was 'insulated from critical legal studies, post-colonial studies, and other efforts to problematize the emancipatory potential of transitional justice institutions and the monopoly that human rights discourse has claimed over struggles'.[57] This can no longer seriously be argued. Nowadays, there is a sustained and self-consciously radical rejection of some of the dominant paradigms in transitional justice (as distinct from mere criticism of certain dimensions of its operation) that takes its cue from the liberal peacebuilding critique it is seen to automatically replicate. This scholarship aims at destabilizing traditional conceptions of transitional justice and challenging its existing *modi operandi*. It reveals concealed interests, ideological limitations and repetition of historical patterns of class domination obscured by its rhetoric. It is sensitive to the inclusions and exclusions, oppression and suppression transitional justice might entail. In a negative sense, many of these critiques 'share the idea that transitional justice is in some sense dangerous or duplicitous in claiming to be a distinct brand of justice that responds to a distinct set of dilemmas. Many strands of such critical thought suggest that this

---

[56] Shahar Hameiri, 'A Reality Check for the Critique of the Liberal Peace' in Campbell, Chandler and Sabaratnam (eds) (n 2) 191 at 192.

[57] Vasuki Nesiah, 'Discussion Lines on Gender and Transitional Justice: An Introductory Essay Reflecting on the ICTJ Bellagio Workshop on Gender and Transitional Justice' (2006) 15 *Columbia Journal of Gender and Law* 799, 801.

duplicity enables evil in the guise of "doing good".'[58] More positively, the critique of transitional justice also aspires to ensure more broadly defined definitions of justice-based society. It is worthwhile, therefore, to consider how the liberal peacebuilding critique has informed and/or reflects that of transitional justice since the first iterations of the critique.

2. THE PARALLEL CRITIQUES

Critical peace studies can be said to have ripened into a semi-coherent tradition comprising a number of fundamental premises – that liberal peacebuilding is (1) an exercise in globalized hegemonic discipline that (2) is unhelpfully technical, (3) creates inherently conservative shell-states, (4) disregards the local and the everyday conceptions of peace and justice and (5) is market-driven and hence tolerant of economic injustice. These complaints find strong echoes and complementarities in recent critiques of transitional justice's inherent liberal-legalism. Taken together, they are assumed to explain why transitional justice and peacebuilding fail to address issues like employment, future prosperity, public safety, clean water, housing, education and healthcare that field-based analysis and surveys of survivor populations suggest are the most essential forms of justice.

2.1 Exercises in Hegemonic Discipline

The critical peacebuilding school interrogates the relationship between liberal peacebuilding and global governance in the post-Cold War era of globalization. Post-structuralist, Foucault-inspired scholars argue that something more subtle than imperialist control of subordinate populations transpires in peacebuilding. They argue that a new, biopolitical hegemony is at work which curbs the self-determination of intervened-upon societies but disavows the open exercise of power and abjures any responsibility for its actions. While interventions target domestic or local structures, the primary interest underlying intercession is the international or regional order which is secured by producing domestic order on its periphery. It is argued that contemporary globalization attempts to cultivate a unified, worldwide economic and political structure by enabling reconstructed sovereign states to have a role as the managers and mediators of

---

[58] Christine Bell, 'Transitional Justice, Interdisciplinarity and the State of the "Field" or "Non-Field"' (2009) 3 *International Journal of Transitional Justice* 5, 12–13.

globalization on the domestic political economy.[59] Indeed, globalization is impossible without the state's liminal role in easing and regulating tensions between the overarching global system and their own potentially restive or resistant populations. To the extent that sovereignty, the territorial state and good governance form part of a worldwide project of international order, peacebuilding naturalizes that order and all the North-South inequalities it fosters. For critics of peacebuilding, its aim is 'to subvert radical challenges to the global and national distribution of power and resources and to stabilize the system' through discursive and material means.[60] Modern peacebuilding is premised on the stabilization of conflicted countries. In so doing, it attempts to secure compliant states from the sorts of instability that would create fall-out for the international community like mass-movements of refugees, organized crime using said states as locations for transit and supply, and use by terrorist groups of these areas for recruitment and training, to say nothing of the disruption of markets.[61] Much-trumpeted deference to local ownership owes less to any genuine desire for national autonomy on the part of peacebuilders than a desire to have domestic stakeholders take responsibility before their own populations for the policy prescriptions that interveners export.[62]

These critiques are replicated in transitional justice, which has always been understood with reference to international power politics and normative change as a global project.[63] Since its earliest days, transitional justice has been associated with an 'end of history' liberal teleology where the end of right–left ideological conflict paved the way for the universalized, post-political discourse of human rights and international justice.[64] Some critics of transitional justice interrogate the hegemonic impulse. For Orford and Sharp, for example, transitional justice and the

---

59 Christopher Clapham, 'The Challenge to the State in a Globalized World' (2002) 33 *Development and Change* 775, 775.

60 Devon Curtis, 'The Contested Politics of Peacebuilding in Africa' in Devon Curtis and Gwinyayi Dzinesa (eds), *Peacebuilding, Power and Politics in Africa* (Ohio University Press 2012) 1 at 13.

61 Neclâ Tschirgi, *Post-conflict Peacebuilding Revisited: Achievements, Limitations, Challenges* (International Peace Academy 2004) ii.

62 Caroline Hughes and Vanessa Pupavac, 'Framing Post-conflict Societies: International Pathologisation of Cambodia and the Post-Yugoslav States' (2005) 26 *Third World Quarterly* 873, 883.

63 Rosemary Nagy, 'Transitional Justice as a Global Project: Critical Reflections' (2008) 29 *Third World Quarterly* 275, 276.

64 Catherine Turner, 'Deconstructing Transitional Justice' (2013) 24 *Law and Critique* 193, 198.

judicialization of politics is a means by which liberal values are transmitted globally from core to periphery and states are produced as reliable subjects in the course of enforcing the new world order.[65] The assumption is that transitional justice adopts institutions to address external security and economic agendas as opposed to local needs.[66]

Others critique transitional justice through an explicitly imperialist lens. Hinton warns that in the context of unequal power relations between international actors and the local state, transitional justice may import a barely concealed neo-imperialism that produces certain forms of knowledge, persons and practices (democracy, free markets, due process).[67] In Africa, in particular, many see transitional justice as a neo-colonial instrument that undermines sovereignty and the domestic ability to resolve governance issues, particularly those of war and peace. A further iteration of the imperialist argument is the concern expressed at the way in which policy-makers in international organizations and governments employ its discourse to legitimate interventions in supposedly rogue or failed states.[68] Overall, transitional justice does little to critique the globally dominant practices it is enmeshed in (though the emerging critique acts as a partial refutation of this) and reinforces existing hierarchies of power.

2.2 De-politicizing Technocratic Approaches

The core goods associated with liberal peacebuilding such as human rights, rule of law, civic association and market rationality are seen by many as being produced by a universalized post-Enlightenment liberal view of the autonomous individual that applies to all mankind. These goods are best secured within the institutional framework of the liberal

---

[65] Dustin Sharp, 'Emancipating Transitional Justice from the Bonds of the Paradigmatic Transition' (2015) *International Journal of Transitional Justice* 150, 162; Anne Orford, 'Commissioning the Truth' (2006) 15 *Columbia Journal of Gender and Law* 851, 852.

[66] Gready and Robins (n 24) 345.

[67] Alexander Laban Hinton, 'Introduction: Toward an Anthropology of Transitional Justice' in Alexander Laban Hinton (ed.), *Transitional Justice: Global Mechanisms and Local Realities after Genocide and Mass Violence* (Rutgers University Press 2010) 1 at 7.

[68] Christine Bell, Colm Campbell and Fionnuala Ní Aoláin, 'The Battle for Transitional Justice: Hegemony, Iraq and International Law' in Kieran McEvoy, John Morrison and Gordon Anthony (eds), *Judges, Transition and Human Rights Cultures: Essays in Honour of Stephen Livingstone* (Oxford University Press 2007) 147.

state under a modern constitution, elections contested by political parties and a bureaucratic apparatus of state to guarantee governance (the civil service), justice (transitional justice and rule of law institutions) and security (police and army). Intervention policy is therefore oriented towards these ends. Because these principles and institutions are presented as universal, they are assumed to be of automatic utility in any post-conflict ecology. Peacebuilding is therefore seen as something essentially mechanical that can be applied irrespective of the idiosyncrasies of a given state. The utilitarian efficiency approach of peacebuilders 'assumes a rational, cost-benefit formula, in which inputs (financial resources, institutional reforms, "sound" policies, troops, donor pledges, international commitment, technical assistance, etc.) are made and from which normative outputs (peace, development, progress, etc) are supposed to emerge'.[69] Divisive and deep-rooted areas of social and political dysfunction are treated as resolvable by largely unproblematic fixes like good governance and other institutional reform programmes readily falling within the expertise of external humanitarian action. Technocratic capacity-building and good governance programmes are naturalized as being non-ideological and beyond politics, disavowing messy involvement in civic controversies and ignoring poverty and structural inequality within society. As such, they can be said to 'depoliticise peace for the sake of managerial rationality',[70] falsely representing contentious questions of allocation of resources as merely problems of rule and control that revolve around state weakness.[71]

This technocratic critique has the most synchronicity between radical critiques of peacebuilding and transitional justice. Transitional justice is presented as the product of a universalizing, expansionary human rights discourse that has fully imbibed the assumption in liberal democratic theory that its institutional order is both natural and neutral.[72] This mindset is manifested in narrow juridical approaches in which the right transitional justice institutions and processes are exported by fiat.

---

[69] Shahrbanou Tadjbakhsh and Oliver Richmond, 'Conclusion: Typologies and Modifications Proposed by Critical Approaches' in Shahrbanou Tadjbakhsh (ed.), *Rethinking the Liberal Peace: External Models and Local Alternatives* (Routledge 2011) 221 at 224.

[70] Laurent Goetschel and Tobias Hagmann, 'Civilian Peacebuilding: Peace by Bureaucratic Means? Analysis' (2009) 9 *Conflict, Security and Development* 55, 56.

[71] Mats Berdal and Dominik Zaum, 'Power After Peace' in Berdal and Zaum (eds) (n 32) 1 at 11.

[72] Franzki and Olarte (n 44) 203.

A one-size-fits-all, apolitical toolkit of trials, truth, lustration and reparations is applied regardless of context to generate outcomes like reconciliation, truth and rehabilitation.[73] The ritual privileging of pre-defined ideas and mechanisms means that transitional justice 'has shrouded itself in a discourse of technical legalism that threatens to obfuscate the underlying politics' of its interventions'.[74] More worryingly, these legal-institutional frameworks do not permit deep engagement with structural injustices or the types of intervention required to address them. As Nesiah puts it:

> In sum, the technical assistance approach to transitional justice encourages de-politicized and de-contextualized engagements. It defines expertise as professionalized and internationally mobile knowledge rather than knowledge that is situated in activist commitments and knowledge of local context; it favours models that are already legible to the field and its 'best practices', rather than innovations that may extend or challenge the field as we know it.[75]

Indeed, to the extent that transitional justice shares the same teleological impulses towards a peaceful democratic future, it depoliticizes debate over social structures by assuming all fundamental dilemmas are either resolved by the sheer fact of liberalizing transition or resolvable soon within the new democratic dispensation.[76] The impetus of transitional justice towards catalysing or affirming political-institutional change makes socio-economic justice 'irrelevant' in terms of the democratic legitimation of the new regime.[77]

2.3 The Conservative Shell-state

Peacebuilders attempt to reconstruct securitized Westphalian frameworks of the sovereign state that can respect boundaries, maintain physical security and implement a peace agreement. However, critics argue that what ultimately transpires is a 'shell' of the liberal state achieving only a 'virtual peace', a superficial overlay of liberal governance directed

---

[73] Rubli (n 15) 10.

[74] Sharp (n 21) 150.

[75] Vasuki Nesiah, *Transitional Justice Practice: Looking Back, Moving Forward* (Impunity Watch 2016) 34.

[76] Rolando Ames Cobián and Felix Reátegui, 'Toward Systemic Social Transformation: Truth Commissions and Development' in Pablo de Greiff and Roger Duthie (eds), *Transitional Justice and Development: Making Connections* (New York 2009) 142 at 155.

[77] Franzki and Olarte (n 44) 203.

externally by interveners and from the top-down by elites above indigenous culture and tradition.[78] The technical project of statebuilding is abstracted from state-society relations, meaning that these institutions of state are disconnected from the everyday needs of the population. As a result, they cannot bridge the gap between the legal state and the sociological nation, undermining any prospect of fostering the sense of legitimacy that lies at the heart of the social contract between them.[79] Critics see good governance models as replacing more turbulent and potentially redistributive politics of self-representation organized along lines of capitalist class division.[80] In a shell-state where leaders are willing to settle for such limited aims, there is a natural tendency to fall back on conservative peace-as-order models of peacebuilding that simply regulate conflict through security, institutions and existing hierarchies, as opposed to social justice, community and everyday life.[81] There is a natural tendency in such a system to rely on elites (invariably portrayed as conservative or oligarchical) to guarantee security to the exclusion of the many.[82] As Darby and Mac Ginty conclude, peacebuilding

> often reinforces power-holders and replicates exclusive patterns of social and political relations … in many peace processes, participants have been unwilling or unable to challenge prevailing patterns of social and political organisation. Although violence ends, patterns of land ownership, patriarchy, and political participation remain unchanged. As a result, the 'peace' is essentially conservative rather than transformative.[83]

Fourth generation critics of transitional justice institutions ('conservative instruments deployed to manage transitions and contain change')[84] have replicated this suspicion of state reconstruction and the reliance on existing power-holders. An early critique of the field assailed its tendency to see the state and state-like institutions as the only practical and metaphorical mechanism by which goals could be rendered 'legible',

---

[78] Richmond (n 53) 564.

[79] Béatrice Pouligny, 'Civil Society and Post-Conflict Peacebuilding: Ambiguities of International Programmes Aimed at Building "New" Societies' (2005) 36 *Security Dialogue* 495, 505.

[80] Hameiri (n 56) 199.

[81] Richmond (n 53) 562.

[82] Belloni (n 35) 31.

[83] John Darby and Roger Mac Ginty, 'Introduction: What Peace? What Process?' in John Darby and Roger Mac Ginty (eds), *Contemporary Peacemaking: Conflict, Violence and Peace Processes* (Palgrave Macmillan 2003) 1 at 6.

[84] Nesiah (n 75) 11.

blinding actors to the role of other non-state agents and forms of knowledge to deliver effective change.[85] This was compounded by the tendency of transitional justice as a form of statebuilding to maintain existing normative and political hierarchies at the national level over the interests of the many. The origins of the field were situated in choices by elite groups and in legal-institutional reform at the expense of inquiry into social conditions and grassroots processes.[86] Therefore, critics regard discourses of transitional justice as empowering elites at the expense of the most disempowered in society, and as diverting attention from the beneficiaries of the existing social system.[87] Muvingi argues that the traditional concern for security that transitional justice shares with peacebuilding has marginalized questions of socio-economic development.[88] In terms of the field's legal-institutional emphasis, the stress on criminal law and incremental reform could only ever offer conservative conceptions of transition when more radical economic change is needed.[89]

2.4 Excluding the Local

As noted earlier, critical approaches problematize dominant frameworks and seek alternatives to them. In the peacebuilding critique, the most commonly proposed alternative frameworks are local, customary and everyday forms of peace, which are assumed to enjoy significant peacebuilding and emancipatory potency by resisting violence and transforming localities.[90] The field of critical peace studies is explicitly premised on the disavowal of elite politics or deal-making or collusion with international actors in favour of expanded decision-making by a genuinely indigenous civil society or the population as a whole.[91] In this

---

[85] Kieran McEvoy, 'Beyond Legalism: Towards a Thicker Understanding of Transitional Justice' (2007) 34 *Journal of Law and Society* 411, 422.

[86] Arthur (n 22) 347.

[87] Gready and Robins (n 24) 343; Aguirre and Pietropaoli (n 23) 367.

[88] Ismael Muvingi, 'Sitting on Powder Kegs: Socio-Economic Rights in Transitional Societies' (2009) 3 *International Journal of Transitional Justice* 163, 167.

[89] Reem Abou-El-Fadl, 'Beyond Conventional Transitional Justice: Egypt's 2011 Revolution and the Absence of Political Will' (2012) 6 *International Journal of Transitional Justice* 318, 320.

[90] A.B. Fetherston, 'Peacekeeping, Conflict Resolution and Peacebuilding: A Reconsideration of Theoretical Frameworks' (2000) 7 *International Peacekeeping* 190, 195 and 201.

[91] Call (n 27) 44 and 224.

view, human needs and potentialities should be determined at the level of communities and individuals, as opposed to the national level.[92] The most consistent iteration of this theme is the comparison of top-down, externally led peacebuilding with bottom-up efforts by civil society, indigenous groups and local populations. Top-down peacebuilding organized around state functionality and mass democracy tends to privilege the needs and interests of international actors and state elites over those of families, religious groups, regional or cultural collectivities or locally associative life. This is troubling because it fails to truly end the conflict (because ostensibly national or regional wars have local roots, only by addressing local issues can violence be ended) and undermines the quality of the emergent peace. The problem is not merely that liberal peacebuilders ignore vital local concerns about welfare, identity and culture, but rather that they exclude or obstruct the emergence of alternative local, everyday and customary agendas for peace.[93] Democratization erodes the space for locally defined political processes, while other forms of liberalization disrupt traditional ways of life.[94]

These positions have been echoed in the critical transitional justice literature. The top-down, high politics, off-the-shelf approach that characterized transitional justice historically seems to preclude reconstruction of social relations and inclusive, intersubjective local dialogues that would allow for the construction of common understandings of peace and mutual existence within local communities.[95] Formalist methods usually preferred by transitional justice policy-makers exclude more legitimate, participatory and effective indigenous approaches that respect the constructive agency of those most affected.[96] By contrast, some models of transformative justice proposed in the literature are presented as context-specific and driven by localized agency and understandings, as opposed

---

[92] Richmond and Mitchell (n 50) 20.

[93] Edward Newman, 'A Human Security Peace-Building Agenda' (2011) 32 *Third World Quarterly* 1737, 1741.

[94] Kristoffer Lidén, 'Building Peace between Global and Local Politics: The Cosmopolitical Ethics of Liberal Peacebuilding' (2009) 16 *International Peacekeeping* 616, 619.

[95] Andrieu (n 21) 537.

[96] Mark Drumbl, 'Collective Violence and Individual Punishment: The Criminality of Mass Atrocity' (2005) 99 *Northwestern University Law Review* 539, 597.

to traditional, purely normative approaches that lack evidence bases.[97] The issue of excluding the local will be considered specifically in Chapter 5.

2.5 The Allowance of Economic Injustice

One of the main criticisms of peacebuilding is that it does little to address discriminatory economic structures. As noted earlier, peacebuilding missions limit their economic activities to supporting employment generation and rehabilitation of basic infrastructure. Though economic liberalization comes to post-conflict states independently of democratization or state-building (indeed, it often precedes conflict and is often a root cause of it), peacebuilding does nothing to challenge fundamentally unfair global economic structures and may even normalize and legitimize them. In the critical peacebuilding literature, institutional governance reform and state-building are seen as core aspects of the globalization of capital,[98] while a liberal market is seen as inextricably bound with democratization:

> In recent years there has been a tendency to associate economic liberalisation – the primary concern of neoliberal capacity building efforts – with democracy, either because it is viewed as the best shell for capitalist development or due to the assumed inherently pacific nature of democracy and free markets – the so-called 'liberal peace' thesis.[99]

The core fundamentals of neo-liberal policy do not facilitate the development and repair of conflict root causes that would underpin a genuine peace. The poor and the marginalized do not prosper from a dogma that promotes a shrunken state, constrained public spending, and self-reliance that leaves their core needs to the mercy of the markets.[100] However, the social contract that emerges from governance reform and democratization accrues legitimacy by emphasizing civil and political rights that serves to

---

[97] Gready and Robins (n 24) 344.

[98] David Roberts, 'Hybrid Polities and Post-Conflict Policy' in David Chandler and Timothy Sisk (eds), *The Routledge Handbook of International Statebuilding* (Routledge 2013) 94 at 94.

[99] Shahar Hameiri, *Regulating Statehood: State Building and the Transformation of the Global Order* (Palgrave Macmillan 2010) 15.

[100] Michael Pugh, 'Towards Life Welfare' in Edward Newman, Roland Paris, and Oliver Richmond (eds), *New Perspectives on Liberal Peacebuilding* (United Nations University Press 2009) 78 at 83.

displace needs and welfare-based approaches.[101] Governments become more accountable to international donors than they are to their own people's desires for development. At all points, those who were most adversely affected by the war are those who bear the greatest burden when the scope of government is reduced, social safety nets are dismantled or public expenditure is cut. State-building shifts the burden of blame and responsibility for the causes of economic breakdown and poverty back to the state. The implicit argument of liberal peace policy-making is that global capitalism in and of itself is not harmful, but is either good or bad depending on whether the state's own institutional framework supports development and prosperity, on the one hand, or rent-seeking and depredation on the other.[102]

Along similar lines, a number of critics contend that transitional justice has acquiesced to the conscious exclusion of economic justice from the democratization and governance processes promoted by liberal peacebuilders.[103] They argue that transitional justice has adopted a policy-oriented research agenda that must fit with the pro-market liberal peacebuilding model. This has resulted in a conscious disavowal of other, more radical, perspectives open to structural analysis of conflict and distinctly different means of organizing society like democratic control of the economy or social equality.[104] As suggested earlier, the liberal-legalist influence on transitional justice means that philosophically it tends to favour freedom and liberty over equality and individual rights over the collective. In this view, individual rights and economic growth are sufficient to permit individuals to pursue their life goals. When this disposition is coupled with the top-down, security-focused approach fostered by peacebuilders, the violence transitional justice is designed to address is inevitably conceived in political and exceptionalist terms, as opposed to more routine structural or economic terms.[105] Critics of transitional justice therefore argue that it can only ever provide victims from marginalized communities one-time victories in 'minor legal battles'.[106] In so doing, it largely precludes more emancipatory justice by

---

[101] Oliver Richmond, 'Resistance and the Post-liberal Peace' (2010) 38 *Millennium: Journal of International Studies* 665, 667.

[102] Chandler (n 36) 7.

[103] Miller (n 1).

[104] Franzki and Olarte (n 44) 201 and 202.

[105] Balint, Evans and McMillan (n 43) 199.

[106] Geoff Dancy and Eric Wiebelhaus-Brahm, 'Bridge to Human Development or Vehicle of Inequality? Transitional Justice and Economic Structures' (2015) 9 *International Journal of Transitional Justice* 51, 57.

'papering over systemic problems with only promises of reform', promoting abstract ideas of rights over concrete improvements in the situation of victims.[107] Truth commissions have proven disempowering because abuses which could not be characterized as criminal (i.e. most socio-economic rights deprivations) have traditionally been ignored, reinforcing a narrative of conflict that violence was political, ideological, ethnic or religious, and not a matter of deliberate economic choice.[108] Reparations partially fulfil the need to 'do something' about inequality by making payments to deserving recipients, but they may detract from more systematic attempts to redistribute wealth.[109] Others go even further. Muvingi, for example, contends that transitional justice does not merely fail to address socioeconomic justice, it appears to exacerbate it by serving to protect the interests of the privileged at the expense of the poor.[110] Makau Mutua sees transitional justice as reproducing the assumption in global human rights of the naturalness of the market and the inevitability of capitalist relationships.[111]

The purpose of this chapter is not to disagree with these critiques. Transitional justice is unduly technocratic; it does little to challenge conservative interests in society. Furthermore, it can exclude more emancipatory forms of local justice, and it tends to elevate civil and political rights over socio-economic concerns. However, this type of critique is limited as a guide for action as it ignores parallel domestic impulses which exert stronger influence on justice outcomes and offers little by way of means–ends proposals for rectification.

3. THE LIMITS OF LIBERAL INFLUENCE ON DOMESTIC POLITICAL ECONOMY

The foregoing section examined current critiques of how the liberalism inherent to transitional justice is reinforced by the broader peacebuilding

---

[107] ibid 58.

[108] Colm Campbell and Catherine Turner, 'Utopia and the Doubters: Truth, Transition and the Law' (2008) 28 *Legal Studies* 374, 377.

[109] Dancy and Wiebelhaus-Brahm (n 106) 59.

[110] Muvingi (n 88) 182.

[111] Makau Mutua, 'A Critique of Rights in Transitional Justice: The African Experience' in Gaby Oré Aguilar and Felipé Gomez Isa (eds), *Rethinking Transitions: Equality and Social Justice in Societies Emerging from Conflict* (Intersentia 2011) 31 at 36–37.

environment. This bias towards interventionary actors, though it diagnoses some clear pathologies in both projects, is problematic. One of the striking things about the parallel critiques of peacebuilding and transitional justice is that because they focus on the norms of the international community in diagnosing problems of the liberal peace and on the sub-state local in devising alternatives to it, the critiques rarely begin from the starting point of peacebuilders and transitional justice policymakers themselves, namely the state-level peace process that compelled their involvement.

As Selby argues, one of the main flaws with the liberal peacebuilding critique is that it treats exogenous peacebuilding as the dominant element of contemporary war-ending practices and endogenous peace negotiations and agreements as merely second-order issues subordinate to liberal logics.[112] By contrast, he argues that individual peace negotiations and settlements are (1) driven by strategic considerations of power and legitimacy, (2) form the foundation of all political and economic opportunity and (3) define the degree to which liberal peacebuilding prescriptions will be applied, instrumentalized or disregarded. Because the liberal peacebuilding critique ignores this reality, it results in significant interpretative errors when trying to understand why post-conflict conditions take the shape they do.[113] Chapter 3 examined how the domestic post-conflict political economy conditions opportunities for justice. It also argued that the ineluctable legacy of instability and division ensures that the content of the peace that is ultimately realized will always represent the product of a national power struggle among the erstwhile conflict principals. Consequently, neither transitional justice nor international peacebuilding that emerges in the aftermath of a peace accord or power-sharing arrangement can straightforwardly embody the mechanical imposition of a standardized liberal blueprint. As the next two sections argue, the 'liberalism' of peacebuilding and transitional justice is consequently modified to the point that the rubric appears inappropriate, calling into question the critical presupposition that norms promoted by multilateral bodies, states and NGOs matter more to outcomes than domestic imperatives. Far from representing the imposition of hegemonic governmentality or civil and political rights in the interests of making the state safe for global capital, most peacebuilding and transitional justice epitomize context-specific responses to the domestic political economy,

---

112 Jan Selby, 'The Myth of Liberal Peacebuilding' (2013) 13 *Conflict, Security and Development* 57, 64.

113 ibid 65.

the security rationales of local actors and an agonistic process of bargaining over which liberalizing impulses enjoy a highly contested influence. None of this is to argue that these responses are successful in sustaining peace, delivering justice or creating a fairer or more functional society. However, the ultimate shape that transitional justice assumes will mainly, if not exclusively, be shaped by domestic design even where projects are supported and funded by international principals.

3.1 Exaggerating the Influence of International Actors

The necessity of peace settlements goes largely ignored in critical transitional justice and peacebuilding literatures that assume a neo-imperial potency to impose liberal solutions on post-conflict states qualified only at the edges by hybridity and resistance.[114] One likely explanation for this notion of liberal peacebuilding as a hegemonic Leviathan imposing liberal regimes on supine national communities is a focus on a small sample of liberal interventions that are markedly different from the garden-variety interventions typical of most peace operations. In the peacebuilding literature, these interventions are ones where external actors enjoyed sovereign or semi-sovereign power or post-conquest interventions in the War on Terror. Here it is credible to speak of interventions driven by external actors, but these examples bear little relation to consensual peacebuilding based on peace agreements with broad (elite) consent and consensus that is characteristic of African and (most) Asian missions. Prominent critics of liberal peacebuilding concentrate on the transitional administrations in Kosovo, East Timor and Bosnia[115] or post-conquest administrations in Iraq and Afghanistan.[116] In these states the international community manifested many of the signs of belligerent occupation, early 20th century international trusteeships and 'benevolent despotism' like assuming sovereignty, putting combat-ready boots on the ground and the full internationalization of politics to impose peace deals on local antagonists. These examples are emphasized to confine case studies to areas the authors are most familiar with instead of presenting 'inauthentic African or Latin American case studies' from places they are not.[117] Though intellectually defensible, the conclusions

---

[114] The concepts of hybridity and resistance are examined in Section 5.

[115] Richmond and Franks (n 5) 2.

[116] E.g., Lidén (n 94) 626; Hameiri (n 99) 44–45 and 117–207; Chandler (n 36) 1; Richmond (n 53) 561–62.

[117] Roger Mac Ginty, *International Peacebuilding and Local Resistance: Hybrid Forms of Peace* (Springer 2011) 13.

drawn are not so limited. They are assumed to apply unproblematically to those other peacebuilding ecologies that they are less familiar with which enjoyed/endured far less international control like Angola, Burundi, Côte d'Ivoire, the DR Congo, El Salvador, Liberia, Mozambique, Namibia, Nicaragua, Rwanda, Sierra Leone. This assumption elides the large gap between the powers exercised in the likes of Iraq and Bosnia, on the one hand, and the likes of Liberia or Mozambique, on the other. Because critics of liberal peacebuilding and transitional justice assume that external actors control peacebuilding outcomes (prominent critics of transitional justice refer to those states where 'liberalization policies grant an extensive role to the international community in restructuring the political, economic and social systems of states emerging from conflict'),[118] they analyse all intervention as if the 'key to the puzzle' lies with external actors even in cases where armed domestic conflict principals are quite clearly defining the parameters of any political settlement.[119] One obvious consequence of this is that only one core independent variable affecting the quality of peace or justice is assessed (the forms of intervention), without examining or demonstrating the relative significance of other factors (military balances, domestic ideologies, spoilers) in shaping the outcomes they criticize.[120] The failure of certain outcomes like peace (or democracy, or economic reform, or redistribution of wealth) will not necessarily result from the acts or omissions of peacebuilders alone, but will also flow from deliberate decisions of domestic actors with the power to resist the pressure of interveners.

Critics writing about peacebuilding and transitional justice outside the familiar examples of UN territorial administrations and post-9/11 occupations labour under fundamental misconceptions as to the degree of influence international agents enjoy on domestic structures. The first, and most serious, misapprehension from which all others flow is that peacebuilding and transitional justice are 'interventionary' acts free to impose universalized principles, as opposed to 'procedural' processes limited to providing support for the reconstruction of a state with its own internally negotiated agreements.[121] While sites of transitional justice like Bosnia, Kosovo and East Timor fit this 'interventionary' paradigm, most transitional justice projects in the likes of the DR Congo, Kenya, El Salvador or Uganda never have; instead they manifest a 'procedural'

---

118 Turner (n 45) 127.
119 Sending (n 2) 56.
120 ibid 56–57.
121 Tadjbakhsh and Richmond (n 69) 223.

essence. In the aftermath of contemporary negotiated settlements 'domestic actors virtually always determine who shall rule and under what interim arrangements … The main logic of international engagement therefore becomes support for the peace agreement, pressure to maintain any powersharing elements, and efforts to keep potential spoilers on board'.[122] This agreement lies at the crux of all future progress (or regression) in political, economic and social life within the state.

Third-party states or the UN have a role to play in mediating these agreements and reaching conclusions about projects like transitional justice, but they rarely define them. The role of peacebuilders and transitional justice actors in most post-conflict states is fundamentally as reactive, secondary actors. This has proven to be the case even in those instances where the inclusion of transitional justice in peace agreements like those in Sierra Leone or Cambodia follow heavy international pressure on the disputants. Unlike transitional administrations or post-9/11 occupations, interventionary actors generally lack the hard power of command, enforcement and coercion and instead rely on the soft power of persuasion and incentivization. These have distinct limitations.

The primary limitation on international influence is the fact that the state maintains its sovereignty, critically undermining interveners' freedom of action and affording domestic leaders a level of autonomy over issues of peace, development, economic distribution and justice. Most importantly, peacebuilders and transitional justice policy-makers must operate through political leaders they have not chosen and who historically demonstrate significant ability to evade and manipulate even the strongest outside pressures to reform domestic structures.[123] Transitional justice and peacebuilding are typically requested by invitation and as such are premised on consent and conditioned by peace agreements. This element of consent compels interveners to negotiate with actors who are central to ensuring security, resulting in a 'culture of principled pragmatism' and compromises in the face of hard realities.[124] This principle of consent also means the host government enjoys far more agency than critics of the liberal peace and transitional justice allow as permission can be revoked if international actors act in ways the post-conflict government disapproves of, a coercive tool that ensures the boundaries are not

---

[122] Call (n 27) 252.

[123] Sending (n 2) 62.

[124] Michael Barnett and Christoph Zürcher, 'The Peacebuilder's Contract: How External Statebuilding Reinforces Weak Statehood' in Roland Paris and Timothy Sisk (eds), *The Dilemmas of Statebuilding: Confronting the Contradictions of Postwar Peace Operations* (Routledge 2009) 23 at 32 and 34.

pushed too far.[125] Transitional justice goals on the spectrum from basic trials to fully transformative conceptions of justice are entirely dependent on the ability of interveners to convince domestic actors with veto power to engage constructively. Language like 'ownership' and 'transfer of responsibility' give a misleading impression of the dynamics of peacebuilding (and, it might be added, transitional justice) inasmuch as they suggest external actors are in the position of de facto rulers with the power to grant more autonomous rule.[126] Much is made of the export of liberal human rights norms by peacebuilders and the impact of a justice cascade in which the prevalence of accountability is primarily due to the impact of transnational human rights networks. However, scholars like Payne, Reiter and Olsen have demonstrated through controlling for old and new regime types, conflict type, duration, democratic history and the presence of a negotiated regime change, that transition-type is ultimately the key deciding factor in determining how far and how expansively transitional justice can be pursued.[127] The decision to adopt trials, truth commissions and reparations in the first place can more usually be explained by domestic political incentives to punish certain individuals, promote certain ideologies or to mitigate particular grievances.[128] Domestic political incentives also explain the initial lack of attention to economic justice. As Chapter 3 argued, consultation and communication with the broader public or responsiveness to popular preferences are often sacrificed as a result of the deference to domestic (elite) preferences in negotiations that are indispensable to securing a settlement between highly motivated armed antagonists.[129] The paramountcy of domestic transition politics and peace agreements must call into question the degree to which the ostensibly Western package of state institutions, democracy and legalistic transitional justice can be attributed solely to liberal ideology. As Bleiker notes, 'there is no doubt that re-establishing order, the rule of law and democracy reflects more than just liberal

---

[125] Susanna Campbell, 'Routine Learning? How Peacebuilding Organisations Prevent Liberal Peace' in Campbell, Chandler and Sabaratnam (eds) (n 2) 89 at 99–100.

[126] Ulrich Schneckener, 'State Building or New Modes of Governance? The Effects of International Involvement in Areas of Limited Statehood' in Thomas Risse (ed.), *Governance Without a State: Policies and Politics in Areas of Limited Statehood* (Columbia University Press 2011) 232 at 254.

[127] Tricia Olsen, Leigh Payne and Andrew Reiter, *Transitional Justice in Balance: Comparing Processes, Weighing Efficacy* (US Institute of Peace 2010).

[128] Padraig McAuliffe, 'The Roots of Transitional Accountability: Interrogating the Justice Cascade' (2013) 9 *International Journal of Law in Context* 106.

[129] This argument is also made in Call (n 27) 252.

political preferences. These are crucial elements if a society is to stop violence, overcome deep-seated antagonisms and establish a lasting peacebuilding process'.[130] The most significant barriers to a transformative vision of peace will be domestic as well as international. Even if transitional justice and peacebuilding transcend their liberal impulses to become attuned to horizontal inequalities, maldistribution and poverty, it cannot be assumed that they can alter domestic preferences in the absence of a pre-existing willingness to address these issues on the part of politically effective actors.

3.2 The Realities of 'Compromised Peacebuilding'

The post-Cold War record demonstrates that peacebuilders have proven effective in promoting objectives like state institutions, some form of power-sharing democracy or generalized commitment to human rights that conflict antagonists find unobjectionable in general and sufficiently vague to allow prolonged bargaining over their exact forms. Similarly, though with less consistent success, transitional justice advocates and policy-makers have succeeded in catalysing trials, truth commissions, reparations and memory projects in diverse post-conflict states. However, it is far from clear that international actors can forcefully direct national leaders to pursue certain aspirations (like women's rights, or tackling corruption, or redistribution of wealth) or dissuade them from courses of action that undermine these aspirations. Domestic politics are more than mere constraints on a prefabricated liberal peace. Instead, what we see is a dyadic relationship between domestic and international actors based on a mix of conflictual and co-operative strategies which explain why grand designs for wider transformation of society give way to bargaining and compromise that often leave pre-war societal structures largely untouched.

The best examination of this dyadic interaction between domestic governing actors and interveners comes from Christoph Zürcher and others in a series of co-authored works on what he calls 'compromised peacebuilding'. He posits that domestic elites may wish to take advantage of the material and symbolic resources international interveners have to offer, but resist full implementation of some of their prescriptions because they fear these might undermine their security, power or economic interests. Peacebuilders (and, it might be added, transitional justice

---

[130] Roland Bleiker, 'Conclusion – Everyday Struggles for a Hybrid Peace' in Richmond and Mitchell (eds) (n 50) 293 at 303.

actors) operate under time, resource and commitment constraints, and so are utterly reliant on co-operation or lack of obstruction from domestic leaders if the projects they promote are to be realized effectively. This gives the latter a loose but definite veto power on policy options, though this diminishes the more reliant that domestic actors are on international support to guarantee their security or power. As a result, if peacebuilders and transitional justice actors are to secure some or all of their goals and if domestic elites are to preserve some or all of their objectives, they must bargain over the type of peace and justice they wish to build.[131] Post-conflict elites on both sides of war will generally come to some agreement about how to resolve the differences that occur through various forms of political, military and economic power-sharing. The peacebuilding record of the last 25 years demonstrates that domestic elites will generally want to preserve at least some of these military, political and economic powers and interests. Consequently, they may only superficially embrace goals like good governance and democracy (to say nothing of progressive taxation or redistribution), which may undermine a leader's power or their ability to extract wealth from the state or to reward patrimonial clients.[132]

As a result, international interveners and elites are in a state of strategic interaction, where the ability of each to secure certain aims is crucially dependent on the strategy of the other.[133] As Barnett and Zürcher note, the most common outcome is compromised peacebuilding which 'reflects the desire of peacebuilders for stability and the legitimacy of peacebuilding and the desire of local elites to ensure that reforms do not threaten their power base' instead of the wider type of structural reform that makes for a higher quality, more sustainable peace.[134] Even if liberal interventionism is tempered or replaced by a commitment to socio-economic equality, interveners may still have to tailor their programme to local conditions, acknowledging the reality of elite interests and power. National power-brokers acquiesce to peacebuilding reforms or transitional justice but will enjoy the power to minimize potential risks to their fundamental interests.[135] Though the concept of 'compromised peacebuilding' is grounded in game theory and rational choice studies, it

---

[131] Christoph Zürcher, Carrie Manning and Kristie Evenson, *Costly Democracy: Peacebuilding and Democratization after War* (Stanford University Press 2013) 5–6.

[132] ibid 23–24.

[133] Barnett and Zürcher (n 124) 24.

[134] ibid.

[135] ibid 25.

captures empirically observable phenomena. For example, the extensive socio-economic provisions in the Guatemalan peace process that international actors midwifed were not implemented as organized landed elites could resist progressive reform.[136] The DR Congo's International Committee to Support Transition established to guarantee the implementation of its Global Accord could not use the considerable authority it enjoyed on paper and was instead controlled entirely by the Congolese government and presidency.[137] Even in the 'near perfect conditions' of RAMSI's deployment to the Solomon Islands or interventions in the likes of East Timor (undisputed territory, small population, consent of the population, no relevant interests of third parties), interveners were limited in their ability to shape domestic politics.[138] Peacebuilders, like transitional justice actors, usually end up tacitly accepting resistance to their prescriptions from domestic actors, reasoning that some progress is better than none at all. As Jones argues:

> [R]esistance from social forces threatened by reform processes … have frequently compelled a compromise settlement that falls well short of the ideal-type state planned by the interveners. In some cases, deeply entrenched social and political coalitions have even been able to capture externally imposed reform processes and use them to reinforce their predatory domination. It is therefore important not to overestimate the power of interveners. State-building interventions have very important effects, providing or limiting resources and opportunities that shift the makeup of the coalitions contesting state power. However, they are often simply intervening variables in struggles which they have no realistic hope of taming.[139]

Compromised peacebuilding makes clear that there may be actors or spoilers who exert veto-power over any settlement or peace, and who can force revision of headquarters blueprints for reform or justice. Transformative justice principles are invariably compromised by the need to co-operate with local elites and the legacy of armed conflict, to say nothing of resource shortages endured by the interveners. State-building projects like transitional justice or rule of law, therefore, are always

---

136 Tony Addison, Abdur Chowdhury and S. Mansoob Murshed, 'Financing Reconstruction' in Gerd Junne and Willemijn Verkoren (eds), *Post-Conflict Development: Meeting New Challenges* (Lynne Rienner 2005) 211 at 212.

137 Davis (n 47) 294.

138 Lars Brozus, 'Applying the Governance Concept to Areas of Limited Statehood' in Risse (ed.) (n 126) 262 at 273.

139 Lee Jones, '(Post-) Colonial State-Building and State Failure in East Timor: Bringing Social Conflict Back In' (2010) 10 *Conflict, Security and Development* 547, 552.

attended by what de Guevara calls state-formation, namely the 'contingent social processes that accompany and deform' original intentions in the process of politics.[140] There can never be a linear, one dimensional, top-down production of peacebuilding rationality or transitional justice as purposeful action to this end is inevitably 'bent' by the domestic reactions intervention catalyses and by the compromises this compels.[141] In all matters, international interveners must balance between objectively desirable policies that can underpin peace and what former belligerents will willingly agree to. 'Policy capture' by national and local actors best explains why the largely illusory asymmetry of bargaining power that critics identify rarely results in outcomes pursued by interveners.[142]

Taking cognizance of compromised peacebuilding in external–internal interactions allows us to see most contemporary peacebuilding and transitional justice interventions not in terms of what critics reject (a virtual peace masquerading as, or undermined by, liberal democracy) or for what they would like them to be (a missed opportunity for radically redistributive state or bottom-up social pacification), but for what they actually are – the safeguarding of a domestically negotiated settlement where international actors are indispensable to implementation but enjoy less influence than is commonly assumed on issues of politics, identity, rights and distribution. The aims of peacebuilders and transitional justice actors are unavoidably embedded deep within local politics, clientelistic modes of rule and the vested interests of national elites to the degree that a liberal vision of peace premised on democracy, human rights and civil society so widely caricatured in the critical literature goes unrealized on the ground. This is evident in policy areas like rule of law reconstruction and democratization. Thick versions of the rule of law premised on rights outlined in UN policy documents consistently give way to thinner versions in the field that concentrate on formal institutions as the most that can be achieved.[143] Governments elected after power-sharing do not truly represent democratic legitimation but instead the effective sociological legitimacy conferred by military mobilization and success.[144] The reality of compromise and policy capture is most evident from the

---

[140] Bliesemann de De Guevara (n 9) 113.

[141] ibid 116.

[142] Miles Kahler, 'Statebuilding After Afghanistan and Iraq' in Paris and Sisk (eds) (n 124) 287 at 296.

[143] Camino Kavanagh and Bruce Jones, *Shaky Foundations: An Assessment of the UN's Rule of Law Support Agenda* (Center on International Cooperation 2011) 27.

[144] Bhuta (n 26) 822.

record of traditionally liberal-legalist transitional justice itself, an unedifying history of stalled or selective trials, ignored truth commission reports and paltry reparations. Far from exporting liberal democracy or trying to remodel post-conflict societies in the Western image, therefore, security and 'keeping a lid' on the pertinent divisions that led to international involvement is the most international peacebuilding on the ground often succeeds in achieving.[145]

Most peacebuilding and transitional justice efforts are essentially ratifications of post-conflict power relations. This creates a sufficiently capacious institutional architecture for deeply divisive issues to be discussed, but rarely are they addressed comprehensively. The goal at all points is more to avoid reversion to violence than to consolidate democracy or restructure society because this is the most that the domestic political economy conduces to within the life-span of intervention. Critics legitimately argue that this is an unduly restrictive or conservative vision of peace. They are, however, on far shakier ground in arguing there is significant potential to change this given what we know about peacebuilding and the reliance on already-powerful domestic actors. As De Coning argues, contemporary post-conflict interventions should be understood not as activities that can generate specific outcomes, but rather as measures that can at best facilitate processes that enable self-organized peace or justice solutions to emerge.[146] This is an aspiration that falls short not only of liberal democracy but also of the necessarily more complex and difficult process of developing social systems that serve the needs of the whole population.

4. BEFORE AND AFTER PEACEBUILDING: THE ENDURING IMPACT OF DOMESTIC INSTITUTIONS AND INFORMAL POWER

Much of the critique of transitional justice is premised on the notion that all-powerful donors and international organizations of the West define transitional justice projects that submissive post-conflict states are supposed to absorb and implement.[147] However, the foregoing examination of compromised peacebuilding makes clear that any critique of transitional justice that is premised on the notion that liberal peacebuilding's

---

[145] Chandler (n 36) 34.

[146] Cedric De Coning, 'Understanding Peacebuilding as Essentially Local' (2013) 2 *Stability: International Journal of Security and Development* 1.

[147] Rubli (n 15) 14.

top-down imposition of external legal frameworks and institutional templates represent the 'foundational' limitations on a more transformative transitional justice must be called into question. This position ignores (1) the salience of domestic politics in the heightened tension of conflict termination and (2) the weakness of most contemporary international interventions in post-conflict states. Critics of contemporary transitional justice are correct to argue that the liberalism of the field limits the transformative imagination of interveners for all the reasons described by critics. A radical transformation in international approaches to transitional justice is necessary if it is to become relevant to the needs and lived experiences of most communities after conflict. However, the liberal-legalism of the field is not the primary underlying reason that transitional justice fails to impact the root causes of socio-economic rights deprivation. The main barriers lie in the domestic political economy and the demonstrable ability of post-conflict leaderships to pursue endogenously generated interests and to resist impositions that do not accord with them.

The philosophical underpinnings of transitional justice may have unduly limited the types of abuse addressed and the types of justice pursued, but the other foundational limitations to transformative justice are in fact domestic. Two stand out. The first is the short-term, essentially ephemeral process of negotiating and implementing peace, which has been examined in Chapter 3. The second limitation comes from the long-term, inherited characteristics of the typical post-conflict state. These provide the background for, and limits to, projects that attempt to fundamentally revise structures of economic injustice. It forms the subject of this section.

One of the least assailable arguments made by critics of transitional justice and liberal peacebuilding is that they help build shell-states that represent a superficial veneer of liberal governance over a largely unchanged state. Nevertheless, the processes of statebuilding that flow from peace rarely fail completely. Successful peacebuilding will generally allow the state to exercise the fundamental functions of the state like security, representation and development, even if imperfectly. However, in most cases like Sierra Leone, Liberia or Libya, state-building falls far short of the institutionally competent, routinized bureaucracy with the capacity to implement and enforce all policies or to secure its grip on state-society relations. Even very intrusive peace missions are frequently unsuccessful at achieving progress in aspects of statehood other than security given the difficulty of imposing coherent political influence over fissiparous post-conflict societies.[148] Other classic Weberian capacities which underpin emancipatory or redistributive visions of peace like mobilizing or managing revenues and providing goods or services to the population may be imperfectly realized. The most typical result of peacebuilding, therefore, is not a Western 'mini-me' state with a deliberately unexercised bureaucratic potential to rectify structural injustice. It is instead a semi-liberal state that is composed of pluricentric power structures mixing the sort of functioning state familiar in the West with residual deep-rooted, traditional forms of government and social organization. The state is characterized by superficial democracy, has low capacity to secure social minima beyond security, and is mediated by non-state institutions that employ their own methods of resolving social problems within the rebuilt state.[149]

Instead of establishing a liberal and democratic peace, international intervention invariably leads to a hybrid condition in which liberal and illiberal, democratic and undemocratic elements coexist.[150] The hybrid condition of liberal and illiberal, democratic and undemocratic means that national and international actors must again co-operate with parastatal and non-state actors to achieve functionality. Any peacebuilding goal on the spectrum from conservative to liberal to emancipatory can only be achieved if these national actors decide to engage constructively with it. Governance in peacebuilding can only ever be realized 'within shifting networks of alliances' and not as a product of the realization of neutral, objective governing interests.[151] Those who would wish for a more socio-economically transformative iteration of transitional justice are left with the task of outlining how their aspirations fit with those diverse social logics, pluricentric power structures and shifting alliances.

The first and most obvious point to remember is that even if we accept that the transformative aspirations sketched in Chapter 2 do not project idealized understandings of the West's own historical development (though, as Sabaratnam convincingly argues, much of the welfarism and

---

[148] Kimberly Zisk Marten, *Enforcing the Peace: Learning from the Imperial Past* (Columbia University Press 2004) 155 and 159.

[149] Berit Bliesemann de Guevara, 'The State in Times of Statebuilding' (2008) 10 *Civil Wars* 348, 349.

[150] Belloni (n 35) 21 and 27.

[151] Les Johnston, 'Transnational Security Governance' in Jennifer Wood and Benoit Dupont (eds), *Democracy, Society and the Governance of Security* (Cambridge University Press 2006) 33 at 34.

poverty alleviation that underpins critical alternatives to liberal peace-building unwittingly represents 'nostalgia' for the liberal social contract),[152] international and domestic actors attempting to transform society-wide structures are effectively aspiring to engineer within the lifetime of even the most long-term transitional justice project what took centuries to achieve in states that currently enjoy even minimal commitments to welfare and provision of services or even basic wealth redistribution. As Hameiri notes, 'Much romanticized welfare and developmental states had only existed for a limited time in the post-war era, in a small part of the world' and bear little relation to the types of hybridized polities state-builders are capable of reconstructing.[153] Historically, post-colonial states assumed much more limited welfare functions which took the form of direct or indirect subsidies on key commodities (like food or fuel) paid for by external or internal rents (e.g. commodity exports, loans and foreign aid) in a distinctly different manner than the Western industrial welfare state model, which was generally premised on redistributive welfare and a functioning taxation system.[154] For reasons outlined below, state capabilities rarely improve dramatically within the time-range of state-building or transitional justice. At the very least, therefore, transformative aspirations may be at odds with the past and present empirical conditions in the state in question (of course, if they were not, they wouldn't be transformative!). Domestically, neither historical developments nor economic incentives generated more equal economies, serious poverty alleviation or welfare, suggesting there are pre-existing domestic impediments to such an order. One of the core arguments of the transitional justice critique, after all, is that social exclusion, inequality and underdevelopment are phenomena that are deliberately sustained.[155] This often very recent historical experience must inform thinking not only about what needs to change, but how difficult it will be. As Bøås points out:

> Most international interventions in fact overlook the deliberate aspect of state failure: the extent to which regimes allow and enable state recession in order

---

[152] Meera Sabaratnam, 'Avatars of Eurocentrism in the Critique of the Liberal Peace' (2013) 44 *Security Dialogue* 259, 268.

[153] Hameiri (n 99) 209.

[154] Jennifer Milliken and Keith Krause, 'State Failure, State Collapse, and State Reconstruction: Concepts, Lessons and Strategies' (2002) 33 *Development and Change* 753, 761.

[155] For example, Amanda Cahill-Ripley, 'Foregrounding Socio-Economic Rights in Transitional Justice: Realising Justice for Violations of Economic and Social Rights' (2014) 32 *Netherlands Quarterly of Human Rights* 183, 191.

> to serve their own financial and security interests, regardless of the best interests of the people ... These interventions are therefore severely compromised, insofar as they are trying to 'fix' that which is probably broken for a reason.[156]

While in general terms it is permissible to argue that transitional justice should transform unequal economic structures, in the context of an individual state such approaches risk ahistoricity if there is no attempt to comprehend the long-term processes whereby traditional economic structures evolved or were negotiated. Many of the root causes of conflict will remain entirely undiminished after war, peace and peacebuilding. Others may change because wars are transformative and create new social realities – some structural elements that led to conflict may be replaced by new ones which may be less, equally or more unconducive to reform of socio-economic structures.

The endurance of deep-seated socio-political realities beyond the reach of government, factions and interveners is important for transitional justice theorists and practitioners to remember. Even in its most traditional and limited forms, transitional justice discourse tends to 'imagine' idealized states that do not exist in much of the developed world.[157] Socially contractarian goals of transformative justice like development, addressing horizontal inequalities and welfare presuppose an at least minimally functional state capable of co-ordinating economic and political power, one with at least some bureaucratic capability to formulate and implement policies to these ends. They also presuppose a critical mass of domestic actors committed to transformation, or at least unwilling to impede it. However, many states that undergo radical shifts in the distribution of political power and/or intensive processes of peacebuilding nevertheless end up being captured for much narrower ends or replicating old forms of unequal resource distribution. For example, the inclusive Guatemalan peace agreement to address the roots of conflict and inequality by giving significantly more power to excluded indigenous groups required a referendum on revision of the constitution. The referendum's defeat has been seen as a victory for elite conservatism over the vast pro-change constituency. The mass media leagued with oligarchs and the military to secure a 'no' vote, consigning most of the most radical features of the peace agreement like land rights to the dustbin of

---

156 Morten Bøås, 'Returning to Realities: A Building-Block Approach to State and Statecraft in Eastern Congo and Somalia' (2010) 10 *Conflict, Security and Development* 443, 444–45.

157 McEvoy (n 42) 39.

history.[158] Beyond this, shadowy networks of ex-military figures, organized crime, the political establishment and organized elites collaborated to prevent other elements of implementation of the agreement and to generate wealth through illegal means.[159] Though the UN-brokered peace agreement stipulated democracy and reform of both army and governmental institutions, El Salvador's ARENA government resisted socio-economic redistribution in negotiations with leftist rebels lest it undermine its power-base in the business community. Wood argues that the peace agreement there reflected an explicit exchange of political inclusion for the rebels for the economic elite's continued control of assets, thereby preventing significant economic redistribution, even if there was ultimately some re-allocation of land.[160] Jean-Bertrand Aristide's first radically egalitarian government in Haiti was overthrown after only seven months by the business community and upper echelons of the military who feared redistribution of wealth.[161] The economic power of whites in South Africa was allied to the risk of collapsing the transition to democratic rule to foreclose an expansive conception of transitional justice.[162] National reconciliation in Namibia and post-Smith Zimbabwe was similarly dictated by the need to avoid antagonizing the white community economically.[163] In Kenya, the 2008 post-election violence peace agreement was designed by the international community and African Union to address longstanding causes of conflict. However, the leadership in Nairobi and the national political elite resisted implementation of its prescriptions, most notably by the simple expedient of not nominating commissioners in crucial implementation mechanisms.[164]

---

158 Thania Paffenholz, 'Unpacking the Local Turn in Peacebuilding: A Critical Assessment Towards an Agenda for Future Research' (2015) 36 *Third World Quarterly* 857, 866–74.

159 Susan Peacock and Adriana Beltrán, *Hidden Powers in Post-conflict Guatemala: Illegal Armed Groups and the Forces Behind Them* (Washington Office on Latin America 2003).

160 Elisabeth Wood, 'Agrarian Reform, Land Occupation, and the Transition to Democracy in El Salvador' in Bergsmo et al. (eds) (n 20) 141 at 175.

161 Alex Dupuy, *The Prophet and Power: Jean-Bertrand Aristide, the International Community and Haiti* (Rowman and Littlefield 2007).

162 Jon Elster, *Closing the Books: Transitional Justice in Historical Perspective* (Cambridge University Press 2004) 197.

163 Rama Mani, *Beyond Retribution: Seeking Justice in the Shadows of War* (Polity Press 2002) 92–93.

164 Paffenholz (n 158) 867.

In these states and elsewhere, three underlying domestic conditions in particular underpin a reality of continual conflict over limited resources beyond the transitional moment, limiting the malleability of post-conflict economic structures and hence the potential success of transitional justice-inspired reforms. They are a mutually reinforcing trifecta of (1) the bureaucratic weakness of the state, (2) the endurance of long-term patterns of patrimonialism, clientelism and corruption, and (3) the prerogatives of elites, and in particular conflict elites.

4.1 The Bureaucratic Weakness of the State

Most of the post-conflict states that this book addresses will fall somewhere between those quasi-states that manifest mere 'juridical statehood'[165] and those that exemplify limited statehood where governments fail to enforce political decisions over time in many different policy areas and only make social goods available selectively.[166] It is tempting to employ 'fragility' as the guiding concept given that it has replaced 'state failure' as the means by which less functional developing states are commonly assessed. Certainly, the state is fragile in the sense that the state endures chronic gaps in its authority (most notably in terms of the monopoly of violence), its capacity to provide basic services and its severely corroded legitimacy.[167] However, the state could accurately have been described as fragile even before conflict. Something materially worse than fragility is being endured, particularly bearing in mind that those conditions of fragility that led to civil war are seldom solved by it and are almost always worsened by the ensuing carnage. As noted in Chapter 1, the particular difficulty of post-conflict states is best captured within the transitional justice literature by de Greiff's concept of 'very imperfect worlds'; namely, those societies characterized not just by the massive and systematic violation of norms, but by the fact that there are enormous disadvantages implicated in any attempt to enforce compliance.[168]

Recent warfare will of course have degraded state capacity, but in most contemporary states in Africa and to a lesser extent other more conflicted

---

165 Robert H. Jackson, *Quasi-states: Sovereignty, International Relations, and the Third World* (Cambridge University Press 1990).

166 Risse (ed.) (n 126).

167 Frances Stewart and Graham Brown, *Fragile States* (University of Oxford CRISE 2009) 3–4.

168 Pablo de Greiff, 'Theorizing Transitional Justice' in Williams, Nagy and Elster (eds) (n 18) 1 at 4–5.

states outside the West like Myanmar, Yemen or Nepal, this capacity will not have been very strong to begin with. Long-term, endogenous state-building is an extremely difficult and costly process that involves the use of force against local resistance to transform individuals into obedient citizens. As a result, it requires significant motivation. To grossly summarize, in Europe's historical evolution from hundreds of medieval polities to the present fifty or so, the motivation to build a state and extract revenue emerged systematically from the need of princely authoritarians and statesmen to face external threat or imperial opportunity by waging wars. War compelled the centralization of control in society, while funding it demanded extraction from the public, which was facilitated by, and exchanged for, the security the emerging state could offer in return via the monopoly of violence.[169] Over centuries, the process of state formation and consolidation saw an increasing differentiation between military and non-military activities as the state became statized (with broadened and deepened duties) and socialized (made subject to law and democracy) as the political institutions of the state gradually became dominant over the military.

Present-day developing states have historically lacked this incentivized, mutually constitutive relationship of motivation between war and the state's development of bureaucratic potential to respond to social need. In the first place, many Asian, African and Middle Eastern states had been subject to colonial rule, meaning state personhood was largely inherited, as opposed to constructed internally. The colonial state was strong in the sense that it had significant despotic power but weak on account of its almost non-existent infrastructural power or public legitimacy.[170] Anti-colonial nationalism proved successful in ending this external rule, but rarely generated a sustained social basis for regularizing political activity or generating public goods. Furthermore, the general post-colonial respect for the norm of fixed borders deprived states of the external threats that compel the development of strong institutions and identification of a jeopardized citizenry with the state, particularly in its periphery. The wars they ended up fighting were of the 'wrong kind' in that they were largely internal and associated with domination of one particular section of the population over the others.[171] Furthermore, the fear of rivals led many post-colonial rulers to emasculate a state

169 Charles Tilly, *Coercion, Capital and European States, AD 990–1992* (Blackwell 1990).

170 Michael Mann, 'The Autonomous Power of the State: Its Origins, Mechanisms and Results' (1984) 25 *European Journal of Sociology* 185.

171 Clapham (n 59) 786.

apparatus that could otherwise have institutionalized their rule.[172] The need to manage these problems of internal diversity through forms of power-sharing and patrimonialism with compliant elites was more characteristic of post-colonial development than the European model. Even the pernicious incentive for elites to develop effective administrative capacity to siphon wealth from the state was weak. Because emerging states were able to finance their rule via clientelistic networks through rents from natural resources or international aid, the rulers of developing states had little incentive to forge ties with the population or undertake the inherently conflictive task of tax collection. The reality that claims for transformative justice must be mediated, institutionalized and in the long-term guaranteed by (or merely within) these types of state should temper some of the more expansive claims about transitional justice's ability to catalyse redistribution or widespread welfare. This is the 'vacuous state' to which Bosire refers, one which has little in the way of institutional strength. As she notes, state vacuity was not really in issue in the European and Latin American transitions that formed the basis for the general understanding and critique of the transition paradigm, but is the context in which most contemporary transitional justice plays out.[173] State vacuity is an issue the transformative turn has neglected to engage with. It may be the case, as one editorial in the *International Journal of Transitional Justice* argued, that the lack of any state law enforcement in many states calls into question the appropriateness of transitional justice's traditional emphasis on criminal determination of responsibility.[174] However, it is tempting (if depressing) to ask if this logic can and should extend to any more ambitious prescriptions for justice that clearly exceeds its short- to medium-term institutional capacity.

Most states that have progressive taxation, provide welfare or can intervene with sufficient penetration to enforce the law against recalcitrant actors in the domestic economy have a managerial and technical state bureaucracy sufficient to formulate and implement planned development. They also tend to have a widely legitimate national identity, a prosperous middle class and a growing economy. Beyond grassroots-level initiatives, only a modern state with functioning bureaucracy, rule of law and institutions to guide elite co-operation can credibly commit to

---

172 Joel Migdal, *Strong Societies, Weak States* (Princeton University Press 1988) 207–38.

173 Lydiah Bosire, *Overpromised, Underdelivered: Transitional Justice in Sub-Saharan Africa* (International Center for Transitional Justice 2006) 8 at footnote 32.

174 An-Na'im (n 12) 201.

the sort of long-term projects needed to secure sustainable development. Only a functional state enjoys power to devise and implement policies against the will of major social actors. Even arch-critics of 'liberal' peacebuilding accept the state is a precondition for development and reject its shrinking as unconducive to taxation and welfare.[175] Because of the weakness of the state's administrative structures, governments in many developing states seldom employ bureaucratic formulae to develop authoritative institutions oriented towards the purposeful achievement of normative goals like development, welfare or redistribution. Many post-conflict states will have achieved neither institutional standardization (where a single set of rules gains dominance within society) nor identity standardization (where socio-cognitive 'rules of the mind' are shared within a politically defined population).[176] In these types of state, factions 'are least inclined to envision government as a progressive problem-solving entity and more likely to see it as a principal means to achieve superiority over rivals'.[177]

Though peacebuilding missions are in theory designed to remedy these problems through processes of state reconstruction, the reform of state institutions is subject to the same problems of compromise and hybridity outlined above. Space precludes a detailed examination of the technical shortcomings of peacebuilding, but the extremely difficult processes of developing institutions that could become more responsive to public needs is complicated by three problems in particular. These are (1) the notorious coherence problem manifest on the ground in erratic policies, irreconcilable programmes and replication of projects, (2) lack of adequate resources and time allocated to missions, and (3) technical and political weakness in creating domestic incentives for reform.[178] For those who wish to significantly transform the politics and culture of post-conflict states in any direction (be it redistributive, welfarist or liberal), it is far from clear that complex peacekeeping operations can

---

[175] Bendaña (n 8) 7–8.

[176] Dominik Balthasar, 'From Hybridity to Standardization: Rethinking State-Making in Contexts of Fragility' (2015) 9 *Journal of Intervention and Statebuilding* 26, 27.

[177] Ian Spears, 'Africa's Informal Power-Sharing and the Prospects for Peace' (2013) 15 *Civil Wars* 37, 44.

[178] One useful survey is Ole Jacob Sending, 'Why Peacebuilders Fail to Secure Ownership and Be Sensitive to Context' (NUPI Working Paper 755, 2009) 22 <http://brage.bibsys.no/xmlui/handle/11250/277766> accessed 21 July 2016.

accomplish much beyond stabilization.[179] An examination of the state's bureaucratic weakness highlights some of the superficiality of the arguments that transitional justice should be judged by its success or failure to deliver welfare or secure socio-economic rights. As Call argues, '[w]here states have historically not been the natural providers of core good and services (i.e. 'weak' states), it is unrealistic to expect any newly recast state to acquire and effectively carry out such services in the space of a few years'.[180]

4.2 Patrimonialism, Clientelism and Corruption

Because the post-conflict state may lack capacity and legitimacy, stability within the state will often be generated only by building ethnic-, religious- or faction-based networks of interest and the distribution of payments and rents to cultivate loyalty. Consequently, many of the hybridized states restored by peacebuilding demonstrate the endurance of elements of patrimonialism. Neopatrimonialist states enjoy political and administrative systems that are formally constructed on a rational-legal basis, but in practice tend to be pervaded by personalized rule, clientelism and little or no ability to restrain private appropriation of public resources.[181] In many sub-Saharan African, Middle Eastern and Asian states, institutional weakness compels governments to exercise authority through personal patronage, rather than through ideology or law – offices of state are performed to acquire and distribute wealth, status, jobs, contracts and projects, clouding any distinction between public and private interests. Short-term reciprocal relationships are built between leaders and their followers (and then between higher-ranking and lower-ranking followers) to compensate for the absence of long-term, generalized relationships within a functioning formal state hierarchy.[182]

As a result, weak states are often accompanied by resilient and highly effective social structures. The weak legal-rational bureaucratic arms of the government are penetrated, compromised and often overshadowed by informal practices. Though many transitional justice scholars are optimistic that these informal practices can generate localized forms of care and reconciliation, many of these structures at the grassroots level may not

---

[179] Marten (n 148).

[180] Charles Call, 'Ending Wars, Building States' in Charles Call (ed.) with Vanessa Wyeth, *Building States to Build Peace* (Lynne Rienner 2008) 1 at 14.

[181] Christopher Clapham, *Third World Politics: An Introduction* (Helm 1985) 48.

[182] Clapham (n 59) 780–81.

enjoy links to state-level development. (This is the subject of Chapter 5.) At a higher level, informal practices often take the form of patrimonial systems that fulfil some useful social functions as the pattern of distribution trickles downward and outward from national leaders to local clients lower in the social hierarchy. However, the very success of these may inhibit the type of state formation that can support welfare, development and reduction of horizontal inequalities.[183] Though one must be wary of reductionist perspectives on developing world politics that deprive non-elite groups of agency in their political and economic lives,[184] in societies exhibiting neopatrimonial features the line between private and public spheres tends to blur. A civic public realm where policy ambitions of general application to all groups of society are collectively bargained between organized state and social interests tends to be under-developed.[185] Political leaders do not use state power to pursue common interests, but rather use the state to bring demands for communities they represent. Policy-making cannot be insulated from political interference by sectoral interests, while clientelistic patronage encourages competition over what are seen as particularistic benefits to the exclusion of a generalized provision of welfare-enhancing public goods.[186] Both governments and peacebuilders may have to tolerate corruption, black markets and illicit economies not only because they are too weak to control them, but also because they are indispensable for sustaining basic livelihoods by providing sources of employment and subsistence that the legal economy cannot.[187] However, overall the effect of patrimonialism, clientelism and corruption is exclusionary, prioritizing and privileging insiders at the expense of outsiders and compounding inequalities. As suggested in the earlier examination of compromised peacebuilding, if the main goal of national political actors is to maintain themselves in power, then the continued ability to secure sufficient wealth and opportunity for the clients and supporters that ultimately

---

[183] Volker Boege et al., 'Building Peace and Political Community in Hybrid Political Orders' (2009) 16 *International Peacekeeping* 599, 612.

[184] Thandika Mkandawire, 'Neopatrimonialism and the Political Economy of Economic Performance in Africa: Critical Reflections' (2015) 67 *World Politics* 563.

[185] Michael Bratton and Nicolas Van de Walle, 'Neopatrimonial Regimes and Political Transitions in Africa' (1994) 46 *World Politics* 453, 458.

[186] Rod Alence, 'Political Institutions and Developmental Governance in Sub-Saharan Africa' (2004) 42 *Journal of Modern African Studies* 163, 167 and 178.

[187] Mats Berdal, *Building Peace After War* (Routledge 2009) 70.

buttress their claim to power is imperative. Processes of statebuilding, peacebuilding or transitional justice that 'dilute those resources among the population at large (or even among a minimum winning coalition) may seem unnecessary or even dangerous'.[188] As the previous chapter noted, this 'patrimonial marketplace' in which a stable political order is produced by inclusive buy-in of factions and elites is compounded by power-sharing in post-conflict agreements. Given the heightened difficulty of post-conflict environments, there is little reason to believe that attempts to expand the focus of transitional justice to the types of corruption or inequality fostered under patrimonial conditions would not incur the same types of automatic political resistance by privileged groups that non-transitional attempts to combat it have traditionally provoked.[189]

4.3 Elites

Neopatrimonialism can be described as the conversion of public good to private gain, but there exists a separate but inter-related problem of private good operating to the detriment of public well-being. This is most obviously manifest in elite control of political and economic resources. In both the social state of nature and, later, the purposeful pursuit of complex goals, human societies enter into collective power relations with each other. In so doing, social organization and divisions of labour are typically established on hierarchical bases that distribute power as authoritative actors emerge by demonstrating the greatest ability or resources to organize security or provide socially useful services.[190] This authority confers on itself the potential to garner riches and abuse power as established elites or coalitions thereof cultivate private interests and act in pursuit of them rather than in the interests of the community, group or nation as a whole. As Hameiri notes, '"state capture" by particular interests and coalitions, predatory and otherwise, is not an aberration, but something that is common to every state, or indeed every political

[188] Kahler (n 142) 294.

[189] Madalene O'Donnell, 'Corruption: A Rule of Law Agenda' in Agnes Hurwitz and Reyko Huang (eds), *Civil War and the Rule of Law: Security, Development and Human Rights* (Lynne Rienner 2008) 225.

[190] Michael Mann, *The Sources of Social Power, Vol. 1, A History of Power from the Beginning to AD 1760* (Cambridge University Press 1986) 6.

structure'.[191] This is true of Western democracies (historically as much the product of oligarchy as of protest against it),[192] but the tendency is pronounced in highly personalized and poorly institutionalized polities. The post-colonial experience in many states has been characterized by the monopolization of political and economic authority by powerful class and identity group leaders. Because of the absence of centralization and bureaucratic reach beyond the metropolis, 'the post-civil war state frequently lacks the capacity to translate its decisions into authoritative rules applicable to society as a whole ... It therefore often has little option but to negotiate with powerful class and identity group leaders to achieve system goals'.[193] These elites can confer advantages on themselves in the accumulation of socially valuable resources, making distribution of wealth a rigged game where inequality is institutionalized by people following the rules, as opposed to breaking them.[194]

Though the phrase is bandied about loosely in the transitional justice literature, characterizing elites is difficult given the amorphousness of the concept and their different manifestations at national and sub-national levels. One of the best descriptions of elites in the post-conflict context is that of Bhuta, who outlines the importance of those individuals or entities who 'organize, contain, and generate political power' and aggregate micro- or meso-level conflicts sufficiently to 'speak for a population and bind it to a resolution'.[195] They are recognizably effective politically and serve as the natural focal points for social co-ordination sufficient to foster the acquiescence of the general public.[196] It is worth pointing out that some elites are horizontally divided by class, as opposed to ethnicity, clan or religion, and may not be directly involved in mass political co-ordination or organize along conflict lines. They may nevertheless independently dominate society's regulatory processes and its 'legitimate' economy, or serve as the access channel for international interests.

---

191 Shahar Hameiri, 'Capacity and Its Follies: International State Building as State Transformation' (2009) 38 *Milennium: Journal of International Studies* 55, 64.

192 Samuel Huntington, 'Will More Countries Become Democratic?' (1984) 99 *Political Science Quarterly* 193, 212.

193 Donald Rothchild, 'Settlement Terms and Postagreement Stability' in Stephen John Stedman, Donald Rothchild and Elizabeth Cousens (eds), *Ending Civil Wars: The Implementation of Peace Agreements* (Lynne Rienner 2002) 117 at 120.

194 Michael Schwalbe, *Rigging the Game: How Inequality is Reproduced in Everyday Life* (Oxford University Press 2008) 5–15.

195 Bhuta (n 26) 848 and 850.

196 ibid 846.

Good examples include the new black elites of South Africa, the emerging Lusophone establishment in East Timor or the old landed interests of Guatemala or El Salvador who gained or retained control over structures of opportunity after hugely turbulent political transitions in which they were bystanders. For these elites, transformative goals like redistributive taxation, nationalization of industry, land reallocation or any policy vaguely referred to as redressing inequality may jeopardize wealth and status.

These are the inevitably conservative upholders of the status quo who are disparaged in the critical transitional justice literature as unrepresentative of their societies' needs. What goes unremarked is the logical corollary of this status, i.e. that they have a significant capacity to secure their share of economic power that strong international assistance or presence in peacebuilding, statebuilding or transitional justice are unlikely to transform. As Chapter 3 illustrated, war pits governments (an institutionalized elite) against leaders of ethnic or religious communities or conflict entrepreneurs. The largely endogenous process of war and negotiating peace tends more towards entrenching elites in power than loosening their hold over society:

> [G]roup elites play a major role. Ideally, they should convince their followers, contain radical opponents and paramilitary groups, build formal and informal coalitions with moderate forces of the other side, stick to the agreed status quo, assure full participation of all relevant groups and, if possible, revive positive traditions of mutual understanding from the past. All this implies a strong commitment to cooperation and the principles of shared rule by elites.[197]

Peace itself can be conceptualized as the move of elites from conflict to co-operation. After war, conflict entrepreneurs who many not already have formed part of the pre-existing elite often form links with it, formalizing a 'political–criminal nexus' between the political establishment and a criminalized economy.[198] For these elites, the post-conflict period is as much, if not more, a matter of consolidating war-time accumulation than it is of imposing reconciliation and peace.[199] Indeed,

[197] Ulrich Schneckener, 'Making Power-sharing Work: Lessons from Successes and Failures in Ethnic Conflict Regulation' (2002) 39 *Journal of Peace Research* 203, 224.

[198] Roy Godson, 'Transnational Crime, Corruption and Security' in Michael Brown (ed.), *Grave New World* (Georgetown University Press 2003) 259 at 260.

[199] David Keen, 'A Rational Kind of Madness' (1997) 25 *Oxford Development Studies* 67.

elites, by virtue of those aspects of power or influence they enjoy independently of war or peace, furthermore stand to benefit from successful peacebuilding. As Cheng points out, after conflict elites 'can combine their political influence to leverage three important advantages: stores of conflict capital, access to insider information, and substantial financial resources' to benefit disproportionately from processes of political and economic liberalization.[200] The peacebuilding record since the Cold War illustrates that in straitened post-conflict circumstances, governments tend to allow those who have gained from the inequities of the pre-transitional period to continue their economic activities because they generate employment. Instead of challenging elites, they attempt to foster their interest in the long-term well-being of the state.[201] This is the case even where the actions of elites run contrary to liberal prescriptions of open politics and open markets. Powerful elites with an interest in perpetuating the status quo of a largely unreformed economy can do so even in the face of strong international pressure for liberalization.[202] Democratization, too, seldom operates as its international promoters intend. Political parties in new democracies seldom represent the views of broad-based constituencies and instead tend to function as tools of entrenched special interests.[203]

The prevalence of elite pacts and the ability of elites to use peace to safeguard their inherited status reinforces the argument of Zürcher, Manning and Evenson that the 'single most important factor' determining the success or failure of any peacebuilding project is whether domestic elites view it as a means to achieve their goals or as an impediment.[204] This begs the very obvious question of where advocates of transformative justice see the potential for redistributing wealth and opportunity or addressing poverty that flows in whole or in part from maldistribution. As Franzki and Olarte observe, one crucial question that is not addressed in

---

[200] Christine Cheng, 'Private and Public Interests: Informal Actors, Informal Influence, and Economic Order after War' in Berdal and Zaum (eds) (n 32) 63 at 73.

[201] Christopher Cramer, 'Trajectories of Accumulation through War and Peace' in Paris and Sisk (eds) (n 124) 129 at 135.

[202] Timothy Donais, 'The Political Economy of Stalemate: Organised Crime, Corruption and Economic Deformation in Post-Dayton Bosnia' (2003) 3 *Conflict, Security and Development* 359.

[203] Eric Bjornlund, Glenn Cowan and William Gallery, 'Election Systems and Political Parties in Post-Conflict and Fragile States' in Derick Brinkerhoff (ed.), *Governance in Post-Conflict Societies: Rebuilding Fragile States* (Routledge 2012) 64 at 66.

[204] Zürrcher, Manning and Evenson (n 131) 144.

critical analyses of transitional justice 'is *why* the societal actors that supported physical violence to secure economic interests would now subscribe to a societal consensus that puts their profits in danger'.[205] The transformative turn in transitional justice, however, has deliberately eschewed such questions by assuming that elite bargaining and structural conditions are separate phenomena in which the conditions can be ameliorated without recourse to bargaining. Critics of traditional liberal-legalist transitional justice denounce the limited worldview imposed by transition through elite bargains on the basis that it that obscures structural conditions. In a widely cited article Arthur posited a traditional preference within transitional justice for legal-institutional reform over transformation at the socio-economic level, which necessarily imported a deference to the interests of the elite over the many.[206] Arthur argued that with a transitional justice discourse rooted in a negotiated, institutionalist paradigm, inequality can be seen 'as a question of time or development rather than the entrenched ideology of elites'.[207] In this view, transitional justice needs to be 'externalized' as far as possible from political elites.[208] Though these critics correctly identify the prejudicial effects of elite bargaining on prospects for transformation, the notion that international and domestic policy-makers administering transitional justice or reconstructing the state have a choice over whether to negotiate with elite interests is highly questionable beyond the most bottom-up of projects.

Transitional justice scholars who present enduring elite control of the economy as willing liberal capitulation in oligarchic capitalism need to demonstrate how and why elites could otherwise be compelled to voluntarily concede that which they have the power not to concede. Such an exercise would not be a novel departure. Jelena Subotic, most notably, has demonstrated how even the traditional accountability goals of transitional justice are contested between three types of elite, namely true believers, instrumentalists and resisters.[209] As noted in Chapter 2, resisters are politically or pragmatically opposed to justice, unable to accept its diagnosis of the roots of conflict or to internalize its norms because this

[205] Franzki and Olarte (n 44) 211.

[206] Arthur (n 22).

[207] Miller (n 1) 268.

[208] Thomas Obel Hansen, 'The Vertical and Horizontal Expansion of Transitional Justice: Explanations and Implications for a Contested Field' in Buckley-Zistel et al. (eds) (n 44) 105 at 119.

[209] Jelena Subotic, 'Bargaining Justice' in Buckley-Zistel et al. (eds) (n 44) 127.

would undermine the basis of their power nationally.[210] Instrumentalists (who use transitional justice to distinguish themselves from other political groups) and true believers (those who fully accept the need for justice) may offer more promising avenues for a strong domestic consensus on economic justice. However, Subotic's schema does not address these dilemmas in the economic context, and few critics of transitional justice's inherent liberalism have adopted such a power-based analysis. One obvious difference is that old-style transitional justice and its newer transformative conception would make radically different demands on theoretically supportive elites – the perceived right to torture, maim or kill are resources antagonists are content to give up in order to secure transition, while land, opportunities and natural resources may not be. Subotic usefully warns that transnational advocates of transitional justice consistently underestimate the ability of domestic elites to resist international norms and overestimate the power of domestic reform constituencies, particularly considering the fact that none of the three groups is likely to enjoy a monopoly of authority.[211]

In transitional justice's transformative turn, there is an implicit image of the post-conflict state that is freed from liberal imposition of democracy, markets and alien institutions. This imagined state serves as an aggregate of individuals and communities with the authority to deliver the needs of communities, to competently provide social goods and to act as neutral arbiter among contending constituencies. However, this image is transformed beyond recognition by the reality of entrenched elite control of political and economic opportunity. Formal political institutions that exist in post-conflict states are invariably shaped by, and reproduce, the primary interests and constituencies of domestic elites. Regardless of what governance arrangements are put in place, the state will remain a site of social conflict, not a purely neutral ground for enlightened policy-making. Without attention to this socio-political logic of domestic governance, it becomes impossible to make robust claims about what external actors' logics of governance can or should aspire towards.[212] Long after the discrete events of peace agreements, transitional justice, elections and so on, elites will mediate, collaborate in and contest the realms of security, capital and opportunities no less than they do in Western societies.[213] Even if formal power is organized in more

---

210 ibid 136.

211 ibid 134, 137.

212 Sending (n 2) 63.

213 Jago Salmon and Catherine Anderson, 'Elites and Statebuilding' in Chandler and Sisk (eds) (n 98) 42 at 44.

democratic ways or cabined by external supervision by the judiciary, much informal power may nevertheless be exercised in ways that reflect a common elite understanding. Failure to confront elite patterns of accumulation is best viewed not as a blind spot of transitional justice, nor as a conscious trade-off to guarantee security. It is instead an acknowledgement that any normative standards (be they traditionally liberal or revised to reflect distributive or transformative goals) through which the international community wishes to bestow legitimacy on a political dispensation may stand in stark contrast to the norms and rules of elites, the pacts they negotiate formally or informally amongst themselves, and their expectant constituencies.[214]

4.4 Why the Post-conflict State Tends to Resemble the Pre-conflict State

Chapter 2 examined how the impact of constructivist thinking, the abstraction of the concept of transition from any really-existing context and the innate optimism over transition have combined to obscure the political economy of transitional justice from theorization. Scholarship and advocacy in fourth generation transitional justice assumes the social world of transitional states is malleable, provided the right theories of justice are applied by the right people at the right time. This discourse, plus the tendency to assume the foundational barriers to transformation lie with the liberalism of interveners, implies that transformation of social structures is an essentially conciliatory process that need not conflict with vying interests or, to the extent that it does, is so unambiguously beneficial for a sufficiently large number of people that the interests of those who stand to lose are easily circumvented. The assumptions underpinning the transformative turn imagine the mechanisms and popular legitimacy of a revised transitional justice as a short cut to development and structural reform that domestic incentives have hitherto not permitted. This discourse has side-stepped engagement with elites, warlords and patrimonial forces that liberally inclined, negotiation-based transitional justice historically engaged with for more limited purposes of stability and political resolution of conflict.

The resources that transitional justice interveners can deploy and the narratives of progress they express and imbibe have always fostered an illusory sense that they can comprehend and influence the post-transitional society. In the transformative turn, this illusion is magnified.

---

[214] ibid 49.

Belief in the rightness of the cause appears to have inhibited reflection on the possibility that national institutions may be too feeble to self-enforce transformation or that powerful local figures might disagree with an interventionary policy. As Coyne argues, projects carried out in the pursuit of humanitarian goals that are bound up in absolute normative commitments like equality, development or redistribution are 'necessarily simple relative to the complexity of the system within which those activities are carried out'.[215] Much critical transitional justice scholarship presumes that transformative outcomes can be produced, legitimized and stabilized as matters of intention and design, and that transitional justice can catalyse desired economic dynamics and outcomes. However, it is intuitively reasonable and empirically justifiable to suggest that those who prosper under the economic status quo will devote some portion of their gains to protecting it. Humanitarian interventions like transitional justice are 'conceived and designed as if the intended recipients, and other actors in the system, are passive and non-strategic in their behaviors' when of course many actors will behave strategically in response to projects that attempt to transform society.[216] It is unlikely that the disturbance to the political equilibrium signalled by peace in and of itself can render malleable the largely informal and sometimes criminalized economies of accumulation and inequality favoured by vested interests.

This section has made clear that the wish-list tendency of transitional justice theorization examined in Chapter 2 and the fixation on the liberalism of transitional justice examined in the present chapter do not contribute to the development of adaptive theories of transformative transitional justice. Adaptive theories are those that can cope with the difficulties imposed by weak state structures, engrained patterns of patrimonialism, and entrenched elite control of the economy. These collectively sub-optimal underlying factors are not the product of deliberate design, and hence theoretically more amenable to conscious counter-design by external actors or domestic reform constituencies. They are produced by rules and orders that follow from the actions of thousands, if not millions, of different people interactively pursuing their own ends over decades. As Mani notes, the agentless and macroeconomic nature of systematic inequality poses distinct problems in conceptualizing responses to damage done – the beneficiaries of many of the practices underpinning social injustice like patrimonialism or elite

---

215 Christopher Coyne, *Doing Bad by Doing Good: Why Humanitarian Action Fails* (Stanford University Press 2013) 145.

216 ibid 150.

control of the economy are more 'amorphous', 'nameless' and 'faceless' than those wrongdoers we are familiar with who commit defined crimes.[217] Most acts or systems entrenching inequality occur beyond the reach of government, sometimes with its imprimatur, but often because it has no choice but to acquiesce given the state's weakness. There is no good reason to expect these phenomena to cease because there has been a transitional alteration in the locus of state power or because interveners would prefer they did not exist.

> [Options for redesign of the state] are limited by the historical, institutional fabric woven over decades or centuries by colonial legacies, land tenure patterns, industrial development … In this context, elites in transitional periods tend not to look very far from previous models … This is true largely because previous forms of governance hold some level of acceptance even among those who are not advantaged by them, whereas any deviation will find opposition from those who think they might possibly be left disadvantaged vis-à-vis familiar prior structures. Prior structures start as an obvious point of convergence in bargaining, be it explicit or tacit.[218]

None of these factors makes transformation impossible or the aspiration for economic justice futile. However, these systemic biases are crucial mediating factors that determine the prospects for altering structures of inequality or poverty. They condition the motivational conditions for collaboration, co-operation and coercion between transitional justice actors and those whose interests are challenged by radical reform.

Though peacebuilders, transnational transitional justice advocacy groups and national reform constituencies can press for transformation, post-conflict states often manifest the 'paradox of weakness' whereby domestic political actors can credibly resist reform and minimize concessions by claiming that internal opposition is too strong and risks either a return to violence or jeopardizes elite buy-in to the peace.[219] Newly developed institutions (most notably the state, but one could include any transitional justice mechanism developed after peace) rarely develop sufficient authority or reach in the short-term to curb the raw power of different factions that are truly determined to resist.[220] What's more,

---

[217] Rama Mani, 'Editorial: Dilemmas of Expanding Transitional Justice, or Forging the Nexus between Transitional Justice and Development' (2008) 2 *International Journal of Transitional Justice* 253, 255.

[218] Call (n 180) 380.

[219] Zürcher, Manning and Evenson (n 131) 28.

[220] Marina Ottaway, 'Rebuilding State Institutions in Collapsed States' (2002) 33 *Development and Change* 1001, 1015.

interventions to strengthen the state's institutional capacity to strengthen a notional social contract may appear to threaten existing privileges of groups who can resort to violence to oppose it.[221] For reasons outlined earlier, local actors can almost always work around formal institutions of state by embracing pre-existing hybrid or patrimonial structures. As Subotic notes, entrenched elites can adapt quickly to the transitional justice preferences of international actors and develop strategies of quasi-compliance, deception, or even counter-mobilization.[222] For these reasons, transitional justice may be no different than any other forms of peacebuilding intervention, which 'begin with grand notions of transformation but nevertheless adopt strategies and strike implicit contracts with local elites that reinforce existing state-society relations'.[223] Acknowledging this reality does not mean absolving liberal peacebuilding or transitional justice interveners of responsibility for the limits of, or damage inflicted by, their approaches. Nor does it mean that the pressure transitional justice actors in particular can bring to bear on post-conflict leaders will never alter domestic policy in relation to economic structures. However, it does mean that those who urge transformative approaches should do so without illusions that they can disregard the very evident limitations on the malleability of socio-economic structures where there is little political will to redress inequalities.

5. THE LIMITS OF CRITICAL APPROACHES: A CRISIS OF RELEVANCE?

This chapter has made clear that while the liberal-legalist impulses that underlie transitional justice advocacy and practice have restricted the possible bounds of justice, the primacy of domestic politics in peace agreements and the enduring impact of state weakness, patrimonialism and elite control of economic opportunity make clear that some of the primary barriers to transformation are domestic. The tempting, if glib, response is to argue that transitional justice should bring these phenomena within its scope of inquiry. However, these are not merely problems to be addressed. They are long-term forms of action purposively undertaken by actors who have the political or informal power to resist action by international interveners or domestic reform constituencies to address

---

[221] Dominik Zaum, 'Beyond the "Liberal Peace"' (2012) 18 *Global Governance* 121, 128.

[222] Subotic (n 209) 139.

[223] Barnett and Zürcher (n 124) 29.

them. It should be clear from the foregoing issues, and the failure of the field to address them even superficially, that the transformative turn in transitional justice fails to account for the social processes that go into the production of countervailing norms and ideas. It lacks awareness of how those aspirations are incompatible with the incentives of those with formal and informal power in post-conflict states. Conflict and resistance are inherent to processes of social change, meaning that even if the field re-orients itself to concentrate on economic injustice, there will be slippage between norms and impact that cannot be explained purely by the biases of international actors. Not all amelioration of inequitable social structures is exclusively dependent on the goodwill of elites – forceful national leadership, international norm penetration and civil society mobilization can achieve much depending on how strong they are, though few transitional justice scholars have explained how this might be so. However, the viability of some transformative justice measures and the maximization of others depend far more on the incentives facing domestic actors than the conceptions of justice promoted by international transitional justice actors. This pragmatic injunction does not assume the resistance of those who benefit from inequality is legitimate, morally tolerable or forever unalterable, but it does recognize that mediation of policy by these figures has acquired the status of an inevitable social fact within any timescale recognizable as transitional. A theory of transformative justice that cannot acknowledge adoption costs for potential losers nor cope with hard cases is of limited utility.

Prospects for transformative justice are best where it can be shown to be of instrumental value to those domestic political actors who organize political power. They can speak for at least some of the population and bind it to a resolution. Almost all theories of peacebuilding, democratization and state-building now emphasize the imperative of increasing elite incentives to pursue policies in the public interest.[224] For example, informal power structures of patrimonialism and elite control of resources structure political behaviour and expectations of politically effective actors, and are extremely resistant to change. As Helmke and Levitsky argue, any body of research or advocacy that fails to consider these structures risks missing many of the most crucial incentives and

---

[224] A good example is Thomas Ohlson and Mimmi Soderberg Kovacs, 'Peace through Democracy? The Challenges of Post-War Democratisation in Weak and War-Torn States' in Ashok Swain, Ramses Amer and Joakim Ojendal (eds), *The Democratization Project: Challenges and Opportunities* (Anthem Press 2008) 165.

constraints that dictate political behaviour and prospects for change.[225] Without understanding how such factors permeate the site of intervention, 'outsiders will grope in the dark and their actions will continue to produce perverse and unintended consequences, at worst creating structures that encourage and reward continuing violence'.[226]

However, very little in a critical discourse of transitional justice that is shaped almost exclusively around the twin poles its own justice imaginary (the focus of Chapter 2) and the rote rejection of liberalism (the focus of the present chapter) provides the appropriate antennae for proposing how the long-term and culturally engrained dynamics of inequality can be shifted through the alliance of external incentives, grassroots pressure and limited political transition manifested in a peace agreement. Nothing in the fourth generation transitional justice literature has even begun to engage with the types of organized opposition posed by those who benefit from unequal socio-economic structures noted above in Kenya, El Salvador, Guatemala and anywhere else transitional justice has been attempted, bar the denigration of elites or the reality of dealing with them. This literature has not engaged with the rationality behind patterns of distribution in exclusionary patron-client pyramids or the limits imposed by state weakness. Critical transitional justice discourse as it has developed is comfortable in the language of equality, transformation and right but not in the register of domestic authority and informal power where the key dilemma of the field's potential to activate core variables in favour of transformation is found.

5.1 A Crisis of Relevance

This chapter has drawn attention to the limits of an approach grounded more in a rejection of liberalism than a concrete engagement with the political economy of post-conflict societies. As such, it is worth pondering the parallels with the more developed critical peacebuilding literature, which itself is struggling with the limitations imposed by such a one-sided scholarship. If, after all, the liberal peacebuilding critique is automatically applied to transitional justice, it is worth considering if its more obvious shortcomings are too. It is relevant, therefore, that many of peacebuilding's own critical theorists have to acknowledge (1) the tendency of its scholarship to focus more on problematizing the ontological or epistemological claims of liberal interveners than on empirical

[225] Gretchen Helmke and Steven Levitsky, 'Informal Institutions and Comparative Politics: A Research Agenda' (2004) 2 *Perspectives on Politics* 725.

[226] Berdal (n 187) 92.

analysis of actual interventions, and (2) that this has left critical theorists at a considerable remove from policy discourse in the field.[227] Like the theorization of the transformative turn, most critical peace studies place the West and the liberal at the centre of analysis, juxtaposing it against the domestic 'rest'.[228] In theoretical terms, critical peacebuilding is focused almost entirely on the policies and beliefs of the interveners, even if there is consistent lip-service to local needs and wants. The major works in this intellectual tradition adopt a critical stance to international power and concentrate more 'on making sense of the genealogies, contradictions and trajectories of the intellectual traditions of the "West" as the key object of intellectual concern' than the states intervened upon. Notwithstanding generic and decontextualized references to hybridity, the local and the everyday, these works do not 'represent or engage with the activities or behaviour of particular peoples targeted by interventions, since these were not considered relevant to the overall framing of this part of the research … [they] were implicitly irrelevant to the conclusions that the research wanted to draw about the West's relationship with post-conflict environments'.[229] Though these criticisms do not apply absolutely to critical approaches to transitional justice (Chapter 5 examines its concern for grassroots justice and everyday lives), it does appear to share the liberal peacebuilding critique's lack of orthodox paradigms of realist analysis and its extreme detachment from the core phenomena affecting national peace processes like power-sharing, institutional strength and elite buy-in.[230]

The liberal peacebuilding critique, like fourth generation transitional justice, is intellectually stimulating and has succeeded in pointing out contradictions, increasing context-sensitivity and extending imaginations of what practitioners could aspire towards. However, the former tends to demonstrate feet of clay when posed with real-world dilemmas. Even sharp critics of liberal peacebuilding have been forced to acknowledge that their body of theory provides no functional way forward to an improved practice beyond deconstructing liberal interventionism.[231]

[227] Susanna Campbell, David Chandler and Meera Sabaratnam, 'Introduction: The Politics of Liberal Peace' in Campbell, Chandler and Sabaratnam (eds) (n 2) 1 at 3.

[228] Jenny Peterson, 'A Conceptual Unpacking of Hybridity: Accounting for Notions of Power, Politics and Progress in Analyses of Aid-driven Interfaces' (2012) 7 *Journal of Peacebuilding and Development* 9, 18.

[229] Sabaratnam (n 152) 263.

[230] Mac Ginty (n 117) 23.

[231] Newman (n 93) 1747.

Because so much of the critical literature does not examine in even the most generic sense the typical relationships among conflict antagonists, the structural characteristics of their antagonism and the historically specific processes of division in war-torn societies, even the most prominent critics of liberal peacebuilding like Richmond and Mac Ginty admit that the most significant failing of the critique 'has been its inability to engage in a fuller way' with the policy mainstream.[232] It is this distance and opacity within the critique that has cemented a notion prevalent even within the critical school itself that scholars in the area are more theoretical than policy-driven.[233] Tadjbakhsh identifies an intrinsic divide between 'optimistic practitioners' and 'pessimist or at least skeptical academics and theoreticians' in which on-the-ground work is dismissed as irrelevant to the scholarly community.[234] Critical peacebuilding scholars acknowledge the need to develop sharper theoretical tools to comprehend the complexities of liberal peacebuilding if they are to remedy their lack of policy influence.[235] Without greater attention to the political economy of post-conflict states, these are problems that critical, fourth generation transitional justice theorists may find themselves parroting after it achieves the prominence in the scholarly discourse (if it has not done so already). Already, as Sharp notes, the critiques of transitional justice that have emerged come 'most strongly from academics working in a critical studies tradition rather than those at the centers of power and decision-making' in the field.[236]

This crisis of relevance is troubling from the perspective of transitional justice because practitioners, as opposed to academics, have always had to take prevailing social relationships and the institutions they are organized into as the given framework for action. Within the traditional remit of trials, truth commissions, reparation and so on, transitional justice was always an essentially reactive, bargained and epiphenomenal

---

232 Oliver Richmond and Roger Mac Ginty, 'Where Now for the Critique of the Liberal Peace?' (2015) 50 *Cooperation and Conflict* 171, 173.

233 An argument suggested in Erin McCandless, Eric Abitbol and Timothy Donais, 'Vertical Integration: A Dynamic Practice Promoting Transformative Peacebuilding' (2015) 10 *Journal of Peacebuilding and Development* 1, 1; Edward Newman, 'The Violence of Statebuilding in Historical Perspective: Implications for Peacebuilding' (2013) 1 *Peacebuilding* 141, 144.

234 Shahrbanou Tadjbakhsh, 'Introduction: Liberal Peace in Dispute' in Tadjbakhsh (ed.) (n 69) 1 at 1. She also speaks of practitioners, on the one hand, and 'abstract theoreticians', on the other (at 2).

235 John Heathershaw, 'Towards Better Theories of Peacebuilding: Beyond the Liberal Peace Debate' (2013) 1 *Peacebuilding* 275, 275.

236 Sharp (n 21) 177.

process within the confines of a single state. There was usually little practical space for approaches that questioned prevailing structures of power and the interests they serve because those powers and structures presented immediate dilemmas that called for immediate resolution. Though there has always been space for moral and critical arguments about what transitional justice should aspire to, the field has always been more policy-oriented and problem-solving than theoretical, cabined by country-specific and historically-configured social structures and the strategic choices of political actors within them. Though critical theorists argue that transitional justice 'is a perspective that sets bounds to the societal projects that can be envisioned through its discourse',[237] the historical reality in places like Argentina, South Africa, Rwanda and Uganda is that transitional justice does not *set* boundaries but rather exists *within* them, albeit occasionally pressing them to the extent possible. Transitional justice, unlike critical peacebuilding, has never been a purely discursive project or a theory of justice in its own right. Though we tend to describe transitional justice as a construct that has a will and exerts active power (transitional justice 'must' or 'should' or 'can'), it has always been an extraordinary form of justice whose parameters are defined by compromises demanded by paradigmatic transitions from authoritarianism or war to some form of democracy or peace. Transitional justice on the ground has always consisted of a series of tools like trials and truth commissions employed by international and domestic professional and donor networks. These have little or no influence over domestic factors like the terms of peace agreements, the informalization of the national economy or domestic governmental decisions on whether to use reparations as substitutes for development or whether to formulate a development plan. Factors relating to the balance of power and availability of moral, human and political capital have constrained the field's ability to address injustices of the past. Indeed, it was the uniqueness of these very restrictive dilemmas and their solutions that made transitional justice distinctive. Idealist theorizations where universalist conceptions of justice apply – regardless of balance of power considerations as a necessary precursor to political change – have always existed in tension with (and usually give way to) realist positions where justice in transition was the epiphenomenal and inevitably compromised product of political or institutional constraints.[238] As noted earlier,

---

[237] Franzki and Olarte (n 44) 204. A similar argument is made in Arthur (n 22).

[238] Ruti Teitel, *Transitional Justice* (Oxford University Press 2001) 3–4.

qualitative and quantitative studies of transitional justice have demonstrated that the largely endogenous factor of transition type is ultimately the key deciding factor in determining whether transitional justice is pursued or not, and how it is pursued.[239]

5.2 A Crisis of Clarity

This chapter has argued that transformative justice is defined not by what it is but by what it is not. When transitional justice theory attempts to escape from the restrictive, bargained problem-solving paradigm it rejects, a seemingly insuperable but under-acknowledged problem of vagueness arises. Transformative visions for justice concentrate primarily on establishing appropriate conceptual frameworks to the neglect of intervention models, policy instruments and methodologies of assistance that grapple with generic conditions in post-conflict states. Much of the transformative discourse is self-referential or self-contained, premised on reconceptualizing the limitations of the field's foundational paradigm of justice to better help practitioners and scholars in the field to understand what they are doing. For example, a recent work by Balint, Evans and McMillan is typical:

> Injustice is conceived of as a product of inequitable structures as well as individual action. In this view, a structural justice model would involve a shift from individualistic and state-focused modes of redress towards a more thoroughgoing evaluation of the structural vestiges of 'past' harms and an openness to deep and wide-ranging reforms, including indigenous jurisprudences, which would transform social, political, legal and economic arrangements that enabled the harms. A structural justice would pay attention to both the causes and the legacies of the initial harms.[240]

Note here the binaried rejection of liberal-legalist approaches, a concentration on the field's own means of evaluation and the implicit confidence that 'openness to reforms' automatically conduces to transformation. This view is typical of a literature characterized by a keenness to depart from traditional approaches, a confidence in the field's efficacy in enabling socio-economic change coupled with an unerring imprecision about how transformative impulses might be manifest in action on the ground.

David Kennedy reminds us that in the field of humanitarian action, there is always a risk of conflating what seem like improvements in the field's ability to respond to things outside itself with what may in fact

239 Olsen, Payne and Reiter (n 127).
240 Balint, Evans and McMillan (n 43) 213.

merely represent improvements in the field's ability to respond to its own internal divisions and contradictions.[241] It would appear that much of the transformative theorizing tends more towards the latter than the former. As noted in Chapter 2, advocates of a role for transitional justice in fundamentally altering the structures of divided societies acknowledge that thus far all we have are 'a series of hypothetical connections to be further researched',[242] 'points of possible interconnection',[243] 'a starting point for a broader conversation'[244] and underdeveloped concepts and boundaries.[245] Even those scholars who explicitly undertake to 'outline concrete ways in which transitional justice can become more transformative'[246] (or suggest conceptions of transformative justice that are analytically distinct from transitional justice)[247] gesture more towards reforming our participation in transitional states than illustrating how this reformed participation would then play out in the context of a specific state against specific opposition. Gready and Robins, for example, encourage a shift from the legal to the social, from the state and institutions to communities, from technical and managerial approaches to advocacy and mobilization.[248] They urge firstly the reframing of issues to resonate with already-accepted norms so as to insert them into the transitional agenda, secondly a form of participation in all elements of the project cycle that transforms victimhood, and thirdly an empowering shift in the focus of rights talk from the metropolis to the new democratic spaces at the interface of state and society where violations occur.[249] Though these recommendations are undoubtedly welcome and contribute to a more imaginative and sensitive practice, they may mean little to the poor,

---

[241] David A. Kennedy, *The Dark Sides of Virtue: Reassessing International Humanitarianism* (Princeton University Press 2004) 24.

[242] Christopher Colvin, 'Purity and Planning: Shared Logistics of Transitional Justice and Development' (2008) 2 *International Journal of Transitional Justice* 412, 414.

[243] ibid.

[244] Miller (n 1) 291.

[245] Lisa Hecht and Sabine Michalowski, 'The Economic Dimensions of Transitional Justice' (University of Essex Transitional Justice Network Concept Paper 2012) 1 <http://www.essex.ac.uk/tjn/documents/Th eeconomicandsocial dimensionsofTJ.pdf> accessed 20 July 2016.

[246] Gready and Robins (n 24) 17.

[247] Most notably ibid and Matthew Evans, 'Structural Violence, Socioeconomic Rights and Transformative Justice' (2016) 15 *Journal of Human Rights* 1.

[248] Gready and Robins (n 24) 355 and 352–53.

[249] ibid 355–60.

victims and civil society unless other broader conditions are in place that allow the gap between better insight and transformation to be bridged. Links between reformed participation and better socio-economic outcomes are assumed, not demonstrated. Gready and Robins explicitly aim to translate ambition into practice,[250] but a genuine theory of change needs to go a step further by exploring how that practice might be translated into outcomes or cope with predictable opposition. This is seldom a characteristic of a literature in which suggested activities ('exposing' discriminatory practices,[251] 'reaching' for deeper justice,[252] 'making connections',[253] 'placing' on a 'broader justice agenda'[254]) are the precursors to effective political strategy, but always at least one or two removes from it. De Greiff has spoken of how truth commission recommendations seem 'utopian' in the sense that they are all-encompassing but seldom contain feasible prescriptions from getting from 'here to there', but it is a criticism that applies to much of the transformative literature.[255]

Transitional justice in the transformative turn is a combination of commendable impulses and fuzzy policy guidance. The targets of transformation are victims, civil society and the social processes they find legitimate, commendably emphasizing their agency but neglecting the political frameworks they operate in. Highlighting economic rights might, as a number of authors argue, serve as a springboard for embedding such rights in transitional societies.[256] However, as one of the few explicitly sceptical treatments of field's ability to affect socio-economic structures puts it, there are lessons in humility for transitional justice in those states where socio-economic rights are already incorporated into the constitutional framework but where poverty nevertheless endures. Formal progress towards socio-economic justice is always mediated by the political

---

250 ibid 355.

251 Louise Arbour, 'Economic and Social Justice for Societies in Transition' (2007) 40 *NYU Journal of International Law and Policy* 1, 3.

252 Tafadzwa Pasipanodya, 'A Deeper Justice: Economic and Social Justice as Transitional Justice in Nepal' (2008) 2 *International Journal of Transitional Justice* 378, 397.

253 See title of de Greiff and Duthie (eds) (n 76).

254 Balint, Evans and McMillan (n 43) 211.

255 Pablo de Greiff, 'Articulating the Links Between Transitional Justice and Development: Justice and Social Integration' in de Greiff and Duthie (eds) (n 76) 28 at 40.

256 Arbour (n 251); Cahill Ripley (n 155).

community and institutional weakness.[257] Truth commissions in South Africa, Chad, Guatemala and Peru had remits to examine socio-economic structures but their lack of impact merely highlighted the gaps between insight and transformation.[258] The belief that an emphasis on rights or redistribution or economic violence on the part of transitional justice actors makes their realization more likely reveals the 'naïve technicism' in transitional justice that critics have railed against in assuming 'that societies can be understood and manipulated, and people behave rationally or at least predictably'.[259]

The real transformation sketched in much of the literature, therefore, is in transitional justice's *approach*, not necessarily in its outcomes. Noting this failure should not be confused with criticism per se, but it does highlight the large gap between rhetoric and means that exists within this literature. As Chapter 2 suggested, there is nothing resembling a theory of change in the sense of a chain of assumptions explaining how these forms of intervention contribute to a desired outcome. Disruptive thinking, bottom-up theorizing and intersectionality may open up discourse to agonism,[260] but they are likely to prove hollow if theorization continues to be divorced from domestic politics. Even the most detailed attempts to outline a concept of transformative justice tend to fall back on a largely motherhood-and-apple-pie vagueness. For example, Lambourne outlines four elements of transformative justice, namely (1) legal justice that reconciles the retributive and the restorative, (2) truth and healing, (3) socio-economic justice (reparation, restitution and distributive justice) and (4) political justice (political reform, governance, democratization), which appear mostly to restate the traditional goals of the field and then merely re-iterate the need for redistribution.[261] Evans writes of the necessary conditions of transformative justice as 'the inclusion of affected communities (not just elites) in shaping the agenda for policy and practice; a focus on addressing economic conditions; emphasis on long-term societal changes; and attention to the historical and structural

---

[257] Frank Haldeman and Rachelle Kouassi, 'Transitional Justice without Economic, Social and Cultural Rights?' in Eibe Riedel, Gilles Giacca and Christophe Golay (eds), *Economic, Social and Cultural Rights: Contemporary Issues and Challenges* (Oxford University Press 2014) 498 at 513–14.

[258] De Greiff (n 255) 36.

[259] Colvin (n 242) 423.

[260] Brown and Ní Aoláin (n 17) 146.

[261] Wendy Lambourne, 'Transformative Justice, Reconciliation and Peacebuilding' in Buckley-Zistel et al. (eds) (n 44) 19 at 33 (list).

roots of contemporary injustices'.[262] Though these approaches are laudable and unobjectionable in principle, they exemplify a tendency to present transitional justice as a purely normative orientation, one which takes for granted a popular consensus among all or most parties for dramatic economic change, assumes a lack of organized opposition and infers a bureaucratic capability to bridge the gap between need and delivery. Others have argued that a revised transitional justice might serve as 'a lobbying tool when it comes to pressing new governments for much needed reforms',[263] a powerful new way to describe the real human impact of abuses[264] and a means of allowing victims to be heard and acknowledged.[265] All of these roles are welcome, but in and of themselves fall short of transformation. As I have elsewhere argued, if all we have lost through transitional justice's narrow concern for civil and political rights is one lobbying tool, a victim platform or information source (among many) in a transitional state, then there is a distinct possibility that the critical pudding has been over-egged.[266]

5.3 Final Observations

Much of fourth generation transitional justice boils down to a simplistic but commendable plea to go beyond the perspective of liberal democracy and to 'be open to alternative options'.[267] However, critiques that originate in the failure of dominant Western worldviews of justice have little to say about what potential success looks like or how it might be achieved. In Chapters 1 and 2, the radically different visions of transformative justice were sketched. However, these goals remain largely undifferentiated, are not prioritized and not considered in a strategic relationship with each other. Incompletely articulated theories of transformative justice have not specified whether need or entitlement forms

---

[262] Evans (n 247) 9.

[263] Sharp (n 21) 171.

[264] Chris Albin-Lackey, 'Corruption, Human Rights and Activism: Useful Connections and Their Limits' in Sharp (ed.) (n 16) 139 at 139.

[265] Sandra Nichols, 'Reimagining Transitional Justice for an Enduring Peace: Accounting for Natural Resources in Conflict' in Sharp (ed.) (n 16) 203 at 214.

[266] Padraig McAuliffe, 'Weighing Domestic and International Impediments to Transformative Justice in Transition' (2015) 3 *London Review of International Law* 169, 181–82.

[267] Suzanne Buckley-Zistel et al., 'Transitional Justice Theories: An Introduction' in Buckley-Zistel et al. (eds) (n 44) 1 at 14, summarizing Olarte and Franzki (n 44).

the basis for justice, or whether justice should be understood comparatively (measuring what everyone is due relative to what is available to distribute) or absolutely (measuring what everyone is due by an absolute standard regardless of what is available to distribute). Elements of economic governance that underpin any strategy for equitable division of society's economic resources go unaddressed in the literature. The almost innumerable technical elements and institutional engineering needed for employment/education quotas, special credit or investment programmes, anti-discrimination legislation, progressive taxation or regional development programmes similarly go unmentioned. Challenges to transformation are not so much underestimated as ignored. Though much is made of all the disciplines transitional justice now incorporates, few of them are useful in acknowledging these types of question, let alone answering them. Backgrounds in law, restorative justice, anthropology and so on provide limited guidance for the resource distribution issues underlying constructive policy to redress inequalities. The words of Haldemann and Kouassi noted in the Foreword are worth repeating:

> It is one thing to explain why socio-economic rights should be integrated into the transitional justice framework; it is quite another to address the question of *how* this could be done. This is a crucial issue. If the ESC rights thesis is to be more than an empty abstraction, one should be able to describe the ways and means of putting it into practice.[268]

To conclude, proposed theoretical reorientations of transitional justice based upon a departure from liberal norms or mimicry of critical peacebuilding theory need to be interrogated for policy relevance. They risk abstracting a theory of transitional justice from the political and cultural context in which it applies through dehistoricized and apolitical frameworks. It could indeed be argued that insofar as it glosses over the interests and motivations of powerful domestic actors, assumes a 'no preconditions' outlook for policy prescriptions and overgeneralizes about the causes of dysfunction, it replicates much of the wishful thinking found in the mainstream liberal peace theory it rejects. It is one thing to oppose any status quo insufficiently supportive of equality, redistribution and development, but entirely another to assume interveners alone or in conjunction with the domestic government or civil society enjoy a largely untrammelled power to modify exploitative systems. We can move issues of reparation and redistribution from the periphery to the centre of transitional justice or embrace actor-oriented approaches that emphasize

---

[268] Haldeman and Kouassi (n 262) 504.

victims over institutional approaches. However, the key to socio-economic justice or structural transformation within a given state lies in the actions and incentives faced by domestic actors who may remain entirely untouched by, unaware of, or resolutely opposed to these reorientations. Understanding transitional justice's potential within a broader process of peacebuilding to address imbalances and injustices requires a careful analysis of power dynamics within post-conflict states in place of generic and reductionist liberal-critical dichotomies. This is most apparent in the area where alternatives to liberal-legalist approaches have been most apparent, namely localized and bottom-up forms of transitional justice, which the next chapter will examine.

5. 'Trickle-up' justice? The impact of bottom-up transitional justice beyond the local

Ethically, attempts to include or privilege the voice and actions of 'the local' are seen as countering a previous focus on the formal, national and international institutions at the expense of those who actually engage in the everyday and lived practices of peace and development.[1]

One strongly cherished idea among civil society peace groups is that of the power of the small example and the linkage between the local or personal level and that of the large-scale violent conflict. Peace in mind will bring peace within the family, which in turn will bring peace to the village, the country, and ultimately the world. If people are harmonic and united locally, this will serve as an example showing that peace is indeed possible, also at a higher level'.[2]

Doubts are often quickly put aside, even by the most critical. The effectiveness of the programs is presented as a wager: a wager based upon the good will of the actors, and above all a wager based, as we will see, upon the ripple effects of local dialogue processes and of the diffusion of various representations. Because they cannot be evaluated, their effectiveness is conceived as "natural" or common sense; that is, as grounded in unquestioned assumptions about social change and interactions. As such, they can be promoted and legitimized as alternatives to dominant practices.[3]

---

[1] Jenny Peterson, 'A Conceptual Unpacking of Hybridity: Accounting for Notions of Power, Politics and Progress in Analyses of Aid-driven Interfaces' (2012) 7 *Journal of Peacebuilding and Development* 9, 20.

[2] Camilla Orjuela, 'Building Peace in Sri Lanka: A Role for Civil Society?' (2003) 40 *Journal of Peace Research* 195, 203.

[3] Sandrine Lefranc, 'A Critique of "Bottom-up" Peacebuilding' in Bruno Charbonneau and Genevieve Parent (eds), *Peacebuilding, Memory and Reconciliation: Bridging Top-Down and Bottom-up Approaches* (Routledge 2013) 34 at 37.

1. TRANSITIONAL JUSTICE'S LOCAL TURN AND PARALLEL PEACEBUILDING DEBATES

Chapters 3 and 4 examined how the people empowered and the incentives created by national peacemaking and peacebuilding often tend to reduce opportunities for transformative justice. However, political settlements flowing from formal negotiations between antagonists who speak for the collectivities they represent and from the institutions fostered by external peacebuilders do not represent the totality of peace. Conflict affects the spectrum of lived experience from the individual to the community to the region, identity group or state. Each stratum incorporates different conflict parties and different levels of analysis. Any resulting peace, therefore, is lived, tested and renegotiated in and against disparate local realities where very different backgrounds, worldviews, resource bases and incentive structures apply. Post-conflict pacification is therefore built by national elites and external peacebuilders establishing top-down, macro-level visions of peace, but also through bottom-up processes stemming from what are variously described in terms of geography as the *local* or the *grassroots* and in terms of ethos as the *everyday*, the *traditional* or the *bottom-up*. One of the fundamental questions all interventionary actors must ask is whether to direct efforts towards the top-down strengthening of central state institutions to enforce the provisions of the earlier agreement or the bottom-up support of localized processes at the level of individuals and communities to foster co-operation across the lines of division.

This question has received considerable attention in transitional justice discourse. Much of the discussion about how to balance 'international' (i.e. truth commissions, trials, reparations, so defined on the empirically dubious basis that they enjoy a primarily exogenous impetus) with local justice mechanisms has been unashamedly normative. The debate, as Hansen points out, is deeply ideological and almost always based on general considerations instead of contextual deliberations.[4] That bottom-up, grassroots and everyday visions of justice are essential to any in-country transitional justice policy approaches the status of an unquestioned mantra in policy documents and praxis. Much of the energy in these debates is directed towards (1) explaining why formal, state-level justice processes alone are insufficient if a relationship is to be drawn

[4] Thomas Obel Hansen, 'The Vertical and Horizontal Expansion of Transitional Justice' in Susanne Buckley-Zistel et al. (eds), *Transitional Justice Theories* (Routledge 2013) 105 at 108.

between justice and social repair, and (2) asserting that local, traditional, everyday or grassroots processes need to be positioned far higher up the justice agenda at the former's expense. This advocacy flows from a strong sense that universalist 'international' justice would otherwise be paramount on account of international actors' role in funding and technically supporting projects.[5] It can be seen as a reaction to the earlier sense in the transitional justice literature that grassroots forms of justice would form a competing locus of accountability which would be found wanting when judged against the human rights standards that informed processes of trials or truth commissions. As Stover and Weinstein put it at the time, 'for many in the international community, what appears crucial is not what makes sense to the people most affected by mass violence but whether the form of justice mirrors that of the developed world'.[6]

This sense of embattledness emerged from an era characterized by an ingrained assumption that chaos must reign where there were no state institutions. It is no longer fully justified, however. Increased engagement with post-conflict states has led to greater sensitivity among peacebuilders towards informal and sub-national forms of rule-making, social organization and conflict resolution.[7] A securitized, mainstream peacebuilding embrace of local-level conflict resolution systems is also apparent, driven by concerns that local violence can escalate.[8] Support to diverse local civil society has been a staple of most major bilateral and multilateral peacebuilding agencies for at least a decade,[9] even if it rarely extends to a relocation of power from the state. A similar process of learning, particularly in Rwanda, East Timor and Uganda, has meant that respect for local ownership and local leadership has been emphasized by transitional justice policy-makers since the seminal *Rule of Law*

---

[5] Jaya Ramji-Nogales, 'Designing Bespoke Transitional Justice: A Pluralist Process Approach' (2010) 32 *Michigan Journal of International Law* 1, 21.

[6] Harvey M. Weinstein and Eric Stover, 'Introduction: Conflict, Justice and Reclamation' in Harvey M. Weinstein and Eric Stover (eds), *My Neighbor, My Enemy: Justice and Community in the Aftermath of Mass Atrocity* (Cambridge University Press 2004) 1 at 12.

[7] For example, Organisation for Economic Co-operation and Development, *From Fragility to Resilience: Concepts and Dilemmas of State Building in Fragile States* (Organisation for Economic Co-operation and Development 2008) 23.

[8] Timothy Sisk, *Statebuilding* (Polity Press 2013) 102 and 149.

[9] Thania Paffenholz, 'Unpacking the Local Turn in Peacebuilding: A Critical Assessment Towards an Agenda for Future Research' (2015) 36 *Third World Quarterly* 857, 867.

and Transitional Justice Report in 2004.[10] This is driven firstly by the realization that traditional or indigenous forms of justice are often the only *via media* between formal justice and impunity, and secondly by the gradual acceptance that they respond best and most legitimately to the needs of the communities in question. The deference to, or at least non-interference with, the types of bottom-up justice sketched in this chapter suggests this is a genuinely held belief and does not merely refer to ownership of 'our' Western ideas. Nevertheless, the consistent juxtaposition of top-down and bottom-up this chapter surveys is a testament to an enduring intuition that local custom, tradition, agencies, rights and needs might be suppressed by a generic transitional justice liberal-legalist toolbox.

1.1 The 'Local Turn'

While the transformative turn examined in Chapters 1 and 2 represents one notable alternative to liberal-legal models of transitional justice as examined in Chapter 4, this 'local turn' represents the other. It is one which also promises accordance with social needs, sustainability and transformation of social structures. The rest of this chapter examines the extent to which the transformative and local turns complement, contradict, or can be reconciled with each other. It asks the question of whether local processes add to, subtract from or have any impact at all on the types of structural change advocated in Chapter 2, or whether localized processes in and of themselves can amount to such transformation. This question is spurred by the tendency of the largely normative, advocatory literature on bottom-up processes to adopt two distinct approaches. Some transitional justice scholars see local justice initiatives as complementing international and national efforts to change conflict-related power dynamics.[11] They reject potentially separatist pluralism to advocate syncretic and place-based transitional justice that mixes familiar retributive and legal models with restorative local approaches.[12] Others, by contrast, seek

---

[10] UN Secretary-General, *The Rule of Law and Transitional Justice in Conflict and Post-Conflict Societies* (2004) UN Doc. S/2004/616, para. 17.

[11] Naomi Roht-Arriaza, 'Human Rights and Strategic Peacebuilding: The Roles of Local, National and International Actors' in Daniel Philpott and Gerard Powers (eds), *Strategies of Peace: Transforming Conflict in a Violent World* (Oxford University Press 2010) 231.

[12] E.g. Wendy Lambourne, 'Transformative Justice, Reconciliation and Peacebuilding' in Buckley-Zistel et al. (eds) (n 4) 19 at 21; Rosalind Shaw and Lars Waldorf, 'Introduction: Localizing Transitional Justice' in Rosalind Shaw

a fundamental transformation of the 'politics, locus and priorities' of transitional justice by shifting the focus 'from the legal to the social and political, and from the state and institutions to communities and everyday concerns', exchanging supposedly external, liberal frameworks and templates for a predominantly bottom-up understanding of justice.[13] These approaches reject any instrumentalization of local conflict resolution to serve macro-level political agendas.[14] While this position is premised on a belief in the efficacy of localized processes, it also emanates to a significant extent from the critical discourse around the supposedly hegemonic liberalism of transitional justice explored in the previous chapter. There is something intuitively and morally appealing about centring reconciliation and justice on grassroots traditional bodies or civil society instead of faction leaders and national politicians whose power-base and supposed legitimacy lie in violence, wealth or the authority conferred by distant state institutions. The supportive literature on localized transitional justice has therefore seen a 180 degree revolution from old formalist, state-based approaches. Much contemporary field-based or ethnographic transitional justice scholarship tends to be locale-centric, focussing on immediate community relations and treating state-level institutions and politics as illegitimate constraints on grassroots justice. One effect of this approach is that it neglects to position the processes they advocate within overarching processes of stabilization and reconciliation.

These dichotomies between technocratic, legalistic, Western transitional justice and locally led initiatives that draw on traditional sources or a more reconciliatory *weltanschauung* are unhelpful in assessing the potential of the latter to effect change in post-conflict structures. First and foremost, there is never a binary choice between one initiative or another. Most localized justice processes emerge organically beyond international influence (a matter examined below in Section 4), while most of those that are supported or catalysed by international actors enjoy a similarly splendid isolation from formal state structures. Much of the discourse on localized transitional justice serves primarily as an elaborate critique of

---

and Lars Waldorf (eds) with Pierre Hazan, *Localizing Transitional Justice: Interventions and Priorities After Mass Violence* (Stanford University Press 2010) 3.

[13] Paul Gready and Simon Robins, 'From Transitional to Transformative Justice: A New Agenda for Practice' (2014) 8 *International Journal of Transitional Justice* 339, 340.

[14] ibid 349. Similar sentiments are expressed in Shaw and Waldorf (n 12) 26.

macro-level processes of punishment or truth, and only secondarily concentrates on what the alternative, bottom-up projects can actually achieve. Though there is consistent lip-service to the notion of avoiding the romanticization of the local, there is nevertheless a strikingly uncritical assessment of the broader impact of grassroots processes that is rarely justified by the empirical record. As Section 3 argues in greater detail, there is an expectation that forms of transitional justice that emphasize local agency and resources are integrally related to attempts to challenge unequal power relationships and structures of exclusion at the local, national and global level.[15] As such, it replicates similar arguments within the critical peacebuilding literature that localized and context-specific peacebuilding 'produces an everyday dynamic that spills over positively into future social, economic, political and cultural well-being'.[16]

It is one thing to assert that there should be enough space and sensitivity in our conception of justice to accommodate alternative visions of punishment, reconciliation and healing, but entirely another to assert they have a broader justice capacity or agency beyond the moment or locality in which they manifest themselves. Though individual-, household- and community-based processes are lauded as inherently legitimate and meaningful, there are few attempts to disaggregate the impact of local processes from national ones and fewer still to concretely assess their aggregated impacts at subnational and national levels. Arguments in favour of the preferability of local justice are drawn from a predominantly anecdotal literature which is often based on single-project or single-locality studies that do not show obvious potential for generalizability. Much of the pro-localization discourse amounts to believing in an 'invisible hand' by which broad, national-level social benefits unintended by the immediate principals in the locality trickle upwards from an accumulation of individual grassroots justice processes. However, there are at least three different types of transition occurring in post-conflict societies – a social transition from internecine fighting to peace, a political transition from the pre-war government to new government arrangements of the sort examined in Chapter 3, and economic transitions

---

15 Gready and Robins (n 13) 340.

16 Oliver Richmond and Jason Franks, *Liberal Peace Transitions: Between Statebuilding and Peacebuilding* (Edinburgh University Press 2009) 184.

from warped war-time patterns of accumulation to different (and hopefully better) patterns of post-conflict development.[17] Localized transitional justice processes make an obvious contribution to the first of these, but may have an at best tangential relationship to the other forms of transition that dictate both the stability of the peace and the prospects for wider justice. Many of the arguments raised in favour of localized processes are cultural, but egalitarian transformation also involves the legal, economic and political dimensions of collective existence.[18] Bearing this in mind, how far can localized justice processes affect local politics and economics within the immediate micro-collective community? What impact can they have on the macro-collective – i.e. the state?

1.2 The Relevance of Local Peacebuilding Debates

In exploring the impact of localized transitional justice on the immediate locale and the wider state, it is useful to look to debates on bottom-up, localized peacebuilding. Not only is much of the same dichotomized vocabulary used (local versus state, traditional versus modern, formal versus informal), but both literatures also refer to a significant extent to the same projects. There is a notable degree of overlap between localized peacebuilding and bottom-up transitional justice, largely because those who analyse them are often talking about the same thing, namely the cultivation of interdependent relationships and the capacity to incorporate non-violent forms of conflict resolution. The leading peacebuilding theorist on mediation and conflict resolution, John Paul Lederach, for example, sees problem-solving workshops, local peace commissions, prejudice-reduction projects and psycho-social work in post-conflict trauma as examples of middle-range and grassroots peacebuilding.[19] The self-same projects could also be considered reconciliation projects within transitional justice. His preference for elicitive conflict resolution that

---

[17] Roland Paris and Timothy Sisk, 'Introduction: Understanding the Contradictions of Postwar Statebuilding' in Roland Paris and Timothy Sisk (eds), *The Dilemmas of Statebuilding: Confronting the Contradictions of Postwar Peace Operations* (Routledge 2009) 1 at 1.

[18] To lightly adapt the formulation in Rolando Ames Cobián and Felix Reátegui, 'Toward Systemic Social Transformation: Truth Commissions and Development' in Pablo de Greiff and Roger Duthie (eds), *Transitional Justice and Development: Making Connections* (Social Science Research Council 2009) 142 at 145.

[19] John Paul Lederach, *Building Peace: Sustainable Reconciliation in Divided Societies* (US Institute of Peace Press 1997) 39.

builds models from cultural resources and local knowledge over prescriptive forms that transfer Western methods to non-Western conflict ecologies bears obvious affinities with much of the transitional justice literature.[20] Both transitional justice and bottom-up peacebuilding would 'claim' micro-techniques such as problem-solving workshops, psychological support for victims, non-violent conflict management dialogues, or facilitative mediation as lying within their particular fields of competence.[21] Mac Ginty, for example, sees processes of story-telling and grievance-airing and an emphasis on relationships as key characteristics of localized peacebuilding,[22] while transitional justice scholars would identify these attributes as core components of their own field of study. Projects that occurred before transitional justice's 'local turn', like the use in Mali by non-governmental facilitators of traditional community decision-making practices to generate localized conflict resolution,[23] or Somalia's employment of traditional *shir* and *guurti* methods of resolving conflict as part of regionally based clan reconciliation conferences,[24] have always been considered types of peacebuilding, but might now also fit conceptually within transitional reconciliation processes.

The emerging interest in grassroots and bottom-up interventions in peacebuilding is essentially inseparable from parallel resurgence of more dovish, therapeutic academic and practitioner discourses on trauma, healing and reconciliation,[25] of which transitional justice is the most obvious proponent in post-conflict states. Conflict resolution theorists

---

[20] John Paul Lederach, *Preparing for Peace: Conflict Transformation Across Cultures* (Syracuse University Press 1995). He is cited, for example, in Jodi Halpern and Harvey Weinstein, 'Rehumanizing the Other: Empathy and Reconciliation' (2004) 26 *Human Rights Quarterly* 561, 565.

[21] See, for example, what is included as 'civil society first' peacebuilding in Ulrich Schneckener, 'State Building or New Modes of Governance? The Effects of International Involvement in Areas of Limited Statehood' in Thomas Risse (ed.), *Governance Without a State: Policies and Politics in Areas of Limited Statehood* (Columbia University Press 2011) 232 at 243.

[22] Roger Mac Ginty, *International Peacebuilding and Local Resistance: Hybrid Forms of Peace* (Palgrave Macmillan 2011) 54.

[23] Kare Lode, 'Mali's Peace Process: Context, Analysis and Evaluation' in Catherine Barnes (ed.), *Owning the Process: Public Participation in Peacemaking* (Accord 2002) 56 at 62.

[24] Tamara Duffey, 'Cultural Issues in Contemporary Peacekeeping' (2000) 7 *International Peacekeeping* 142, 162.

[25] Meera Sabaratnam, 'The Liberal Peace? An Intellectual History of International Conflict Management, 1990–2010' in Susanna Campbell, David Chandler and Meera Sabaratnam (eds), *A Liberal Peace? The Problems and Practices of Peacebuilding* (Zed Books 2011) 13 at 13–14 and 19–20.

like Burton and Lederach are found in both literatures and are drawn on to make similar points.[26] Transitional justice scholars urge the field to concentrate on everyday restorative and reparative activities and local needs like social services, shelter, clean energy and jobs at the micro-level, borrowing at least some of the trappings of 'local' peacebuilding.[27] With many programmes, it is unclear where local peacebuilding ends and transitional justice begins; consider for example the creation of 'dialogue tables' in the Congolese district of Ituri to bring women from different communities together to devise and disseminate reconciliation strategies.[28] One rough distinction that might be drawn is that while localized peacemaking addresses prospective crimes (e.g. peace committees that attempt to reduce violence between local groups), localized transitional justice addresses them retrospectively, but there are always elements of the prospective and retrospective in both. As Rubli notes, in order to receive funds local humanitarian and peacebuilding organizations 'have started to place and frame their projects under the heading of transitional justice and/or transitional justice has been mainstreamed into existing humanitarian and peace-building programs'.[29]

Drawing on localized peacebuilding debates is useful because they have gone much further than those within transitional justice in terms of assessing how far 'up' bottom-up justice has an impact. The argument that justice interventions need re-orientation towards sensitive engagement with local processes instead of imposing external notions of what justice should look like has largely been won in transitional justice debates. However, more complex and perhaps underwhelming arguments about their wider reach and emancipatory potency have yet to be even partially elaborated. In a literature in which domestic and international practitioners or researchers rely on their own personal experiences of a process or anecdotal evidence provided by other counterparts to advocate for grassroots approaches, there are seldom any systematic efforts to

---

[26] Wendy Lambourne, 'Outreach, Inreach and Civil Society Participation in Transitional Justice' in Nicola Palmer, Phil Clark and Danielle Granville (eds), *Critical Perspectives in Transitional Justice* (Intersentia 2012) 235 at 237; Roht-Arriaza (n 11) 232.

[27] Dustin Sharp, 'Emancipating Transitional Justice from the Bonds of the Paradigmatic Transition' (2014) 9 *International Journal of Transitional Justice* 150, 164.

[28] Sara Hellmüller, 'The Power of Perceptions: Localizing International Peacebuilding Approaches' (2013) 20 *International Peacekeeping* 219, 227.

[29] Sandra Rubli, *Transitional Justice: Justice by Bureaucratic Means?* (Swiss Peace Working 2012) 6.

synthesize knowledge about these localized processes with macro-level research on parallel national peacebuilding. By contrast, localized peacebuilding debates have grappled with whether and how bottom-up processes can catalyse wider transformation. In particular, the policy-oriented, 'problem-solving' literature has moved away from dichotomies of the liberal (usually a synonym for state-level institutions) and the local that characterize transitional justice discourse as unhelpfully crude insofar as it neglects the plethora of intermediary relationships between them. It is something of a commonplace that there are at least three levels of domestic actors in peacebuilding, namely grassroots (indigenous leaders, small-scale civil society leaders, gang leaders), mid-range (civil society and NGOs) and top leadership (political, religious or military power-brokers), all of which admit of their own vertical subdivisions.[30] As Hofmann points out, most scholars and practitioners of peacebuilding are agreed that local or state-level approaches alone cannot succeed without the other. He observes that macro-level peacebuilding processes establish a framework in which bottom-up initiative can flourish and result in more genuine forms of local governance and social contracting.[31] Most peacebuilding theorization welcomes localized processes but emphasizes that prospects for peace or justice cannot be fully understood by analysing this single constituent part, and so promotes systematic approaches that understand localized processes as elements of an interrelated whole.[32]

1.3 Horizontal and Vertical Impacts of Grassroots Transitional Justice

On the basis of the foregoing, it would appear necessary to comprehend not just the social meanings of a given justice process in a given locality,

---

[30] John Paul Lederach, 'Levels of Leadership' in Luc Reychler and Thania Paffenholz (eds), *Peacebuilding: A Field Guide* (Lynne Rienner 2001) 145.

[31] Bjoern Hofmann, 'Are Hybrid Political Orders an Appropriate Concept for State Formation? Timor-Leste Revisited' in Martina Fischer and Beatrix Schmelzle (eds), *Handbook for Conflict Transformation Dialogue Series* 8 (Berghof Research Centre 2009) 79 at 81.

[32] See, for example, Daniela Körppen and Norbert Ropers, 'Introduction: Addressing the Complex Dynamics of Conflict Transformation' in Daniela Körppen, Norbert Ropers and Hans Giessemann (eds), *The Non-Linearity of Peace Processes: Theory and Practice of Systemic Conflict Transformation* (Verlag Barbara Budrich 2011) 11 at 13; Robert Ricigliano, 'Networks of Effective Action: Implementing an Integrated Approach to Peacebuilding' (2003) 34 *Security Dialogue* 445.

but the networks of regional and national relationships, institutions and structures within which they fit or do not fit. As Talentino argues,

> Bottom-up processes try to bring individuals together by focusing on the benefits of inter-group relations. But that effort to transcend divisions and encourage interactions cannot be sustained without first developing the state itself and building structures for stable administration. Efforts to bridge social divides may not spring up naturally, but often need political development to provide a reason for integration.[33]

As a result, for many peace scholars, localized processes are never the starting point for peace, but rather can only consolidate the political settlement negotiated at a national level.[34] These approaches tend towards a perhaps idealized view of peace in a state whose effective sovereignty is restored by peacebuilding intervention and which is in turn empowered by the agency of local communities. However, they do take seriously the question of vertical integration of the local with the national or the society with the state in a way that largely normative or ideological advocacy of localism in transitional justice debates has yet to do. With the expansion of the concept of local peacebuilding, the key question they ask is whether and how the 'peace writ little' at a local or grassroots level contributes to the broader society-level 'peace writ large'.[35]

Going beyond the trite, ouroboros-like mantra that the local affects the national and the national affects the local, this chapter examines whether the repair of social relationships among conflicting social groups on a horizontal level has any effect on the vertical relationship between the localized society in question and the state, which of course has a follow-on impact on the prospects for socio-economic transformation. In particular, it questions the suppositions that local legitimacy implies a broader agency or that meaningfulness automatically facilitates wider impact. It begins in Section 2 by dispatching some definitional questions – what is meant by 'local' for the purposes of this chapter, and what sorts of transitional justice activities it refers to. Section 3 goes on to outline the faith in localized justice in the transitional justice literature as an

---

[33] Andrea Kathryn Talentino, 'The Two Faces of Nation-Building: Developing Function and Identity' (2004) 17 *Cambridge Review of International Affairs* 557, 558.

[34] Carrie Manning, 'Local Level Challenges to Post-Conflict Peacebuilding' (2003) 10 *International Peacekeeping* 25, 26–27.

[35] Anita Ernstorfer, Diana Chigas and Hannah Vaughan-Lee, 'From Little to Large: When Does Peacebuilding Add Up?' (2015) 10 *Journal of Peacebuilding and Development* 72, 72.

agent not only of local reconciliation, but of broader transformation and emancipation, and shows how this fits within broader peacebuilding debates. Section 4 examines the limitations of grassroots justice imposed by the enduring influence or control of subnational elites. Section 5 draws attention to the crucially different spatial and motivational dynamics of national and local conflict. Section 6 explores the lack of linkages between micro-level reconciliation and macro-level change. It concludes by arguing that the enthusiasm for localized transitional justice as a change agent beyond that locale needs to be tempered.

The chapter does not argue that local efforts should be devalued if they are not vertically linked or do not have broader regional or national level effects, nor is it argued that only the state can guarantee peace or represent the symbolic identity of those within it. Bottom-up, grassroots justice processes are (generally) good in and of themselves, but it is necessary to question the apparent faith that they represent a genuinely transformative alternative to state-based approaches of truth, reparations or human rights campaigning, given their lack of macro-level instrumentality. The chapter concludes that if the widely assumed relationship between local transitional justice processes and national reconciliation or social transformation is to become a reality, it needs to be consciously planned. Debates on vertical integration and hybridity may help transitional justice practitioners to develop an improved analysis of the links between local-level and national-level dynamics. Only with attention to them can the type of improved project design emerge that would allow localized processes to not merely contribute to achieving immediate objectives but also provide a basis for wider social change beyond the specific process in question.

2. DEFINING THE 'LOCAL'

As Goodale has argued, beyond the academy and policy literature, there is no one, definable place we can identify as 'the local'.[36] It is a social construction, more a 'floating signifier' used and produced through

[36] Mark Goodale, 'Introduction: Locating Rights, Envisioning Law Between the Global and the Local' in Mark Goodale and Sally Engle Merry (eds), *The Practice of Human Rights: Tracking Law Between the Global and the Local* (Cambridge University Press 2007) 5 at 15–16.

practices of representation than a clearly defined concept.[37] In transitional justice discourse it is used both promiscuously and polysemically. For some the local is inherently relational, a specific socio-geographic space defined by its connection (or lack thereof) to other political scales like the individual, the national and international. In other depictions the local is a more open-ended, deterritorialized concept, referring less to spatially bounded places than to ethoses of ownership and resistance or everyday concerns.

2.1 An Equivocal Concept

For most, embracing the local is something of a motherhood statement, a sweeping platitude that all concerned would agree is good but lacking somewhat in specified content. What once appeared useful insofar as it captured a novel facet of transitional justice may in fact have become problematic, as it obscures a crisp understanding of complex situations. There is a calculated ambiguity in discussing the local – after all, it is much easier to assert the local or the people or the community are the root of all peace or justice when these concepts are not defined. The only unity in the concept of 'local' we see in the transitional justice literature is an almost rote juxtaposition to the global. This juxtaposition is employed to advocate a shift in attention from the international or state realm to that of society as the primary domain for policy intervention.[38] This 'stark and mutually exclusive binary opposition'[39] contrasts the norms and institutions of international actors and those of individuals or communities experiencing violence who have their own sources of social, economic and political order and legitimacy. Implicit within this opposition is the notion that the local 'is a shorthand for those who are on the receiving end of applications of overwhelming concentrations of military

---

[37] Andreas Hirblinger and Claudia Simons, 'The Good, the Bad, and the Powerful: Representations of the Local in Peacebuilding' (2015) 46 *Security Dialogue* 422, 434.

[38] For example, Alexander Laban Hinton (ed.), *Transitional Justice: Global Mechanisms and Local Realities after Genocide and Mass Violence* (Rutgers University Press 2010); Colm Campbell and Fionnuala Ní Aoláin, 'Local Meets Global: Transitional Justice in Northern Ireland' (2002) 26 *Fordham International Law Journal* 871; Diane Orentlicher, '"Settling Accounts" Revisited: Reconciling Global Norms with Local Agency' (2007) 1 *International Journal of Transitional Justice* 10.

[39] Patricia Lundy, 'Paradoxes and Challenges of Transitional Justice at the "Local" Level: Historical Enquiries in Northern Ireland' (2011) 6 *Contemporary Social Science* 89, 93.

might and economic resources, and whose voices are least likely to be heard'.[40] Though this binary is usually caveated with boilerplate acceptance that the dichotomy cannot capture the full complexity of what is happening, pleas to find a balance between the two and references to the likelihood that the global and local are mutually transformative, there are serious problems with it. First, it essentializes actors that are neither ideologically monolithic nor politically homogenous.[41] The poles of the local and the global serve as automatic indicators of the extent to which a policy or norm is legitimate, representative and people-centric, on the one hand, or imposed, alien and institution-centric on the other. This reductive imagery of the global as the realm of domination and the local as the realm of solution fosters the 'facile embrace of the local or the community' that Theidon identifies in the literature.[42]

Second, the binary obscures the diversity inherent in the local, which in critiques of transitional justice and peacebuilding is almost invariably conceptualized as a source or form of resistance against hegemonic international liberal actors. Where the local and the global are constructed in opposition to each other, the former may refer to any level within the state subject to intervention, from the national government to other units like municipalities, regions or villages.[43] To understand the potency of the local, it is necessary to unpack the concept into the macro-local (the state), the meso-local (regions, autonomous units) and micro-local (towns, villages, communities, households). The local frequently refers to the national in peace discourse, for example when one speaks of local ownership informing the exercise of political authority, governance models or development assistance. This macro-level use of the local is prevalent in transitional justice, too. Local ownership is usually discussed in the context of inherently state-level processes like

---

[40] Caroline Hughes, Joakim Öjendal and Isabell Schierenbeck, 'The Struggle Versus the Song – The Local Turn in Peacebuilding: An Introduction' (2015) 36 *Third World Quarterly* 817, 818.

[41] Dustin Sharp, 'Addressing Dilemmas of the Global and the Local in Transitional Justice' (2014) 29 *Emory International Law Review* 71, 106.

[42] Kimberley Theidon, 'Editorial Note' (2009) 3 *International Journal of Transitional Justice* 295, 296.

[43] Bruce Mazlish, 'The Global and the Local' (2005) 53 *Current Sociology* 93, 93.

truth commissions[44] and hybrid courts.[45] The oft-cited distinction between 'distanced' and 'embedded' forms of transitional justice refers primarily to international and national forms of justice.[46]

Though this conceptualization of local as national is perfectly acceptable, this is not the definition of local that informs this chapter. Here, the 'local' applies to the bottom-up micro-local or what Richmond labels the 'deeper local-local', those spaces 'where individuals and communities live and develop political strategies in their local environment'.[47] This is what most transitional justice scholars mean when they speak of the 'local', reproducing the traditional, scale-based, inter- and intra-community understandings of the concept as 'bottom-up', 'on the ground', 'subnational', 'indigenous', 'customary', and 'micro-level', even if most of these concepts can also have some national-scale connotations.[48] This is the area where the state dimensions are limited and distant, through rarely non-existent. Issues of justice and politics are relocated away from state actors to community participants exercising their own agency to resolve disputes, to reconcile, to reach *modi vivendi*. As previously interdependent communities fracture along the lines of conflict, the relevant antagonists are not factions or ethnic groups, but brothers, neighbours, old schoolmates or the village over the river that ended up in different alliances during the prior conflict. It is here that post-conflict impunity, division and impoverishment are felt most acutely. The local turn is therefore associated with a focus on the 'everyday', understood by Riaño Alcalá and Baines as the means by which survivors, families and communities 'reconstruct their worlds, work towards social coexistence, justice and repair' and 'pursue mundane activities and practices to restore the basic fabrics of meaningful social relations, negotiate or recreate protective mechanisms and provide some sense of continuity in their lives and sense of self in relation to other'.[49] It draws attention to the insufficiency of state and international initiatives to

---

44 Rachel Kerr and Eirin Mobekk, *Peace and Justice: Seeking Accountability after War* (Polity Press 2007) 139.

45 Ellen Emilie Stensrud, 'New Dilemmas in Transitional Justice: Lessons from the Mixed Courts in Sierra Leone and Cambodia' (2009) 46 *Journal of Peace Research* 5, 9–12.

46 Paul Gready, 'Analysis: Reconceptualising Transitional Justice: Embedded and Distanced Justice' (2005) 5 *Conflict, Security and Development* 3.

47 Oliver Richmond, 'Resistance and the Post-liberal Peace' (2010) 38 *Millennium: Journal of International Studies* 665, 670.

48 Hirblinger and Simons (n 37) 423–24.

49 Pilar Riaño Alcalá and Erin Baines, 'Editorial Note' (2012) 6 *International Journal of Transitional Justice* 385, 385 and 386.

ground justice and social repair where fear and interpersonal insecurity have become a normal psycho-social reality. Everyday perspectives also shift attention from the apparent exceptionalism of abuses in conflict to the normality of ongoing structural violence[50] and to the intimate spaces in which gendered experiences of power are encountered.[51]

2.2 Bottom-up Projects

Though the 'local' is often conflated with traditional, indigenous or customary forms of justice, it also refers to novel, locally based projects like psychological support and trauma therapy for victims, exhumations and reburials, non-violent conflict management dialogues, reconciliation workshops and victim-offender mediation. These projects can be entirely autonomous, supported by national and international NGOs, or backed by the state and supranational peacebuilding bodies. They include anything that leads antagonistic individuals within communities or individual communities within localities to co-operate or reconcile. The most familiar examples in the literature are those of traditional or indigenous justice, including *mato oput* in Uganda, *nahe biti* in East Timor, *bashingantahe* in Burundi and the *palava hut* dispute resolution mechanism in Liberia. In Mozambique, where health is defined as good relations between human beings and their ancestors, rituals to appease the spirits of fighters and civilians killed during war were performed by local spirit mediums. Symbolically charged purification rituals reintegrated those who had suffered during the war to heal some wounds and stabilize communities.[52] Similar ritual and non-verbal cleansing processes were used to absolve perpetrators of crimes in Angola.[53] In Peru, rituals of confession and repentance, communal labour agreements and land redistribution were used to rehabilitate former Shining Path *arrepentidos* and foster co-existence.[54] As Arriaza and Roht-Arriaza note,

---

[50] Sarah Maddison and Laura Shepherd, 'Peacebuilding and the Postcolonial Politics of Transitional Justice' (2014) 2 *Peacebuilding* 253, 264.

[51] Kris Brown and Fionnuala Ní Aoláin, 'Through the Looking Glass: Transitional Justice Futures through the Lens of Nationalism, Feminism and Transformative Change' (2014) 9 *International Journal of Transitional Justice* 127, 149.

[52] Alcinda Honwana, 'Healing and Social Reintegration in Mozambique and Angola' in Elin Skaar, Siri Gloppen and Astri Suhrke (eds), *Roads to Reconciliation* (Lexington Books 2005) 83.

[53] ibid.

[54] Kimberly Theidon, 'Justice in Transition: The Micropolitics of Reconciliation in Postwar Peru' (2006) 50 *Journal of Conflict Resolution* 433.

these processes rely to a significant extent on specific cultural traditions and mass community involvement, and they are usually initiated organically by local actors without state or international involvement.[55] It should be noted that these are never merely atomized or episodic actions, but fit within wider cultural worldviews. These actors understand how customary law, kinship and spirituality as well as societal structures and authorities like tribes, village communes, elders, *bigmen*, clans or healers exercise persuasive and consensual authority over everyday social reality beyond the reach of the state. Indeed, they amount to forms of ad hoc governance, welfare and social control in areas of limited statehood. Other communities, it should be noted, reintegrate and heal through forms of voluntary amnesia on the basis that publicly acknowledging violence is unconducive to reconciliation.[56]

In other cases, national civil society and external transitional justice experts or groups provide support for more ad hoc, non-traditional or non-customary dialogue and reconciliation between groups. This often takes the form of organized encounters between national or international NGOs and 'ordinary' individuals who come from a community or communities in conflict. The main objective is longer-term relationship-building across the lines of conflict and the building of a sustainable capacity for future conflict resolution. A good example of ad hoc civil society action is the way in which the South African TRC's macro-discourses on apartheid were complemented by micro-level projects like the Cape Town Trauma Centre for Survivors of Violence and Torture, a Torture Project and the Khulumani (Western Cape) Support Group.[57] A Sierra Leonean human rights NGO and a US NGO co-operated to launch *Fambul Tok*, a face-to-face, village-level project to help communities organize events like truth-telling bonfires and traditional cleansing ceremonies.[58] Even without any wider results, mobilization and participation like this 'allows victims to meet others in the same position and to

---

[55] Laura Arriaza and Naomi Roht-Arriaza, 'Social Reconstruction as a Local Process' (2008) 2 *International Journal of Transitional Justice* 152, 164.

[56] See, for example, Craig Etcheson, 'The Limits of Reconciliation in Cambodia's Communes' in Skaar, Gloppen and Suhrke (eds) (n 52) 201.

[57] Christopher Colvin, *'We are Still Struggling': Storytelling, Reparations and Reconciliation after the TRC* (Centre for the Study of Violence and Reconciliation 2000).

[58] Andrew Iliff, 'Root and Branch: Discourses of "Tradition" in Grassroots Transitional Justice' (2012) 6 *International Journal of Transitional Justice* 253, 261–65.

construct the meaning and identities that permit them to cope'.[59] Sometimes these local projects are less traditional than improvised and more about intra-community remembrance than cross-community reconciliation. In the Colombian municipality of Granada, a victims association created a *Salon del Nunca Mas*, literally a 'Hall of Never Forgetting', in the main square where the families of victims installed images of their murdered and missing relatives with brief biographies to maintain their memory among the general population.[60] In other instances, formal, state-based DDR processes have fostered local informal agreements for voluntary disarmament and reintegration within communities in states as diverse as Papua New Guinea, South Africa and the Solomon Islands.[61] The scale on which these processes operate is important – by working on a community level, these projects can engage dozens, hundreds and even thousands of people in face-to-face communion. Anecdotally, this tends to foster a sense of ownership over agreements reached and a sense of responsibility for their endurance. There is also a wider optimism that civil society can empower individuals and communities to create social movements that can shape the broader society to reflect their interests or their own conceptions of the good.

3. THE LOCAL IN TRANSITIONAL JUSTICE DISCOURSE: TOP-DOWN STASIS VERSUS BOTTOM-UP EMANCIPATION

In academic analysis, NGO reports and policy documents, those involved in the field of transitional justice communicate a discourse on community-led or participatory approaches to justice and broader social outcomes. This discourse has encouraged a broader view of where and how justice should be imagined, commendably moving beyond top-down northern research epistemologies. Much of it amounts to a conscious

---

59 Simon Robins, 'Addressing the Needs of Families of the Missing: A Test of Contemporary Approaches to Transitional Justice' (PhD diss., University of York 2011) 286 <http://etheses.whiterose.ac.uk/1971/1/Robins_-_Needs_of_the_Missing_A_test_of_TJ.pdf> accessed 21 July 2016.

60 Gabriel Ruiz Romero, 'Voices Around Us: Memory and Community Empowerment in Reconstruction Efforts in Colombia' (2012) 6 *International Journal of Transitional Justice* 547.

61 Béatrice Pouligny, 'Civil Society and Post-Conflict Peacebuilding: Ambiguities of International Programmes Aimed at Building "New" Societies' (2005) 36 *Security Dialogue* 495, 498.

disavowal of the field's traditional politics of scale in which the local was positioned as the lowest rung in the hierarchy of knowledge and power as indigenous and community practices were subjugated by universal conceptions of justice.[62] The study of localized justice is characterized primarily by ideographic case studies with detailed description of individual processes from *in loco* participant observation, actual participation, or personal first-hand interviews. Beyond the purely descriptive aspects, much of the literature attempts to conceptualize observed experiences. These are then converted into training concepts and project skills for international actors or local justice agents as intermediaries or facilitators of processes that aim to give communities power over their attempts at justice.

There is, however, another strain of more abstract meditation about the broader virtues of localism which posits the relevance of grassroots processes for the success or failure of national transitional justice and peacebuilding outcomes. This strain is supported by little systematic evidence, employing arguments based on personal observation which tends to be ad hoc and tied to that immediate process, with sketchy articulation of potential influence on the wider society. As Macdonald argues:

> Individual pieces of research can be very high in quality but the overall picture is less satisfying. Once the evidence is reviewed, we are left with a patchwork, fragmented understanding of how transitional justice is understood and experienced in local spaces ... Micro-level research which examines local engagement and responses to transitional justice tends to be qualitative; is much more likely to have an interpretative approach and is therefore rarely comparative in any systematic sense ... There is very little comparative research interrogating how transitional justice plays out at the sub-national level, especially across communities and administrative units.[63]

One of the main pitfalls of social research is an enthusiasm for generalization on the basis of limited case-study material, to make claims of a wider capacity or validity than the inquiry might strictly justify. This is particularly the case with localized research in post-conflict communities. Here, the 'intimate connection' of those facilitating communications with, mediating between, or training local groups 'can distort and shape their perception of the conflict, and limit their ability to understand

62 Riaño Alcalá and Baines (n 49) 386.

63 Anna Macdonald, 'From the Ground Up: What Does the Evidence Tell Us about Local Experiences of Transitional Justice?' (2015) 3 *Transitional Justice Review* 72, 112 and 117.

the conflict dynamics beyond the confines of a local situation … they might see the conflict only from the perspective of the particular groups they are dealing with, and fail to take into account wider, national developments and dynamics'.[64] There are distinct signs that the tendency to mix analysis with advocacy may have may impeded an appropriately sceptical attitude towards localized justice's wider promise. In particular, the exuberance with which traditional or indigenous mechanisms were endorsed in the transitional justice literature may have occasioned a degree of myth-making, knowledge gaps and decision-making 'based on weak data, ex-ante evaluation and speculation'.[65] Many of the claims made for local justice are proven. Others are essentially unverifiable but accord with commonsense notions, for example that local-level initiatives should be a core element of post-conflict justice planning, that international initiatives should not undermine them, that they can compensate for some of the limitations of other transitional justice measures and that for many victims the local organizers of violence are far more pertinent objects of justice than national leaders.[66] However, other claims lack sufficient evidence to suggest anything beyond a threshold plausibility, e.g. that they can serve as 'crucial precursors' for wider-scale national projects or as clues for what would resonate at the national level,[67] or that transitional justice automatically become transformative when it 'emphasizes the principles of local participation and empowerment'.[68]

The argument that localized transitional justice is imperative has solid foundations in the truism that justice cannot originate solely in elite settlements or concessions. War undoubtedly has micro-foundations rooted in neighbourhood and personal antipathies to which justice must respond. Empirical evidence suggests that survivors think more in terms of relationships with past friends or colleagues within their own communities when they speak of reconciliation than a larger, collective sense of reconciliation with all members of an ethnic, religious or linguistic

---

[64] Dominik Zaum, 'International Non-Governmental Organisations and Civil Wars' (2009) 11 *Civil Wars* 22, 25–26.

[65] Luc Huyse, 'Introduction: Tradition-based Approaches in Peacemaking, Transitional Justice and Reconciliation Policies' in Luc Huyse and Mark Salter (eds), *Traditional Justice and Reconciliation after Conflict: Learning from African Experience* (International Institute for Democracy and Electoral Assistance 2008) 1 at 6.

[66] All of these arguments are made in Arriaza and Roht-Arriaza (n 55) 153, 157, 159.

[67] ibid 152 (abstract) and 170.

[68] Lambourne (n 26) 238.

group.[69] Historically specific grievances 'about who did what horrible thing to whom' are of greater concern to local participants at transitional justice conferences than cosmopolitan notions of national healing or accountability.[70] The focus on small groups of national leaders and egregious criminals in trials and truth commissions, therefore, left an obvious geographical impunity gap for so-called small fish left behind in survivor communities. Where once transitional justice was the domain of state officials, lawyers and the international community, there has emerged a realization that to be successful, transitional justice needs to work at the level of the individual and the community, to resituate justice through everyday needs and empathy, to transform identities and relationships at all levels of society. Community-based forms of transitional justice can be seen as a re-situation of deviance within a 'nested paradigm of human interaction that is negotiated through relationship ties, and the norms and mores of community networks', as opposed to within legally codified behaviour. Where it is more contextually situated, deviance can be more effectively sanctioned.[71] Insisting on the centrality of local justice also accords with broader political and ethical values of understanding, empathy and self-determination. Transitional justice discourse sees vulnerable subjects in need of empowering agency, not passive victims to be externally protected. It accords with the notion that 'any framework for engaging people across ethnic or ideological divides' conduces to altering mind-sets and undercutting problematic political identities.[72]

3.1 The Local as the Agent of Socio-economic Transformation

These beliefs underpin the conviction that uniquely tailored local processes of justice, dialogue and mutual recognition are crucial for long-term reconciliation by repairing the social fabric of post-conflict communities. It is no exaggeration to say that consultation and involvement with civil society and local communities have emerged as core

---

69 Eric Stover and Harvey M. Weinstein, 'Conclusion: A Common Objective, a Universe of Alternatives' in Stover and Weinstein (eds) (n 6) 323 at 323.

70 Mark Osiel, 'The Banality of Good: Aligning Incentives Against Mass Atrocity' (2005) 105 *Columbia Law Review* 1751, 1756.

71 Carl Stauffer, 'Transitional Justice' in *Encyclopedia of Criminology and Criminal Justice* (Springer 2014) 5272 at 5273.

72 David Chandler, *International Statebuilding: The Rise of Post-Liberal Governance* (Routledge 2010) 185.

'benchmarks for the legitimacy' of any transitional justice project.[73] The argument that localized justice should serve as 'building blocks' and 'complements' to a national approach is by now well established.[74] However, others go further, positing a revised relationship with top-down transitional justice not as complementary to it but as having primacy over it, guaranteeing not merely local reconciliation, but better social outcomes for the entire post-conflict population. Andrieu, for example, argues that transitional justice should focus on civil society 'first' and that the field as a whole should 'aim less at the rebuilding of state institutions and more at the reconstruction of social relations and unfettered dialogue between communities'.[75] In this view, the reconstruction of society and social legitimacy should take precedence over top-down processes of conflict management and state-building.[76] This echoes the call elsewhere for a shift in the locus and priorities of transitional justice from the legal to the social and from statist, institutional concerns to those of communities and the everyday.[77] This new approach is based on an apparently widely shared confidence that bottom-up approaches can exert an effect vertically to state level as well as horizontally among communities. It is assumed that successful local initiatives can 'create wider, self-sustaining regions of peace', that individual dialogues can restructure broader social arrangements, and that localized peacebuilding 'can establish a basis for new national structures'.[78] Just as transitional justice theory once assumed that individual accounts of suffering or abuse became woven into the larger national collective narrative, so now is it assumed that individual justice processes at local level automatically feed into the wider national process of transformation.

This approach also appears to be premised on the notion that localized justice processes are analogous to, or constitutive of, civil society movements. It assumes that local communities will emphasize needs-based agendas and welfare, and that this feeds upwards into wider demand for reform. The expectation is that 'from below' approaches

---

73 Hansen (n 4) 108.

74 Arriaza and Roht-Arriaza (n 55) 154.

75 Kora Andrieu, 'Civilizing Peacebuilding: Transitional Justice, Civil Society and the Liberal Paradigm' (2010) 41 *Security Dialogue* 537, 537.

76 ibid 540.

77 For example, Gready and Robins (n 13) 340; Rosalind Shaw, opening remarks at 'Living Through Violence' workshop in Vancouver, February 2012, as cited in Riaño Alcalá and Baines (n 49) 387.

78 Andrieu (n 75) 545 and 547.

increase the legitimacy of the demands of those involved and encourages them to be more proactive in the process of social reconstruction.[79] Indeed, bottom-up perspectives are equated with resistance on the part of non-state actors and civil society to hegemonic social, political and economic forces.[80] Gready and Robins argue that 'transformative change should be locally driven because such change is most likely to be informed by the local and particular needs of people in communities where legacies of violence play out'.[81] Pointing to the example of reparations campaigns, they argue that the localized articulation of need can transform the wider normative parameters of human rights debates, expanding the range of valid claims and developing new skills, building reform constituencies and creating new patterns of engagement.[82] The belief that civil society naturally represents the needs and concerns of the population is a staple of much critical transitional justice theorization, as is the presumption that localized processes automatically generate inclusion, empowerment and agency.[83] It is a belief that is also apparent in broader peacebuilding debates. As Nadarajah and Rampton note with some scepticism, there is a widespread belief that the delivery of justice 'should be more responsive and effective as supply gets closer to the source of demand ... Anything that is explicitly non-elite and that therefore addresses social, psychological or other dimensions of justice at the local or community level must therefore benefit non-elites at this level'.[84] However, the causality by which improved interpersonal

---

[79] Patricia Lundy and Mark McGovern, 'Community, Truth-Recovery and Conflict Transformation "From Below"' in Libby Chapman et al. (eds), *A Sustainable Peace? Research as a Contribution to Peace-Building in Northern Ireland* (Community Relations Council 2008) 155.

[80] Kieran McEvoy and Lorna McGregor, 'Transitional Justice from Below: An Agenda for Research, Policy and Praxis' in Kieran McEvoy and Lorna McGregor (eds), *Transitional Justice from Below: Grassroots Activism and the Struggle for Change* (Hart Publishing 2008) 1 at 3; Chandra Lekha Sriram, 'Post-Conflict Justice and Hybridity in Peacebuilding' in Oliver Richmond and Audra Mitchell (eds), *Hybrid Forms of Peace: From Everyday Agency to Post-Liberalism* (Palgrave Macmillan 2012) 58.

[81] Gready and Robins (n 13) 349.

[82] ibid 354 and 358.

[83] See somewhat sceptical iterations of these beliefs in Rubli (n 29) 15 and Patricia Lundy, 'Exploring Home-Grown Transitional Justice and its Dilemmas: A Case Study of the Historical Enquiries Team, Northern Ireland' (2009) 3 *International Journal of Transitional Justice* 321, 327.

[84] Suthaharan Nadarajah and David Rampton, 'The Limits of Hybridity and the Crisis of Liberal Peace' (2015) 41 *Review of International Studies* 49, 65.

co-existence or localized articulation of need feeds into wider national transformation is conspicuously underspecified. Gready and Robins, for example, admit that one of the main challenges for a transformative theory of intervention that prioritizes the local is the question of how it can 'scale-up' to address structures of inequality at national and international levels.[85]

Instead of answering this question, however, the discourse on localized processes of justice essentially replicates the problem identified in the previous chapter, namely that of negative identification. Once one goes beyond the descriptive tasks of depicting local justice processes and highlighting their congruence with restorative or emancipatory concepts of justice, more energy is expounded in outlining what localized justice is not (i.e. top-down, liberal, institutional) than theorizing the wider cumulative effect it can have. Though the usual caveats not to romanticize the local and to guarantee some level of procedural protection are consistently invoked, the literature re-iterates the grossly simplified position canvassed in the last chapter that transitional justice is unduly liberal and top-down, imposed as part of a rule of law package on communities where these values are alien.[86] Much of this impetus comes from the aforementioned tendency to pitch the local versus the global in some very politicized disputes, most notably the paradigmatically dichotomized division between the imposition of ICC jurisdiction in Uganda and essentialized traditional reconciliation ceremonies.[87] This orientation is further informed by qualitative studies of the views of citizens on the ground to discover what optimal peace and justice would look like from a local perspective. These surveys reach strikingly different conclusions to the theories of victim satisfaction on which orthodox national-level transitional justice were founded.[88] The stated needs and desires expressed by victims within communities rarely align with the abstract

---

[85] Gready and Robins (n 13) 360.

[86] For example, Laura Grenfell, 'Legal Pluralism and the Challenge of Building the Rule of Law in Post-Conflict States: A Case Study of Timor-Leste' in Brett Bowden, Hillary Charlesworth and Jeremy Farrall (eds), *The Role of International Law in Rebuilding Societies after Conflict: Great Expectations* (Cambridge University Press 2009) 157.

[87] Orentlicher (n 38) 19–21.

[88] For example, Gearoid Millar, 'Local Evaluations of Justice through Truth Telling in Sierra Leone: Postwar Needs and Transitional Justice' (2011) 12 *Human Rights Review* 515; Simon Robins, 'Transitional Justice as an Elite Discourse: Human Rights Practice Where the Global Meets the Local in Post-Conflict Nepal' (2012) 44 *Critical Asian Studies* 3.

attribution of criminal responsibility to individuals in the capital. Similarly, top-down truth commissions may have an impact on state stability and the national conflict narrative, but seldom look in minute detail at localized experiences or the sentiments that characterized relations there. Privileging the rule of law, human rights and democratization as the dominant transitional justice discourse thereby 'sidelines the perspectives and practices of survivors and ordinary people'.[89] Just as state-centric transitional justice inevitably fails to recognize local customs and practical knowledge, it also fails to appreciate local needs and developmental priorities[90] and ignores local dynamics that reinforce (or could potentially transform) people's lives.[91]

The apparent but under-theorized corollary to this line of criticism is an assumption that bottom-up processes automatically operate as an antidote to its economically unconcerned, inherently unequal, top-down liberalism of transitional justice. There is an implied logic that if transitional justice has neglected both the economic roots of conflict and local communities, then an emphasis on one axiomatically redounds to the benefit of the other. A further supposition is made that if justice is made less distant to the lived realities of people, it has an inherent potency to socio-economically improve those lived realities. Balint, Evans and McMillan, for example, argue that opening up to indigenous worldviews and jurisprudences instead of privileging Western frameworks automatically offer 'new possibilities for understanding structural injury and responding to historical injustices'.[92] For other transitional justice scholars, popular grassroots participation equates with mobilization and effective local agency to develop new social movements that can shape the broader society to achieve emancipatory ends identified in transitional justice discourse.[93] Sharp, for example, is optimistic that a focus in transitional jutice on everyday issues and local needs like social services, shelter, clean energy and jobs at the micro-level can 'trickle up' to the macro level by generating legitimacy for those international,

---

[89] Riaño Alcalá and Baines (n 49) 386.

[90] Kieran McEvoy, 'Letting Go of Legalism: Developing a "Thicker" Version of Transitional Justice' in McEvoy and McGregor (eds) (n 80) 15 at 28.

[91] Arriaza and Roht-Arriaza (n 55) 152 (abstract).

[92] Jennifer Balint, Julie Evans and Nesam McMillan, 'Rethinking Transitional Justice, Redressing Indigenous Harm: A New Conceptual Approach' (2014) 8 *International Journal of Transitional Justice* 194, 196–97.

[93] Patricia Lundy and Mark McGovern, 'Whose Justice? Rethinking Transitions from the Bottom Up' (2008) 35 *Journal of Law and Society* 265, 265 (abstract); McEvoy (n 90) 36; Andrieu (n 75) 549.

national or local actors who participate and grounding a potentially workable scheme for reform.[94]

3.2 Support from the Peacebuilding Literature

In making this argument, Sharp draws on critical peace theories that call for interveners to shift their focus from the needs of the state to the needs of localities and communities.[95] His emphasis is appropriate as the critical peacebuilding literature has gone much further in theorizing potential links from the local to the overall peace through concepts like popular peace, multicultural peace and the 'everyday peace'. The concepts of the local and the everyday draw on post-structural and post-colonial discourses to reveal structural forms of violence and emphasize resistance and social solidarity against the influence of conservative or liberal power structures.[96] In these empathetic discourses the liberal and local are presented as coherent but distinct entities, and dichotomies of external imposition and local ownership are prevalent. For many, the emphasis on the local derives from a post-modern suspicion of progressist meta-narratives of the universal and global and the identification of virtue in the local and particular instead.[97] For others, it stems from the reality that processes of democratization, rule of law or civil service reform overlook local specificities and so have little impact in the peripheries. Critics of liberal peacebuilding identify the existence of a chasm between interventionary conceptions of violence and peace and those of the host communities. The most commonly proposed alternative framework to the liberal mixture of parliaments, constitutional reform and rule of law is the local, the customary and the everyday, which are assumed to enjoy significant peacebuilding and emancipatory potency by resisting violence and transforming localities.[98] Peace is envisioned as a non-linear process emerging from local agents, practices and interrelationships, and so a larger role is given to bottom-up agency and those

---

[94] Sharp (n 27) 164.

[95] Most notably David Roberts, 'Beyond the Metropolis? Popular Peace and Post-Conflict Peacebuilding' (2011) 37 *Review of International Studies* 2535, cited in Sharp (n 27).

[96] Shahrbanou Tadjbakhsh, 'Introduction: Liberal Peace in Dispute' in Shahrbanou Tadjbakhsh (ed.), *Rethinking the Liberal Peace: External Models and Local Alternatives* (Routledge 2011) 1 at 7.

[97] Mazlish (n 43) 96.

[98] A.B. Fetherston, 'Peacekeeping, Conflict Resolution and Peacebuilding: A Reconsideration of Theoretical Frameworks' (2000) 7 *International Peacekeeping* 190, 195 and 201.

able to express or shape opinion within the relevant communities. It is argued that top-down peace, like top-down justice, cannot exercise an effect over those social subjectivities and accumulated fears or resentments that condition life beyond elite bargaining.

Critics of liberal peacebuilding agree that human needs and potentialities should be determined at the level of communities and individuals, not at national level.[99] The problem is not merely that liberal peacebuilders ignore vital local concerns about welfare, identity and culture, but rather that they exclude or obstruct the emergence of alternative local, everyday and customary agendas for peace.[100] The 'politics of the everyday' is juxtaposed against a conservative politics that perpetuates the types of unequal domestic power relations described in Chapter 4 or a liberal politics that focuses on distant state institutions.[101] The implication in much of the critique is that community cultures with inherent concern for identity and welfare are 'displaced' in favour of external discourses of expert knowledge.[102] Bottom-up perspectives are presumed to cultivate moderate leaders, 'progressive' voices and positive peace.[103] Advocates of what are variously described as social, hybrid, emancipatory and everyday peacebuilding argue that culturally adapted, bottom-up forms of peacebuilding devoid of any political conditions (except inclusion and non-violence) inevitably incorporate economic rights, needs-based activity and stronger concern for social justice as sources of peace.[104] In this view, effective, consensual forms of social security can be formed on the basis of local preferences, traditions and cultures of care.[105]

---

[99] Oliver Richmond and Audra Mitchell, 'Introduction: Towards a Post-Liberal Peace: Exploring Hybridity via Everyday Forms of Resistance, Agency and Autonomy' in Richmond and Mitchell (eds) (n 80) 1 at 20.

[100] Edward Newman, 'A Human Security Peace-Building Agenda' (2011) 32 *Third World Quarterly* 1737, 1741.

[101] Richmond and Mitchell (n 99) 15–16.

[102] Oliver Richmond, 'A Post-Liberal Peace: Eirenism and the Everyday' (2009) 35 *Review of International Studies* 557, 575.

[103] Edward Newman, '"Liberal" Peacebuilding Debates' in Edward Newman, Roland Paris and Oliver Richmond (eds), *New Perspectives on Liberal Peacebuilding* (United Nations University Press 2009) 26 at 37–38.

[104] Kristoffer Lidén, 'Building Peace Between Global and Local Politics: The Cosmopolitical Ethics of Liberal Peacebuilding' (2009) 16 *International Peacekeeping* 616, 621; Oliver Richmond, *The Transformation of Peace* (Palgrave Macmillan 2005) 215.

[105] Ken Bush, 'Beyond Bungee Cord Humanitarianism: Towards a Developmental Agenda for Peacebuilding' (1996) 17 *Canadian Journal of Development Studies* 75, 86.

3.3 Unproven Assumptions

However, drawing on critical peacebuilding theory to demonstrate that top-down approaches to transitional justice fail to foster needed structural transformation in and of itself is insufficient to prove that the bottom-up can achieve it instead. The urge on the part of critics from the Global North to reach out to institutions of justice, reconciliation or conflict resolution that are alien to Western experiences is a double edged-sword – interventions may enjoy a more legitimate situational rationality, but the lack of familiarity with these customs and locales means their downstream consequences cannot be fully anticipated. The softer social-psychological and relational dynamics of grassroots justice presumably can influence the harder aspects of peacemaking, state-building and democratization, but, as noted earlier, even advocates of this approach have admitted that the causal pathways are rarely spelled out. Neither transitional justice nor the critical peacebuilding literatures on which it draws have been able to do so. In many respects, the literature replicates that which it hoped to depart from. In place of a trickle-down liberal peace, we see an equally amorphous implication that localized justice can 'trickle up'. The confidence that the roots of local peace lie entirely at the community level, and that this community-level justice contributes to a wider peace, is called into question by what we know about conflict dynamics and about informal justice processes.

The rest of this chapter goes on to explain why localized justice processes that originate in indigenous groups or the interactions of communities with transitional justice NGOs, though immensely valuable in and of themselves, may have little 'transformative' effect on socio-economic structures within that sphere of action or beyond it, either alone or in combination. The first argument is that most localized forms of justice occur organically without any international involvement or need only minimal external support, meaning that they are unlikely to depart significantly from their purely local and traditionally non-transformational remits. The second argument is that the roots of conflict are never purely local. Local inequalities may be symptomatic of larger divisions and iniquities, but local justice processes alone or in combination can do little to affect them. The third argument is a related one, namely that transitional justice theorization has not been able to articulate vertical links between bottom and top. It may be the case that transitional justice is ill-suited to establishing such links, because the simplified discourses of transformation and localization it has adopted pull in distinctly different (top-down and bottom-up) directions. In particular, the distance from statist, macro-level processes that underpin the bottom-up discourse can only serve to restrict any transformative effect to the immediate locale.

4. THE LIMITS OF THE LOCAL: REPLICATION OF EXISTING POWER STRUCTURES

The purpose of this section is to examine the potential for grassroots forms of justice to impact socio-economic conditions within their own community. The local turn in transitional justice has been motivated by a belief that state-based transitional justice interventions systematically 'exclud[e] local communities or traditionally disenfranchised groups as active participants in transitional justice and peacebuilding measures', thereby raising questions of legitimacy, local ownership and sustainability.[106] However, one of the curious but underexplored facets of this position is that much of it effectively amounts to the advocacy of processes that would in many cases occur organically in these communities regardless of either international/state support or opposition. While developed polities can exclude or disenfranchise groups by tightly controlling justice processes even at community level, this is rarely an option within the government's (or peacebuilders') range of possible policy outcomes in post-conflict areas of limited statehood where ad hoc, localized, indigenous or substate justice processes emerge as core elements of governance. Though Na'im and Sriram are correct to argue that individual judicial determinations of criminal responsibility should not be the main approach to justice in areas where there is little or no presence of state law or legal enforcement,[107] the obvious corollary of this is that formal structures can rarely, if ever, impinge on localized justice processes. Formal state structures or liberal peacebuilding could only challenge local forms of social administration with great effort, which they are unlikely to be financially or organizationally capable of immediately after conflict (see Chapter 4). The question is not one of exclusion or disenfranchisement. Instead, it is whether there is any political

---

[106] Lundy (n 83) 325.

[107] Abdullahi Ahmed An-Na'im, 'Editorial Note: From the Neocolonial "Transitional" to Indigenous Formations of Justice' (2013) 7 *International Journal of Transitional Justice* 197, 201; Chandra Lekha Sriram, 'Justice as Peace? Liberal Peacebuilding and Strategies of Transitional Justice' (2007) 21 *Global Society* 579, 589.

incentive or administrative capacity on the part of the state or non-state transitional justice actors to embrace processes that are mostly already ongoing.

In countries where the state bureaucracy proves unwilling or unable to provide collective goods like security and services, long-existing traditional or indigenous social structures in rural areas and ad hoc community-based groups in urban areas endure or emerge to answer fundamental questions of justice. They also deliver physical and economic security for communities on the basis of custom, convention and mutual self-interest. This tendency becomes even more imperative in war as communities and individuals similarly develop practical daily responses to the conflict to originate or renew sub-state systems of informal governance based on bonds of trust or loyalty or necessity. Local communities and neighbourhoods continue, or learn how, to provide core services and informal pacts or truces necessary for everyday life. Where civil conflict destroys formal institutions, it often spurs a 'radical localisation' of politics and economic relationships.[108] In such instances, a pragmatic peace may develop that allows for some co-existence, security and development even in the absence of reconciliation. Even in refugee camps, social life can be reorganized through community networks of co-operation and control.[109]

This adaptability extends to transitional justice even before the end of conflict – as Vandeginste observes, 'There is no reason why tradition would "wait" for an agreement between the government and the UN to be signed before rendering justice'.[110] In the aftermath of conflict communities evince a pragmatic willingness to get on with life.[111] Communities embrace spontaneous initiatives to address local legacies of violence that are invisible to national and international constituencies.[112] Forms of customary, indigenous and transitional justice have been dusted off as micro-level societies come to terms with the past in the likes of Somalia, East Timor and Mozambique.[113] On other occasions, ethnically

---

[108] Mats Berdal, *Building Peace After War* (Routledge 2009), 123, citing Peter Little, *Somalia: Economy Without State* (James Currey 2003) 167.

[109] Pouligny (n 61) 498.

[110] Stef Vandeginste, 'Transitional Justice for Burundi: A Long and Winding Road' in Kai Ambos, Judith Large and Marieke Wierda (eds), *Building a Future on Peace and Justice* (Springer 2009) 393 at 419.

[111] Riaño Alcalá and Baines (n 49) 391.

[112] Gready and Robins (n 13) 349.

[113] Ken Menkhaus, 'Traditional Conflict Management in Contemporary Somalia' in I. William Zartman (ed.), *Traditional Cures for Modern Conflicts:*

divided communities have employed long-established modes of co-existence based on tacit agreements to remain silent about the violence of the past. Perpetrators of crimes have been observed being reintegrated into their communities in the absence of trial, truth-telling or even traditional ritual simply by exhibiting social values of humility, industriousness and reciprocity in Sierra Leone, or via informal negotiation with neighbours in Uganda.[114] In all of these situations, transitional justice has 'unwittingly provided the scaffolding of language'[115] for actions that would have occurred anyway for those left out of national or international justice responses. This reality is distinct from, if not entirely incompatible with, the widespread but undertheorized notion that top-down transitional justice either implicitly or explicitly demands the cessation of grassroots forms of justice or a re-ordering of the world-views that underpin them. One example of this simplified discourse goes as follows:

> The traditional Timorese confronted with human rights discourse is told that she should abandon her belief in the agency of the spirits that have long sustained her community and rather pursue the legal and political routes to action that underlie modern notions of political causality. Liberal modernity constructs her not as a member of a community, linked to family, clan and ancestors through blood and spirit, but as an autonomous agent whose humanity alone determines what she can be.[116]

Along similar lines, An-Na'im argues that indigenous or traditional practices are deemed 'unacceptable' by the international community because they are inconsistent with universal human rights norms.[117] These positions are problematic because they clearly over-state the case. At the level of UN policy on transitional justice, it has been accepted that traditional and informal mechanisms are often the best available recourse

---

African Conflict 'Medicine' (Lynne Rienner 2000) 183; Dionisio Babo-Soares, 'Nahe Biti: The Philosophy and Process of Grassroots Reconciliation (and Justice) in East Timor' (2004) 5 *Asia Pacific Journal of Anthropology* 15; Victor Igreja, 'Multiple Temporalities in Indigenous Justice and Healing Practices in Mozambique' (2012) 6 *International Journal of Transitional Justice* 404.

[114] See Rosalind Shaw, 'Linking Justice with Reintegration? Ex-Combatants and the Sierra Leone Experiment' and Ann Nee and Peter Uvin, 'Silence and Dialogue: Burundians' Alternatives to Transitional Justice', both in Shaw and Waldorf (eds) (n12) at 111 and 157.

[115] Stauffer (n 71) 5272.

[116] Simon Robins, 'Mapping a Future for Transitional Justice by Learning from Its Past' (2015) 9 *International Journal of Transitional Justice* 181, 188.

[117] An-Na'im (n 107) 197.

to serve the public's justice needs, a position that is further apparent in projects supported by bilateral and multi-lateral donors.[118] They are also problematic because they assume a fundamentally 'hydraulic' relationship between top-down ('liberal') and bottom-up forms of justice in which as one goes up the other must go down, and vice versa.[119] As Heathershaw argues, this binary 'maintains the myth that they are naturally oppositional' when in fact co-constitutive relationships between the two are as common, or more common, than competitive ones.[120]

Given the prevalence of ad hoc transitional justice responses at the micro-level and the reality that external actors can seldom sufficiently understand the complex identities and ethics incorporated by the notion of local justice, action by outside transitional justice actors to catalyse micro-level justice or render indispensable support for it will typically occur mostly in those communities where war has severely damaged or destroyed social and economic life. Though there are some examples of grassroots justice driven to a significant degree by external actors (see the examples in Section 2), in most cases where the transitional justice 'industry' deploys to localized processes, this deployment can at most co-ordinate interactions with other processes, provide advice, facilitate access to peacebuilding or state resources, mediate or provide cover for difficult decisions, or lay out additional soft-skills or human rights training. With or without this assistance, there are links between local justice and transformation on the basis that the former can outline the co-existence and legitimacy of multiple social meanings or can open critical space to redefine the social meaning of the good. One of the most common depictions of externally supported localized justice or peacebuilding is where NGOs facilitate antagonistic groups to co-operate through truth-telling, reconciliation workshops or joint economic ventures, given their rootedness in tradition or local relations. Local forms of justice and co-operation not only reflect pre-existing, context-specific values, but can work discursively to transform those values and incorporate inclusive actors over exclusionary power-brokers over time. Grassroots forms of justice are intuitively understood to be inclusive,

118 UN Secretary-General, *The Rule of Law and Transitional Justice in Conflict and Post-Conflict Societies* (2011) UN Doc. S/2011/634, para. 39.

119 To adapt a formulation in relation to security and liberty outlined in Andrew Ashworth, 'Security, Terrorism and the Value of Human Rights' in Benjamin Goold and Liora Lazarus (eds), *Security and Human Rights* (Hart Publishing 2007) 203 at 208.

120 John Heathershaw, 'Towards Better Theories of Peacebuilding: Beyond the Liberal Peace Debate' (2013) 1 *Peacebuilding* 275, 279–80.

progressive and legitimate – 'those who have been excluded will be included ... the voiceless will be heard and empowered ... locals will inform policy and practice appropriate to local needs'.[121]

However, regardless of whether localized forms of transitional justice are self-started or assisted by international actors, there is little reason to believe that ad hoc, localized justice processes will be able to avoid the traditional limitations of purely organic micro-level forms of conflict resolution. As noted earlier, the assumption appears to be that anything that is explicitly non-elite and that addresses social, psychological or other dimensions of justice at the local or community level must as a matter of course benefit non-elites at this level. However, 'locals' are not unitary actors. They mix the most needy with those who benefit significantly from pre-war and war-time patterns of accumulation/ distribution. No commonality of purpose can be assumed beyond the resumption of normal life (if even this can be assumed) at the community level. Many of the most legitimate and durable local social orders entrench sub-national elites through whom unjust structures originate. Indeed, in states where liberal peacebuilding is hybridized with local structures, the functioning of the latter often depends entirely on the interests of local elites, which obviously calls into question the extent to which the local can be considered an empowering alternative to top-down peacebuilding or transitional justice.[122] While local justice activities can build bonding capital among groups and even transform relations between participants, they can seldom compel. It is questionable whether these activities can transform the values underpinning the community's economic relationships with those that benefit from existing economic inequalities.

Because local elites often emerge even stronger at the end of conflict and because peacebuilding and state actors are often out of their depth beyond the capital, local elites frequently capture peacebuilding in a manner that does more to reproduce than transform existing patrimonial or economically regressive structures at the micro-level.[123] One obvious barrier to the potential of grassroots justice to transform the most locally damaging phenomena (most notably unregulated taxation and types of clientelism where patronage, resources and jobs are exchanged for political support) is the degree of control local elites enjoy over

---

[121] Lundy (n 83) 326.

[122] Paffenholz (n 9) 864.

[123] Michael Barnett and Christoph Zürcher, 'The Peacebuilder's Contract: How External Statebuilding Reinforces Weak Statehood' in Paris and Sisk (eds) (n 17) 23 at 36.

bottom-up processes, particularly those rooted in traditional authority. As Pouligny argues, community leaders will often also fulfil the role of faction representative after war, reducing the space for organizing interests autonomous of conflict parties.[124] The often laudatory literature on community-based processes 'can overlook divisions and conflict' and 'conceals power-struggles and networks, exclusionary tactics by local elites', meaning that many voices will not be heard equally.[125] Much of what is seen as deference to custom may in fact be the cynical invocation of tradition on the part of local elites with vested interests in protecting the status quo though mechanisms they already control or strongly influence – 'we see not so much resistance "from below" from ordinary citizens, but rather resistance from traditional providers of justice to incursions upon their sources of legitimacy, income and power'.[126] For example, post-transitional commune councils in Cambodia restored hierarchical social relations in a manner paradigmatically opposed to the sort of responsive and participatory decision-making domestic and international supporters of the processes intended.[127] The traditional elderates (*guurti*) who were incorporated into the governance structure of Somaliland and made responsible for managing internal conflicts reinforced regressive patronage patterns.[128] In Sierra Leone, the reconstituted authority of paramount chiefs who monopolized land and were instrumental in corrupt politico-economic networks surrounding diamond extraction risks once again alienating the same groups that rebelled against the government in the civil war.[129] There is strong anecdotal evidence that traditional grassroots leaders in Northern Uganda 'lean towards' those who are relatively well-off.[130] Those who assume grassroots transitional justice has some inherent potential to transform

---

124 Pouligny (n 61) 500.

125 Lundy (n 83) 327.

126 Sriram (n 80) 63.

127 Peter Blunt and Mark Turner, 'Decentralisation, Democracy and Development in a Post-Conflict Society: Commune Councils in Cambodia' (2005) 25 *Public Administration and Development* 75.

128 Marleen Renders and Ulf Terlinden, 'Negotiating Statehood in a Hybrid Political Order: The Case of Somaliland' (2010) 41 *Development and Change* 723, 742.

129 Paul Jackson, 'Chiefs, Money and Politicians: Rebuilding Local Government in Post-war Sierra Leone' (2005) 25 *Public Administration and Development* 49.

130 Valarie Vat Kamatsiko, 'Grassroots Peacebuilding and Vertical Integration: A Case Study of the Peace-Rings Approach' (2015) 10 *Journal of Peacebuilding and Development* 56, 66.

social structures would do well to bear in mind the warning by Chetail and Jütersonke:

> [T]he offices of local and international NGOs and other 'grassroots' organisations are themselves populated with members of the local elites, who may well see their involvement in an internationally support 'civil society' as a convenient and effective means through which to pursue their own political agendas. Projects aimed at empowering local people may thus inadvertently foster social exclusion and help entrench local rivalries, thereby fraying the fragile social fabric even further.[131]

This should not be overstated. Time and again, we see local elites exert their agency to rebuild peace and systems of exchange in divided communities, though this also illustrates the indispensability of political will. Where grassroots justice is not co-opted by local elites, there exists the further problem of non-participation. Bottom-up approaches to justice need to enjoy a socio-cultural legitimacy in which all parties understand and honour its methods, which raises obvious difficulties in the case of out-group members. Grassroots actors, be they traditional or civil-society based, can affect intangible factors like animosities and relationships. However, they do not have the resources or the authority to bring parties who are not ready or willing to relinquish economic or social power to negotiation, settlement or mediation. Urbanization and the consumerist and proprietorial rationalities of globalization play a role in the disintegration of moral sanctions that work in closed communities, but it may also be due to the fact that locally legitimate authorities break down in conflict. Traditional forms of caste management of Nepalese society were fundamentally challenged by Maoist insurgents, just as armed youths transformed cultural assumptions about the authority of male lineage-based elders and chiefs in Ugandan Acholiland.[132] Sometimes the process is more deliberate. In the Sudanese civil war, for example, military factions deliberately undermined and even in some cases obliterated any mediating kinship or community authorities perceived to stand between them and the loyalty of those they recruited to fight.[133] Afghanistan's tribal structures were in many instances replaced by warlords who gained

---

[131] Vincent Chetail and Oliver Jütersonke, *Peacebuilding: A Review of the Academic Literature* (Geneva Peacebuilding Platform 2015) 7.

[132] Andries Odendaal, *A Crucial Link: Local Peace Committees and National Peacebuilding* (US Institute of Peace Press 2013) 28.

[133] Sharon Hutchinson, 'Spiritual Fragments of an Unfinished War' in Niels Kastfelt (ed.), *Religion and African Civil Wars* (Hurst 2005) 28.

their authority from military strength and contraband activity.[134] Even where local authorities persist, they may have little control over local power-brokers. Arriaza and Roht-Arriaza note that in Guatemala 'the continuing stranglehold on local power by those who committed atrocities has limited the extent' of cultural traditions of justice and mass community involvement, while some ex-perpetrators show no interest in acknowleding past violations or re-integrating.[135] Local authorities, NGOs and religious leaders in DR Congo proved completely incapable of mediating or controlling violence in the face of recalcitrant groups.[136] Traditional mechanisms of conflict management that worked to pacify northwestern Somalia could not be exported to the south where new gangs, new militias and new clan factions held sway.[137]

Much of transitional justice's imaginary of bottom-up justice appears to involve a 'let a thousand flowers bloom' mosaic of local justice processes operating in tandem to ground culturally relevant peace across the post-conflict territory. However, this vision sits uneasily with the reality of many grassroots peaces, which are characterized by re-negotiation, the inability to bind all relevant parties, temporariness and the shadow of violent self-help from local power-brokers.[138] As Hyden laments:

> Because African societies are so structured that customary values embrace not only those living in villages or urban slums but also members of the elite who serve as their elected representatives and 'brokers', there are few, if any, places where subalterns act in resistance to what they perceive as oppressive structures.[139]

Of course, some forms of local justice will prove open, non-elitist and genuinely cross-community. However, scholars of hybrid orders acknowledge that one of the core challenges of deferring to local authority is to

---

134 Susanne Schmeidl with Masood Karokhail, '"Prêt-a-Porter States": How the McDonaldization of State-Building Misses the Mark in Afghanistan' in Fischer and Schmelzle (eds) (n 31) 67 at 71–72.

135 Arriaza and Roht-Arriaza (n 55) 170.

136 Séverine Autesserre, 'Hobbes and the Congo: Frames, Local Violence and International Intervention' (2009) 63 *International Organization* 249, 261.

137 Ken Menkhaus, 'International Peacebuilding and the Dynamics of Local and National Reconciliation in Somalia' (1996) 3 *International Peacekeeping* 42, 51–52.

138 Trutz Von Trotha, 'The "Andersen Principle": On the Difficulty of Truly Moving Beyond State-Centrism' in Fischer and Schmelzle (eds) (n 31) 37 at 44.

139 Goran Hyden, 'Rethinking Justice and Institutions in African Peacebuilding' (2015) 36 *Third World Quarterly* 1007, 1009.

avoid strengthening the wrong local actors who can revive forms of patrimonialism and instability without careful monitoring.[140] Many transitional justice scholars acknowledge the dangers of romanticizing bottom-up processes and pay lip-service to the risks of exclusionary, discriminatory or human rights-abusive conduct. However, they have insufficiently acknowledged how these inherited downsides fundamentally limit any wider transformative potential they have, either in their own locales or cumulatively within the state at large.

5. THE LIMITS OF THE LOCAL: MICRO-LEVEL JUSTICE AND MACRO-LEVEL CONFLICT CAUSALITIES

It is unclear if greater optimism is warranted if we look beyond purely local–local transformation to the question of whether an emphasis on local justice can cumulatively amount to, or catalyse, wider social transformation. Much of the transitional justice literature in its local turn is dedicated to specifying *why* grassroots justice is crucial to transformation of unequal structures but comparatively little, if any, attention is dedicated to explaining *how* bottom-up processes can achieve or contribute to such outcomes. The primary limitation of micro-level justice processes is that which all forms of sub-state justice suffer from, namely that even the most successful substantive outcomes can only address localized symptoms as opposed to structural causes. Micro-level justice can resolve conflict between figures or groups interacting within the relatively intimate grounding of a community, town or region. However, if we take the economic roots of conflict seriously, then it becomes apparent that there are long-term, macro-level processes at the level of state weakness and institutional viability that grassroots justice cannot even begin to comprehend, let alone affect, even where it deals comprehensively with localized manifestations of these phenomena. This reality is usually as evident before conflict as after. As Jarstad and Olsson argue, while sustainable progress in development and stability might need to be based on local power structures, contemporary peacebuilding takes place

[140] Martina Fischer and Beatrix Schmelzle, 'Introduction' in Fischer and Schmelzle (eds) (n 31) 5 at 10 and 11.

in contexts where local authorities have clearly failed to establish such progress on their own by this point.[141]

As argued in Chapter 3, both centralized state discrimination within an institutional framework and the struggle by the government or mass rebel coalitions to capture key state resources are the fundamental cause of most conflicts. Familiar civil conflicts in the likes of Darfur, Mindanao and Aceh can be traced to widespread distributive polarization among distinct groups of rich and poor or state fiscal imbalances between regions that local authorities within those regions have no control over. This lack of control is something which can also be said of those conflicts that flow from climate change, mass scarcity of resources (or its mirror image, resource abundance), external occupation/marketization of indigenous land, the organization of the national market or national disenfranchisement of certain groups.

The most salient units of analysis in conflict and peace are those identity groups that transcend a local–local locus like ethnicity, religion, culture and class. Highly esteemed and legitimate forms of local authority have thrived within their own communities for centuries in the likes of Burma and Nepal. However, they provided no answer to the most widely identified core conflict root causes that emerged from outside the community like ethno-religious discrimination in public appointments, corruption, language rights deprivations or unequal access to land resource benefits in the former, or feudal land tenure systems and caste-based discrimination in the latter. Localized peace committees lack leverage in their relations with figures who enjoy greater formal power, particularly those found at a higher vertical level such as political leaders and government, and so can be ignored with impunity.[142] The political positions and access to resources enjoyed by national figures responsible for such policies seldom depend on relationships with local authority figures or popular legitimacy, nor can they suffer significant social sanction locally for failing to address national problems. As Roht-Arriaza notes, even where local mechanisms may be able to cope with horizontal-level disputes between neighbours at the same socio-economic level who need to live together in the aftermath of conflict, local forms of justice may not be able to process vertical conflict involving state agents

[141] Anna Jarstad and Louise Olsson, 'Hybrid Peace Ownership in Afghanistan: International Perspectives of Who Owns What and When' (2012) 18 *Global Governance* 105, 106.

[142] Andries Odendaal, 'The Political Legitimacy of National Peace Committees' (2012) 7 *Journal of Peacebuilding and Development* 40.

pursuing extra-community agendas.[143] Even violent crime can explode the limits of systems designed primarily to deal with family or conflict-related disputes, calling in to question any wider potential to develop solutions to local manifestations of structural problems. The penetration of the local by regional and even global actors means that a simplified discourse of 'local solutions to local problems' cannot adequately capture the demands of justice.[144]

This is most apparent if we consider the different spatial and motivational lenses of local and national conflict. Militarized civil wars *among factions* occur between historically specific coalitions of interest like classes, ethnic/religious/linguistic groups or territories at a mass level, to which local–local processes of justice and repair *among communities* can respond to, or map onto, imperfectly. One obvious consequence of this is that the latter cannot respond to all, or even a significant proportion, of the problems caused by the former. It has long been recognized within the transitional justice literature that most contemporary conflicts mix vertical violence that runs from the state (or rebels that would replace it) downwards to the citizenry and horizontal violence that pitches communities, or elements within them, against each other. The local turn in transitional justice can be attributed to a renewed focus on interpersonal, horizontal micro-cleavages between and within communities at the expense of an emphasis on top-down macro-cleavages at state level that inevitably glossed over the political dynamics that local communities represent. Only by embracing these dynamics and designing justice interventions accordingly could context-appropriate accountability and reconciliation be secured beyond the metropolis. However, in making such arguments, scholars have isolated the projects and localities they observe from the surrounding conflict. They rarely, if ever, consider whether the settlements reached through informal forms of justice and reconciliation to address micro-cleavages can (1) be insulated from or (2) affect the macro-cleavage. Though most transitional justice scholars are enthusiastic about grassroots forms of justice, repair or rehabilitation, the focus has been more on their legitimacy or cultural value than their causal significance to wider conditions of peace or justice. This is important because few policy-oriented scholars of war and peace find local violence or local reconciliation to be of causal significance to either war or peace. Communities are more likely to follow national peace or justice initiatives than they are to catalyse them – Theidon, for example,

143 Roht-Arriaza (n 11) 242.
144 A point made in Sharp (n 41) 104–05.

notes how the greater sense of security that came with the introduction of militarized security emboldened communities to attempt rehabilitation of Senderistas in Peru.[145]

The conflict divisions between 'us' and 'them' run through towns, villages and families. Much war-time violence at local level is driven by the agendas of overlapping micro-societies in districts, communities, towns and villages relating to land, resources or power. Some even suggest that most localized violence is unrelated to dominant discourses of the war or that many civil wars are actually amorphous agglomerations of multiple, overlapping localized conflicts.[146] This bottom-up view of conflict has left an imprint on transitional justice. Dancy, for example, argues that 'individual and group behaviour collects to form state-level characteristics ... if local people re-arm, organize and fight, the expression of this will be macro-social instances of violence'.[147] Furthermore, after civil war settlements, local areas remain vulnerable if parties to it treat localities as a reserve domain of revanchist power or resource exploitation, if key provisions are not implemented at grassroots level by unable or unwilling authorities, or if local politics prove more zero-sum than endlessly fungible national power-sharing agreements. As Manning points out, 'Local level instability creates tempting exit possibilities for national level actors who find that they have signed onto an agreement that no longer serves their interests'.[148] Sometimes local violence erupts even after a national agreement. In areas of the DR Congo like Ituri and South Kivu after the 2005 peace agreement, ethnic and political macro-cleavages declined as engines of violence, but parties continued to fight on a localized basis over militia leadership, land, resources and administrative positions that traditionally belonged to identifiable ethnic groups even where a national peace was supposedly in place.[149] Much of the tribal violence between Afghan warlords has little to do with the fate of the government in Kabul or the Taliban, and instead relates more to control of contraband substances and smuggling routes.

---

[145] Theidon (n 54) 445–46.

[146] These options are canvassed, but not accepted, in Stathis Kalyvas, 'The Ontology of "Political Violence": Action and Identity in Civil Wars' (2003) 1 *Perspectives on Politics* 475, 479.

[147] Geoff Dancy, 'Choice and Consequence in Strategies of Transitional Justice' in Christopher Coyne and Rachel Mathers (eds), *Handbook on the Political Economy of War* (Edward Elgar 2011) 397 at 413.

[148] Manning (n 34) 38.

[149] Autesserre (n 136) 259–60.

There are, however, compelling reasons why peacebuilders like those in the DR Congo 'never consider … that working at the local level could be an appropriate strategy'.[150] Local agendas sustain national and regional violence, but seldom start it and rarely are causally significant to its resolution. Chapters 3 and 4 noted that the state is the most significant site of conflict over power and resources for rebels and governments. Wars like those in Sudan, Guatemala or Myanmar have seen the state attempt to use its apparatus to destroy communities. State-driven differential development patterns in the likes of Sri Lanka and Nepal lead to the alienation and grievances that underpinned Sinhalese–Tamil conflict in the former and the 'People's War' against the government in the latter. Ideological conflicts over the nature and scope of state authority like those in Nicaragua, Syria, Algeria and Peru are triggered by elite-level activities or macro-level structural problems and have no obvious local–local origins, only local-local manifestations. Ostensibly community-based conflict driven by local agendas in the DR Congo could not be separated from top-down manipulation of relationships between a Rwandophone minority and the 'indigenous' peoples of Kivu.[151] Much of the horizontal violence perpetrated by indigenous Civil Defense Force members in Guatemala against their neighbours were organized by the national army and *ladino* commanding officers.[152] As Jackson and Dexter argue, 'The narratives employed by conflict entrepreneurs to produce violence are initiated from the top-down … [p]articularly in times of (perceived) crisis, national leaders can draw upon a 'toolbox' of cultural resources as both an interpretive framework for problem definition and a resonant frame to legitimize or 'sell' policies to the collective'.[153] Though the phrase itself is unduly simplistic, these 'conflict entrepreneurs' are the interlocking individuals and elites who can transform structural division or resentments into active participation in violence, co-ordinating a message and organization to create the necessary widespread consensus that war is necessary.[154] The most common of the narratives they employ relate to top-down ethnic exclusion – ethnic wars are always based on competing claims over sovereignty or autonomy. Core factors underpinning ethnic conflict like exclusion from state power, mobilizational

---

[150] ibid 256, though Autesserre disagrees with this position.

[151] ibid 256 and 258–59.

[152] Arriaza and Roht-Arriaza (n 55) 156.

[153] Richard Jackson and Helen Dexter, 'The Social Construction of Organised Political Violence: An Analytical Framework' (2014) 16 *Civil Wars* 1, 6.

[154] ibid 7.

ability or recent experience of conflict have top-down causalities.[155] Well-established risk factors for warfare like poverty or share of GDP from primary commodities have localized manifestations but do not originate in communities, nor do the finance or mobilization warfare needs. Even sub-nationalist movements are typically organized on a far larger scale than the local–local, drawing on region-wide and often inter-ethnic alliances among many social actors and communities.[156]

Of course, as Kalyvas argues, there is a crucial distinction between the causes of civil war and the causes of violence within it. Conflict within communities is ontologically embedded in fundamentally personal and local discourses or conditions that explain much of this violence, not the causal master-narratives of macropolitics propounded by those prosecuting the war.[157] However, while community-level conflict dynamics worsen the violence and polarization caused by the master cleavage, the majority of the most vicious local conflicts are essentially opportunistic. Pointing to the way that national wars in Liberia and Sudan served to re-open feuds and disputes about cattle theft, he argues that civil wars provide a medium for localized grievances to be realized within the wider conflict and a language in which violence that most people would otherwise abhor can be justfied.[158] Local grievances seldom cause wars because in peacetime, state sanctions or community mechanisms of social control prevent local grudges from erupting into wider violence.[159] In war, where infrastructures of war (armies, transportation, communications systems, media, propaganda) penetrate localities, these mechanisms can fail. Though local actors proactively appropriate the narratives of the macro-cleavage to prosecute localized conflict, the external cause of national war is needed to 'activate the fault lines' as the narratives of the macro-cleavage are employed to clothe local struggles.[160] Even if national causes are cynically co-opted or instrumentalized in the prosecution of micro-level conflict, local alliance with supra-local actors is a

---

[155] Lars-Erik Cederman, Andreas Wimmer and Brian Min, 'Why Do Ethnic Groups Rebel? New Data and Analysis' (2010) 62 *World Politics* 87, 88.

[156] Joshua Forrest, 'Subnationalism and Post-conflict Governance: Lessons from Africa' in Derick Brinkerhoff (ed.), *Governance in Post-conflict Societies: Rebuilding Fragile States* (Routledge 2007) 226 at 234.

[157] Stathis Kalyvas, *The Logic of Violence in Civil War* (Cambridge University Press 2006).

[158] Kalyvas (n 146) 479.

[159] ibid 485.

[160] ibid 480–85.

precondition and cause of community-level violence – 'top-down mechanisms are likely to do most of the "heavy lifting" before the war, during its initial stages, or after the war has ended'.[161] None of this is to argue that local violence is a mere emanation of national conflicts that can be routinely addressed by a pacified and reconstructed state. However, to argue that addressing local issues is essential to end national-level violence and ensure sustainable positive peace, or to argue that there are automatic and unproblematic aftereffects of localized justice on broader structures, is to exaggerate the causal significance of local reconciliation and local peace to national conditions.

It is unlikely that the success or failure of some or all local justice can either bolster or threaten macro-level settlements to a causally significant extent, and the more likely relationship is the reverse – the failure of macro-level peace may negate micro-level accommodations. On the one hand, the fact that the motivations for conflict are significantly different between core and periphery should mean that localized, ad hoc self-help processes of truth, accountability, healing and reparation can have a strongly beneficial effect within the periphery and may be easier to conclude even in the absence of a national process. On the other hand, this can serve to atomize local justice processes from anything broader, more meaningful or more sustainable on a wider level. Any wider peace involves multiple and deeply imbricated conflicts and, consequently, a plethora of different agendas to which an individual local justice process (or accumulation thereof) cannot respond comprehensively. Given that local-level violence often needs national-level conflict to start, there are good reasons to believe that in many cases the potential for local justice to spread or influence wider communities is dependent on national peace and statebuilding, as opposed to the other way round. As one practitioner puts it:

> Bottom-up processes try to bring individuals together by focusing on the benefits of inter-group relations. But that effort to transcend divisions and encourage interactions cannot be sustained without first developing the state itself and building structures for stable administration. Efforts to bridge social divides may not spring up naturally, but often need political development to provide a reason for integration.[162]

While some state support is necessary for success to spread, its absence may guarantee failure. Talentino points to the way in which state collapse

---

[161] ibid 487.

[162] Talentino (n 33) 558.

in Somalia prevented successful grassroots community development projects by women 'from being a springboard to the development of broader, state-based community' and how state opposition from the Sudanese government prevented a cross-ethnic Women's Action Group 'from being a catalyst for something larger'.[163]

The limitations of even highly fruitful forms of local justice or memorialization may be demonstrated by considering a paradigmatic example of a successful grassroots project in action:

> In Bong County, Liberia ... in a village where a massacre occurred during the war, an individual dreamed repeatedly of dead ancestors who came to him pleading that they did not want to be forgotten. After a visit to a traditional healer, it was determined that a memorial needed to be erected on behalf of those killed. Once the monument was in place and a proper ceremony conducted, the ancestor dreams ceased. For the community, it was reported that hope replaced despair, residents developed a greater sense of purpose, and community solidarity flourished.[164]

This illustrates how local justice processes respect community autonomy, welfare and conceptions of the good life. However, it is far from clear that grassroots processes that generate changed feelings, ways of thinking and behaviour can endure under top-down stress if spoilers or those with a vested interest in continued instability work towards renewed conflict. Though we can readily accept that the state is largely irrelevant to daily life in communities, it creates a larger social order and a larger social product beyond the local. Where this breaks down before or after conflict, there is little reason to believe that even the most harmonious or restorative process can endure under the attendant pressures. In wartime, discourses of hatred and difference accumulate and are institutionalized in ideologies that can support a return to localized conflict if the types of peace agreement and peacebuilding examined in Chapters 3 and 4 break down. Society-wide meta-narratives and discursive practices of revanchists or spoilers can ignite violence by stereotyping or dehumanizing others within the community as an enemy. As armies, transportation, communications systems and propaganda penetrate localities once more and people are forced to take sides defined from above, those moral scruples which before conflict existed to regulate social interaction may once more become overwhelmed and replaced by a willingness to

163 ibid 568 and 569.

164 Patricia Mauldeen, 'The Post-Conflict Paradox: Engaging War, Creating Peace' in Parent and Charbonneau (eds) (n 3) 19 at 30.

exclude or even exterminate 'the other'.[165] At the same time, war brings large agglomerations like the state and rebel armies to the fore instead of individuals or communities. As Lefranc argues, 'neither a "cognitive" relation to the past – knowledge of prior periods of extreme violence or civic education – nor adherence to humanistic values can provide reliable fortification from political collective violence'.[166] Alterations in micro-level psychological dispositions towards the other can do little to alter the fundamental macro-level security dilemma examined in Chapter 3 that elites from one side to the conflict will renege on a peace agreement. Studies of peace education and training initiatives by NGOs reveal that they often prove ineffective in the face of deeply ingrained, radical in-group identities – the 'scattered, short-term and fragmented nature' of most NGO initiatives in the likes of Bosnia or Israel–Palestine often can do little to compensate for, or counter-balance, radicalization.[167] Indeed, the binary divisions between the local/everyday and the international/liberal divorces interpersonal relations from the larger social identities of survivor communities, 'ignor[ing] the salience and force within the "everyday" and "local" of identity-based aspirations to, and contestations over, nationhood, statehood and modernisation'.[168]

Even where local processes can reconcile communities, there is no guarantee they can survive stresses from above. War and violence abruptly create new relationships and new traumas that take societies by surprise and may overwhelm apparently reconciled communities. For example, East Timor's relatively extensive Community Reconciliation Process seemed to be highly successful in pacifying and reconciling divided communities after the violence surrounding the independence referendum. However, the accommodations agreed proved to be of little effect once the national peace appeared to break down during the 2006 Crisis as 150,000 people became displaced on account of 'a deeply

---

[165] Glenn Bowman, 'Xenophobia, Fantasy and the Nation: The Logic of Ethnic Violence in Former Yugoslavia' in Victoria Goddard, Josep Llobera and Cris Shore (eds), *The Anthropology of Europe: Identity and Boundaries in Conflict* (Berg 1994) 143.

[166] Lefranc (n 3) 51.

[167] Thania Paffenholz, 'Civil Society Beyond the Liberal Peace and Its Critique' in Campbell, Chandler and Sabaratnam (eds) (n 25) 138 at 147–48.

[168] Nadarajah and Rampton (n 84) 69.

ingrained fear of any form of political contention' at a national level.[169] In the years following the 2002 ceasefire, the Sri Lanka Monitoring Mission succeeded in solving numerous disputes regarding local-level violence, but many of these benefits were lost once the state returned to war in 2006.[170] Localized processes cannot insulate themselves from national divisions regardless of how hard they try.

Any local solution in deeply divided countries can be undone if there are no state institutions to regulate or control the lawful exercise of force by external actors. If violence is co-produced by local and national actors, then peace cannot be produced solely or predominantly from the bottom-up. The inherent downside to local-level solutions is that they may eventually be destabilized by subsequent national-level developments. It is for these reasons that von Trotha contends that 'peacebuilding by non-state orders has to be paid for by curtailments in the reliability of that peace'.[171] Even strong advocates for localized peacebuilding and conflict resolution remain more aware than their transitional justice counterparts of the limitations of grassroots solutions. Both Bleiker and Belloni, for example, argue that state-level order and rule of law are imperative if violence is to be stopped even if full respect is given to localized agency or if a healthy civil society exists.[172] Simply put, localized processes remain too hostage to exogenous fortunes to justify an exclusive or predominant focus on horizontal violence within and between communities as the source of causally significant justice outcomes on a broader level. If vertical linkages between the state and the grassroots drive civil war and fragility, it stands to reason that vertical linkages between the two offer better entry points for thinking about justice.

---

169 UN Secretary-General, *Report of the Secretary-General on Timor-Leste Pursuant to Security Council Resolution* 1690 (2006), UN Doc. S/2006/628, 8 August 2006, para. 31.

170 Kristine Hoglund, 'Violence in War-to-Democracy Transitions' in Anna Jarstad and Timothy Sisk (eds), *From War to Democracy: Dilemmas of Peacebuilding* (Cambridge University Press 2008) 80 at 101.

171 Von Trotha (n 138) 44.

172 Roland Bleiker, 'Conclusion – Everyday Struggles for a Hybrid Peace' in Richmond and Mitchell (eds) (n 80) 293 at 293; Roberto Belloni, 'Civil Society in War-to-Democracy Transitions' in Jarstad and Sisk (eds) (n 170) 182 at 208.

6. THE LIMITS OF THE LOCAL: THE MISSING MIDDLE

It is possible to point to the widespread impact of local justice processes in East Timor and Sierra Leone, to successful mediation in 'crucibles of conflict' in Mozambique, and to alternative dispute resolution mechanisms for the land allocation issues that formed a important driver of Liberia's conflict.[173] However, if bottom-up grassroots projects are to have any effect on wider structures of conflict or inequality, these processes need to be conceptualized as an element of a politics of strategic interaction or strategic influence in which local, national and international actors exist in a condition of mutual interdependence. There is little evidence to suggest that bottom-up processes can, without any intent to aggregate their consequences, incrementally ground sustainable peace or shape the wider national justice environment. While it is arguable that 'the sum of disaggregated, unco-ordinated and fragmented, hidden disguised and marginal agencies represents a significant totality', it must also be admitted that it is not unidirectional and is impossible to consciously direct.[174] Though optimistic transitional justice scholars have imbued grassroots justice with significant agency beyond the immediate locale, most local peacebuilding or reconciliatory activity is rarely strategic in the sense of having specific national objectives or explicit connections to policy options for broader transformation. For example, in Haiti international and local actors launched a vast range of community dialogues and local peace accords to address the root causes of insecurity in the Port-au-Prince slums, but failed to make much sustainable difference to patterns of life because they lacked integration with wider institutional frameworks there, most notably the police.[175] Though Serbs and Muslims in the city of Brcko came together to reconstruct and parcel out homes devastated by conflict, the project did not filter horizontally or vertically beyond this in the absence of positive reinforcement from state structures.[176] Community-driven reconstruction programmes in Northern Liberia positively affected community cohesion, social inclusion of the

---

173 Ernstorfer, Chigas and Vaughan-Lee (n 35) 74.

174 Oliver Richmond, 'Critical Agency, Resistance and a Post-colonial Civil Society' (2011) 46 *Cooperation and Conflict* 419, 434.

175 Timothy Donais and Geoff Burt, 'Peace-building in Haiti: The Case for Vertical Integration' (2015) 15 *Conflict, Security and Development* 1, 3.

176 Talentino (n 33) 564.

marginalized and democratic values, but little attempt was made to scale them up to the national level.[177]

Local-level and community-based projects can be conceived of as a 'more people' approach, working with large numbers of individuals in a locality but not necessarily with those 'key people' who can say yes or no to social change.[178] Consequently, though those NGO figures involved presume these efforts will 'add up' someday, this does not automatically or inevitably occur in the absence of explicit efforts to achieve this.[179] As Chigas puts it:

> Peacebuilding efforts that focus on building relationships and trust across conflict lines, increasing tolerance, building skills in conflict management ... often produce dramatic transformations in attitudes, perceptions and trust of individuals participating. But evidence shows that impacts for the broader peace are significant only if these personal transformations are translated into actions at the sociopolitical level – the public, political and institutional sphere of activity.[180]

She contends that grassroots and middle-level approaches that concentrate mostly on ordinary people as a whole risk irrelevance to the extent that they are not linked to key decision-makers who control the levers of the broader peace.[181] The plethora of initiatives and workshops sponsored by international interveners bear testimony to their 'bepuzzlement' in trying to relate macro-level projects like peace agreements or state-building with the local in a meaningful way.[182] Critics of localized peacebuilding note that predefined activities like dialogue and other reconciliation-oriented projects are implemented 'regardless of their relevance in the context and phase of peacebuilding in question'.[183] The civil society actors on whom processes of reconciliation and justice depend focus their analysis on how the things they know how to do can

---

[177] Thomas Flores and Irfan Nooruddin, 'Credible Commitment in Post-conflict Recovery' in Coyne and Mathers (eds) (n 147) 474 at 491.

[178] Ernstorfer, Chigas and Vaughan-Lee (n 35) 75.

[179] Diana Chigas, 'Capacities and Limits of NGOs as Conflict Managers' in Chester Crocker, Fen Osler Hampson and Pamela Aall (eds), *Leashing the Dogs of War: Conflict Management in a Divided World* (US Institute of Peace Press 2007) 553 at 570 and 573.

[180] ibid 574.

[181] ibid.

[182] Chetail and Jütersonke (n 131) 9.

[183] Thania Paffenholz, 'International Peacebuilding Goes Local: Analysing Lederach's Conflict Transformation Theory and its Ambivalent Encounter with 20 Years of Practice' (2014) 2 *Peacebuilding* 11, 24.

be applied to a given context, but do not undertake any wider conflict analysis that might identify how their intervention might affect factors driving the conflict.[184] A lack of power analysis and the limited attention paid to the overall political system are characteristic features of the local in peacebuilding no less than in transitional justice.[185] This problem is exacerbated by the tendencies in both fields to present the local as deterritorialized webs of empathy or potentiality to reshape lived lives. The idea that local justice or community dialogues can be transformational in a broader sense relies too heavily on a Lederachian notion of 'critical yeast' in which interactions amongst a small group of individuals mechanically spreads to larger groups,[186] a post-war analogue of the 'reckless extrapolation from the micro to the macro level' that characterizes some of the more exuberant bottom-up theorizing of civil war ecologies.[187] Much of transitional justice's local turn is a commendable reaction against the simplistic top-down consensus that a centralized, state-level form of accountability, truth or reparation inevitably spreads outwards from the metropolis to the local. However, the faith in its transformative efficacy risks merely inverting this threadbare supposition by positing an inevitable trickle-up effect of localized healing and restoration.

To reduce approaches to peace, justice or transformation merely to alliances or reconciliation between active localized agents is to court irrelevance and reversal. As noted at the outset of this chapter, policy-focused analysis of grassroots peacebuilding assumes that bottom-up and people-centred approaches need conceptual and operational links to top-down processes. Even some of the strongest advocates of deference to indigenous, traditional or localized ad hoc forms of rule accept that states reliant on them must authorize, mediate and regulate private providers of state functions to at least minimally address concerns about exclusion in political or justice-based arrangements and guarantees of physical security.[188] Similarly, approaches to peacebuilding premised on

---

184 Chigas (n 179) 573.

185 Paffenholz (n 9) 860.

186 Lefranc (n 3) 43 and 45.

187 Stathis Kalyvas, 'Promises and Pitfalls of an Emerging Research Program: The Microdynamics of Civil War' in Stathis Kalyvas, Ian Shapiro and Tarek Masoud (eds), *Order, Conflict, Violence* (Cambridge University Press 2014) 397 at 398.

188 For example, Donais and Burt (n 175) 2–3; Ken Menkhaus, 'Somalia: Governance vs State-Building' in Charles Call with Vanessa Wyeth (eds), *Building States to Build Peace* (Lynne Rienner 2008) 187, 208 and 209–210.

secular, bottom-up civil society projects like women's and children's rights, education or culture inevitably adjust to broader political and economic pressures, and therefore successively widen their engagements with the state in the face of newly emergent problems.[189] Top-down and bottom-up integration usually accords with public sentiment. Participants in bottom-up land disputes and legal empowerment initiatives in Liberia 'seemed to feel that true progress to peace could only be achieved at a larger level and is dependent ultimately on the government's actions'.[190] Justice or peace initiatives at grassroots level that are disconnected from wider political dynamics are more likely to be palliative than transformative.[191]

However, bottom-up and grassroots strategies of transitional justice do not consciously develop spaces or opportunities for state or international efforts to interact in a meaningful way (though I fully accept that the reverse also applies). If anything, as the shift towards localism is underpinned by a rejection of the liberalism, state-centricity and alien nature of 'top-down' justice, the field is moving away from systemic analysis of the interactions between internationalized or state-level justice and grassroots variants. This is unfortunate, as this type of analysis would help to understand how, and under what conditions, micro-level justice and macro-level justice do or do not mutually reinforce the other to effect useful social change. Illustrating this mutual empowerment may prove a difficult task. In peacebuilding overall, those who study potential linkages admit that 'conceptually, empirically and strategically, our knowledge remains limited about relational dynamics of and between the "top-down" and "bottom-up", and what forms of interaction between them are likely to produce constructive results'.[192] Even strong advocates of deference to local initiatives admit that 'it is not at all clear how "bottom-up" processes actually move upwards, influencing top-level processes'.[193] This is a problem that also affects other top-down and bottom-up processes. Rule of law reconstruction policy, for example,

---

189 Schneckener (n 21) 244.

190 Christof Kurz, *The Cumulative Impacts of Peacebuilding in Liberia* (CDA Collaborative Learning Projects 2010) 45.

191 Erin McCandless, Eric Abitbol and Timothy Donais, 'Vertical Integration: A Dynamic Practice Promoting Transformative Peacebuilding' (2015) 10 *Journal of Peacebuilding and Development* 1, 3.

192 ibid 3–4.

193 ibid 4.

endures a 'missing middle' where scholars and practitioners have developed instructive guidelines on the political economy of effective institutional forms at state-level and a thoroughgoing anthropological understanding of indigenous dispute resolution systems from 'below', but struggle to usefully integrate the two perspectives.[194] Transmitting the values and example of locally negotiated justice horizontally into myriad other localities or vertically towards regional or national levels must involve complex processes of co-operation and communication with meso-level leaders, government officials and other shapers of widespread influence.

Peacebuilding and conflict resolution theorists like Lederach (who illustrates that conflict resolution exists in nested paradigms where local problems are enclosed within those of larger geographical subsystems),[195] McCandless, Abitbol and Donais (who have begun preliminary exploration of 'vertical integration' strategies to effectively link actors and programmes for society-wide peacebuilding and development)[196] and Odendaal (discussing integrated infrastructures for peace)[197] have begun to explore these potential links. The UN Development fund for Women (UNIFEM), notably, has adopted a multilayered approach that aims to foster changes in development capacity at macro-, meso- and micro-levels as part of a single theory of change.[198] Vertically integrated transitional justice processes could map how social organization at community level could be linked with existing subnational and national political networks. Any such linkages need to be consciously and strategically planned in transitional justice interventions, albeit with due attention to the risks of co-option or coercion. There are some ready examples. East Timor's Community Reconciliation Process had a coherent, mutually empowering, if ultimately under-used, linkage to the parallel Serious Crimes Process.[199] A few years later, UNDP and the East

---

[194] Deval Desai, Rosie Wagner, and Michael Woolcock, 'The Missing Middle: Reconfiguring Rule of Law Reform as if Politics and Process Mattered' (2014) 6 *Hague Journal on the Rule of Law* 230, 253.

[195] Lederach (n 19) 55–58.

[196] McCandless, Abitbol and Donais (n 191).

[197] Odendaal (n 132).

[198] UNIFEM, 'UNIFEM Framework Guidance Note for Capacity Development' (2010) <http://www.undp.md/employment/2010/50–100/092/Annex_2_UNIFEM_HQ_Capacity_Dev_Strategy_March_2010.PDF> accessed 21 July 2016.

[199] Padraig McAuliffe, 'East Timor's Community Reconciliation Process as a Model for Legal Pluralism in Criminal Justice' (2008) 12 *Law, Social Justice and Global Development* 1.

Timorese Ministry of Social Solidarity worked assiduously to harness culturally appropriate dialogue and mediation processes to reintegrate the 70,000 internally displaced persons caused by the 2006–2007 crisis.[200] Though more controversial in the sense that there was an obviously coercive element, Rwanda's *gacaca* process can be seen as an attempt to marry community-level justice to a national pacificatory vision. Another useful example that straddles the transitional justice–peacebuilding divide is the successful Northern Uganda Early Recovery Project, which was premised on grassroots-level peace rings that facilitated dialogue and mediation of local conflicts on a voluntary basis but which cohered with, assisted and benefited from the Kampala government's Peace Recovery and Development Plan for the region.[201] The North Kenyan Peace and Development Committees offer another relevant example. These were established to deal with intercommunal and interethnic disputes relating to land and livestock and became progressively rationalized as the state started to review and standardize them to make them compatible with national law and human rights standards, combining local legitimacy with anti-discrimination values.[202]

None of this is to argue localized justice should always be formalized or must always have links with the state, merely that without such links any activity will have little benefit beyond the immediate community. Even though models for interaction must inevitably be context-dependent, if the local turn in transitional justice is to remain aligned with the broader contract between the state and society, it must go beyond romanticized visions of micro-level emancipatory potential and stylized top-down versus bottom-up debates. Advocates of grassroots justice could develop sophisticated needs analysis to understand the countless ways communities, towns, regions and states are interconnected, even where those connections are tenuous and often resented. Grassroots transitional justice can only contribute to social transformation if its more widely applicable values and practices are linked with national projects like justice, statebuilding, rule of law and development, facilitating interaction between micro-level actors and the state through consultative mechanisms, some measure of mutual accountability and modes of collaboration. Would local justice be more effective if bottom-up actors consulted or accommodated the conflict analysis

---

[200] Hofmann (n 31) 83.

[201] See, generally, Kamatsiko (n 130).

[202] Tanja Chopra, 'Peace versus Justice in Northern Kenya: Dialectics of State and Community Law' in Yash Ghai and Jill Cottrell (eds), *Marginalized Communities and Access to Justice* (Routledge 2010) 185.

and strategic peace planning of state-level actors in the post-conflict government? Can local justice have any broader effect if its initiation, objective-setting and project design/management/monitoring/evaluation relate only to the expectations of a geographically or culturally enclosed community?

There is little evidence to suggest that transitional justice theorists or policy-makers are equipped or prepared to answer these questions in a discourse characterized by the enchantment of the local and reductive liberal–local binaries. As Paffenholz points out, integrated visions of peacebuilding revolve not only around rebuilding relationships but also infrastructures and processes which include the state. By contrast, more critical peacebuilding approaches (on which transitional justice's local turn to some extent draws on) understand localized approaches as forms of resistance against the dominant 'liberal' approach, seeking instead an alternative order based on grassroots agency.[203] Even the strongest voices for the prioritization of local approaches admit the state eventually 'must be brought back in'.[204] However, without some connecting intellectual cartilage between central government and peripheral sources of moral and social authority, transitional justice provides no sense of an overall architecture through different levels at which it can be achieved. This conceptual cartilage may be difficult to develop. Macro-level studies of transitional justice's impact on systemic goals like stability or democratization (or economic transformation) tend to be strongly positivist and employ quantitative techniques, while micro-level studies are more qualitative, interpretative and eschew comparative analysis, making it difficult to reconcile methodologies or co-ordinate the conclusions derived.[205]

7. CONCLUSION: WHY TRANSFORMING RELATIONSHIPS DOES NOT MEAN TRANSFORMING STRUCTURES

That transitional justice actors and scholars now emphasize broad-based community involvement, deference to local traditions and co-operation

203 Paffenholz (n 9) 859.

204 Andrieu (n 75) 551. See also McEvoy (n 90) 32.

205 Macdonald (n 63) 117, building on Geoff Dancy, 'Impact Assessment, Not Evaluation: Defining a Limited Role for Positivism in the Study of Transitional Justice' (2010) 4 *International Journal of Transitional Justice* 355, 366.

with socially legitimate NGOs has been one of the most important developments in the field in the course of its often halting development. The consistent repetition of these messages has served to counteract the ever-present (if diminishing) risk of alienating formalism or monomaniacal concentration on the national goals and international aspirations. It represents a preference for inductive, grassroots knowledge about what works over external imposition of unfamiliar rationalist and statist blueprints. It favours a communitarian emphasis on tradition and popular legitimacy in determining a vision of justice over assumptions of universal appropriateness. Bottom-up transitional justice interventions treat communities not as victims, but as the co-producers of peace (and violence). Grassroots justice appears as a way of empowering active citizens and communities, enabling them as political subjects to take some measure of societal responsibility for repair, restoration and reintegration. Calls to engage with the local–local 'imply a decolonisation of knowledge and a disaggregation of power, not the reconstitution of the Enlightenment project as a Northern example to the rest of the world'.[206] The notion of the local as a self-regulating entity capable of mobilizing the community population to fundamentally transform everyday life is an attractive one, but so attractive that the field has become blind to its limitations. The local turn's emphasis on community agency divorced from overarching order-producing systems represents something of a 'forest versus trees' phenomenon in which scholars or practitioners are so close to the actual practice of the local that they have not drawn back to examine the larger picture. There is not always a clear link between the activities of justice actors at grassroots level and the hazy theoretical utterances about the virtues of such enterprises. The notion that peaceful individuals or peaceful communities do not automatically make peaceful societies or states is one that has been elaborated throughout this chapter, as has the distinction between the intersubjective processes implicated in building grassroots peace and the material dimensions of political economy that affect them. Amidst an aestheticized optimism regarding the local, transitional justice scholars have insufficiently acknowledged how the constrictions of bottom-up processes fundamentally limit any wider transformative agency they might enjoy outside statist or institutional domains, either in their own locales or cumulatively within the state at large.

---

[206] David Chandler and Oliver Richmond, 'Contesting Postliberalism: Governmentality or Emancipation?' (2015) 18 *Journal of International Relations and Development* 1, 10.

In the literature on bottom-up approaches to accountability and reconciliation, the local is more a normative notion than an analytic concept. The rush to embrace the virtues of the local and the everyday has operated to the exclusion of a critical assessment of their limitations and potential in a post-conflict ecology where many other types of power relations and cross-cutting needs exist. None of this is to argue that bottom-up approaches to issues of economic and social justice cannot succeed in altering local conditions or catalysing effective social movements. However, this potential will be limited by (1) the tendency of bottom-up justice to become captured by local elites, (2) the different distribution of macro-level and micro-level cleavages, and (3) the lack of any links between bottom-up and top-down peacebuilding. It is one thing to argue that localized processes offer commendably contextualized alternatives to liberal-legalist criminal justice and truth commissions. It is another entirely to suggest they should replace or take precedence over them. While 'justice writ little' initiatives do great work in improving the day-to-day lives of communities (at least in relation to those issues they can cope with), they usually do little to positively impact on the bigger picture of 'justice writ large'.[207] If bottom-up processes are to promote socio-economic change at the community level or cumulatively at the national level, the discourse of the local needs to go beyond the enchantment of the grassroots and binaried opposition to formal avenues for justice. It must establish whether and how the bargaining power of local groups or communities can be increased in the formulation and development of local and national development plans. This requires far more strategic, vertically integrated thinking than has characterized the local turn thus far.

---

[207] To adapt the formulation of Ernstorfer, Chigas and Vaughan-Lee (n 35) 72.

6. Conclusion: lessons learned, lessons spurned?

The normative case that transitional justice should address the structural causes of conflict like underdevelopment, maldistribution and systematic denial of socio-economic rights has become increasingly prevalent in transitional justice discourse. It may become the mainstream position, if it has not done so already. This transformative turn is a commendable reaction against the prior 'stay in your lane' ethos in which the field was expected to concern itself solely with traditional remits of combatting impunity or reconciliation, and not the 'bigger picture' conditions that made them necessary. It is now unproblematically accepted that transitional justice actors can and should 'turn the majority of their attention and resources to efforts that directly target existing structural and cultural violence'[1] or formulate a 'holistic and comprehensive settlement addressing the foundational problems' that unleashed conflict.[2] It is assumed that transitional justice can 'assure outcomes based on the third generation right to development[3] or 'actively reverse the systems and attitudes that discriminate and dehumanize' across the entire society.[4] As the theoretical case for the transformative turn has been outlined, scholars have turned their attention to the reasons such self-evidently necessary and legitimate outcomes have not become the priority in practice. In exploring this question, the explanation is found to lie not with the inadequacy of the field's existing mechanisms (trials, truth commissions or reparations) as catalysts for macro-economic reforms, nor the strictly negotiated

[1] Matthew Mullen, 'Reassessing the Focus of Transitional Justice: The Need to Move Structural and Cultural Violence to the Centre' (2015) 28 *Cambridge Review of International Affairs* 462, 471.

[2] Makau Mutua, 'A Critique of Rights in Transitional Justice: The African Experience' in Gaby Oré Aguilar and Felipé Gomez Isa (eds), *Rethinking Transitions: Equality and Social Justice in Societies Emerging from Conflict* (Intersentia 2011) 31 at 39.

[3] Daniel Aguirre and Irene Pietropaoli, 'Gender Equality, Development and Transitional Justice: The Case of Nepal' (2008) 2 *International Journal of Transitional Justice* 356, 356.

[4] Mullen (n 1) 477.

nature of transition, nor the limited statehood evident in the post-conflict environment. Instead, the explanation is found in the conception of justice within the discipline. As Chapter 4 outlined, most scholars identify the limits of transitional justice in its promotion and export as an integral part of a globalized human rights discourse linked to hegemonic liberalism that promotes liberal democracy and open markets as the only valid endpoint for post-conflict societies. Chapter 2 made clear that arguments to the effect that structural transformation is impaired by the narrowness of the concept of justice presuppose a wide latitude for transitional justice actors to define their fields of action and a high degree of efficacy once they act.

As Stover and Weinstein argue, the assumptions we most wish are true deserve the most careful scrutiny of the grounds for optimism.[5] This book has explored the arguments underpinning fourth generation transitional justice by analyzing how a state's specific post-conflict conditions and inherited characteristics contribute to the malleability of inherited structural inequalities. It argues that research in the transformative turn suffers from a lack of theories of change and empirical evidence from post-conflict states. Many of the assumptions made about the malleability of post-conflict social structures are based on rather elementary concepts and causal claims that neglect the complexity of post-conflict states and the domestic political incentives that shape opportunities for change. The failure of transitional justice to seriously engage with issues of economic justice cannot be explained solely by the liberal legalism or top-down state-centricity of the field. Any analysis of transitional justice's potential to address economic injustice that neglects the deep domestic politics of peacemaking and peacebuilding and the incremental interplay of action and reaction must be shallow and misleading.

1. TAKING THE AGENCY OF *ALL* DOMESTIC ACTORS SERIOUSLY

Though the international community exports transitional justice models, the decision to embrace them and to pursue justice in good faith to the extent possible, lies primarily with the domestic post-conflict leadership (this is not to deny the limitations that exist beyond the control of

[5] Harvey M. Weinstein and Eric Stover, 'Introduction: Conflict, Justice and Reclamation' in Harvey M. Weinstein and Eric Stover (eds), *My Neighbor, My Enemy: Justice and Community in the Aftermath of Mass Atrocity* (Cambridge University Press 2004) 1 at 4.

peacebuilders, transitional justice actors or governments like globalization or structural adjustment policies). Many of them will have a genuine interest in seeking fundamental transformation of structures that gave rise to the earlier conflict. Others, however, will not. Much of the transformative turn is premised on the optimism that post-conflict transition represents a change from a society based on insecurity and fear to one based at least temporarily on a minimum of trust and co-operation. However, the study of the vagaries of largely endogenous peace negotiation in Chapter 3 made clear that domestic agreements on peacebuilding and transitional justice are not freely negotiated rational-choice options for improving society augmented by the re-vindication of human rights norms. They are instead conditioned by the state's need to ensure that institutions and policy are at least some way congruent with (1) the dispersal of power within the state and (2) the compromises agreed among social forces who inevitably have contradictory ideas about what stability and development depend on.[6] Much of the transformative turn is based on the fundamental assumption that the structures of post-conflict societies are malleable if only we understand the nature of socio-economic injustice comprehensively. However, the reality of compromised liberal intervention in Chapter 4 should make clear that reformed views of justice can never be translated in a linear fashion into reformed social conditions as purposeful action to this or any other end is inevitably warped by the domestic reactions and resistance such activities set in motion. Similarly, as Chapter 5 argues, the limits to localism are not solely set by traditional transitional approaches 'that prioritize institutional change and often instrumentalize local conflict resolution to serve national, state agendas'.[7] They are also set by local–local politics and traditions, the different distribution of macro-level and micro-level cleavages, as well as the failure to integrate local projects with wider emancipatory politics at the meso- and macro-levels.

Though international interveners and national/local reform constituencies can alter the balance of forces between actors and incentivize certain outcomes, their policies inevitably interact with strategies for political hegemony and economic accumulation that emerge from the resolution of domestic contestation. The apparent failures of transitional justice may be

---

[6] Lee Jones, '(Post-) Colonial State-Building and State Failure in East Timor: Bringing Social Conflict Back In' (2010) 10 *Conflict, Security and Development* 547, 563.

[7] Paul Gready and Simon Robins, 'From Transitional to Transformative Justice: A New Agenda for Practice' (2014) 8 *International Journal of Transitional Justice* 339, 349.

locked-in or over-determined on account of phenomena that even the most contextually appropriate transitional justice policy could not reasonably be expected to circumvent, like the division of power and resources in the prior peace agreement, the outright veto of transformation by emerging post-conflict elites or opportunist sabotage of the peace. This makes it self-defeating to attribute blame primarily to transitional justice or even the liberal peacebuilding framework it is embedded in, even if we accept that this framework exacerbates the problem.

The literature so far has provided few answers to the question of how to avoid the predictable consequences of peace pacts and sovereign manipulation of interventionary impulses. The last three chapters have made clear that meaningful transitional justice, like any form of governance in peacebuilding, can only ever be realized within mutually suspicious networks of alliances where goals of security and accumulation jostle with aspirations to improve the commonweal, and not as the inevitable product of objective norms or governing interests. Transitional justice can, at most, modify or influence power that lies elsewhere. To be viable, it must reflect at least partially the distribution of this power.[8] Those who advocate forms of transitional justice that highlight inequality, discrimination or deprivation of socio-economic rights must show how their prescriptions fit with those diverse social logics, pluricentric power structures and shifting alliances that characterize post-conflict states. The prior historical evolution of the state (the impact of geography, colonialism, post-colonial governance patterns, under-development and the impact of the most recent conflict) all have a bearing on the ability of the polity to transform itself. Fourth generation transitional justice is premised on the purposeful achievement of things we take for granted in more functional states like using taxation to provide welfare, redressing maldistribution in the face of recalcitrant elites or employing a state machinery to tackle poverty, but which may not be possible in highly mediated states with little social trust and institutions degraded by war. As Bøås and Jennings argue:

> Every state is a culmination of unique historical processes. Problematising them not on the basis of their own merits, needs, and particular pathologies of state and regime formation, but against the norms and standards of a specific

[8] To lightly adapt Przeworki's formulation in relation to political institutions in Adam Przeworski, 'Institutions Matter?' (2004) 39 *Government and Opposition* 527, 528–29.

type of advanced, northern state results in misguided and self-referential policy responses.[9]

It is clear that critical transitional justice theorists have failed to make visible the political framework within which their aspirations for transformation are to be realized, to say nothing of the manner in which this framework sets opposition in motion to radical reform of economic structures. The speed and ease with which concepts like 'transformation', 'economic violence' and 'justice from below' have been embraced within scholarly discourse is encouraging, but they do not readily offer policy-makers a tool for a better understanding of the political economy within which they will act. To the extent that transitional justice scholars have considered economic issues, an intellectual monoculture that paints all shortcomings in the same light (i.e. the liberal-legalism of our interventions) has developed that implicitly exaggerates the field's capacity for deliverance in the absence of politics.

The ever-present risk in transitional justice that the linking of concepts can be reiterated so often that it achieves the status of a truism may very well be the case with the constant invocation of the field's inherent potential to transform economic injustice.[10] It is hard to shake the conclusion that much of the transformative turn's exuberant theorizing reflects the status of transitional justice as a proxy battleground for wider debates about the status of socio-economic rights (i.e. that they are indivisible[11] or deserve parity of esteem[12]) or the pathologies of globalized liberalism[13] than a sober application of norms to context. Many of the debates that pitch traditional liberal impulses against transformative aspirations come to resemble turf battles over turf no side has ever shown the aptitude to actually fill. Other scholars largely sympathetic to

---

[9] Morten Bøås and Kathleen Jennings, '"Failed States" and "State Failure": Threats or Opportunities?' (2007) 4 *Globalizations* 475, 477.

[10] To adapt the argument in Tristan Anne Borer, *Telling the Truths: Truth Telling and Peace Building in Post-Conflict Societies* (University of Notre Dame Press 2006) 30.

[11] Lisa Laplante, 'On the Indivisibility of Rights: Truth Commissions, Reparations and the Right to Development' (2007) 10 *Yale Human Rights and Development Law Journal* 141.

[12] Louise Arbour, 'Economic and Social Justice for Societies in Transition' (2007) 40 *NYU Journal of International Law and Policy* 1, 4.

[13] Makau Mutua, 'What Is the Future of Transitional Justice?' (2015) 9 *International Journal of Transitional Justice* 1; Ismael Muvingi, 'Sitting on Powder Kegs: Socio-Economic Rights in Transitional Societies' (2009) 3 *International Journal of Transitional Justice* 163.

the impulses underlying the transformative turn have noted the 'basket approach' that scholars, campaigners and practitioners take towards transitional justice where 'the broad parameters of a normative imperative exist; all that awaits is the substance that will bring it to life.'[14] They also observe the risk of giving an overextended transitional justice 'quasimagical powers to "transform" or "regenerate" societies' inasmuch as it attempts to contribute to resolving deep social, cultural, and economic inequities'.[15] Without attention to the dynamics of transition and the weakness of the state, arguments that transitional justice practitioners should address mass poverty as an object of justice[16] or 'elaborate remedial actions that comprehensively address grievances in societies emerging from conflict'[17] may simply replicate the simplistic rhetoric and sloganeering that characterize much of the discourse on socio-economic rights realization.[18] An 'add structural inequality and stir' ethos is most apparent in the fuzzier elements of a literature that takes refuge in vague platitudes devoid of means–end articulation that serve as surrogates for strategy in any given state.

As argued above, transitional justice's impact will not be straightforwardly manifest in purposive, top-down practices designed externally. There are limits to social engineering that is led either by external transitional justice actors or by domestic reform actors who lie wholly or partly outside the loci of effective political power. Instead, a transitional justice practice that takes seriously socio-economic rights deprivations will be haphazard, contradictory and deeply compromised. It will replicate the tendency evident in development politics that 'any intentional

---

[14] Anna Macdonald, 'From the Ground Up: What Does the Evidence Tell Us about Local Experiences of Transitional Justice?' (2015) 3 *Transitional Justice Review* 72, 115.

[15] Kora Andrieu, 'Dealing with a "New" Grievance: Should Anticorruption Be Part of the Transitional Justice Agenda?' (2012) 11 *Journal of Human Rights* 537, 553–54.

[16] Ruben Carranza, 'Plunder and Pain: Should Transitional Justice Engage with Corruption and Economic Crimes?' (2008) 2 *International Journal of Transitional Justice* 310, 315.

[17] Japan International Co-operation Society and International Center for Transitional Justice, 'Workshop on Transitional Justice and Development in Africa: Enhancing Socio-Economic Justice in Societies in Transition: Case Studies on the African Continent' (2008) 7 <http://ictj.org/sites/default/files/ICTJ-JICA-Africa-Justice-Development-2008-English.pdf> accessed 21 July 2016.

[18] Kenneth Roth, 'Defending Economic, Social and Cultural Rights: Practical Issues Faced by an International Human Rights Organization' (2004) 26 *Human Rights Quarterly* 63, 63 and 65.

deployment only takes effect through a convoluted route involving unacknowledged structures and unpredictable outcomes ... The whole mechanism is ... a "mushy mixture" of the discursive and the non-discursive, of the intentional plans and the unacknowledged social world with which they are engaged'.[19] If prescriptions are to take account of this 'mushy mixture', it is imperative that transitional justice policy-making takes account of the national and subnational hardwiring that comes from the history, the conflict legacy, prior governmental norms, socio-cultural practices, physical conditions and institutional capacity.

Transformative approaches to transitional justice that disregard the frequent absence of political will or the paucity of institutional preconditions may offer little beyond platitudes. Over a decade ago, Bosire argued that for transitional justice to be effective in vacuous states 'the gap between expectations and reality must be narrowed by cultivating modest expectations about what justice-seeking measures can deliver [and] assessing realistically the institutional conditions necessary for their successful implementation'.[20] Her conclusion called for 'a thorough assessment of the institutional basis of countries in transition prior to embarking on transitional justice' and 'cultivation of extremely modest expectations about what can be delivered'.[21] This caution applied to a much more circumspect set of unmet expectations in relation to accountability and reconciliation, and is of evident relevance to more ambitious aspirations to fundamentally alter social structures. Transformative transitional justice must proceed from a penetrating assessment of the core opportunities and restraints that define the political life of the state in question and how justice interventions can capitalize on, or alter, them. It must take cognizance of the agency of all people within the state – not simply the victims, NGOs and grassroots actors we sympathize and work with. Only when this is done can theories of change be developed that would articulate how and why a transitional justice intervention would trigger a specific transformation of economic structures or enjoyment of socio-economic rights.

---

[19] James Ferguson, 'The Anti-Politics Machine' in Aradhana Sharma and Akhil Gupta (eds), *The Anthropology of the State: A Reader* (Blackwell 2006) 270 at 283–84.

[20] Lydiah Bosire, *Overpromised, Underdelivered: Transitional Justice in Sub-Saharan Africa* (International Center for Transitional Justice 2006) 3.

[21] ibid 34–35.

2. FUTURE RESEARCH AGENDAS: ADAPTING TRANSFORMATIVE ASPIRATIONS TO THE LIMITS OF POLITICS AND CAPACITY

While scholars in the transformative turn have advanced a number of arguments about how the field might address economic injustice, one of the most common is that of drawing attention to abuses, discrimination and inequalities that have hitherto passed below the disciplinary radar with reference to international human rights standards. However, it is not merely enough to highlight structures of poverty. The intuition that transitional justice can catalyse significant change to structures of injustice or socio-economic rights-deprivation needs more solid academic and empirical foundations. Deep and detailed historical analyses of settlements underpinning peace, the domestic political coalitions set in motion and the administrative strength of the state are also needed if transitional justice is to become socio-economically prescriptive in any meaningful sense. Though concerned with many different types of economic injustice, scholars in the field have not done obvious things like developing typologies of post-conflict states and using them to explain the endurance of economic violence with reference to obvious causally significant factors like institutional strength, patterns of elite economic control, power-sharing or conflict legacy. Hypotheses have not been formed to link proposed activities like employing truth commissions and reparations or empowerment of local communities to specific outcomes like positive discrimination or welfare promotion. The field is far from developing a contextually disaggregated, politically nuanced perspective on post-conflict states that captures the key variations in the malleability of the structures that underpin inequality, poverty and discrimination.

This book sought to contribute a more context-specific discourse on economic violence by providing a framework and language with which to analyse the experiences of structural harms in post-conflict justice. While (hopefully) improving on or complementing prior studies of transitional justice and economic violence, this book has limitations that can only be addressed in the future by collecting data on peace agreements, the administrative capacities and political motivations of post-conflict leaderships and the make-up of transitional justice and peacebuilding deployments. We need more knowledge about how socio-economic rights are meaningfully included in peace agreement implementation, how patrimonial economies reform or mitigate harms, how power-sharing gives way to greater openness to non-conflict elites, how international interveners can avoid or mitigate the stasis of compromised peacebuilding and compromised transitional justice. Such studies would have clear policy relevance as they can propose lessons that can be applied to transitional justice. They may generate a clearer account of the agents of transformation – who they are, what responsibilities or duties they need to be given, by what metrics they should be judged if they are not given them. At the same time, they might cause us to theoretically revise some of our most fundamental assumptions about the potential of the field or the malleability of the societies it applies to. When it comes to in-country policy proposals, we need information on the exact character of the governing coalition, the pathologies of the economic structures and the enforcement ability of existing institutions. Methodologically, approaches that integrate transitional justice with civil war theory, peacebuilding and developmental economics should significantly advance our knowledge of the malleability of existing structures of injustice given that we know the interplay of conflict legacies, international intervention and domestic institutions will matter decisively.

The normative theories this type of analysis can generate need to be supplemented with the sort of statistical analysis that would permit macro-hypotheses about transformation. Future research could mix quantitative studies in multiple post-conflict states that identify opportunity and risk factors with qualitative approaches that go beyond monocausal attributions of blame to the field's liberal-legalism to examine how and why transitional justice actors succeeded or failed in a given state. Quantitative studies may help to develop a taxonomy of context and opportunity to influence the formulation of policy regarding what might be achievable, under what circumstances, and by what means in a given post-conflict environment. It would permit better reference to, and consideration of, the post-war ecology in any analysis of structural malleability. Qualitative case studies would permit scholars to explore in detail a small number of instances where the activities of transitional justice actors and mechanisms had an impact on rights delivery, economic structures or distribution patterns in a given state or locality, and learn more about the processes by which a specific outcome had been reached. Comparative analysis can bridge the gap between general reflections and broad prescriptions that characterize the transformative turn and specific country- or locale-based studies. Of course, given the diversity of development levels, conflict types, conflict-resolution types, levels of intervention and political-psychological circumstances of ruling coalitions, broader lessons or trends may be difficult to extrapolate. Apparently failed transitional justice is a phenomenon clouded by equifinality – different confluences of factors can lead to the outcome criticized. The causes of discrimination, inequality and poverty are distinctly idiosyncratic combinations of history, geography, demographics and *fortuna*. It may be the case that no patterns can be identified across different post-conflict transitions and that no parsimonious narrative about the contribution of transitional justice to transformation can be gleaned. Intellectual modesty in the face of unfathomable complexity and diverse opposition may be the surest wisdom.

3. THE NEED FOR MODESTY

This book has argued that the claims made, and the goals asserted, by scholars and advocates in transitional justice's transformative turn are too broad and need refinement. They derive more from the social constructivist nature of transitional justice theorization than a sober analysis of the general structures of malleability and stasis that characterize areas of limited statehood after civil war. Only if the field can improve the alignment between the political incentives facing the governments of post-conflict states and redistributive or developmental objectives may it produce more constructive justice concepts. However, even if fourth generation transitional justice adopts a research agenda that allows it to calibrate the approach and prescriptions of a given intervention to context, more informed policy-making and practice cannot guarantee transformation given the limitations of political will, institutional capacity and the sheer scale of historical inequality and post-conflict destruction. Transitional justice may not be able to prescribe realistic means to address all deficits and dysfunctions, nor promote local processes that can catalyse change in communities. The best it might achieve is to discern and engage with progressive elements of government or national reform constituencies with the goal of promoting the right struggles – i.e. those economic, social and political processes that actively challenge elite control of the economy, the failure to provide services or differential development. The appropriate goal may not be transformation, but rather the more modest one of identifying which among the wide range of potential contests most clearly offer a pathway to equitable social change in a context of conservative peace agreements, the stasis of power-sharing and the inherited infirmities of fragile states. While it is imperative to take advantage of every possible opportunity to examine structures of inequality or socio-economic rights deprivation, we may need a humbler approach to our discipline, one based on evidence of what works (or has the potential to work), rather than one based on a simplistic telos of revised norm articulation to transformation.

Transitional justice might be most successful in addressing economic issues when, with an awareness of the limits of available mechanisms and opportunities, it encourages political leadership to maintain inclusive coalitions, incentivizes them to reach out to broader constituencies and empowers domestic reform constituencies to articulate socio-economic human rights obligations. This necessarily falls short of those inspiring but vague pleas to directly target existing structural and cultural violence[22] or formulate comprehensive settlements to address the root causes of conflict.[23] It does, however, accept that mediating factors exist between insight and transformation, between norms and realization. Recognizing this state of affairs does not mean exonerating transitional justice interveners (or the liberal peacebuilding apparatus they exist within) of responsibility for the blind spots and pathologies of their approaches. It does not imply that domestic or international transitional justice can never mobilize people or public sentiment sufficiently to alter domestic policy in relation to economic structures. It does, however, mean that scholars and policy-makers who advocate the reorientation of the field towards issues of inequality, subsistence and discrimination can do so effectively only by recognizing the distinct limitations on the malleability of socio-economic structures in the absence of a unified domestic political will to address them. Without such will, many structures of economic injustice can at best be managed, not resolved.

Elizabeth Cousens has argued that one of the most difficult challenges for the international community is to be 'ruthlessly modest' about its ambitions for positive peace in divided, underdeveloped states with weak capacity.[24] Even in the most propitious environments, the existing mechanisms of transitional justice may be better suited to those aspects of cultural violence ('values, traditions and beliefs that justify exclusion and marginalization of particular groups in society') where insight combats irrational bias, than they are to structural violence ('institutions and societal structures that suggest exclusive rules and norms that prevent participation of the entire population particularly in decision-making

22 Mullen (n 1) 10.

23 Mutua (n 2) 39.

24 Elizabeth Cousens, 'Introduction' in Elizabeth Cousens and Chetan Kumar (eds), *Peacebuilding as Politics: Cultivating Peace in Fragile Societies* (Lynne Rienner 2001) 1 at 15.

processes') where insight combats rational and stoutly defended interests.[25] It may also be the case that in the most difficult environments, all interventionary actors fulfil is a much more limited remit of creating 'a space, both real and perceived, for hope or learned optimism to overcome anomie, disaffection, or learned pessimism'.[26] It may further be the case that while transformation is necessary in all post-conflict states, we should become most exercised about the failure of transitional justice to foster it only in those cases where pre-existing conditions, domestic political will and external support are such that genuine transformation is possible. None of this is to counsel despair. It is instead to counsel pragmatism over rigid principle and undue pessimism.

Like the field of human rights as a whole, transitional justice in its transformative turn should couple a fallibilist pragmatism that 'welcomes the discomfort of undergoing a crisis of faith' and travels in the 'productive space that lies between states of doubt and belief,' with a melioristic pragmatism that focuses on what can be done to hasten progress and mitigate decline, preferring the art of the possible over the pursuit of perfect justice.[27] Even partial successes should be emphasized, recognizing that many more years will be required for genuine transformation. As Williams and Nagy note, second-best justice is better than nothing at all, and it is better to do what we can, even if imperfect, than to permit injustice to stand entirely unaddressed.[28] With a renewed attention to limitations imposed by the political economy of post-conflict states (to say nothing of issues this book has not addressed, like the

[25] Definitions, but not argument, taken from Briony Jones, Elisabeth Baumgartner and Sidonia Gabriel, *A Transformative Approach to Dealing with the Past* (SwissPeace 2015) 18.

[26] Patricia Mauldeen, 'The Post-Conflict Paradox: Engaging War, Creating Peace' in Bruno Charbonneau and Genevieve Parent (eds), *Peacebuilding, Memory and Reconciliation: Bridging Top-Down and Bottom-up Approaches* (Routledge 2013) 19 at 24–25.

[27] To adapt Geoff Dancy, 'Human Rights Pragmatism: Belief, Inquiry, and Action' (2016) 22 *European Journal of International Relations* 512 at 516, citing Jack Knight and James Johnson, *The Priority of Democracy: Political Consequences of Pragmatism* (Princeton University Press 2011) 26 (fallibilism) and Colin Koopman, 'Pragmatism as a Philosophy of Hope: Emerson, James, Dewey, Rorty' (2006) 20 *Journal of Speculative Philosophy* 106, 107 (meliorism).

[28] Melissa Williams and Rosemary Nagy, 'Introduction' in Melissa Williams, Rosemary Nagy and Jon Elster (eds), *Transitional Justice* (New York University Press 2012) 1 at 13.

destructive irrationalities of global trade patterns and structural adjustment policies), the argument that transitional justice risks losing credibility unless it improves overall living conditions for citizens in the transitional state may seem exaggerated. It represents yet another example of the field's characteristic mix of narcissism (the assumption that the discipline can make an impact on the distribution of economic wealth) and hand-wringing (that in practice it does not) when everything we know about the malleability of post-conflict states suggests that transitional justice has neither the potential ascribed to it to change structures of injustice nor the complicity in them it damns itself with.[29] One must take care neither to exaggerate nor to deprecate the effects of transitional justice as a force for political and social change.

This book may help to identify those instances where transitional justice actors stand a real chance of informing development patterns, successfully promoting socio-economic rights or converting the insights of truth commissions or inquiries into genuinely transformational policy. Nevertheless, transitional justice can only ever be a limited element of what is a much larger and more multifaceted challenge that peacebuilders, development agencies, local communities, the international community and a post-conflict government address over time. The exuberant theorizing of the transformative turn must give way to a more sober reflection on the opportunities for – and barriers to – transformation in a reality of ongoing contestation.

---

[29] I have made this point elsewhere: Padraig McAuliffe, 'Weighing Domestic and International Impediments to Transformative Justice in Transition' (2015) 3 *London Review of International Law* 169, 171.

Bibliography

BOOKS AND PUBLISHED REPORTS

Alexander, J. *A Scoping Study of Transitional Justice and Poverty Reduction* (DFID 2003).

Ammitzboll, K. and Torjesen, S. *Maximum or Minimum? Policy Options for Democratisation Initiatives in UN Peace Operations* (Norsk Utenrikspolitisk Institutt 2006).

Bekoe, D. *Implementing Peace Agreements: Lessons from Mozambique, Angola and Liberia* (Palgrave Macmillan 2008).

Bell, C. *Peace Agreements and Human Rights* (Oxford University Press 2003).

Bell, C. *On the Law of Peace: Peace Agreements and the Lex Pacificatoria* (Oxford University Press 2008).

Berdal, M. *Building Peace After War* (Routledge 2009).

Bergsmo, M. et al. (eds). *Distributive Justice in Transitions* (Torkel Opsahl 2010).

Boraine, A. *A Country Unmasked: Inside South Africa's Truth and Reconciliation Commission* (Oxford University Press 2000).

Borer, T.A. *Telling the Truths: Truth Telling and Peace Building in Post-Conflict Societies* (University of Notre Dame Press 2006).

Bosire, L. *Overpromised, Underdelivered: Transitional Justice in Sub-Saharan Africa* (International Center for Transitional Justice 2006).

Boulding, K. *Conflict and Defense: A General Theory* (Torch Books 1962).

Brams, S. and Taylor, A. *Fair Division: From Cake-cutting to Dispute Resolution* (Cambridge University Press 1996).

Buckley-Zistel, S. et al. (eds). *Transitional Justice Theories* (Routledge 2013).

Call, C. *Why Peace Fails: The Causes and Prevention of Civil War Recurrence* (Georgetown University Press 2012).

Kavanagh, C. and Jones, B. *Shaky Foundations: An Assessment of the UN's Rule of Law Support Agenda* (Center on International Cooperation 2011).

Chandler, D. *International Statebuilding: The Rise of Post-Liberal Governance* (Routledge 2010).

Chetail, V. and Jütersonke, O. *Peacebuilding: A Review of the Academic Literature* (Geneva Peacebuilding Platform 2015).

Chinkin, C. *Peace Agreements as a Means for Promoting Gender Equality and Ensuring Participation of Women* (UN Division for the Advancement of Women 2003).

Clapham, C. *Third World Politics: An Introduction* (Helm 1985).

Collier, P. *The Challenge of Ugandan Reconstruction, 1986–98* (World Bank Development Research Group 1999).

Colvin, C. *'We are Still Struggling': Storytelling, Reparations and Reconciliation after the TRC* (Centre for the Study of Violence and Reconciliation 2000).
Coyne, C. *Doing Bad by Doing Good: Why Humanitarian Action Fails* (Stanford University Press 2013).
Darby, J. *The Effects of Violence on Peace Processes* (US Institute of Peace Press 2001).
De Greiff, P. and Duthie, R. (eds). *Transitional Justice and Development: Making Connections* (Social Science Research Council 2009).
Doyle, M. *UN Peacekeeping in Cambodia: UNTAC's Civil Mandate* (Lynne Rienner 1995).
Doyle, M. and Sambanis, N. *Making War and Building Peace: United Nations Peace Operations* (Princeton University Press 2006).
Duffield, M. *Development, Security and Unending War: Governing the World of Peoples* (Polity Press 2007).
Dupuy, A. *The Prophet and Power: Jean-Bertrand Aristide, the International Community and Haiti* (Rowman and Littlefield 2007).
Elster, J. *Closing the Books: Transitional Justice in Historical Perspective* (Cambridge University Press 2004).
Fischer, M. *Civil Society in Conflict Transformation: Ambivalence, Potentials and Challenges* (Berghof Research Center for Constructive Conflict Management 2006).
Fisher, K. and Stewart, R. (eds). *Transitional Justice and the Arab Spring* (Routledge 2015).
Fritz, V. and Rocha Menocal, A. *Understanding State-Building from a Political Economy Perspective* (Overseas Development Institute 2007).
Haas, R. *Conflicts Unending* (Yale University Press 1990).
Hameiri, S. *Regulating Statehood: State Building and the Transformation of the Global Order* (Palgrave Macmillan 2010).
Hampson, F.O. *Nurturing Peace: Why Peace Settlements Succeed or Fail* (US Institute of Peace Press 1996).
Hardin, R. *Liberalism, Constitutionalism, and Democracy* (Oxford University Press 2003).
Hartzell, C. and Hoddie, M. *Crafting Peace: Power-Sharing Institutions and the Negotiated Settlement of Civil Wars* (Pennsylvania State University Press 2007).
Hayner, P. *Negotiating Justice: Guidance for Mediators* (HD Centre for Humanitarian Dialogue 2009).
Hinton, A.L. (ed.). *Transitional Justice: Global Mechanisms and Local Realities after Genocide and Mass Violence* (Rutgers University Press 2010).
Horowitz, D. *Ethnic Groups in Conflict* (University of California Press 1985).
Inter-Congolese Dialogue, Resolution DIC/CPR/04 and Truth and Reconciliation Commission, *Witness to Truth: Report of the Sierra Leone Truth and Reconciliation Commission* (Freetown 2004).
Jackson, R.H. *Quasi-states: Sovereignty, International Relations, and the Third World* (Cambridge University Press 1990).
Jackson, R. and Rosberg, C. *Personal Rule in Black Africa: Prince, Autocrat, Prophet, Tyrant* (University of California Press 1982).

Jarstad, A. and Sisk, T. (eds). *From War to Democracy: Dilemmas of Peacebuilding* (Cambridge University Press 2008).
Jessop, B. *State Theory: Putting the Capitalist State in its Place* (Penn State Press 1990).
Jones, B., Baumgartner, E. and Gabriel, S. *A Transformative Approach to Dealing with the Past* (SwissPeace 2015).
Kalyvas, S. *The Logic of Violence in Civil War* (Cambridge University Press 2006).
Kavanagh, C. and Jones, B. *Shaky Foundations: An Assessment of the UN's Rule of Law Support Agenda* (Center on International Cooperation 2011).
Keen, D. *The Economic Functions of Violence in Civil Wars, Adelphi Paper 320* (Oxford University Press 1998).
Kennedy, D. *The Dark Sides of Virtue: Reassessing International Humanitarianism* (Princeton University Press 2005).
Kerr, R. and Mobekk, E. *Peace and Justice: Seeking Accountability after War* (Polity Press 2007)
Knight, J. and Johnson, J. *The Priority of Democracy: Political Consequences of Pragmatism* (Princeton University Press 2011).
Kurz, C., *The Cumulative Impacts of Peacebuilding in Liberia* (CDA Collaborative Learning Projects 2010).
Lederach, J.P. *Preparing for Peace: Conflict Transformation Across Cultures* (Syracuse University Press 1995).
Lederach, J.P. *Building Peace: Sustainable Reconciliation in Divided Societies* (US Institute of Peace Press 1997).
Little, P. *Somalia: Economy Without State* (James Currey 2003).
Mac Ginty, R. *International Peacebuilding and Local Resistance: Hybrid Forms of Peace* (Palgrave Macmillan 2011).
Mani, R. *Beyond Retribution – Seeking Justice in the Shadows of War* (Polity Press 2002).
Mann, M. *The Sources of Social Power, Vol. 1, A History of Power from the Beginning to AD 1760* (Cambridge University Press 1986).
Marten, K.Z. *Enforcing the Peace: Learning from the Imperial Past* (Columbia University Press 2004).
McAuliffe, P. *Rule of Law and Transitional Justice: A Contentious Relationship* (Routledge 2013).
Mehler, A. *Not Always in the People's Interest: Power-Sharing Arrangements in African Peace Agreements* (German Institute of Global and Area Studies 2008).
Mehler, A. and Ribaux, C. *Crisis Prevention and Conflict Management in Technical Cooperation* (Deutsche Gesellschaft Technische Zusammenarbeit 2000).
Meister, R. *After Evil: A Politics of Human Rights* (Columbia University Press 2011).
Miall, H., Ramsbotham, O. and Woodhouse, T. *Contemporary Conflict Resolution* (Polity Press 2011).
Migdal, J. *Strong Societies, Weak States* (Princeton University Press 1988).

Mobekk, E. *Transitional Justice and Security Sector Reform: Enabling Sustainable Peace* (Geneva Centre for the Democratic Control of Armed Forces 2006).

Moulier-Boutang, Y. *Cognitive Capitalism* (Polity Press 2011).

Nesiah, V. *Transitional Justice Practice: Looking Back, Moving Forward* (Impunity Watch 2016).

Odendaal, A. *A Crucial Link: Local Peace Committees and National Peacebuilding* (US Institute of Peace Press 2013).

Okello, M.C. et al. (eds). *Where Law Meets Reality: Forging African Transitional Justice* (Pambazuka Press 2012).

Olsen, T., Payne, L. and Reiter, A. *Transitional Justice in Balance: Comparing Processes, Weighing Efficacy* (US Institute of Peace Press 2010).

Oré Aguilar, G. and Gomez Isa, F. (eds), *Rethinking Transitions: Equality and Social Justice in Societies Emerging from Conflict* (Intersentia 2011) 31.

Organisation for Economic Co-operation and Development. *From Fragility to Resilience: Concepts and Dilemmas of State Building in Fragile States* (Organisation for Economic Co-operation and Development 2008).

Palmer, N., Clark, P. and Granville, D. (eds). *Critical Perspectives in Transitional Justice* (Intersentia 2012).

Paris, R. and Sisk, T. (eds). *The Dilemmas of Statebuilding: Confronting the Contradictions of Postwar Peace Operations* (Routledge 2009).

Peacock, S. and Beltrán, A. *Hidden Powers in Post-conflict Guatemala: Illegal Armed Groups and the Forces Behind Them* (Washington Office on Latin America 2003).

Poulantzas, N. *State, Power, Socialism* (Verso 1978).

Prunier, G. *From Genocide to Continental War: The Congolese Conflict and the Crisis of Contemporary Africa* (C. Hurst and Co. 2009).

Reychler, L. and Langer, A. *Researching Peace Building Architecture* (Centrum voor Vredesonderzoek en Strategische 2006).

Richmond, O. *The Transformation of Peace* (Palgrave Macmillan 2005).

Richmond, O. and Franks, J. *Liberal Peace Transitions: Between Statebuilding and Peacebuilding* (Edinburgh University Press 2009).

Rubli, S. *Transitional Justice: Justice by Bureaucratic Means?* (SwissPeace 2012).

Sandole, D. *Capturing the Complexity of Conflict: Dealing with Violent Ethnic Conflicts in the Post-Cold War Era* (Pinter 1999).

Schwalbe, M. *Rigging the Game: How Inequality is Reproduced in Everyday Life* (Oxford University Press 2008).

Sharp, D. (ed.). *Justice and Economic Violence in Transition* (Springer 2013).

Sikkink, K. *The Justice Cascade: How Human Rights Prosecutions Are Changing World Politics* (W.W. Norton and Co. 2011).

Sisk, T. *Statebuilding* (Polity Press 2013).

Sklar, J. *Legalism* (Harvard University Press 1964).

Sriram, C.L. *Peace as Governance: Power-sharing, Armed Groups and Contemporary Peace Negotiations* (Palgrave Macmillan 2008).

Sriram, C.L. et al. (eds). *Transitional Justice and Peacebuilding on the Ground: Victims and Ex-Combatants* (Routledge 2012).

Stahn, C., Easterday, J. and Iverson, J. (eds). *Jus Post Bellum: Mapping the Normative Foundations* (Oxford University Press 2014).
Stein, D. and Valters, C. *Understanding Theory of Change in International Development* (Justice and Security Research Programme and Asia Foundation 2012).
Stewart, F. and Brown, G. *Fragile States* (University of Oxford CRISE 2009).
Suhrke, A., Wimpelmann, T. and Dawes, M. *Peace Processes and Statebuilding: Economic and Institutional Provisions of Peace Agreements* (Chr. Michelsen Institute 2007).
Teitel, R. *Transitional Justice* (Oxford University Press 2000).
Tilly, C. *Coercion, Capital and European States, AD 990–1992* (Blackwell 1990).
Tschirgi, N. *Post-conflict Peacebuilding Revisited: Achievements, Limitations, Challenges* (International Peace Academy 2004).
Unger, R.M. *False Necessity: Anti-necessitarian Social Theory in the Service of Radical Democracy* (Cambridge University Press 1987).
van der Merwe, H., Baxter, V. and Chapman, A. (eds). *Assessing the Impact of Transitional Justice: Challenges for Empirical Research* (US Institute of Peace Press 2009).
Vollan, K., Butenschøn, N. and Stiansen, O. *Power-sharing in Conflict-ridden Societies: Challenges for Building Peace and Democratic Stability* (Ashgate 2015).
Weick, K. *Sensemaking in Organizations* (Sage Publications 1995).
Whaites, A. *States in Development: Understanding State-building* (DFID 2008).
Zartman, I.W. (ed.). *Elusive Peace: Negotiating an End to Civil Wars* (Brookings Institution 1995).
Zartman, I.W. *Ripe for Resolution: Conflict Resolution in Africa* (Oxford University Press 1989).
Zürcher, C., Manning, C. and Evenson, K. *Costly Democracy: Peacebuilding and Democratization After War* (Stanford University Press 2013).

ARTICLES

Abou-El-Fadl, R. 'Beyond Conventional Transitional Justice: Egypt's 2011 Revolution and the Absence of Political Will' (2012) 6 *International Journal of Transitional Justice* 318.
Aguirre, D. and Pietropaoli, I. 'Gender Equality, Development and Transitional Justice: The Case of Nepal' (2008) 2 *International Journal of Transitional Justice* 356.
Alence, R. 'Political Institutions and Developmental Governance in Sub-Saharan Africa' (2004) 42 *Journal of Modern African Studies* 163.
An-Na'im, A.A. 'Editorial Note: From the Neocolonial "Transitional" to Indigenous Formations of Justice' (2013) 7 *International Journal of Transitional Justice* 197.
Andrieu, K. 'Civilizing Peacebuilding: Transitional Justice, Civil Society and the Liberal Paradigm' (2010) 41 *Security Dialogue* 537.

Andrieu, K. 'Dealing with a "New" Grievance: Should Anticorruption Be Part of the Transitional Justice Agenda?' (2012) 11 *Journal of Human Rights* 537.

Arbour, L. 'Economic and Social Justice for Societies in Transition' (2007) 40 *NYU Journal of International Law and Policy* 1.

Arnold, W. 'Bureaucratic Politics, State Capacity, and Taiwan's Automobile Industrial Policy' (1989) 15 *Modern China* 178.

Aroussi, S. and Vandeginste, S. 'When Interests Meet Norms: The Relevance of Human Rights for Power-sharing' (2013) 17 *International Journal of Human Rights* 183.

Arriaza, L. and Roht-Arriaza, N. 'Social Reconstruction as a Local Process' (2008) 2 *International Journal of Transitional Justice* 152.

Arthur, P. 'How "Transitions" Reshaped Human Rights: A Conceptual History of Transitional Justice' (2009) 31 *Human Rights Quarterly* 321.

Asmal, K. 'Truth, Reconciliation and Justice: The South African Experience in Perspective' (2000) 63 *Modern Law Review* 1.

Atlas, P. and Licklider, R. 'Conflict among Former Allies after Civil War Settlement: Sudan, Zimbabwe, Chad and Lebanon' (1999) 36 *Journal of Peace Research* 35.

Atzili, B. 'When Good Fences Make Bad Neighbors: Fixed Borders, State Weakness and International Conflict' (2006–2007) 31 *International Security* 139.

Autesserre, S. 'Hobbes and the Congo: Frames, Local Violence, and International Intervention' (2009) 63 *International Organization* 249.

Autesserre, S. 'Construire la Paix: Conceptions Collectives de son Etablissement, de son Maintien et de sa Consolidation' (2011) 51 *Critique Internationale* 153.

Babo-Soares, D. 'Nahe Biti: The Philosophy and Process of Grassroots Reconciliation (and Justice) in East Timor' (2004) 5 *Asia Pacific Journal of Anthropology* 15.

Balasco, L.M. 'The Transitions of Transitional Justice: Mapping the Waves from Promise to Practice' (2013) 12 *Journal of Human Rights* 198.

Balcells, L. and Kalyvas, S. 'Does Warfare Matter? Severity, Duration and Outcomes of Civil Wars' (2014) 58 *Journal of Conflict Resolution* 1390.

Balint, J., Evans, J. and McMillan, N. 'Rethinking Transitional Justice, Redressing Indigenous Harm: A New Conceptual Approach' (2014) 8 *International Journal of Transitional Justice* 194.

Balthasar, D. 'From Hybridity to Standardization: Rethinking State-Making in Contexts of Fragility' (2015) 9 *Journal of Intervention and Statebuilding* 26.

Bekoe, D. 'Mutual Vulnerability and the Implementation of Peace Agreements: Examples from Mozambique, Angola and Liberia' (2005) 10 *International Journal of Peace Studies* 43.

Bell, C. 'Transitional Justice, Interdisciplinarity and the State of the "Field" or "Non-Field"' (2009) 3 *International Journal of Transitional Justice* 5.

Bell, C. and O'Rourke, C. 'The People's Peace? Peace Agreements, Civil Society, and Participatory Democracy' (2007) 28 *International Political Science Review* 293.

Belloni, R. 'Hybrid Peace Governance: Its Emergence and Significance' (2012) 18 *Global Governance* 21.

Bendaña, A. 'From Peacebuilding to Statebuilding: One Step Forward and Two Steps Back?' (2005) 48 *Development* 5.
Berg, L.-A. 'Guns, Laws and Politics: The Political Foundations of Rule of Law and Security Sector Reform' (2012) 4 *Hague Journal on the Rule of Law* 4.
Bhuta, N. 'New Modes and Orders: The Difficulties of a *Jus Post Bellum* of Constitutional Transformation' (2010) 60 *University of Toronto Law Journal* 799.
Binningsbø, H.M. 'Power Sharing, Peace and Democracy: Any Obvious Relationships?' (2013) 16 *International Area Studies Review* 89.
Bliesemann de Guevara, B. 'The State in Times of Statebuilding' (2008) 10 *Civil Wars* 348.
Bliesemann de Guevara, B. 'Introduction: The Limits of Statebuilding and the Analysis of State-Formation' (2010) 4 *Journal of Intervention and Statebuilding* 111.
Blunt, P. and Turner, M. 'Decentralisation, Democracy and Development in a Post-Conflict Society: Commune Councils in Cambodia' (2005) 25 *Public Administration and Development* 75.
Bøås, M. 'Returning to Realities: A Building-Block Approach to State and Statecraft in Eastern Congo and Somalia' (2010) 10 *Conflict, Security and Development* 443.
Bøås, M. and Jennings, K. '"Failed States" and "State Failure": Threats or Opportunities?' (2007) 4 *Globalizations* 475.
Boege, V. et al. 'Building Peace and Political Community in Hybrid Political Orders' (2009) 16 *International Peacekeeping* 599.
Boesenecker, A. and Vinjamuri, L. 'Lost in Translation? Civil Society, Faith-Based Organizations and the Negotiation of International Norms' (2011) 5 *International Journal of Transitional Justice* 345.
Boraine, A. 'Transitional Justice: A Holistic Interpretation' (2006) 60 *Journal of International Affairs* 17.
Bratton, M. and Van de Walle, N. 'Neopatrimonial Regimes and Political Transitions in Africa' (1994) 46 *World Politics* 453.
Brown, K. and Ní Aoláin, F. 'Through the Looking Glass: Transitional Justice Futures through the Lens of Nationalism, Feminism and Transformative Change' (2015) 9 *International Journal of Transitional Justice* 125.
Brown, M. and Zahar, M.-J. 'Social Cohesion as Peacebuilding in the Central African Republic and Beyond' (2015) 10 *Journal of Peacebuilding and Development* 10.
Burgerman, S. 'Building the Peace by Mandating Reform: United Nations-mediated Human Rights Agreements in El Salvador and Guatemala' (2000) 27 *Latin American Perspectives* 63.
Bush, K. 'Beyond Bungee Cord Humanitarianism: Towards a Developmental Agenda for Peacebuilding' (1996) 17 *Canadian Journal of Development Studies* 75.
Cahill-Ripley, A. 'Foregrounding Socio-Economic Rights in Transitional Justice: Realising Justice for Violations of Economic and Social Rights' (2014) 32 *Netherlands Quarterly of Human Rights* 183.
Cain, K. 'The Rape of Dinah: Human Rights, Civil War in Liberia, and Evil Triumphant' (1999) 21 *Human Rights Quarterly* 265.

Call, C. and Cook, S. 'On Democratization and Peacebuilding' (2003) 9 *Global Governance* 233.

Cammett, M. and Malesky, E. 'Power Sharing in Postconflict Societies Implications for Peace and Governance' (2012) 56 *Journal of Conflict Resolution* 982.

Campbell, C. and Ní Aoláin, F. 'Local Meets Global: Transitional Justice in Northern Ireland' (2002) 26 *Fordham International Law Journal* 871.

Campbell, C. and Turner, C. 'Utopia and the Doubters: Truth, Transition and the Law' (2008) 28 *Legal Studies* 374.

Carothers, T. 'The End of the Transition Paradigm' (2002) *Journal of Democracy* 5.

Carranza, R. 'Plunder and Pain: Should Transitional Justice Engage with Corruption and Economic Crimes?' (2008) 2 *International Journal of Transitional Justice* 310.

Cederman, L.E., Wimmer, A. and Min, B. 'Why Do Ethnic Groups Rebel? New Data and Analysis' (2010) 62 *World Politics* 87.

Chandler, D. 'Hollow Hegemony: Theorising the Shift from Interest-Based to Value-Based International Policy-Making' (2007) 35 *Millennium: Journal of International Studies* 703.

Chandler, D. 'International Statebuilding and the Ideology of Resilience' (2013) 33 *Politics* 276.

Chandler, D. 'Peacebuilding and the Politics of Non-Linearity: Rethinking "Hidden" Agency and "Resistance"' (2013) 1 *Peacebuilding* 17.

Chandler, D. and Richmond, O. 'Contesting Postliberalism: Governmentality or Emancipation?' (2015) 18 *Journal of International Relations and Development* 1.

Cheeseman, N. and Tendi, B.M. 'Power-sharing in Comparative Perspective: The Dynamics of "Unity Government" in Kenya and Zimbabwe' (2010) 48 *Journal of Modern African Studies* 203.

Clapham, C. 'The Challenge to the State in a Globalized World' (2002) 33 *Development and Change* 775.

Colvin, C. 'Purity and Planning: Shared Logics of Transitional Justice and Development' (2008) 2 *International Journal of Transitional Justice* 412.

Cunningham, D. 'Veto Players and Civil War Duration' (2006) 50 *American Journal of Political Science* 875.

Dancy, G. 'Impact Assessment, Not Evaluation: Defining a Limited Role for Positivism in the Study of Transitional Justice' (2010) 4 *International Journal of Transitional Justice* 355.

Dancy, G. 'Human Rights Pragmatism: Belief, Inquiry, and Action' (2016) 27 *European Journal of International Relations.*

Dancy, G. and Wiebelhaus-Brahm, E. 'Bridge to Human Development or Vehicle of Inequality? Transitional Justice and Economic Structures' (2015) 9 *International Journal of Transitional Justice* 51.

Dann, P. and Al-Ali, Z. 'The Internationalized *Pouvoir Constituant*: Constitution-making under External Influence in Iraq, Sudan and East Timor' (2006) 10 *Max Planck Yearbook of United Nations Law* 423.

Davis, L. 'Power Shared and Justice Shelved: The Democratic Republic of Congo' (2013) 17 *International Journal of Human Rights* 289.

De Coning, C. 'Understanding Peacebuilding as Essentially Local' (2013) 2 *Stability: International Journal of Security and Development* 1.
De Greiff, P. 'Transitional Justice Gets Its Own Encyclopedia: Vitamins or Steroids for a Developing Field?' (2013) 7 *International Journal of Transitional Justice* 547.
DeRouen, K., Lea, J. and Wallensteen, P. 'The Duration of Civil War Peace Agreements' (2009) 26 *Conflict Management and Peace Science* 367.
de Soto, A. and del Castillo, G. 'Obstacles to Peace Building' (1994) 94 *Foreign Policy* 69.
Desai, D., Wagner, R. and Woolcock, M. 'The Missing Middle: Reconfiguring Rule of Law Reform as if Politics and Process Mattered' (2014) 6 *Hague Journal on the Rule of Law* 230.
De Waal, A. 'Mission Without End? Peacekeeping in the African Political Marketplace' (2009) 85 *International Affairs* 99.
Diamond, L. 'Promoting Democracy in Post-Conflict and Failed States: Lessons and Challenges' (2006) 2 *Taiwan Journal of Democracy* 93.
Dixon, J. 'Emerging Consensus: Results from the Second Wave of Statistical Studies on Civil War Termination' (2009) 11 *Civil Wars* 121.
Donais, T. 'The Political Economy of Stalemate: Organised Crime, Corruption and Economic Deformation in Post-Dayton Bosnia' (2003) 3 *Conflict, Security and Development* 359.
Donais, T. 'Empowerment or Imposition? Dilemmas of Local Ownership in Post-Conflict Peacebuilding Processes' (2009) 34 *Peace and Change* 3.
Donais, T. and Burt, G. 'Peace-building in Haiti: The Case for Vertical Integration' (2015) 15 *Conflict, Security and Development* 1.
Drumbl, M. 'Collective Violence and Individual Punishment: The Criminality of Mass Atrocity' (2005) 99 *Northwestern University Law Review* 539.
DuBois, F. and Czarnota, A. 'The Transitional Rule of Law' (1999) 24 *Alternative Law Review* 9.
Duffey, T. 'Cultural Issues in Contemporary Peacekeeping' (2000) 7 *International Peacekeeping* 142.
Duthie, R. 'Toward a Development-Sensitive Approach to Transitional Justice' (2008) 2 *International Journal of Transitional Justice* 292.
Englebert, P. and Tull, D. 'Postconflict Reconstruction in Africa: Flawed Ideas about Failed States' (2008) 32 *International Security* 106.
Ernstorfer, A., Chigas, D. and Vaughan-Lee, H. 'From Little to Large: When Does Peacebuilding Add Up?' (2015) 10 *Journal of Peacebuilding and Development* 72.
Evans, M. 'Structural Violence, Socioeconomic Rights and Transformative Justice' (2016) 15 *Journal of Human Rights* 1.
Fetherston, A.B. 'Peacekeeping, Conflict Resolution and Peacebuilding: A Reconsideration of Theoretical Frameworks' (2000) 7 *International Peacekeeping* 190.
Finnemore, M. and Sikkink, K. 'International Norm Dynamics and Political Change' (1998) 52 *International Organization* 887.
Fletcher, L. and Weinstein, H.M. 'Violence and Social Repair: Rethinking the Contribution of Justice to Reconciliation' (2002) 24 *Human Rights Quarterly* 573.

Fletcher, L., Weinstein, H.M. and Rowen, J. 'Context, Timing and the Dynamics of Transitional Justice: A Historical Perspective' (2009) 31 *Human Rights Quarterly* 163.

Fourlas, G. 'No Future Without Transition: A Critique of Liberal Peace' (2015) 9 *International Journal of Transitional Justice* 109.

Fuller, L. 'Burdened Societies and Transitional Justice' (2012) 15 *Ethical Theory and Moral Practice* 369.

Galtung, J. 'Violence, Peace and Peace Research' (1969) *Journal of Peace Research* 167.

Gent, S. 'Relative Rebel Strength and Power Sharing in Intrastate Conflicts' (2011) 37 *International Interactions* 215.

Gheciu, A. and Welsh, J. 'The Imperative to Rebuild: Assessing the Normative Case for Postconflict Reconstruction' (2009) 23 *Ethics and International Affairs* 121.

Goetschel, L. and Hagmann, T. 'Civilian Peacebuilding: Peace by Bureaucratic Means? Analysis' (2009) 9 *Conflict, Security and Development* 55.

Gready, P. 'Analysis: Reconceptualising Transitional Justice: Embedded and Distanced Justice' (2005) 5 *Conflict, Security and Development* 3.

Gready, P. and Robins, S. 'From Transitional to Transformative Justice: A New Agenda for Practice' (2014) 8 *International Journal of Transitional Justice* 339.

Greig, M. 'Moments of Opportunity Recognizing Conditions of Ripeness for International Mediation between Enduring Rivals' (2001) 45 *Journal of Conflict Resolution* 691.

Greig, M. and Regan, P. 'When Do They Say Yes? An Analysis of the Willingness to Offer and Accept Mediation in Civil Wars' (2008) 52 *International Studies Quarterly* 759.

Grindle, M. 'Good Enough Governance: Poverty Reduction and Reform in Developing Countries' (2004) 17 *Governance* 525.

Guilhot, N. '"The Transition to the Human World of Democracy": Notes for a History of the Concept of Transition, from Early Marxism to 1989' (2002) 5 *European Journal of Social Theory* 219.

Gurses, M. and Mason, T.D. 'Democracy Out of Anarchy: The Prospects for Post-Civil-War Democracy' (2008) 89 *Social Science Quarterly* 315.

Hagmann, T. and Péclard, D. 'Negotiating Statehood: Dynamics of Power and Domination in Africa' (2010) 41 *Development and Change* 539.

Halpern, J. and Weinstein, H. 'Rehumanizing the Other: Empathy and Reconciliation' (2004) 26 *Human Rights Quarterly* 561.

Hameiri, S. 'Capacity and Its Follies: International State Building as State Transformation' (2009) 38 *Millennium: Journal of International Studies* 55.

Hansen, T.O. 'Kenya's Power-Sharing Arrangement and its Implications for Transitional Justice' (2013) 17 *International Journal of Human Rights* 307.

Hart, V. 'Constitution-making and the Transformation of Conflict' (2001) 26 *Peace and Change* 153.

Hartzell, C. 'Explaining the Stability of Negotiated Settlements to Intrastate Wars' (1999) 43 *Journal of Conflict Resolution* 3.

Hartzell, C. and Hoddie, M. 'Institutionalizing Peace: Power-sharing and Post-Civil War Conflict Management' (2003) 47 *American Journal of Political Science* 318.

Hartzell, C. and Hoddie, M. 'The Art of the Possible: Power Sharing and Post-Civil War Democracy' (2015) 67 *World Politics* 37.

Heathershaw, J. 'Towards Better Theories of Peacebuilding: Beyond the Liberal Peace Debate' (2013) 1 *Peacebuilding* 275.

Hellmüller, S. 'The Power of Perceptions: Localizing International Peacebuilding Approaches' (2013) 20 *International Peacekeeping* 219.

Helmke, G. and Levitsky, S. 'Informal Institutions and Comparative Politics: A Research Agenda' (2004) 2 *Perspectives on Politics* 725.

Hirblinger, A. and Simons, C. 'The Good, the Bad, and the Powerful: Representations of the Local in Peacebuilding' (2015) 46 *Security Dialogue* 422.

Hovil, L. and Okello, M. 'Editorial Note' (2011) 5 *International Journal of Transitional Justice* 333.

Hughes, C., Öjendal, J. and Schierenbeck, I. 'The Struggle Versus the Song – The Local Turn in Peacebuilding: An Introduction' (2015) 36 *Third World Quarterly* 817.

Hughes, C. and Pupavac, V. 'Framing Post-conflict Societies: International Pathologisation of Cambodia and the Post-Yugoslav States' (2005) 26 *Third World Quarterly* 873.

Huntington, S. 'Will More Countries Become Democratic?' (1984) 99 *Political Science Quarterly* 193.

Hyden, G. 'Rethinking Justice and Institutions in African Peacebuilding' (2015) 36 *Third World Quarterly* 1007.

Igreja, V. 'Multiple Temporalities in Indigenous Justice and Healing Practices in Mozambique' (2012) 6 *International Journal of Transitional Justice* 404.

Iliff, A. 'Root and Branch: Discourses of "Tradition" in Grassroots Transitional Justice' (2012) 6 *International Journal of Transitional Justice* 253.

Iverson, J. 'Transitional Justice, Ius Post Bellum and International Criminal Law: Differentiating the Usages, History and Dynamics' (2013) 7 International *Journal of Transitional Justice* 413.

Jackson, P. 'Chiefs, Money and Politicians: Rebuilding Local Government in Post-war Sierra Leone' (2005) 25 *Public Administration and Development* 49.

Jackson, R. and Dexter, H. 'The Social Construction of Organised Political Violence: An Analytical Framework' (2014) 16 *Civil Wars* 1.

Jarstad, A. and Olsson, L. 'Hybrid Peace Ownership in Afghanistan: International Perspectives of Who Owns What and When' (2012) 18 *Global Governance* 105.

Jones, L. '(Post-) Colonial State-Building and State Failure in East Timor: Bringing Social Conflict Back In' (2010) 10 *Conflict, Security and Development* 547.

Jung, J.K. 'Power-Sharing and Democracy Promotion in Post-Civil War Peacebuilding' (2012) 19 *Democratization* 486.

Kalyvas, S. 'The Ontology of "Political Violence": Action and Identity in Civil Wars' (2003) 1 *Perspectives on Politics* 475.

Kamatsiko, V.V. 'Grassroots Peacebuilding and Vertical Integration: A Case Study of the Peace-Rings Approach' (2015) 10 *Journal of Peacebuilding and Development* 56.

Kayser-Whande, U. and Schell-Faucon, S. 'Transitional Justice and Conflict Transformation in Conversation' (2010) 50 *Politorbis* 97.

Keen, D. 'A Rational Kind of Madness' (1997) 25 *Oxford Development Studies* 67.

Kirschner, S. and Von Stein, J. 'The Pieces of Peacemaking: Understanding Implementation of Civil War Settlements' (2009) 11 *Civil Wars* 279.

Kleiboer, M. 'Ripeness of Conflict: A Fruitful Notion?' (1994) 31 *Journal of Peace Research* 109.

Koopman, C. 'Pragmatism as a Philosophy of Hope: Emerson, James, Dewey, Rorty' (2006) 20 *Journal of Speculative Philosophy* 106.

Koskenniemi, M. 'The Politics of International Law – 20 Years Later' (2009) 20 *European Journal of International Law* 7.

Kreutz, J. 'How and When Armed Conflicts End: Introducing the UCDP Conflict Termination Dataset' (2010) 47 *Journal of Peace Research* 243.

Kurtenbach, S. 'Why is Liberal Peacebuilding So Difficult? Some Lessons from Central America' (2007) 88 *European Review of Latin American and Caribbean Studies* 95.

Kurtenbach, S. and Mehler, A. 'Introduction: Institutions for Sustainable Peace? Determinants and Effects of Institutional Choices in Divided Societies' (2013) 15 *Civil Wars* 1.

Lanz, D. 'Who Gets a Seat at the Table? A Framework for Understanding the Dynamics of Inclusion and Exclusion in Peace Negotiations' (2011) 16 *International Negotiation* 275.

Laplante, L. 'On the Indivisibility of Rights: Truth Commissions, Reparations and the Right to Development' (2007) 10 *Yale Human Rights and Development Law Journal* 141.

Laplante, L. 'Transitional Justice and Peace Building: Diagnosing and Addressing the Socioeconomic Roots of Violence through a Human Rights Framework' (2008) 2 *International Journal of Transitional Justice* 331.

Leftwich, A. 'Bringing Politics Back in: Towards a Model of the Developmental State' (1995) 31 *Journal of Development Studie*s 400.

Levitt, J. 'Illegal Peace: An Inquiry into the Legality of Power-Sharing with Warlords and Rebels in Africa' (2005) 27 *Michigan Journal of International Law* 495.

Lidén, K. 'Building Peace between Global and Local Politics: The Cosmopolitical Ethics of Liberal Peacebuilding' (2009) 16 *International Peacekeeping* 616.

Ludsin, H. 'Peacemaking and Constitution-Drafting: A Dysfunctional Marriage' (2011) 33 *University of Pennsylvania Journal of International Law* 239.

Lundy, P. and McGovern, M. 'Whose Justice? Rethinking Transitions from the Bottom Up' (2008) 35 *Journal of Law and Society* 265.

Lundy, P. 'Exploring Home-Grown Transitional Justice and its Dilemmas: A Case Study of the Historical Enquiries Team, Northern Ireland' (2009) 3 *International Journal of Transitional Justice* 321.

Lundy, P. 'Paradoxes and Challenges of Transitional Justice at the "Local" Level: Historical Enquiries in Northern Ireland' (2011) 6 *Contemporary Social Science* 89.
McAuliffe, P. 'East Timor's Community Reconciliation Process as a Model for Legal Pluralism in Criminal Justice' (2008) 12 *Law, Social Justice and Global Development* 1.
McAuliffe, P. 'From Molehills to Mountains (and Myths?): A Critical History of Transitional Justice Advocacy' (2011) 22 *Finnish Yearbook of International Law* 85.
McAuliffe, P. 'Rhetoric and Realpolitik: Interrogating the Relationship between Transitional Justice and Socio-Economic Justice' (2012–13) 23 *Finnish Yearbook of International Law* 239.
McAuliffe, P. 'The Roots of Transitional Accountability: Interrogating the Justice Cascade' (2013) 9 *International Journal of Law in Context* 106.
McAuliffe, P. 'Weighing Domestic and International Impediments to Transformative Justice in Transition' (2015) 3 *London Review of International Law* 169.
McCandless, E., Abitbol, E. and Donais, T. 'Vertical Integration: A Dynamic Practice Promoting Transformative Peacebuilding' (2015) 10 *Journal of Peacebuilding and Development* 1.
McEvoy, K. 'Beyond Legalism: Towards a Thicker Understanding of Transitional Justice' (2007) 34 *Journal of Law and Society* 411.
Macdonald, A. 'From the Ground Up: What Does the Evidence Tell Us about Local Experiences of Transitional Justice?' (2015) 3 *Transitional Justice Review* 72.
Mac Ginty, R. and Richmond, O. 'Myth or Reality? Opposing Views on the Liberal Peace and Post-War Reconstruction' (2007) 21 *Global Society* 491.
Maddison, S. and Shepherd, L. 'Peacebuilding and the Postcolonial Politics of Transitional Justice' (2014) 2 *Peacebuilding* 253.
Mani, R. 'Editorial: Dilemmas of Expanding Transitional Justice, or Forging the Nexus Between Transitional Justice and Development' (2008) 2 *International Journal of Transitional Justice* 253.
Mann, M. 'The Autonomous Power of the State: Its Origins, Mechanisms and Results' (1984) 25 *European Journal of Sociology* 185.
Manning, C. 'Local Level Challenges to Post-Conflict Peacebuilding' (2003) 10 *International Peacekeeping* 25.
Martin, P. 'Coming Together: Power-Sharing and the Durability of Negotiated Settlements' (2013) 15 *Civil Wars* 332.
Mattes, M. and Savun, B. 'Fostering Peace after Civil War: Commitment Problems and Agreement Design' (2009) 53 *International Studies Quarterly* 737.
Mazlish, B. 'The Global and the Local' (2005) 53 *Current Sociology* 93.
Mehler, A. 'Consociationalism for Weaklings, Autocracy for Muscle Men? Determinants of Constitutional Reform in Divided Societies' (2013) 15 *Civil Wars* 21.
Mehler, A. 'Peace and Power Sharing in Africa: A Not So Obvious Relationship' (2009) 108 *African Affairs* 453.
Mendeloff, D. 'Truth-Seeking, Truth-Telling, and Postconflict Peacebuilding: Curb the Enthusiasm?' (2004) 6 *International Studies Review* 355.

Menkhaus, K. 'International Peacebuilding and the Dynamics of Local and National Reconciliation in Somalia' (1996) 3 *International Peacekeeping* 42.

Meyer, J. and Rowan, B. 'Institutionalized Organizations: Formal Structure as Myth and Ceremony' (1977) *American Journal of Sociology* 340.

Millar, G. 'Local Evaluations of Justice through Truth Telling in Sierra Leone: Postwar Needs and Transitional Justice' (2011) 12 *Human Rights Review* 515.

Miller, Z. 'Effects of Invisibility: In Search of the "Economic" in Transitional Justice' (2008) 2 *International Journal of Transitional Justice* 266.

Miller, Z. '(Re)Distributing Transition' (2013) 7 *International Journal of Transitional Justice* 370.

Milliken, J. and Krause, K. 'State Failure, State Collapse, and State Reconstruction: Concepts, Lessons and Strategies' (2002) 33 *Development and Change* 753.

Mitchell, C. 'The Right Moment: Notes on Four Models of "Ripeness"' (1995) 9 *Paradigms* 38.

Mkandawire, T. 'Neopatrimonialism and the Political Economy of Economic Performance in Africa: Critical Reflections' (2015) 67 *World Politics* 563.

Mullen, M. 'Reassessing the Focus of Transitional Justice: The Need to Move Structural and Cultural Violence to the Centre' (2015) 28 *Cambridge Review of International Affairs* 462.

Mutua, M. 'What Is the Future of Transitional Justice?' (2015) 9 *International Journal of Transitional Justice* 1.

Muvingi, I. 'Sitting on Powder Kegs: Socio-Economic Rights in Transitional Societies' (2009) 3 *International Journal of Transitional Justice* 163.

Nadarajah, S. and Rampton, D. 'The Limits of Hybridity and the Crisis of Liberal Peace' (2015) 41 *Review of International Studies* 49.

Nagy, R. 'Transitional Justice as a Global Project: Critical Reflections' (2008) 29 *Third World Quarterly* 275.

Nagy, R. 'The Scope and Bounds of Transitional Justice and the Canadian Truth and Reconciliation Commission' (2013) 7 *International Journal of Transitional Justice* 52.

Nesiah, V. 'Discussion Lines on Gender and Transitional Justice: An Introductory Essay Reflecting on the ICTJ Bellagio Workshop on Gender and Transitional Justice' (2006) 15 *Columbia Journal of Gender and Law* 799.

Newman, E. 'A Human Security Peace-Building Agenda' (2011) 32 *Third World Quarterly* 1737.

Newman, E. 'The Violence of Statebuilding in Historical Perspective: Implications for Peacebuilding' (2013) 1 *Peacebuilding* 141.

Ní Aoláin, F. and Campbell, C. 'The Paradox of Transition in Conflicted Democracies' (2005) 27 *Human Rights Quarterly* 172.

Ní Aoláin, F., O'Rourke, C. and Swaine, A. 'Transforming Reparations for Conflict-Related Sexual Violence: Principles and Practice' (2015) 28 *Harvard Human Rights Journal* 97.

Nickson, R. and Braithwaite, J. 'Deeper, Broader, Longer Transitional Justice' (2014) 11 *European Journal of Criminology* 445.

Nixon, R. 'The Crisis of Governance in New Subsistence States' (2006) 36 *Journal of Contemporary Asia* 75.

Odendaal, A. 'The Political Legitimacy of National Peace Committees' (2012) 7 *Journal of Peacebuilding and Development* 40.
O'Neill, O. 'Agents of Justice' (2001) 32 *Metaphilosophy* 180.
O'Rourke, C. 'Feminist Scholarship in Transitional Justice: A De-Politicising Impulse?' (2015) 51 *Women's Studies International Forum* 118.
Orentlicher, D. '"Settling Accounts" Revisited: Reconciling Global Norms with Local Agency' (2007) 1 *International Journal of Transitional Justice* 10.
Orford, A. 'Commissioning the Truth' (2006) 15 *Columbia Journal of Gender and Law* 851.
Orjuela, C. 'Building Peace in Sri Lanka: A Role for Civil Society?' (2003) 40 *Journal of Peace Research* 195.
Osiel, M. 'The Banality of Good: Aligning Incentives Against Mass Atrocity' (2005) 105 *Columbia Law Review* 1751.
Ottaway, M. 'Rebuilding State Institutions in Collapsed States' (2002) 33 *Development and Change* 1001.
Ottaway, M. 'Promoting Democracy After Conflict: The Difficult Choices' (2003) 4 *International Studies Perspectives* 314.
Paffenholz, T. 'International Peacebuilding Goes Local: Analysing Lederach's Conflict Transformation Theory and its Ambivalent Encounter with 20 Years of Practice' (2014) 2 *Peacebuilding* 11.
Paffenholz, T. 'Unpacking the Local Turn in Peacebuilding: A Critical Assessment Towards an Agenda for Future Research' (2015) 36 *Third World Quarterly* 857.
Papagianni, K. 'Political Transitions after Peace Agreements: The Importance of Consultative and Inclusive Political Processes' (2009) 3 *Journal of Intervention and Statebuilding* 47.
Pappalardo, A. 'The Conditions for Consociational Democracy: A Logical and Empirical Critique (1981) 9 *European Journal of Political Research* 365.
Pasipanodya, T. 'A Deeper Justice: Economic and Social Justice as Transitional Justice in Nepal' (2008) 2 *International Journal of Transitional Justice* 378.
Peceny, M. and Stanley, W. 'The Resolution of Civil Wars in Central America' (2001) 55 *International Organization* 149.
Peterson, J. 'A Conceptual Unpacking of Hybridity: Accounting for Notions of Power, Politics and Progress in Analyses of Aid-driven Interfaces' (2012) 7 *Journal of Peacebuilding and Development* 9.
Pettersson, T. and Wallensteen, P. 'Armed Conflicts, 1946–2014' (2015) 52 *Journal of Peace Research* 536.
Pouligny, B. 'Civil Society and Post-Conflict Peacebuilding: Ambiguities of International Programmes Aimed at Building "New" Societies' (2005) 36 *Security Dialogue* 495.
Przeworski, A. 'Institutions Matter?' (2004) 39 *Government and Opposition* 527.
Ramji-Nogales, J. 'Designing Bespoke Transitional Justice: A Pluralist Process Approach' (2010) 32 *Michigan Journal of International Law* 1.
Reilly, B. 'Political Parties and Post-Conflict Peacebuilding' (2013) 15 *Civil Wars* 88.
Renders, M. and Terlinden, U. 'Negotiating Statehood in a Hybrid Political Order: The Case of Somaliland' (2010) 41 *Development and Change* 723.
Reynolds, A. 'Constitutional Medicine' (2005) 16 *Journal of Democracy* 54.

Riaño Alcalá, R. and Baines, E. 'Editorial Note' (2012) 6 *International Journal of Transitional Justice* 385.

Richmond, O. 'Devious Objectives and the Disputants' View of International Mediation: A Theoretical Framework' (1998) 35 *Journal of Peace Research* 707.

Richmond, O. 'Patterns of Peace' (2006) 20 *Global Society* 367.

Richmond, O. 'A Post-Liberal Peace: Eirinism and the Everyday' (2009) 35 *Review of International Studies* 557.

Richmond, O. 'Resistance and the Post-liberal Peace' (2010) 38 *Millennium: Journal of International Studies* 665.

Richmond, O. 'Critical Agency, Resistance and a Post-colonial Civil Society' (2011) 46 *Cooperation and Conflict* 419.

Richmond, O. 'Peace During and After the Age of Intervention' (2014) 21 *International Peacekeeping* 509.

Richmond, O. and Mac Ginty, R. 'Where Now for the Critique of the Liberal Peace?' (2015) 50 *Cooperation and Conflict* 171.

Ricigliano, R. 'Networks of Effective Action: Implementing an Integrated Approach to Peacebuilding' (2003) 34 *Security Dialogue* 445.

Roberts, D. 'Beyond the Metropolis? Popular Peace and Post-Conflict Peacebuilding' (2011) 37 *Review of International Studies* 2535.

Robins, S. 'Transitional Justice as an Elite Discourse: Human Rights Practice Where the Global Meets the Local in Post-Conflict Nepal' (2012) 44 *Critical Asian Studies* 3.

Robins, S. 'Mapping a Future for Transitional Justice by Learning from its Past' (2015) 9 *International Journal of Transitional Justice* 181.

Romero, G.R. 'Voices Around Us: Memory and Community Empowerment in Reconstruction Efforts in Colombia' (2012) 6 *International Journal of Transitional Justice* 547.

Roth, K. 'Defending Economic, Social and Cultural Rights: Practical Issues Faced by an International Human Rights Organization' (2004) 26 *Human Rights Quarterly* 63.

Rothchild, D. 'Reassuring Weaker Parties after Civil Wars: The Benefits and Costs of Executive Power-sharing Systems in Africa' (2005) 4 *Ethnopolitics* 247.

Sabaratnam, M. 'Avatars of Eurocentrism in the Critique of the Liberal Peace' (2013) 44 *Security Dialogue* 259.

Samset, I. 'Building a Repressive Peace: The Case of Post-Genocide Rwanda' (2011) 5 *Journal of Intervention and Statebuilding* 265.

Sankey, D. 'Towards Recognition of Subsistence Harms: Reassessing Approaches to Socioeconomic Forms of Violence in Transitional Justice' (2013) 8 *International Journal of Transitional Justice* 121.

Schmid, E. and Nolan, A. '"Do No Harm"? Exploring the Scope of Economic and Social Rights in Transitional Justice' (2014) 8 *International Journal of Transitional Justice* 362.

Schneckener, U. 'Making Power-sharing Work: Lessons from Successes and Failures in Ethnic Conflict Regulation' (2002) 39 *Journal of Peace Research* 203.

Selby, J. 'The Myth of Liberal Peace-building' (2013) 13 *Conflict, Security and Development* 57.
Selim, Y. and Murithi, T. 'Transitional Justice and Development: Partners for Sustainable Peace in Africa?' (2011) 6 *Journal of Peacebuilding and Development* 58.
Sharp, D. 'Interrogating the Peripheries: The Preoccupations of Fourth Generation Transitional Justice' (2013) 26 *Harvard Human Rights Journal* 149.
Sharp, D. 'Addressing Dilemmas of the Global and the Local in Transitional Justice' (2013) 29 *Emory International Law Review* 71.
Sharp, D. 'Emancipating Transitional Justice from the Bonds of the Paradigmatic Transition' (2014) 9 *International Journal of Transitional Justice* 150.
Sisk, T. 'Power-Sharing in Civil War: Puzzles of Peacemaking and Peacebuilding' (2013) 15 *Civil Wars* 7.
Spears, I. 'Africa's Informal Power-Sharing and the Prospects for Peace' (2013) 15 *Civil Wars* 37.
Sriram, C.L. 'Justice as Peace? Liberal Peacebuilding and Strategies of Transitional Justice' (2007) 21 *Global Society* 579.
Sriram, C.L. 'Making Rights Real? Minority and Gender Provisions and Power-Sharing Arrangements' (2013) 17 *International Journal of Human Rights* 275.
Strasheim, J. and Fjelde, H. 'Pre-designing Democracy: Institutional Design of Interim Governments and Democratization in 15 Post-conflict Societies' (2014) 21 *Democratization* 335.
Steenkamp, C. 'The Legacy of War: Conceptualizing a "Culture of Violence" to Explain Violence after Peace Accords' (2005) 94 *The Round Table* 253.
Stensrud, E.E. 'New Dilemmas in Transitional Justice: Lessons from the Mixed Courts in Sierra Leone and Cambodia' (2009) 46 *Journal of Peace Research* 5.
Suhrke, A. and Samset, I. 'What's in a Figure? Estimating Recurrence of Civil War' (2007) 14 *International Peacekeeping* 195.
Szoke-Burke, S. 'Not Only Context: Why Transitional Justice Programs Can No Longer Ignore Violations of Economic and Social Rights' (2015) 50 *Texas International Law Journal* 465.
Talentino, A.K. 'The Two Faces of Nation-Building: Developing Function and Identity' (2004) 17 *Cambridge Review of International Affairs* 557.
Talentino, A.K. 'Perceptions of Peacebuilding: The Dynamic of Imposer and Imposed Upon' (2007) 8 *International Studies Perspectives* 152.
Taylor, D. '"We Have No Influence": International Discourse and the Instrumentalisation of Transitional Justice in Burundi' (2013) 2 *Stability* 1.
Teitel, R. 'Transitional Justice in a New Era' (2002) 26 *Fordham International Law Journal* 893.
Teitel, R. 'Transitional Justice Genealogy' (2003) 16 *Harvard Human Rights Journal* 69.
Teitel, R. 'Rethinking *Jus Post Bellum* in an Age of Global Transitional Justice: Engaging with Michael Walzer and Larry May' (2013) 24 *European Journal of International Law* 335.
Theidon, K. 'Justice in Transition: The Micropolitics of Reconciliation in Postwar Peru' (2006) 50 *Journal of Conflict Resolution* 433.
Theidon, K. 'Editorial Note' (2009) 3 *International Journal of Transitional Justice* 295.

Themnér, L. and Wallensteen, P. 'Armed Conflicts, 1946–2012' (2013) 50 *Journal of Peace Research* 509.

Thoms, O. and Ron, J. 'Do Human Rights Violations Cause Internal Conflict?' (2007) 29 *Human Rights Quarterly* 674.

Thoms, O., Ron, J. and Paris, R. 'State-Level Effects of Transitional Justice: What Do We Know?' (2010) 4 *International Journal of Transitional Justice* 329.

Tiernay, M. 'Which Comes First? Unpacking the Relationship Between Peace Agreements and Peacekeeping Missions' (2015) 32 *Conflict Management and Peace Science* 135.

Tull, D. and Mehler, A. 'The Hidden Costs of Power-sharing: Reproducing Insurgent Violence in Africa' (2005) 104 *African Affairs* 375.

Turner, C. 'Delivering Lasting Peace, Democracy and Human Rights in Times of Transition: The Role of International Law' (2008) 1 *International Journal of Transitional Justice* 126.

Turner, C. 'Deconstructing Transitional Justice' (2013) 24 *Law and Critique* 193.

UN Secretary-General, *The Rule of Law and Transitional Justice in Conflict and Post-Conflict Societies*, UN Doc. S/2004/616 of 3 August 2004.

UN Secretary-General's High Level Panel on Threats, Challenges and Change, *A More Secure World: Our Shared Responsibility*, UN Doc. A/59/565 of 2 December 2004.

United Nations, *Report of the Panel on United Nations Peace Operations*, UN Doc. A/55/305-S/2000/809 of 21 August 2000.

Vandeginste, S. and Sriram, C.L. 'Power Sharing and Transitional Justice: A Clash of Paradigms?' (2011) 17 *Global Governance* 489.

Vat Kamatsiko, V. 'Grassroots Peacebuilding and Vertical Integration: A Case Study of the Peace-Rings Approach' (2015) 10 *Journal of Peacebuilding and Development* 56.

Visoka, G. 'Peace is What We Make of It? Peace-shaping Events and "Non-Events"' (2016) 4 *Peacebuilding* 54.

Waldorf, L. 'Anticipating the Past: Transitional Justice and Socio-Economic Wrongs' (2012) 21 *Social and Legal Studies* 1.

Wallensteen, P. and Sollenberg, M. 'Armed Conflict, 1989–98' (1999) 36 *Journal of Peace Research* 593.

Wanis-St. John, A. and Kew, D. 'Civil Society and Peace Negotiations: Confronting Exclusion' (2008) 13 *International Negotiation* 11.

Wielbelhaus-Brahm, E. 'Transitional Justice, Civil Society, and the Development of the Rule of Law in Post-Conflict Societies' (2007) 9 *International Journal of Not-For-Profit Law* 1.

Wilson, R.A. 'Anthropological Studies of National Reconciliation Processes' (2003) 3 *Anthropological Theory* 367.

Woodward, S. 'Do the Root Causes of Civil War Matter? On Using Knowledge to Improve Peacebuilding Interventions' (2007) 1 *Journal of Intervention and Statebuilding* 143.

Zaum, D. 'International Non-Governmental Organisations and Civil Wars' (2009) 11 *Civil Wars* 22.

Zaum, D. 'Beyond the "Liberal Peace"' (2012) 18 *Global Governance* 121.

CHAPTERS IN EDITED VOLUMES

Aall, P. 'The Power of Non-Official Actors in Conflict Management' in Chester A. Crocker and Fen Osler Hampson (eds) with Pamela Aall, *Managing Global Chaos: Sources of and Responses to International Conflict* (US Institute of Peace 1996) 477.

Addison, T., Chowdhury, A. and Murshed, S.M. 'Financing Reconstruction' in Gerd Junne and Willemijn Verkoren (eds), *Post-Conflict Development: Meeting New Challenges* (Lynne Rienner 2005) 211.

Aggestam, K. 'Internal and External Dynamics of Spoiling: A Negotiation Approach' in Edward Newman and Oliver Richmond (eds), *Challenges to Peacebuilding: Managing Spoilers During Conflict Resolution* (United Nations University Press 2006) 23.

Albin, C. 'Peace vs. Justice – and Beyond' in Jacob Bercovitch, Victor Kremenyuk and I. William Zartman (eds), *The SAGE Handbook of Conflict Resolution* (Sage 2008) 580.

Albin-Lackey, V. 'Corruption, Human Rights, and Activism: Useful Connections and Their Limits' in Dustin Sharp (ed.), *Justice and Economic Violence in Transition* (Springer 2013) 139.

Alvarez, E. with Palencia Prado, T. 'Guatemala's Peace Process: Context, Analysis and Evaluation' in Catherine Barnes (ed.), *Owning the Process: Public Participation in Peacemaking* (Accord 2002) 38.

Ames Cobián, R. and Reátegui, F. 'Toward Systemic Social Transformation: Truth Commissions and Development' in Pablo de Greiff and Roger Duthie (eds), *Transitional Justice and Development: Making Connections* (Social Science Research Council 2009) 142.

Arnson, C. and Azpuru, D. 'From Peace to Democratization: Lessons from Central America' in John Darby and Roger Mac Ginty (eds), *Contemporary Peacemaking* (Palgrave Macmillan 2008) 271.

Ashworth, A. 'Security, Terrorism and the Value of Human Rights' in Benjamin Goold and Liora Lazarus (eds), *Security and Human Rights* (Hart Publishing 2007) 203.

Backer, D. 'Cross-national Comparative Analysis' in Hugo van der Merwe, Victoria Baxter and Audrey Chapman (eds), *Assessing the Impact of Transitional Justice: Challenges for Empirical Research* (US Institute of Peace Press 2009) 23.

Baker, P. 'Conflict Resolution Versus Democratic Governance: Divergent Paths to Peace' in Chester A. Crocker and Fen Osler Hampson (eds) with Pamela Aall, *Managing Global Chaos: Sources of and Responses to International Conflict* (US Institute of Peace 1996) 753.

Barnett, M. and Zürcher, C. 'The Peacebuilder's Contract: How External Statebuilding Reinforces Weak Statehood' in Roland Paris and Timothy Sisk (eds), *The Dilemmas of Statebuilding: Confronting the Contradictions of Postwar Peace Operations* (Routledge 2009).

Bell, C. 'Negotiating Human Rights' in John Darby and Roger Mac Ginty (eds), *Contemporary Peacemaking: Conflict, Violence and Peacemaking* (Palgrave Macmillan 2003) 210.

Bell, C. 'Of Jus Post Bellum and Lex Pacificatoria: What's in a Name?' in Carsten Stahn, Jennifer Easterday and Jens Iverson (eds), *Jus Post Bellum: Mapping the Normative Foundations* (Oxford University Press 2014) 181.

Bell, C., Campbell, C. and Ní Aoláin, F. 'The Battle for Transitional Justice: Hegemony, Iraq and International Law' in Kieran McEvoy, John Morrison and Gordon Anthony (eds), *Judges, Transition and Human Rights Cultures: Essays in Honour of Stephen Livingstone* (Oxford University Press 2007) 147.

Belloni, R. 'Civil Society in War-to-Democracy Transitions' in Anna Jarstad and Timothy Sisk (eds), *From War to Democracy: Dilemmas of Peacebuilding* (Cambridge University Press 2008) 182.

Belmont, K., Mainwaring, S. and Reynolds, A. 'Introduction: Institutional Design, Conflict Management, and Democracy in Divided Societies' in Andrew Reynolds (ed.), *The Architecture of Democracy: Institutional Design, Conflict Management and Democracy in the Late Twentieth Century* (Oxford University Press 2002) 1.

Bercovitch, J. 'Mediation and Conflict Resolution' in Jacob Bercovitch, Victor Kremenyuk and I. William Zartman (eds), *The SAGE Handbook of Conflict Resolution* (Sage 2008) 340.

Bercovitch, J., Kremenyuk, V. and Zartman, I.W. 'Introduction: The Nature of Conflict and Conflict Resolution' in Jacob Bercovitch, Victor Kremenyuk and I. William Zartman (eds), *The SAGE Handbook of Conflict Resolution* (Sage 2008) 1.

Berdal, M. and Zaum, D. 'Power After Peace' in Mats Berdal and Dominik Zaum (eds), *Political Economy of Statebuilding: Power after Peace* (Routledge 2013) 1.

Bergsmo, M. et al., 'Introduction' in Morten Bergsmo et al. (eds), *Distributive Justice in Transitions* (Torkel Opsahl 2010) 1.

Bhuta, N. 'Democratization, State-Building and Politics as Technology' in B. Bowden, H. Charlesworth and J. Farrall (eds), *The Role of International Law in Rebuilding Societies after Conflict: Great Expectations* (Cambridge University Press 2009) 38.

Bjornlund, E., Cowan, G. and Gallery, W. 'Election Systems and Political Parties in Post-Conflict and Fragile States' in Derick Brinkerhoff (ed.), *Governance in Post-Conflict Societies: Rebuilding Fragile States* (Routledge 2012) 64.

Bleiker, R. 'Conclusion – Everyday Struggles for a Hybrid Peace' in Oliver Richmond and Audra Mitchell (eds), *Hybrid Forms of Peace* (Palgrave Macmillan 2011) 293.

Bowman, G. 'Xenophobia, Fantasy and the Nation: The Logic of Ethnic Violence in Former Yugoslavia' in Victoria Goddard, Josep Llobera and Cris Shore (eds), *The Anthropology of Europe: Identity and Boundaries in Conflict* (Berg 1994) 143.

Brenk, M. and van de Veen, H. 'Development: No Development Without Peace, No Peace Without Development' in Paul van Tongeren et al. (eds), *People Building Peace II: Successful Stories of Civil Society* (Lynne Rienner 2005) 399.

Brozus, L. 'Applying the Governance Concept to Areas of Limited Statehood' in Thomas Risse (ed.), *Governance Without a State: Policies and Politics in Areas of Limited Statehood* (Columbia University Press 2011) 262.

Buckley-Zistel, S. et al., 'Transitional Justice Theories: An Introduction' in Susanne Buckley-Zistel et al. (eds), *Transitional Justice Theories* (Routledge 2013) 1.

Call, C. 'Assessing El Salvador's Transition from Civil War to Peace' in Stephen John Stedman, Donald Rothchild and Elizabeth Cousens (eds), *Ending Civil Wars: The Implementation of Peace Agreements* (Lynne Rienner 2002) 383.

Call, C. 'Ending Wars, Building States' in Charles Call (ed.) with Vanessa Wyeth, *Building States to Build Peace* (Lynne Rienner 2008) 1.

Campbell, S. 'Routine Learning? How Peacebuilding Organisations Prevent Liberal Peace' in Susanna Campbell and David Chandler (eds), *A Liberal Peace? The Problems and Practices of Peacebuilding* (Zed Books 2011) 89.

Campbell, S., Chandler, D. and Sabaratnam, M. 'Introduction: The Politics of Liberal Peace' in Susanna Campbell and David Chandler (eds), *A Liberal Peace? The Problems and Practices of Peacebuilding* (Zed Books 2011) 1.

Cavallaro, J. and Albuja, S. 'The Lost Agenda: Economic Crimes and Truth Commissions in Latin America and Beyond' in Kieran McEvoy and Lorna McGregor (eds), *Transitional Justice from Below: Grassroots Activism and the Struggle for Change* (Hart Publishing 2008) 121.

Cheng, C. 'Private and Public Interests: Informal Actors, Informal Influence, and Economic Order after War' in Mats Berdal and Dominik Zaum (eds), *Political Economy of Statebuilding: Power after Peace* (Routledge 2013) 63.

Chigas, D. 'Capacities and Limits of NGOs as Conflict Managers' in Chester A. Crocker, Fen Osler Hampson, and Pamela Aall (eds), *Leashing the Dogs of War: Conflict Management in a Divided World* (US Institute of Peace Press 2007) 553.

Chopra, T. 'Peace versus Justice in Northern Kenya: Dialectics of State and Community Law' in Yash Ghai and Jill Cottrell (eds), *Marginalized Communities and Access to Justice* (Routledge 2010) 185.

Clark, P. and Palmer, N. 'Challenging Transitional Justice' in Nicola Palmer, Phil Clark and Danielle Granville (eds), *Critical Perspectives in Transitional Justice* (Intersentia 2012) 1.

Collins, C. 'The End of Impunity? Late Justice and Post-transitional Prosecutions in Latin America' in Nicola Palmer, Phil Clark and Danielle Granville (eds), *Critical Perspectives in Transitional Justice* (Intersentia 2012) 399.

Cousens, E. 'Introduction' in Elizabeth Cousens and Chetan Kumar (eds), *Peacebuilding as Politics: Cultivating Peace in Fragile Societies* (Lynne Rienner 2001) 1.

Cramer, C. 'Trajectories of Accumulation through War and Peace' in Roland Paris and Timothy Sisk (eds), *The Dilemmas of Statebuilding: Confronting the Contradictions of Postwar Peace Operations* (Taylor and Francis 2009) 129.

Curtis, D. 'The Contested Politics of Peacebuilding in Africa' in Devon Curtis and Gwinyayi Dzinesa (eds), *Peacebuilding, Power and Politics in Africa* (Ohio University Press 2012) 1.

Dancy, G. 'Choice and Consequence in Strategies of Transitional Justice' in Christopher Coyne and Rachel Mathers (eds), *The Handbook on the Political Economy of War* (Edward Elgar 2011) 397.

Darby, J. and Mac Ginty, R. 'Conclusion: Peace Processes, Present, and Future' in John Darby and Roger Mac Ginty (eds), *Contemporary Peacemaking* (Palgrave Macmillan 2008) 352.

Darby, J. and Mac Ginty, R. 'Introduction: What Peace? What Process?' in John Darby and Roger Mac Ginty (eds), *Contemporary Peacemaking* (Palgrave Macmillan 2008) 1.

De Greiff, P. 'Articulating the Links Between Transitional Justice and Development: Justice and Social Integration' in Pablo de Greiff and Roger Duthie (eds), *Transitional Justice and Development: Making Connections* (Social Science Research Council 2009) 28.

De Greiff, P. 'Theorizing Transitional Justice' in Melissa Williams, Rosemary Nagy and Jon Elster (eds), *Transitional Justice* (New York University Press 2012) 31.

Easterday, J. 'Peace Agreements as a Framework for Jus Post Bellum' in Carsten Stahn, Jennifer Easterday and Jens Iverson (eds), *Jus Post Bellum: Mapping the Normative Foundations* (Oxford University Press 2014) 380.

Etcheson, C. 'The Limits of Reconciliation in Cambodia's Communes' in Elin Skaar, Siri Gloppen and Astri Suhrke (eds), *Roads to Reconciliation* (Lexington Books 2005) 201.

Evans, M. 'At War's End: Time to Turn to *Jus Post Bellum*?' in Carsten Stahn, Jennifer Easterday and Jens Iverson (eds), *Jus Post Bellum: Mapping the Normative Foundations* (Oxford University Press 2014) 26.

Ferguson, J. 'The Anti-Politics Machine' in Aradhana Sharma and Akhil Gupta (eds), *The Anthropology of the State: A Reader* (Blackwell 2006) 270.

Ferrer, M.C. 'Philippines National Unification Commission: National Consultation and the "Six Paths to Peace"' in Catherine Barnes (ed.), *Owning the Process: Public Participation in Peacemaking* (Accord 2002) 82.

Fischer, M. and Schmelzle, B. 'Introduction' in Martina Fischer and Beatrix Schmelzle (eds), *Handbook for Conflict Transformation Dialogue Series* 8 (Berghof Research Centre 2009) 5.

Flores, T. and Nooruddin, I. 'Credible Commitment in Post-conflict Recovery' in Christopher Coyne and Rachel Mathers (eds), *Handbook on the Political Economy of War* (Edward Elgar 2011) 474.

Follesdal, A. 'Methods of Philosophical Research on Human Rights' in Fons Coomans, Fred Grunfeld and Menno Kamminga (eds), *Methods of Human Rights Research* (Intersentia 2009) 233.

Forrest, 'Subnationalism and Post-conflict Governance: Lessons from Africa' in Derick Brinkerhoff (ed.), *Governance in Post-conflict Societies: Rebuilding Fragile States* (Routledge 2007) 226.

Franzki, H. and Olarte, M.C. 'Understanding the Political Economy of Transitional Justice: A Critical Theory Perspective' in Susanne Buckley-Zistel et al. (eds), *Transitional Justice Theories* (Routledge 2013) 201.

Godson, R. 'Transnational Crime, Corruption and Security' in Michael Brown (ed.), *Grave New World* (Georgetown University Press 2003).

Goodale, M. 'Introduction: Locating Rights, Envisioning Law Between the Global and the Local' in Mark Goodale and Sally Engle Merry (eds), *The Practice of Human Rights: Tracking Law Between the Global and the Local* (Cambridge University Press 2007) 5.

Grenfell, L. 'Legal Pluralism and the Challenge of Building the Rule of Law in Post-Conflict States: A Case Study of Timor-Leste' in Brett Bowden, Hillary Charlesworth and Jeremy Farrall (eds), *The Role of International Law in Rebuilding Societies after Conflict: Great Expectations* (Cambridge University Press 2009) 157.
Guelke, A. 'Negotiations and Peace Processes' in John Darby and Roger Mac Ginty (eds), *Contemporary Peacemaking* (Palgrave Macmillan 2008) 63.
Haldeman, F. and Kouassi, R. 'Transitional Justice without Economic, Social and Cultural Rights?' in Eibe Riedel, Gilles Giacca and Christophe Golay (eds), *Economic, Social and Cultural Rights: Contemporary Issues and Challenges* (Oxford University Press 2014) 498.
Hameiri, S. 'A Reality Check for the Critique of the Liberal Peace' (2011) in Susanna Campbell and David Chandler (eds), *A Liberal Peace? The Problems and Practices of Peacebuilding* (Zed Books 2011) 191.
Hansen, T.O. 'The Vertical and Horizontal Expansion of Transitional Justice: Explanations and Implications for a Contested Field' in Susanne Buckley-Zistel et al. (eds), *Transitional Justice Theories* (Routledge 2013) 105.
Hinton, A.L. 'Introduction: Toward an Anthropology of Transitional Justice' in Alexander Laban Hinton (ed), *Transitional Justice: Global Mechanisms and Local Realities after Genocide and Mass Violence* (Rutgers University Press 2010) 1.
Hoddie, M. and Hartzell, C. 'Power Sharing in Peace Settlements: Initiating the Transition from Civil War' in Donald Rothchild and Philip Roeder (eds), *Sustainable Peace: Power and Democracy after Civil Wars* (Cornell University Press 2005) 83.
Hofmann, B. 'Are Hybrid Political Orders an Appropriate Concept for State Formation? Timor-Leste Revisited' in Martina Fischer and Beatrix Schmelzle (eds), *Handbook for Conflict Transformation Dialogue Series* 8 (Berghof Research Centre 2009) 79.
Hoglund, K. 'Violence in War-to-Democracy Transitions' in Anna Jarstad and Timothy Sisk (eds), *From War to Democracy: Dilemmas of Peacebuilding* (Cambridge University Press 2008) 80.
Holl, J. 'When War Doesn't Work: Understanding the Relationship between the Battlefield and the Negotiating Table' in Roy Licklider (ed.), *Stopping the Killing: How Civil Wars End* (New York University Press 1993) 269.
Holmes, S. 'Lineages of the Rule of Law' in Jose Maria Maravall and Adam Przeworski (eds), *Democracy and the Rule of Law* (Cambridge University Press 2003) 19.
Honwana, A. 'Healing and Social Reintegration in Mozambique and Angola' in Elin Skaar, Siri Gloppen and Astri Suhrke (eds), *Roads to Reconciliation* (Lexington Books 2005) 83.
Hutchinson, S. 'Spiritual Fragments of an Unfinished War' in Niels Kastfelt (ed.), *Religion and African Civil Wars* (Hurst 2005) 28.
Huyse, L. 'Introduction: Tradition-based Approaches in Peacemaking, Transitional Justice and Reconciliation Policies' in Luc Huyse and Mark Salter (eds), *Traditional Justice and Reconciliation After Conflict: Learning from African Experience* (International Institute for Democracy and Electoral Assistance 2008) 1.

Ignatieff, M. 'Human Rights, Power and the State' in Simon Chesterman, Michael Ignatieff and Ramesh Thakur (eds), *Making States Work: State Failure and the Crisis of Governance* (UN University Press 2005) 59.

Inbal, A.B. and Lerner, H. 'Constitutional Design, Identity, and Legitimacy in Post-Conflict Reconstruction' in Derick Brinkerhoff (ed.), *Governance in Post-Conflict Societies: Rebuilding Fragile States* (Routledge 2012) 45.

Jacobsen, K., Young H. and Osman, A. 'Refugees and IDPs in John Darby and Roger Mac Ginty (eds), *Contemporary Peacemaking* (Palgrave Macmillan 2008) 313.

Jarstad, A. 'Power Sharing: Former Enemies in Joint Government' in Anna Jarstad and Timothy Sisk (eds), *From War to Democracy: Dilemmas of Peacebuilding* (Cambridge University Press 2008) 105.

Johnston, L. 'Transnational Security Governance' in Jennifer Wood and Benoit Dupont (eds), *Democracy, Society and the Governance of Security* (Cambridge University Press 2006) 33.

Kahler, M. 'Statebuilding after Afghanistan and Iraq' in Roland Paris and Timothy Sisk (eds), *The Dilemmas of Statebuilding: Confronting the Contradictions of Postwar Peace Operations* (Taylor and Francis 2009) 287.

Kalmanovitz, P. 'Corrective Justice versus Social Justice in the Aftermath of War' in Morten Bergsmo et al. (eds), *Distributive Justice in Transitions* (Torkel Opsahl 2010) 71.

Kalyvas, S. 'Promises and Pitfalls of an Emerging Research Program: The Microdynamics of Civil War' in Stathis Kalyvas and Ian Shapiro (eds), *Order, Conflict and Violence* (Cambridge University Press 2008) 397.

Keen, D. 'Incentives and Disincentives for Violence' in Mats Berdal and David Malone (eds), *Greed and Grievance: Economic Agendas in Civil Wars* (Lynne Rienner 2000) 19.

Körppen, D. and Ropers, N. 'Introduction: Addressing the Complex Dynamics of Conflict Transformation' in Daniela Körppen, Norbert Ropers and Hans Giessemann (eds), *The Non-Linearity of Peace Processes: Theory and Practice of Systemic Conflict Transformation* (Verlag Barbara Budrich 2011) 11.

Kritz, N. 'Policy Implications of Empirical Research on Transitional Justice' in Hugo van der Merwe, Victoria Baxter and Audrey Chapman (eds), *Assessing the Impact of Transitional Justice: Challenges for Empirical Research* (US Institute of Peace Press 2009) 13.

Lambourne, W. 'Outreach, Inreach and Civil Society Participation in Transitional Justice' in Nicola Palmer, Phil Clark and Danielle Granville (eds), *Critical Perspectives in Transitional Justice* (Intersentia 2012) 235.

Lambourne, W. 'Transformative Justice, Reconciliation, and Peacebuilding' in Susanne Buckley-Zistel et al. (eds), *Transitional Justice Theories* (Routledge 2013) 19.

Lazar, S. 'Skepticism about Jus Post Bellum' in Larry May and Andrew Forcehimes (eds), *Morality, Jus Post Bellum, and International Law* (Cambridge University Press 2012) 204.

Lederach, J.P. 'Levels of Leadership' in Luc Reychler and Thania Paffenholz (eds), *Peacebuilding: A Field Guide* (Lynne Rienner 2001) 145.

Lederach, J.P. 'Cultivating Peace: A Practitioner's View of Deadly Conflict and Negotiations' in John Darby and Roger Mac Ginty (eds), *Contemporary Peacemaking* (Palgrave Macmillan 2008) 36.

Lefranc, S. 'A Critique of "Bottom-up" Peacebuilding' in Bruno Charbonneau and Genevieve Parent (eds), *Peacebuilding, Memory and Reconciliation: Bridging Top-Down and Bottom-up Approaches* (Routledge 2013) 34.

Lefranc, S. and Vairel, F. 'The Emergence of Transitional Justice as a Professional International Practice' in Liora Israël and Guillaume Mouralis (eds), *Dealing with Wars and Dictatorships* (T.M.C. Asser Press 2014) 235.

Lenzen, M. 'Roads Less Travelled: Conceptual Pathways (and Stumbling Blocks) for Development and Transitional Justice and Development' in Pablo de Greiff and Roger Duthie (eds), *Transitional Justice and Development: Making Connections* (Social Science Research Council 2009) 76.

Licklider, R. 'Obstacles to Peace Settlements' in Chester Crocker and Fen Osler Hampson (eds), *Turbulent Peace: The Challenges of Managing International Conflict* (US Institute of Peace Press 2001) 697.

Lode, K. 'Mali's Peace Process: Context, Analysis and Evaluation' in Catherine Barnes (ed.), *Owning the Process: Public Participation in Peacemaking* (Accord 2002) 56.

Lundy, P. and McGovern, M. 'Community, Truth-Recovery and Conflict Transformation "From Below"' in Libby Chapman et al. (eds), *A Sustainable Peace? Research as a Contribution to Peace-Building in Northern Ireland* (Community Relations Council 2008) 155.

Lutz, E. 'Transitional Justice: Lessons Learned and the Road Ahead' in Naomi Roht-Arriaza and Javier Mariezcurrena (eds), *Transitional Justice in the Twenty-First Century: Beyond Truth Versus Justice* (Cambridge University Press 2006) 325.

Mamdani, M. 'A Diminished Truth' in Wilmot James and Linda Van de Vijer (eds), *After the TRC: Reflections on Truth and Reconciliation in South Africa* (Ohio University Press 2001) 58.

Mauldeen, P. 'The Post-Conflict Paradox: Engaging War, Creating Peace' in Bruno Charbonneau and Genevieve Parent (eds), *Peacebuilding, Memory and Reconciliation: Bridging Top-Down and Bottom-up Approaches* (Routledge 2013) 19.

McDougal, T. 'The Trilemma of Promoting Economic Justice at War's End' in Dustin Sharp (ed.), *Justice and Economic Violence in Transition* (Springer 2014) 51.

McEvoy, K. and McGregor, L. 'Transitional Justice from Below: An Agenda for Research, Policy and Praxis' in Kieran McEvoy and Lorna McGregor (eds), *Transitional Justice from Below: Grassroots Activism and the Struggle for Change* (Hart Publishing 2008) 1.

McEvoy, K. 'Letting Go of Legalism: Developing a "Thicker" Version of Transitional Justice' in Kieran McEvoy and Lorna McGregor (eds), *Transitional Justice from Below: Grassroots Activism and the Struggle for Change* (Hart Publishing 2008) 15.

Menkhaus, K. 'Somalia: Governance vs State-Building' in Charles Call with Vanessa Wyeth (eds), *Building States to Build Peace* (Lynne Rienner 2008) 187.

Mutua, M. 'A Critique of Rights in Transitional Justice: The African Experience' in Gaby Oré Aguilar and Felipé Gomez Isa (eds), *Rethinking Transitions: Equality and Social Justice in Societies Emerging from Conflict* (Intersentia 2011) 31.

Nee, A. and Uvin, P. 'Silence and Dialogue: Burundians' Alternatives to Transitional Justice', in Rosalind Shaw, Lars Waldorf with Pierre Hazan (eds), *Localizing Transitional Justice: Interventions and Priorities After Mass Violence* (Stanford University Press 2010) 157.

Newman, E. '"Liberal" Peacebuilding Debates' in Edward Newman, Roland Paris and Oliver Richmond (eds), *New Perspectives on Liberal Peacebuilding* (United Nations University Press 2009) 26.

Nichols, S. 'Reimagining Transitional Justice for an Enduring Peace: Accounting for Natural Resources in Conflict' in Dustin Sharp (ed.), *Justice and Economic Violence in Transition* (Springer 2013) 203.

O'Donnell, M. 'Corruption: A Rule of Law Agenda' in Agnes Hurwitz and Reyko Huang (eds), *Civil War and the Rule of Law: Security, Development and Human Rights* (Lynne Rienner 2008) 225.

O'Flynn, I. 'Democratic Values and Power-Sharing' in Ian O'Flynn, David Russell and Donald Rothchild (eds), *Power Sharing: New Challenges for Divides Societies* (Pluto Press 2005) 15.

Ohlson, T. and Kovacs, M.S. 'Peace through Democracy? The Challenges of Post-War Democratisation in Weak and War-Torn States' in Ashok Swain, Ramses Amer and Joakim Ojendal (eds), *The Democratization Project: Challenges and Opportunities* (Anthem Press 2008) 165.

Oomen, B. 'Justice Mechanisms and the Question of Legitimacy: The Example of Rwanda's Multi-layered Justice Mechanisms' in Kai Ambos, Judith Large and Marieke Wierda (eds), *Building a Future on Peace and Justice: Studies on Transitional Justice, Peace and Development* (Springer 2009) 175.

Ottaway, M. 'From Political Opening to Democratisation' in Marina Ottaway (ed.), *Democracy in Africa: The Hard Road Ahead* (Lynne Rienner 1997) 1.

Paffenholz, T. 'Civil Society Beyond the Liberal Peace and Its Critique' in Susanna Campbell, David Chandler and Meera Sabaratnam (eds), *A Liberal Peace? The Problems and Practices of Peacebuilding* (Zed Books 2011) 138.

Papagianni, K. 'Participation and State Legitimation' in Charles Call (ed.) with Vanessa Wyeth, *Building States to Build Peace* (Lynne Rienner 2008) 49.

Paris, R. and Sisk, T. 'Introduction: Understanding the Contradictions of Postwar Statebuilding' in Roland Paris and Timothy Sisk (eds), *The Dilemmas of Statebuilding: Confronting the Contradictions of Postwar Peace Operations* (Routledge 2009) 1.

Pillay, S. 'Conclusion' in Chandra Lekha Sriram and Suren Pillay (eds), *Peace Versus Justice? The Dilemma of Transitional Justice in Africa* (James Currey 2010) 347.

Pugh, M. 'The Political Economy of Peacebuilding: A Critical Theory Perspective' in Alex Bellamy and Paul Williams (eds), *Peace Operations and Global Order* (Routledge 2005) 39.

Pugh, M. 'Towards Life Welfare' in Edward Newman, Roland Paris, and Oliver Richmond (eds), *New Perspectives on Liberal Peacebuilding* (United Nations University Press 2009) 78.

Putnam, T. 'Human Rights and Sustainable Peace' in Stephen John Stedman and Donald Rothchild (eds), *Ending Civil Wars: The Implementation of Peace Agreements* (Lynne Rienner 2002) 237.
Restrepo Amariles, D. 'Reassessing the Boundaries of Transitional Justice: An Inquiry on Political Transitions, Armed Conflicts, and Human Rights Violations' in Liora Israël and Guillaume Mouralis (eds), *Dealing with Wars and Dictatorships* (T.M.C. Asser Press 2014) 20.
Richmond, O. and Mitchell, A. 'Introduction: Towards a Post-Liberal Peace: Exploring Hybridity via Everyday Forms of Resistance, Agency and Autonomy' in Oliver Richmond and Audra Mitchell (eds), *Hybrid Forms of Peace* (Palgrave Macmillan 2011) 1.
Risse, T. 'Governance in Areas of Limited Statehood' in Thomas Risse (ed.), *Governance Without a State: Policies and Politics in Areas of Limited Statehood* (Columbia University Press 2013) 1.
Risse, T. and Sikkink, K. 'The Socialization of International Human Rights Norms into Domestic Practices: Introduction' in Thomas Risse, Stephen Ropp and Kathryn Sikkink (eds), *The Power of Human Rights: International Norms and Domestic Change* (Cambridge University Press 1999) 1.
Roberts, D. 'Hybrid Polities and Post-Conflict Policy' in David Chandler and Timothy Sisk (eds), *The Routledge Handbook of International Statebuilding* (Routledge 2013) 94.
Roeder, P. 'Power Dividing as an Alternative to Ethnic Power Sharing' in Donald Rothchild and Philip Roeder (eds), *Sustainable Peace: Power and Democracy after Civil Wars* (Cornell University Press 2005) 51.
Roht-Arriaza, N. 'Human Rights and Strategic Peacebuilding: The Roles of Local, National and International Actors' in Daniel Philpott and Gerard Powers (eds) *Strategies of Peace: Transforming Conflict in a Violent World* (Oxford University Press 2010) 231.
Roht-Arriaza, N. and Orlovsky, K. 'A Complementary Relationship: Reparations and Development' in Pablo de Greiff and Roger Duthie (eds), *Transitional Justice and Development: Making Connections* (Social Science Research Council 2009) 170.
Rothchild, D. 'Settlement Terms and Postagreement Stability' in Stephen John Stedman, Donald Rothchild and Elizabeth Cousens (eds), *Ending Civil Wars: The Implementation of Peace Agreements* (Lynne Rienner 2002) 117.
Rothchild, D. and Foley, M. 'African States and the Politics of Inclusive Coalitions' in Donald Rothchild and Naomi Chazan (eds), *The Precarious Balance: State and Society in Africa* (Westview 1988) 233.
Rothchild, D. and Roeder, P. 'Power Sharing as an Impediment to Peace and Democracy' in Donald Rothchild and Philip Roeder (eds), *Sustainable Peace: Power and Democracy after Civil Wars* (Cornell University Press 2005) 29.
Sabaratnam, M. 'The Liberal Peace? An Intellectual History of International Conflict Management, 1990–2010' in Susanna Campbell, David Chandler and Meera Sabaratnam (eds), *A Liberal Peace? The Problems and Practices of Peacebuilding* (Zed Books 2011) 13.
Salmon, J. and Anderson, C. 'Elites and Statebuilding' in David Chandler and Timothy Sisk (eds), *Routledge Handbook of International Statebuilding* (Routledge 2013) 42.

Sambanis, N. 'How Strategic is UN Peacebuilding?' in Daniel Philpott and Gerard Powers (eds), *Strategies of Peace: Transforming Conflict in a Violent World* (Oxford University Press 2010) 141.

Samuels, K. 'Postwar Constitution Building: Opportunities and Challenges' in Roland Paris and Timothy Sisk (eds), *The Dilemmas of Statebuilding: Confronting the Contradictions of Postwar Peace Operations* (Taylor and Francis 2009) 173.

Schmeidl, S. with Karokhail, M. '"Prêt-a-Porter States": How the McDonaldization of State-Building Misses the Mark in Afghanistan' in Martina Fischer and Beatrix Schmelzle (eds), *Handbook for Conflict Transformation Dialogue Series* 8 (Berghof Research Centre 2009) 67.

Schneckener, U. 'State Building or New Modes of Governance? The Effects of International Involvement in Areas of Limited Statehood' in Thomas Risse (ed.), *Governance Without a State: Policies and Politics in Areas of Limited Statehood* (Columbia University Press 2011) 232.

Selby, J. 'The Political Economy of Peace Processes' in Michael Pugh, Neil Cooper and Mandy Turner (eds), *Whose Peace? Critical Perspectives on the Political Economy of Peacebuilding* (Palgrave Macmillan 2008) 13.

Sending, O.J. 'The Effects of Peacebuilding: Sovereignty, Patronage and Power' in Susanna Campbell, David Chandler and Meera Sabaratnam (eds), *A Liberal Peace? The Problems and Practices of Peacebuilding* (Zed Books 2011) 55.

Sharp, D. 'Introduction: Addressing Economic Violence in Transition' in Sharp, D. (ed.), *Justice and Economic Violence in Transition* (Springer 2013) 1.

Shaw, R. 'Linking Justice with Reintegration? Ex-Combatants and the Sierra Leone Experiment' in Rosalind Shaw, Lars Waldorf with Pierre Hazan (eds), *Localizing Transitional Justice: Interventions and Priorities After Mass Violence* (Stanford University Press 2010) 111.

Shaw, R. and Waldorf, L. 'Introduction: Localizing Transitional Justice' in Rosalind Shaw, Lars Waldorf with Pierre Hazan (eds), *Localizing Transitional Justice: Interventions and Priorities After Mass Violence* (Stanford University Press 2010) 3.

Sisk, T. 'Power Sharing After Civil Wars: Matching Problems to Solutions' in John Darby and Roger Mac Ginty (eds), *Contemporary Peacemaking* (Palgrave Macmillan 2008) 195.

Skaar, E. and Malca, C.G. 'Transitional Justice Alternatives: Claims and Counterclaims' in Elin Skaar, Camila Gianella Malca and Trine Eide (eds), *After Violence: Transitional Justice, Peace, and Democracy* (Routledge 2015) 1.

Sriram, C.L. 'Post-Conflict Justice and Hybridity in Peacebuilding' in Oliver Richmond and Audra Mitchell (eds), *Hybrid Forms of Peace: From Everyday Agency to Post-Liberalism* (Palgrave Macmillan 2012) 58.

Stanley, W. and Holiday, D. 'Broad Participation, Diffuse Responsibility: Peace Implementation in Guatemala' in Stephen John Stedman, Donald Rothchild and Elizabeth Cousens (eds), *Ending Civil Wars: The Implementation of Peace Agreements* (Lynne Rienner 2002) 421.

Stauffer, C. 'Transitional Justice' in *Encyclopedia of Criminology and Criminal Justice* (Springer 2014) 5272.

Subotic, J. 'Bargaining Justice' in Susanne Buckley-Zistel et al. (eds), *Transitional Justice Theories* (Routledge 2013) 127.

Szablewska, N. and Baumann, S.D. 'Current Issues and Future Challenges in Transitional Justice' in Natalia Szabalewska and Sascha-Dominik Baumann (eds), *Current Issues in Transitional Justice: Towards a More Holistic Approach* (Springer 2014) 339.

Tadjbakhsh, S. 'Introduction: Liberal Peace in Dispute' in Shahrbanou Tadjbakhsh (ed.), *Rethinking the Liberal Peace: External Models and Local Alternatives* (Routledge 2011) 1.

Tadjbakhsh, S. and Richmond, O. 'Conclusion: Typologies and Modifications Proposed by Critical Approaches' in Shahrbanou Tadjbakhsh (ed.), *Rethinking the Liberal Peace: External Models and Local Alternatives* (Routledge 2011) 221.

Tansey, O. 'Statebuilding and the Limits of Constitutional Design' in Mats Berdal and Dominik Zaum (eds), *Political Economy of Statebuilding: Power after Peace* (Routledge 2013) 17.

Terreblanche, S. 'Dealing with Systematic Injustice' in Charles Villa-Vicencio and Wilhelm Verwoerd (eds), *Looking Back, Reaching Forward: Reflections on the Truth and Reconciliation Commission in South Africa* (Zed Books 2000) 265.

Thomason, K. 'Transitional Justice as Structural Justice' in Claudio Corradetti, Nir Eisikovits and Jack Volpe Rotondi (eds) *Theorizing Transitional Justice* (Ashgate 2015) 71.

Torjesen, S. 'Transition from War to Peace: Stratification, Inequality and Post-war Economic Reconstruction' in Mats Berdal and Dominik Zaum (eds), *Political Economy of Statebuilding: Power after Peace* (Routledge 2013) 48.

Torpey, J. 'Introduction: Politics and the Past' in John Torpey (ed.), *Politics and the Past: On Repairing Historical Injustices* (Rowman and Littlefield 2003) 1.

Van der Merwe, 'Delivering Justice During Transition: Research Challenges' in Hugo van der Merwe, Victoria Baxter and Audrey Chapman (eds), *Assessing the Impact of Transitional Justice: Challenges for Empirical Research* (US Institute of Peace Press 2009) 115.

Van der Merwe, H., Baxter, V. and Chapman, A. 'Introduction' in Hugo van der Merwe, Victoria Baxter and Audrey Chapman (eds), *Assessing the Impact of Transitional Justice: Challenges for Empirical Research* (US Institute of Peace Press 2009) 1.

Vandeginste, S. 'Transitional Justice for Burundi: A Long and Winding Road' in Kai Ambos, Judith Large and Marieke Wierda (eds), *Building a Future on Peace and Justic*e (Springer 2009) 393.

Von Trotha, T. 'The "Andersen Principle": On the Difficulty of Truly Moving Beyond State-Centrism' in Martina Fischer and Beatrix Schmelzle (eds), *Handbook for Conflict Transformation Dialogue Series* 8 (Berghof Research Centre 2009) 37.

Wagner, R.H. 'The Causes of Peace' in Roy Licklider (ed.), *Stopping the Killing: How Civil Wars End* (New York University Press 1993) 235.

Webber, J. 'Forms of Transitional Justice' in Melissa Williams, Rosemary Nagy and Jon Elster (eds), *Transitional Justice* (New York University Press 2012) 98.

Weinstein, H.M. and Stover, E. 'Introduction: Conflict, Justice and Reclamation' in Harvey M. Weinstein and Eric Stover (eds), *My Neighbor, My Enemy:*

Justice and Community in the Aftermath of Mass Atrocity (Cambridge University Press 2004) 1.

Williams, M. and Nagy, R. 'Introduction' in Melissa Williams, Rosemary Nagy and Jon Elster (eds), *Transitional Justice* (New York University Press 2012) 1.

Woodward, S. 'The IFIs and Post-Conflict Political Economy' in Mats Berdal and Dominik Zaum (eds), *Political Economy of Statebuilding: Power after Peace* (Routledge 2013) 140.

Wood, E. 'Agrarian Reform, Land Occupation, and the Transition to Democracy in El Salvador' in Morten Bergsmo et al. (eds), *Distributive Justice in Transitions* (Torkel Opsahl 2010) 141.

Zahar, M.J. 'Understanding the Violence of Insiders: Loyalty, Custodians of Peace, and the Sustainability of Conflict Settlement' in Edward Newman and Oliver Richmond (eds), *Challenges to Peacebuilding: Managing Spoilers During Conflict Resolution* (United Nations University Press 2006) 40.

Zartman, I.W. 'Dynamics and Constraints in Negotiations in International Conflicts' in I. William Zartman (ed.), *Elusive Peace: Negotiating an End to Civil Wars* (Brookings Institution 1995) 3.

Zartman, I.W. 'Ripeness: The Hurting Stalemate and Beyond' in Paul Stern and Daniel Druckman (eds), *International Conflict Resolution after the Cold War* (National Academy Press 2000) 225.

Zartman, I.W. 'The Timing of Peace Initiatives: Hurting Stalemates and Ripe Moments' in John Darby and Roger Mac Ginty (eds), *Contemporary Peacemaking* (Palgrave Macmillan 2008) 22.

ONLINE MATERIALS

Arthur, P. 'Identities in Transition: Developing Better Transitional Justice Initiatives in Divided Societies' (International Center for Transitional Justice, 2009) <https://www.ictj.org/sites/default/files/ICTJ-Global-Divided-Societies-2009-English.pdf> accessed 21 July 2016.

Basedau, M. 'Managing Ethnic Conflict: The Menu of Institutional Engineering (German Institute for Global and Area Studies, 2011) <https://www.giga-hamburg.de/en/system/files/publications/wp171_basedau.pdf> accessed 21 July 2016.

Chinkin, C. 'The Protection of Economic, Social and Cultural rights in Post-Conflict (United Nations High Commissioner for Human Rights Women's Human Rights and Gender Unit, 2008) 5 <http://www2.ohchr.org/english/issues/women/docs/Paper_Protection_ ESCR.pdf> accessed 21 July 2016.

Di John, J. 'Conceptualizing the Causes and Consequences of Failed States: A Critical Review of the Literature' Crisis States Research Centre Working Paper No. 25, 2010) 31 and 15 <http://www.lse.ac.uk/internationalDevelopment/research/crisisStates/download/wp/wpSeries2/wp252.pdf> accessed 21 July 2016.

Gready, P. et al. 'Transformative Justice – A Concept Note' (unpublished manuscript, October 2010) <http://www.wun.ac.uk/files/transformative_justice_-_concept_note_web_version.pdf> accessed 20 July 2016.

Hecht, L. and Michalowski, S. 'The Economic Dimensions of Transitional Justice' (University of Essex, Transitional Justice Network Concept Paper 2012), 5 <www.essex.ac.uk/tjn/documents/TheeconomicandsocialdimensionsofTJ.pdf> accessed 20 July 2016.

Human Security Centre, 'Human Security Brief' (2006) 19 <http://www.hsrgroup.org/docs/Publications/HSB2006/2006HumanSecurityBrief-FullText.pdf> accessed 21 July 2016.

Integrated Regional Information Networks, 'Peace Unsustainable Without Democratization—Think-tank' (2004) <http://www.irinnews.org/report/50200/sudan-peace-unsustainable-without-democratisation-think-tank> accessed 21 July 2016.

Japan International Co-Operation Society and International Center for Transitional Justice, 'Workshop on Transitional Justice and Development in Africa: Enhancing Socio-Economic Justice in Societies in Transition: Case Studies on the African Continent' (2008) 7 <http://ictj.org/sites/default/files/ICTJ-JICA-Africa-Justice-Development-2008-English.pdf> accessed 20 July 2016.

Khan, M. 'Political Settlements and the Governance of Growth-Enhancing Institutions' (unpublished monograph, University of London, School of Oriental and African Studies, 2010) <http://core.ac.uk/download/files/103/2792198.pdf> accessed 20 July 2016.

Lund, M. 'What Kind of Peace Is Being Built? Taking Stock of Post-conflict Peacebuilding and Charting Future Directions' (paper presented on the 10th Anniversary of Agenda for Peace, International Development Research Centre, Ottawa, Canada, 2003) <http://web.idrc.ca/uploads/user-S/10527469720lund_final_mar_20.pdf> accessed 20 July 2016.

Mehler, A. 'Peace Through Constitutional Amendment? Opportunities and Tendencies' (German Institute of Global and Area Studies, 2011) 2 <https://giga.hamburg/en/system/files/publications/gf_international_1102.pdf> accessed: 21 July 2016.

Miller, B., Pournik, M. and Swaine, A. 'Women in Peace and Security through United Nations Security Resolution 1325: Literature Review, Content Analysis of National Action Plans, and Implementation' (Institute for Global and International Studies, 2014) <https://ggp.elliott.gwu.edu/sites/ggp.elliott.gwu.edu/files/downloads/igis_wp13_ggp_wp09.pdf> accessed 21 July 2016.

OECD, 'Political Economy Analysis' (2009) as cited in DFID, 'Political Economy Analysis How to Note' (2009) 4 <https://www.odi.org/sites/odi.org.uk/files/odi-assets/events-documents/3797.pdf> accessed 21 July 2016.

Political Instability Task Force Problem Set Codebook (2014) <http://www.systemicpeace.org/inscr/PITFProbSetCodebook2013.pdf> accessed 21 July 2016.

Robins, S. 'Addressing the Needs of Families of the Missing: A Test of Contemporary Approaches to Transitional Justice' (PhD diss., University of York, 2011) 286 <http://etheses.whiterose.ac.uk/1971/1/Robins_-_Needs_of_the_Missing_A_test_of_TJ.pdf> accessed 21 July 2016.

Sending, O.J. 'Why Peacebuilders Fail to Secure Ownership and Be Sensitive to Context' (NUPI Working Paper 755, 2009) 22 <http://brage.bibsys.no/xmlui/handle/11250/277766> accessed 21 July 2016> accessed 21 July 2016.

UN Office of the High Commissioner for Human Rights, 'Transitional Justice and Economic, Social and Cultural Rights' (2014) 6 <http://www.ohchr.org/Documents/Publications/HR-PUB-13-05.pdf> accessed 20 July 2016.

UN Secretary-General, *Report of the Secretary-General on Timor-Leste Pursuant to Security Council Resolution* 1690 (2006), UN Doc. S/2006/628, 8 August 2006.

UN Secretary-General, *Guidance Note of the UN Secretary-General: United Nations Approach to Transitional Justice* (2010) <http://www.unrol.org/files/TJ_Guidance_Note_March_2010FINAL.pdf> accessed 20 July 2016.

UN Secretary-General, *The Rule of Law and Transitional Justice in Conflict and Post-Conflict Societies* (2011) UN Doc. S/2011/634.

UN Secretary-General, *No Exit without Strategy: Security Council Decision-making and the Closure or Transaction of United Nations Peacekeeping Operations,* Security Council UN Doc. S/2001/39 of 20 April 2001.

United Nations, 'UN Peacebuilding: An Orientation' (2010) 12 <http://www.un.org/en/peacebuilding/pbso/pdf/peacebuilding_orientation.pdf> accessed 21 July 2016.

UNIFEM, 'UNIFEM Framework Guidance Note for Capacity Development' (2010) <http://www.undp.md/employment/2010/50-100/092/Annex_2_UNIFEM_HQ_Capacity_Dev_Strategy_March_2010.PDF> accessed 21 July 2016.

Weinstein, J. 'Autonomous Recovery and International Intervention Comparative Perspective' (Center for Global Development Working Paper 57, 2005) <http://www.cgdev.org/files/2731_file_WP57.pdf> accessed 20 July 2016.

Index